出版说明

应用型人才是指能够将专业知识和技能应用于所从事的专业岗位的一种专门人才。应用型人才的本质特征是具有专业基本知识和基本技能，即具有明确的职业性、实用性、实践性和高层次性。加强应用型人才的培养，是"十一五"时期我国教育发展与改革的重要目标，也是协调高等教育规模速度与市场人才需求关系的重要途径。

教育部要求今后需要有相当数量的高校致力于培养应用型人才，以满足市场对应用型人才需求量的不断增加。为了培养高素质应用型人才，必须建立完善的教学计划和高水平的课程体系。在教育部有关精神的指导下，我们组织全国高校的专家教授，努力探求更为合理有效的应用型人才培养方案，并结合我国当前的实际情况，编写了这套"高等学校应用型特色规划教材 经管系列"丛书。

为使教材的编写真正切合应用型人才的培养目标，我社编辑在全国范围内走访了大量高等学校，拜访了众多院校主管教学的领导，以及教学一线的系主任和教师，掌握了各地区各学校所设专业的培养目标和办学特色，并广泛、深入地与用人单位进行交流，明确了用人单位的真正需求。这些工作为本套丛书的准确定位、合理选材、突出特色奠定了坚实的基础。

✧ 教材定位

➢ 以就业为导向。在应用型人才培养过程中，充分考虑市场需求，因此本套丛书充分体现"就业导向"的基本思路。

➢ 符合本学科的课程设置要求。以高等教育的培养目标为依据，注重教材的科学性、实用性和通用性。

➢ 定位明确。准确定位教材在人才培养过程中的地位和作用，正确处理教材的读者层次关系，面向就业，突出应用。

➢ 合理选材、编排得当。妥善处理传统内容与现代内容的关系，大力补充新知识、新技术、新工艺和新成果。根据本学科的教学基本要求和教学大纲的要求，制订编写大纲(编写原则、编写特色、编写内容、编写体例等)，突出重点、难点。

➢ 建设"立体化"的精品教材体系。提倡教材与电子教案、学习指导、习题解答、课程设计、毕业设计等辅助教学资料配套出版。

✧ 丛书特色

➢ 围绕应用讲理论，突出实践教学环节及特点，包含丰富的案例，并对案例作详细解析，强调实用性和可操作性。

➢ 涉及最新的理论成果和实务案例，充分反映岗位要求，真正体现以就业为导向的培养目标。

➢ 国际化与中国特色相结合，符合高等教育日趋国际化的发展趋势，部分教材采用双语形式。

➢ 在结构的布局、内容重点的选取、案例习题的设计等方面符合教改目标和教学大纲的要求，把教师的备课、授课、辅导答疑等教学环节有机地结合起来。

✧ 读者定位

本系列教材主要面向普通高等院校和高等职业技术院校，适合应用型人才培养的高等院校的教学需要。

✧ 关于作者

丛书编委特聘请执教多年且有较高学术造诣和实践经验的教授参与各册教材的编写，其中有相当一部分的教材主要执笔者是精品课程的负责人，本丛书凝聚了他们多年的教学经验和心血。

✧ 互动交流

本丛书的编写及出版过程，贯穿了清华大学出版社一贯严谨、务实、科学的作风。伴随我国教育改革的不断深入，要编写出满足新形势下教学需求的教材，还需要我们不断地努力、探索和实践。我们真诚希望使用本丛书的教师、学生和其他读者提出宝贵的意见和建议，使之更臻成熟。

清华大学出版社

高等学校应用型特色规划教材　经管系列

国际结算实训教程

主　编　秦　定　徐　明

副主编　罗小力　王　茜

清华大学出版社

北　京

内 容 简 介

"国际结算"是国际贸易和国际金融从业人员的必修课程,因此本书紧扣应用型国际贸易与金融人才的培养目标,按照其工作语言是英语的特点,结合国际贸易惯例、西方国家法律和我国的实际,模拟实际工作场景进行练习,并采取小组讨论、案例分析、实战练习等手段来强化学生对国际结算的认识和理解。学生可以根据本书各章节的知识,独立操作和演练国际结算的业务环节,从而达到进行全面综合技能训练,掌握实际业务能力的目的,为以后的实际工作打下基础。

本书可作为应用型本科院校的国际贸易、金融专业学生的教材,也可作为国际贸易、国际金融领域内从业人员的参考用书。

图书在版编目(CIP)数据

国际结算实训教程/秦定,徐明主编;罗小力,王茜副主编. —北京:清华大学出版社,2011.6(2019.9重印)

(高等学校应用型特色规划教材 经管系列)
ISBN 978-7-302-25752-3

Ⅰ. ①国… Ⅱ.①秦… ②徐… ③罗… ④王… Ⅲ. ①国际结算—高等学校—教材 Ⅳ. ①F830.73

中国版本图书馆 CIP 数据核字(2011)第 098509 号

责任编辑:温 洁 汤涌涛
封面设计:杨玉兰
版式设计:北京东方人华科技有限公司
责任校对:李玉萍
责任印制:刘祎淼

出版发行:清华大学出版社   地　　址:北京清华大学学研大厦 A 座
　　　　　http://www.tup.com.cn   邮　　编:100084
　　　　　社 总 机:010-62770175   邮　　购:010-62786544
　　　　　投稿与读者服务:010-62776969, c-service@tup.tsinghua.edu.cn
　　　　　质量反馈:010-62772015, zhiliang@tup.tsinghua.edu.cn
印 装 者:北京九州迅驰传媒文化有限公司
经　　销:全国新华书店
开　　本:185mm×230mm   印　张:21.25   字　数:476 千字
版　　次:2011 年 6 月第 1 版   印　次:2019 年 9 月第 5 次印刷
定　　价:48.00 元

产品编号:038965-02

序

随着世界经济一体化和贸易全球化向纵深方向发展，我国改革开放的步伐不断加快，外向型经济逐步深化，越来越多的公司和企业走向国际舞台，对外经济交往日渐频繁。为了适应国际贸易发展形势的需要，进出口企业和银行发展了新的国际结算方式，国际结算方式呈现出多样化和个性化发展的特点，结算手段更灵活，资金划拨更快捷，安全更有保障。

但由于国际结算涉及的知识面广、政策性强，如果对国际结算中的程序、规则还不熟悉，对于国际结算中的国际惯例还不清楚，那么经常会导致货物运出后货款不能按时收回或不能如数收回，进口货物不能保质保量等问题。尤其是步入后危机时代，国际结算的经济和法律环境均有了很大变化，加上国际业务所具有的多样性、复杂性和风险性等特点，对企业加强贸易全球化经营、银行业加强本外币一体化经营以及国际结算从业人员加强自身业务能力建设，都提出了更高的要求。只有主动学习，不断更新知识来充实自己，才能在未来的竞争中把握主动，抢抓先机。

为了普及国际结算方面的知识，方便参与国际结算的当事人根据自身的实际情况选择合适的国际结算方式，从而减少风险，保证国际结算工作的顺利进行，同时方便外贸公司从业人员了解国际结算环节，避免国际贸易收付风险，四位有着丰富从业经验和长期实践经历的同志以交通银行为例子从国际业务产品角度，分别对业务流程、风险控制、实际操作等方面进行描述，从而形成本书。我认为，本书的编写突出了以下几个特点。

一、系统性

作者对本书的设计思路是，按照国际惯例的专业要求，结合管理理论与实践发展的状况，力求在操作层面上，使读者能够完整、系统、熟练地操作整个国际业务的相关流程，叙做主要产品。同时，为了使学生学习的知识更能结合社会与市场的需求，设计出"业务场景与操作"、"风险控制"、"总结思考"与"实训操练"等不同知识模块，力图铺陈国际贸易市场现状，看准交易过程中的潜在风险，符合具体职业领域的要求，使读者能从更宏观的视角对国际结算有全面的把握和全景式理解。

二、实践性

国际结算的实务操作性较强，为了一改同类书籍中出现的理论与实践脱节的问题，本书在创作过程中有意识地选择了来自银行从事国际业务的一线人员。他们有着丰富的从业经验和认真求实的态度，因而使本书能够最大限度地贴近实务。本书在阐述基本理论的同时，也穿插了较多的相关典型案例，将国际结算的理论与实践结合起来，使其具有很强的指导性。大量的实训操练有利于培养读者分析和解决实际问题的能力，丰富的总结与思考方便读者迅速掌握和运用国际结算的要点。

三、超前性

本书是由实际操作的一线人员结合自身工作经验，并对大量的资料进行归纳整理后完成的，从不同角度反映了当前国际结算中最前沿的业务运作基本流程和大体框架。可以说，本书大到所涉及的国际惯例或规则，小到具体数据都做到了及时更新，最大限度地确保了内容上与时俱进，充分展现了目前国际结算中最新的内容，具有较强的超前性。

四、创新性

本书的编写打破常规，体例创新，视角独特，让读者对国际结算产生耳目一新的感觉。它紧密结合了国际结算业务运作的实际情况，对国际结算理论的阐述图文并茂、清晰顺畅。本书在介绍国际结算时，尽量使用通俗流畅的业务术语，并适时加入示意图、流程图、单证票据示样，对相关知识点和业务流程进行对应分析解释，使枯燥的文字变得生动形象，使操作知识的介绍具有直观性，从而增强了阅读者的感性认识，帮助他们更好地理解国际结算的操作知识。例如，票据多采用表格以便进行对比分析，让读者更容易理解。而在部分需要特别标明的章节更是结合相关业务条款进行分析，便于读者更深入地领会具体业务。

上述四个特点，使得该书具备较强的实用价值，是一本有关国际贸易实务操作的好教材。借此书付印之机，我谨在此向作者表示感谢，感谢他们为读者奉献的心血；同时向清华大学出版社的编辑表示感谢，感谢他们用点睛之笔使此书更臻完美。

作为专业书籍，希望它能得到外贸公司、银行系统从业者的欢迎；作为教材，希望它能受到高等院校师生的喜爱。

"路漫漫其修远兮，吾将上下而求索。"

交通银行江苏省分行

行长　顾生

2011 年 5 月

前　言

当今中国的经济已逐步地融入世界经济发展之中，中国和世界各国的贸易往来和非贸易往来日益频繁，由此而产生的资金划拨和资金流动也日益增加。因此，国际结算在全球经济贸易中发挥的作用也日益显著，银行等金融中介机构能否为各类贸易企业提供方便、快捷、安全的跨国资金结算将成为决定其在未来竞争中是否取胜的一个重要因素。近年来，随着电子信息技术和通信技术的突飞猛进，国际结算业务也不断改革和创新，呈现出明显的复杂、多样的特征。本书正是基于这样的背景，从实际业务的每个环节出发，来编排各个章节的内容，使学生一开始就进入一个真实的国际结算业务场景之中，并随着业务的一步步展开，独立操作和演练国际结算的各个主要业务环节，从而达到进行全面综合技能训练，掌握实际业务能力的目的。

例如，本书通过让学生实际参与开证行开立信用证和来单付汇这两个环节的操作，让他们亲身体验了解国际结算核心内容是如何通过信用证来体现的。另外通过让学生根据信用证的要求缮制各项单据，让学生理解和掌握信用证业务"单证相符，单单相符"的基本原则，并清楚了解每一单据中的各项要素。

为了培养学生解决问题的能力，使他们在实际工作中灵活运用所学的知识，我们在本书中以国际结算的业务品种为主线，在每一个章节里都安排了"业务场景与操作"、"风险控制"、"总结思考"和"实训操作"四个栏目，目的是要让学生在实际的业务场景中通过处理相关业务把所学的知识和实践结合起来，以检验自己的真实水平。

本书的编写除针对应用型本科院校国际金融和国际贸易专业的学生外，还分别从金融和国际贸易行业从业人才培养的不同要求出发，安排了相应的功能模块训练，以提高学生实际操作和灵活运用所学知识的能力。特别是在世界经济日趋融合的今天，各家银行都制定了国际业务的发展战略。尤其是国际业务向前台平移后，对银行业的竞争力和服务水平提出了更高的要求。因此，银行要求营销人员集本外币立体营销于一身，要求银行柜面人员本币外币业务都要掌握。这本由资深银行国际业务专家主编的国际结算实训教材正好迎合了各家银行在对新员工培训时加大国际业务培训的需要。

本书由秦定总体策划，并负责全书的提纲拟订、编排和布局以及最后的统稿。徐明负责编写本书的"风险控制"和"总结思考"部分，并编写了"实训操作"的习题与答案；罗小力负责编写本书的"业务场景与操作"部分，完成本书中大量单据的收集和录入工作；王茜负责全书的修改和格式统一。

　　另外，本书配有电子课件，以适应多媒体教学的需要。课件下载网址：www.tup.com.cn。

　　我们希望通过本书能够为广大读者提供更多、更有益的帮助，但由于编者水平有限，书中难免存在不足和遗漏，敬请读者批评和指正。

编　者

目　　录

汇　款

学习目标:

　　熟悉汇款业务的流程并学会编写相关文件电文; 知晓如何把握和控制汇款业务中的相关风险; 掌握汇款业务中的每一个环节和步骤。

第一节　电　汇

一、业务场景与操作

案例 1.1

　　南京康宝公司(KOMPAL CORP.)因为业务需要对加拿大的市场做市场调查工作据以确定业务发展规划, 该司委托 CANADIAN CONSULATE GENERAL 公司进行相关调查并出具调研报告, 调研相关费用共计 4000 美元。2010 年 6 月 25 日, KOMPAL CORP.的业务人员来到汇款银行(例如: 交通银行), 准备通过电汇的方式将该笔款项汇至 CANADIAN CONSULATE GENERAL 公司开在美国银行(BANK OF AMERICA, SWIFT No.为 BOFAUS3NXXX)的账号 4615127。

1. 银行柜面接单

　　以交通银行为例来说明, 汇款相关人员请 KOMPAL CORP.经办人员填具汇款申请书(汇款方式是电汇, 需选择 T/T)并盖单位公章。

2. 客户填写汇款申请书

　　汇款人应仔细看清银行所出具的汇款申请书的每一个栏位, 并将业务场景中的汇款有关要素填写清楚。

银行业务编号 Bank Transac. Ref. No.		收电行/付款行 Receiver/Drawn on	
汇款币种及金额 Currency & Interbank Settlement Amount	USD4000.00	金额大写 Amount in Words	美元肆仟元整
汇款人名称及地址 Remitter's Name & Address	KOMPAL CORP., NANJING, CHINA		
收款银行之代理行名称及地址 Correspondent of Beneficiary's Bank Name & Address			
收款人开户银行名称及地址 Beneficiary's Bank Name & Address	收款人开户银行在其代理行账号 Bene's Bank A/C No. BANK OF AMERICA, 239 MADISON STREET NY, 01002 USA (ACCOUNT NO. 4615127)		
收款人名称及地址 Beneficiary's Name & Address	CANADIAN CONSULATE GENERAL, 235 EAST STREET NY, USA		
汇款附言	只限 140 个字位 RESEARCH FEE	国内外费用承担 SHA	
收款人常驻国家(地区)名称及代码	美国	□□□	
交易编码	□□□□□	相应币种及金额	USD4000.00	交易 附言

购汇汇率	请按照贵行背页所列条款代办以上汇款并进行申报	
等值人民币		
手续费		
电报费		
合计		
支付费用 方式	现金 支票 账户	申请人姓名：KOMPAL CORP. 公章 电话：65651111 日期：20100625	核准人签字 日期：20100625
核印		经办	复核

3. 电汇方式

采用电汇方式时，交行作为汇出行审核汇款申请书和相关证明材料，在确认其资料准确无误后，依据汇款申请书，交行便制作并发出下列电文给其纽约交行(即账户行)。

1)　MT103 电文

------------------------- Message Header -------------------------

Swift Output	: FIN 103 Single Customer Credt Transfer
Sender	: COMMCNSHNJG
Receiver	: COMMUS33XXX

------------------------- Message Text -------------------------

20　Sender's Reference
TT201005906

23B　Bank Operation Code
CRED

32A　Val Dte/Curr/Interbnk Settld Amt
Date　　　　　100625
Currency　　　USD
Amount　　　　4000

50K　Ordering Customer-Name & Address
Account　　　/32181426216299
Name And Address　KOMPAL CORP.
　　　　　　　　　NANJING, CHINA

53A　Sender's Correspondent – BIC
BIC　　　　　COMMCNSHXXX

57A　Account With Institution - BIC
BIC　　　　　BOFAUS3NXXX

59　Beneficiary Customer-Name & Addr
Account　　　/4615127
Name And Address　CANADIAN CONSULATE GENERAL
　　　　　　　　235 EAST STREET NY, USA

71A　Details of Charges
SHA

2)　业务处理要点

编写上述电文，需正确地理解报文的每个栏目。20 是汇款银行自身编号。32A 是起息日、币种和金额，电文中 Date 100625 Currency USD Amount 4000 需与申请书一致。50K 是汇款人信息，请见申请书。提请注意的是，汇款人在填写申请书时应填写公司的准确英文名称以免翻译有误，如康宝公司的英文是 KOMPAL CORP.，如果翻译成其他内容，则会给查询等方面带来不必要的麻烦。32181426216299 是汇款人在交行的公司账号。53A 和 57A

是此汇款的路径，我们可以看出此汇款是通过交通银行纽约分行借记其总行 COMMCNSHXXX 在 BOFAUS3NXXX 的账户来完成款项的划拨的。59 是收款人名称、地址和账号，信息取自于申请书。71A 是费用承担方式，SHA 表示汇款人和收款人对于汇款中银行所产生的费用是平分的。

图 1.1 为此业务的资金流程图。

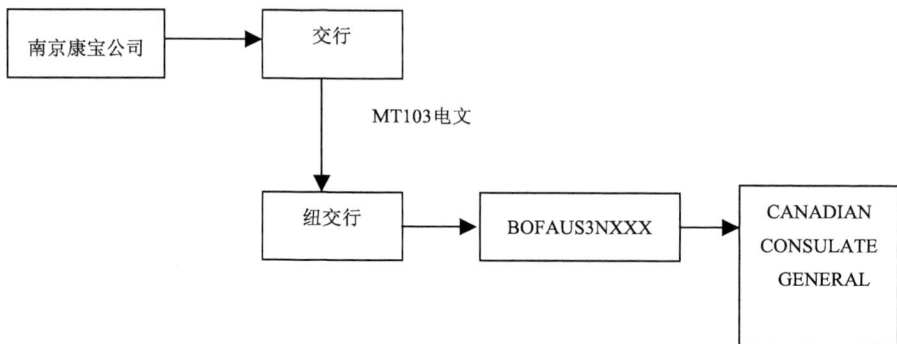

图 1.1　案例 1.1 的资金流程图

案例 1.2

2010 年 6 月 25 日，CHINA TEXTILE CO., LTD.公司来交行欲给 JIANGSU RESOURCES NANJING CO., LTD.在上海银行南京分行(SWIFT No.：BOSHCNSHNJA)的账号 30200140550228 汇 USD199264.22。

1. 银行柜面接单

以交通银行为例，汇款相关人员请 CHINA TEXTILE CO., LTD.经办人员填具汇款申请书(汇款方式为电汇，需选择 T/T)并盖单位公章。

2. 客户填写汇款申请书

汇款人应仔细看清银行所出具的汇款申请书的每一个栏位，并将业务场景中的汇款有关要素填写清楚。

银行业务编号 Bank Transac. Ref. No.		收电行/付款行 Receiver/Drawn on	
汇款币种及金额 Currency & Interbank Settlement Amount	USD199264.22	金额大写 Amount in Words	美元壹拾玖万玖仟贰佰陆拾肆元贰拾贰美分

汇款人名称及地址 Remitter's Name & Address	CHINA TEXTILE CO., LTD. NANJING, CHINA		
收款银行之代理行名称及地址 Correspondent of Beneficiary's Bank Name &Address			
收款人开户银行名称及地址 Beneficiary's Bank Name & Address	收款人开户银行在其代理行账号 Bene's Bank A/C No. BANK OF SHANGHAI, NANJING BRANCH 30200140550228		
收款人名称及地址 Beneficiary's Name & Address	JIANGSU RESOURCES NANJING CO., LTD.		
汇款附言	只限 140 个字位	国内外费用承担 SHA	

收款人常驻国家(地区)名称及代码		中国		□□□	
交易 编码	□□□□□□	相应币种及金额	USD199264.22	交易 附言	
购汇汇率		请按照贵行背页所列条款代办以上汇款并进行申报 申请人姓名：CHINA TEXTILE CO., LTD. NANJING, CHINA			
等值人民币					
手续费					
电报费					
合计					
支付费用 方式	现金 支票 账户	公章 电话：11112334 日期：20100625		核准人签字 日期：20100625	
核印		经办		复核	

3. 电汇方式

一般汇款过程中会有银行扣费，但有些情况下客户要求汇款资金全额到账。为避免扣费，汇款银行在发 MT103 电文的同时，加发 MT202 电文进行银行间款项的划拨。假设上海银行总行 SWIFT No. 为 BOSHCNSHXXX，上海银行南京分行 SWIFT No. 为 BOSHCNSHNJA。

1) MT103 电文

```
----------------------- Message Header -----------------------
Swift Output      : FIN 103 Single Customer Credt Transfer
Sender            : COMMCNSHNJG
Receiver          : BOSHCNSHXXX
------------------------ Message Text -------------------------
```

20	Sender's Reference	
	TT201005822	
23B	Bank Operation Code	
	CRED	
32A	Val Dte/Curr/Interbnk Settld Amt	
	Date	100625
	Currency	USD
	Amount	199,264.22
50K	Ordering Customer-Name & Address	
	Account	/32000661014630000103
	Name And Address	CHINA TEXTILE CO., LTD.
		.FLOOR 4, 187 ZHUJIANG ROAD,
		NANJING, 210008, CHINA
		FAX: 025-83367394
53A	Sender's Correspondent - BIC	
	BIC	CITIUS33XXX
57A	Account With Institution - BIC	
	BIC	BOSHCNSHNJA
59	Beneficiary Customer-Name & Addr	
	Account	/30200140550228
	Name And Address	JIANGSU RESOURCES NANJING CO. , LTD.
70	Remittance Information	
	CHUKOU JIAGONGQU HUOKUAN	
71A	Details of Charges	
	SHA	

2) MT202 电文

```
----------------------- Message Header -----------------------
Swift Output      : FIN 202 General Fin Inst Transfer
Sender            : COMMCNSHNJG
Receiver          : CITIUS33XXX
------------------------ Message Text -------------------------
```

20	Transaction Reference Number
	TT201005822
21	Related Reference
	TT201005822
32A	Value Date, Currency Code, Amt

	Date	100625
	Currency	USD
	Amount	199,264.22

53A	Sender's Correspondent - BIC
	BIC　　　　　COMMCNSHXXX
58A	Beneficiary Institution - BIC
	BIC　　　　　BOSHCNSHXXX

4. 业务处理要点

在处理这笔汇款业务，尤其在编写上述两个电文时，需注意这些内容的正确性并要加以理解。MT103 电文是发给 BOSHCNSHXXX(上海银行总行)的，该电文是汇款银行通知上海银行汇款相关信息的电文。

MT202 电文是发给 CITIUS33XXX(中间银行)用于资金划拨的，编写时要注意的是：20 是汇款银行自身编号，同 MT103 电文；32A 同 MT103 电文，53A 和 58A 是此汇款头寸的调拨路径。至此，我们可以看出整个资金的走向是从 COMMCNSHXXX(交行总行)划到 CITIUS33XXX(中间银行)，再由 CITIUS33XXX 划给汇入行 BOSHCNSHXXX(上海银行总行)，之后通过其南京分行解付给收款人 JIANGSU RESOURCES NANJING CO., LTD.来完成款项的划拨的。

此外还需注意，如果是贸易项下的汇款，汇款方式下的货物款项是由进口企业直接支付给出口企业，而代表货物的单据则由出口企业直接提交给进口企业。因而款项支付和货物发运的先后，直接决定着进出口双方承担风险的大小。在实际业务中某些进口企业根据其业务的需要，将汇款业务区分为前 T/T 和后 T/T。前 T/T 大致相当于预付货款，后 T/T 大致相当于货到付款。那么，如果出口企业的产品有市场竞争力，也可以适当要求进口企业前 T/T 付款；如果进出口双方资信良好，后 T/T 和赊销也是稳定和争取订单的有力手段。在做此类汇款业务时，除上述的注意事项外，还要注意汇款申请书等资料要与合同内容相匹配，这样才能把前期风险控制好。

图 1.2 为此业务的资金流程图。

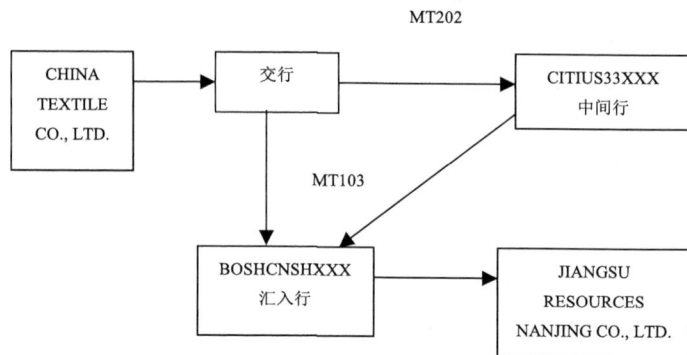

图 1.2　案例 1.2 的资金流程图

图 1.3 为汇款业务的业务流程图。

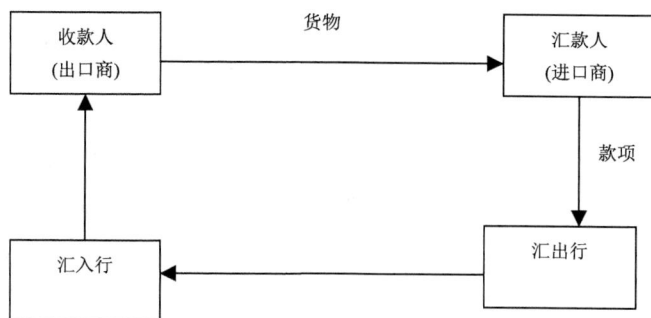

图 1.3　汇款业务的业务流程图

二、风险控制

汇款是汇款人指示其往来银行，以一定的方式将一定的金额支付给收款人。其性质属于商业风险，银行在这种方式的结算过程中不提供任何付款保证。目前银行界普遍使用的汇款方式，是通过 SWIFT 系统处理的电汇(T/T)。与托收、信用证等其他支付方式相比，汇款业务只是收付款人之间的结算安排，双方银行参与程度比较低，但如果银行操作不当，仍会有一定风险。

1. 汇款申请书的审核

由于汇出汇款申请书是汇款人和银行之间的一项契约，是汇款人授权银行办理扣账付款的凭证，因此，汇款人需特别注意汇款申请书内容的准确完整。如果由于汇款人疏忽，填错汇款申请书内容，其后果自负。下面把银行审核的要求介绍如下，请汇款人在实际业务中准确操作，排除不必要的风险隐患。

(1) 办理汇出汇款业务必须提供正本汇出汇款申请书。如是对公客户，汇款申请书上必须加盖预留印鉴；如是私人客户，必须由本人在汇款申请书上签名。

境内/境外两栏汇款的选择要正确，汇款方式的选择要明确电汇还是票汇。

(2) 申请书应由汇款人填写，其中涉及的汇款人、收款人、收款银行等汇款信息必须用英文填写。国内汇款可用中文填写，但汇款路径跨境的国内汇款必须用英文填写。

(3) 汇款方式的选择是否明确，银行目前的汇款方式主要有电汇和票汇。

(4) 汇款币种、金额的大小写是否正确并且一致。

(5) 收款人的姓名、国别及账号填写是否准确无误并清晰可辨。例如：欧洲地区要求填写完整的 IBAN(INTERNATIONAL BANK ACCOUNT NUMBER)账号，若无，常会被拒绝、退回或加收额外费用。

(6) 收款人的往来银行信息填写必须完整，最好能提供银行的 SWIFT 代码。收款人银行在美国地区的，如不能提供 SWIFT 代码，可以提供 9 位的 FED(FEDWIRE)号；汇往英国的英镑汇款也可提供收款人银行相应的 6 位 SC(SORT CODE)号。如不能提供银行的相关代码，必须将收款行全称、所在城市和国家填写清楚。

(7) 汇款申请人的印鉴及账号是否真实准确。如系原币出账，则应填写支取凭条；如系人民币购汇出账，则相应地填写购汇申请书。

(8) 国外银行转汇费承担人的选择是否明确。

国内外银行费用承担人的选择要明确：OUR/BEN/SHA。

- OUR——所有的费用由汇款人承担
- BEN——所有的费用由收款人承担
- SHA——所有的费用由汇款人和收款人共同承担

(9) 国际收支申报信息和核销信息填写要完整、准确。

(10) 汇款申请人的印鉴及账号必须真实有效。

2. 汇款路线的选择

实际业务中比较常见的问题是收款银行名称、地址或账号等错误影响汇路的合理选择，造成汇路中的额外中间行扣费及影响汇款速度。下面介绍一个案例。

2010 年 1 月 25 日，南京 JIANGSU ANIMA CORP.因为业务需要从美国 ICOM 公司进口一批零部件，共计 3000 美元，该司业务人员来到交行准备办理相关业务，因金额不大但比较紧急，所以决定通过电汇方式将该笔款项汇至 ICOM 公司开在美国纽约银行(BANK OF NEW YORK)的账号 00003457。假设交行的 SWIFT 号是 COMMCNSHNJG，收报行的 SWIFT 号是 COMMUS33XXX。客户填写汇款申请书如下：

银行业务编号 Bank Transac. Ref. No.		收电行/付款行 Receiver/Drawn on	
汇款币种及金额 Currency & Interbank Settlement Amount	USD3000.00	金额大写 Amount in Words	美元叁仟元整
汇款人名称及地址 Remitter's Name & Address	JIANGSU ANIMA CORP.		
收款银行之代理行 名称及地址 Correspondent of Beneficiary's Bank Name & Address			
收款人开户银行 名称及地址 Beneficiary's Bank Name & Address	收款人开户银行在其代理行账号 Bene's Bank A/C No.　000003457 BANK OF NEW YORK, 239 SANWAY STREET NY, 03054 USA		
收款人名称及地址 Beneficiary's Name & Address	ICOM CORP.　P. O. BOX 339 NY, USA		
汇款附言	只限 140 个字位	国内外费用承担 SHA	

收款人常驻国家(地区)名称及代码			美国		□□□	
交易 编码	□□□□□	相应币种及金额	USD3000.00		交易 附言	
购汇汇率		请按照贵行背页所列条款代办以上汇款并 进行申报				
等值人民币						
手续费						
电报费						
合计						
支付费用 方式	现金 支票 账户	申请人姓名：JIANGSU ANIMA CORP. 公章 电话：54452222 日期：20100125			核准人签字 日期：20100125	
核印		经办			复核	

　　银行审核汇款申请书和相关证明材料无误，依据汇款申请书，交行作为汇出行制作并发出下列电文。

MT103 电文

```
------------------------- Message Header -------------------------
Swift Output    : FIN 103 Single Customer Credt Transfer
Sender          : COMMCNSHNJG
Receiver        : COMMUS33XXX
------------------------- Message Text -------------------------
```

20　　Sender's Reference

　　　TT201004307(汇款银行自身编号)

23B　Bank Operation Code

　　　CRED

32A　Val Dte/Curr/Interbnk Settld Amt

　　　Date　　　　　100125

　　　Currency　　　USD

　　　Amount　　　　3000

50K　Ordering Customer-Name & Address

　　　Account　　　　/3201426216299

　　　Name And Address　　JIANGSU ANIMA CORP.

　　　　　　　　　　　　　NANJING, CHINA

53A　Sender's Correspondent - BIC

　　　BIC　　　　　　COMMCNSHXXX

57A　Account With Institution - BIC

　　　BIC　　　　　　IRVTUS3NXXX

59　　Beneficiary Customer-Name & Addr

　　　Account　　　/000003457

　　　Name And Address　ICOM CORP.　P. O. BOX 339 NY, USA

71A　Details of Charges

　　　SHA

但是因为业务较紧急，汇款人在提供银行账号时出现了错误，将账号 00003457 误提供为 000003457，导致款项汇出后不能及时入账，BANK OF NEW YORK 发来查询电文，交通银行又向汇款人核实账号后向国外发出以下更正电文。

MT499 电文

```
------------------------- Message Header -------------------------
Swift Output    : FIN 499 Free Format Message
Sender          : COMMCNSHNJG
Receiver        : COMMUS33 XXX
------------------------- Message Text -------------------------
```

RE OUR T/T REF: TT201004307 FOR USD3000 DATED 25 JAN 2010

PLS BE ADVISED THE BENE'S ACCOUNT SHOULD BE 00003457 I/O 000003457.

THANKS FOR CO-OP

B.RGDS

很明显，这样来回耽误了汇款速度，而实际业务中也有些银行在遇到此类问题时会将错误款项直接退回，这时汇款银行只能再次汇出，视同新汇款，从而造成汇款人支付双重手续费，且耽误了时间。由此可见，汇款要素的准确对汇款人来说是十分重要的。

如前文"风险控制"中所述，因为美元是国际结算中最广泛使用的货币，在实际业务中一些涉及受美国制裁的国家、公司、人名的汇款申请，汇款银行应特别注意，如果选择美国的账户行，则款项会在路经美国银行时被冻结而不能顺利流转，这种情况下银行人员可以选择非美国的账户行清算，如欧洲的银行，请看以下案例。

2010年2月2日，南京 FONCHEM CORP.因为业务需要向伊朗客户 HAKAN TURIZM (TRAVEL E22) SEYAHAT ITH IHR VE INT YAZ LTD STI 公司汇款 45000 美元，收款人开户行为 TURK EKONOMI BANKASI A.S.(SWIFT No.：TEBUTRISXXX)，账号为5700032000013200000023552。

客户填写汇款申请书如下：

银行业务编号 Bank Transac. Ref. No.		收电行/付款行 Receiver/Drawn on	
汇款币种及金额 Currency &Interbank Settlement Amount	USD45000.00	金额大写 Amount in Words	美元肆万伍仟元整
汇款人名称及地址 Remitter's Name & Address	FONCHEM CORP.		
收款银行之代理行 名称及地址 Correspondent of Beneficiary's Bank Name & Address			
收款人开户银行 名称及地址 Beneficiary's Bank Name & Address	收款人开户银行在其代理行账号 Bene's Bank A/C No. TURK EKONOMI BANKASI A.S. 5700032000013200000023552		
收款人名称及地址 Beneficiary's Name & Address	HAKAN TURIZM (TRAVEL E22) SEYAHAT ITH IHR VE INT YAZ LTD STI　IRAN		

汇款附言	只限 140 个字位	国内外费用承担
		SHA

收款人常驻国家(地区)名称及代码		伊朗	□□□		
交易 编码	□□□□□	相应币种及金额	USD45000.00	交易 附言	
购汇汇率		请按照贵行背页所列条款代办以上汇款并进行申报			
等值人民币					
手续费					
电报费					
合计					
支付费用方式	现金 支票 账户	申请人姓名：FONCHEM　CORP. 公章 电话：38964445 日期：20100202		核准人签字 日期：20100202	
核印		经办		复核	

MT103 电文

```
-------------------------- Message Header --------------------------
Swift Output     : FIN 103 Single Customer Credt Transfer
Sender           : COMMCNSHNJG
Receiver         : BARCGB22XXX
-------------------------- Message Text --------------------------
    20      Sender's Reference
            TT201007130
    23B     Bank Operation Code
            CRED
    32A     Val Dte/Curr/Interbnk Settld Amt
            Date          100202
            Currency      USD
            Amount        45000
    50K     Ordering Customer-Name & Address
            Account         /320382620100006399
            Name And Address    FONCHEM CORP.
                                NO.100 YUDAO STREET, NANJING, CHINA
```

53A   Sender's Correspondent - BIC

   BIC   COMMCNSHXXX

57A   Account With Institution - BIC

   BIC   TEBUTRISXXX

59   Beneficiary Customer-Name & Addr

   Account   /570003200013200000023552

   Name And Address   HAKAN TURIZM (TRAVEL E22) SEYAHAT

                ITH IHR VE INT YAZ LTD STI

71A   Details of Charges

   OUR

由于伊朗属于被美国制裁的国家，因此，交行在选择账户行时，选择位于英国伦敦的Barclays Bank PLC, London (SWIFT No.为 BARCGB22XXX)发送报文来完成款项的划拨。因此提醒汇款人在汇款时，如果不确定或不清楚时，应及时向汇款银行咨询。

三、总结思考

电汇相比其他汇款方式更加安全、快捷，一般多用于金额大、时间紧迫的情况。选择电汇，汇款人支付的电报费等相关费用较高，其操作风险及如何控制前面已言及，在此还需强调的是，对汇款人来说，需注意申请书填写的准确完整，以便于汇款银行选择合理汇路，这样既避免了汇出过程中出现额外的中间银行扣费，也保障了安全。

四、实训操练

练习 1.1

2010 年 7 月 16 日，南京 SUNRIS CO., LTD.公司因进料加工，需要向 KINGSTATE ELECTRONICS CORPORATION 开在 INTERNATIONAL COMMERCIAL BANK OF CHINA, THE TAIPEI 的账号 101005001230 汇款 13 585.00 美元购买原料，双方各自负担银行费用。

如果你是汇款行(假设是交通银行，SWIFT No.为 COMMCNSHNJG)的经办人员，应如何编制报文？

请参照前文的案例编制下面的报文，假设银行编号是 TT201006774，汇款人 SUNRIS CO., LTD.公司在交行的账号是 3266371461000002211，收款行 SWIFT No.为 ICBCTWTPXXX，中间行 SWIFT No.为 CHASUS33XXX。

MT103 电文

```
-------------------------- Message Header --------------------------
Swift Output    : FIN 103 Single Customer Credt Transfer
Sender          :
Receiver        :
-------------------------- Message Text --------------------------
    20      Sender's Reference

    23B     Bank Operation Code

    32A     Val Dte/Curr/Interbnk Settld Amt
            Date
            Currency
            Amount
    50K     Ordering Customer-Name & Address
            Account
            Name And Address
    53A     Sender's Correspondent - BIC
            BIC
    57A     Account With Institution - BIC
            BIC
    59      Beneficiary Customer-Name & Addr
            Account
            Name And Address
    71A     Details of Charges
```

MT202 电文

```
-------------------------- Message Header --------------------------
Swift Output    : FIN 202 General Fin Inst Transfer
Sender          :
Receiver        :
-------------------------- Message Text --------------------------
    20      Transaction Reference Number

    21      Related Reference
```

32A	Value Date, Currency Code, Amt

32A　　Value Date, Currency Code, Amt

　　　　Date

　　　　Currency

　　　　Amount

53A　　Sender's Correspondent - BIC

　　　　BIC

58A　　Beneficiary Institution - BIC

　　　　BIC

参考答案：

MT103 电文

-------------------------- Message Header ------------------------

Swift Output　　: FIN 103 Single Customer Credt Transfer

Sender　　　　: COMMCNSHNJG

Receiver　　　　: ICBCTWTPXXX

-------------------------- Message Text ------------------------

20　　Sender's Reference

　　　TT201006774

23B　Bank Operation Code

　　　CRED

32A　Val Dte/Curr/Interbnk Settld Amt

　　　Date　　　　　100716

　　　Currency　　　USD

　　　Amount　　　　13585

50K　Ordering Customer- Name & Address

　　　Account　　　/326637146100002211

　　　Name And Address　　SUNRIS CO., LTD.

　　　　　　　　　　　　NO.53 SUYUAN DADAO, JNDZ

　　　　　　　　　　　　NANJING, CHINA

53A　Sender's Correspondent - BIC

　　　BIC　　　　　CHASUS33XXX

57A　Account With Institution - BIC

　　　BIC　　　　　ICBCTWTP010

59　　Beneficiary Customer-Name & Addr

Account   /101005001230

Name And Address   KINGSTATE ELECTRONICS CORPORATION

71A   Details of Charges

SHA

MT202 电文

------------------------- Message Header -------------------------

Swift Output   : FIN 202 General Fin Inst Transfer

Sender   : COMMCNSHNJG

Receiver   : CHASUS33XXX

------------------------- Message Text -------------------------

20   Transaction Reference Number

TT201006774

21   Related Reference

TT201006774

32A   Value Date, Currency Code,   Amt

Date   100716

Currency   USD

Amount   13585

53A   Sender's Correspondent - BIC

BIC   COMMCNSHXXX

58A   Beneficiary Institution - BIC

BIC   ICBCTWTPXXX

练习 1.2

2010 年 4 月 15 日韩光需要向李子兵开在汇丰银行(SWIFT No.：MIDLGB22XXX)的账号 31692100 汇款 500 英镑。

如果你是汇款行(假设交通银行的 SWIFT No.为 COMMCNSHNJG)的经办人员,如何编制报文?

请参照前文的案例编制下面的报文,假设汇丰银行是交行英镑账户行,汇款人负担银行费用,银行编号是 TT201006726。

MT103 电文

```
------------------------- Message Header -------------------------
Swift Output      : FIN 103 Single Customer Credt Transfer
Sender           :
Receiver         :
------------------------- Message Text -------------------------
```

20   Sender's Reference

23B   Bank Operation Code

32A   Val Dte/Curr/Interbnk Settld Amt
     Date
     Currency
     Amount

50K   Ordering Customer-Name & Address

     Name And Address

53A   Sender's Correspondent - BIC
     BIC

57A   Account With Inst -Name & Addr

     Name And Address

59   Beneficiary Customer-Name & Addr
     Account
     Name And Address

71A   Details of Charges

参考答案:

MT103 电文

```
------------------------- Message Header -------------------------
Swift Output      : FIN 103 Single Customer Credt Transfer
Sender           : COMMCNSHNJG
Receiver         : MIDLGB22XXX
------------------------- Message Text -------------------------
```

20　　Sender's Reference

　　　TT201006726

23B　Bank Operation Code

　　　CRED

32A　Val Dte/Curr/Interbnk Settld Amt

　　　Date　　　　　　100415

　　　Currency　　　　GBP

　　　Amount　　　　　500

50K　Ordering Customer-Name & Address

　　　Name And Address　　HAN GUANG

　　　　　　　　　　　　　GONGJIAOYICUN 41-404

53A　Sender's Correspondent - BIC

　　　BIC　　　　　　　COMMCNSHXXX

57A　Account With Inst -Name & Addr

　　　Name And Address　　MIDLGB22XXX

59　　Beneficiary Customer-Name & Addr

　　　Account　　　　　/31692100

　　　Name And Address　　MR ZIBING LI

71A　Details of Charges

　　　OUR

第二节　票　　汇

一、业务场景与操作

案例 1.3

2010 年 1 月 5 日，客户王晓梅因儿子张新在美国 UNIVERSITY OF CALIFORNIA LOS ANGELES 学习需交学费来到银行(假设交通银行)汇款，欲将 10 000.00 美元学费通过票汇的方式汇给儿子。

1. 银行柜面接单

交通银行汇款相关人员请王晓梅填具汇款申请书。

2. 客户填写汇款申请书

汇款人王晓梅应仔细看清银行所出具的汇款申请书的每一个栏位，并将业务场景中的汇款有关要素填写清楚。此时客户在填写汇款申请书时选择票汇。

电汇	票汇 X	信汇	
银行业务编号 Bank Transac. Ref. No.	DD201000341	收电行/付款行 Receiver/Drawn on	
汇款币种及金额 Currency & Interbank Settlement Amount	USD10000.00	金额大写 Amount in Words	美元壹万元整
汇款人名称及地址 Remitter's Name & Address	王晓梅 WANGXIAOMEI 南京市荣庄街 75 号 No. 75 RONGZHUANG STREET, NANJING, CHINA		
□对公 组织机构代码 　　　　Unit Code	□□□□□□□□	[X]对私	个人身份证件号码 Individual ID No.
			□中国居民个人 　Resident Individual □中国非居民个人 Non-Resident Individual
收款人名称及地址 Beneficiary's Name & Address	ZHANGXIN 893 WEST STREET AMHERST LOS ANGELES, CA, USA		
汇款附言	学费	国内外费用承担 SHA	
收款人常驻国家(地区)名称及代码	美国	□□□	
相应币种及金额	USD10000.00	交易附言	非居民向境外付款
银行专用栏	请按照贵行背页所列条款代办以上汇款并进行申报 申请人姓名：王晓梅 电话：55354455 日期：20100105		核准人签字(银行填写) 日期：20100105

3. 银行出票

银行需查验客户身份证明，在符合外管政策的情况下，开立以下汇票交于王晓梅，王晓梅可以将汇票邮寄至张新，由张新向银行提示付款，也可以自行携带出境取款给张新。

汇票样本如下：

BANK OF COMMUNICATIONS
DRAFT NO.　10062927
ISSUING OFFICE　　　　JIANGSU PROVINCIAL BRANCH
REF　　DD201000341　　　　　　　　　　DATE 2010 JAN. 05
PAY TO THE ORDER OF TO ZHANGXIN 893 WEST STREET AMHERST LOS ANGELES, CA, USA
THE SUM OF　USD10000.00　US DOLLARS TEN THOUSAND ONLY
DRAWN ON　　　BANK OF AMERICA, 390 COLLEGE STREET 01002, LOS ANGELES

4. 票汇电文

银行(如交行，SWIFT No.为 COMMCNSHNJG)在出票的同时，给清算银行 BANK OF AMERICA SAN FRANCISCO, CA (SWIFT No.为 BOFAUS6SXXX)发电，电文格式如下。

MT110 电文

```
-------------------------- Message Header --------------------------
Swift Output          : FIN 110 Advice of Cheque(s)
Sender                : COMMCNSHNJG
Receiver              : BOFAUS6SXXX
-------------------------- Message Text --------------------------
    20     Sender's Reference
           CK201000127
    21     Cheque Number
           10063020
    30     Date of Issue
           100105
    32B    Amount
           Currency      USD
           Amount        10000
    59     Payee－Name & Address
           ZHANGXIN 893 WEST STREET AMHERST
           LOS ANGELES, CA, USA
```

5. 业务处理要点

交行同时向清算银行 BANK OF AMERICA SAN FRANCISCO, CA 发出通知电文 MT110，通知其交行已经开出此汇票。该清算银行收到电文后应记录相关信息，以便当持票人来兑付时核对信息，经核对无误后给予兑付。

该电文 30 是汇票开出日期；32B 是交行出具汇票的金额；59 是收款人。

图 1.4 为此业务的资金流程图。

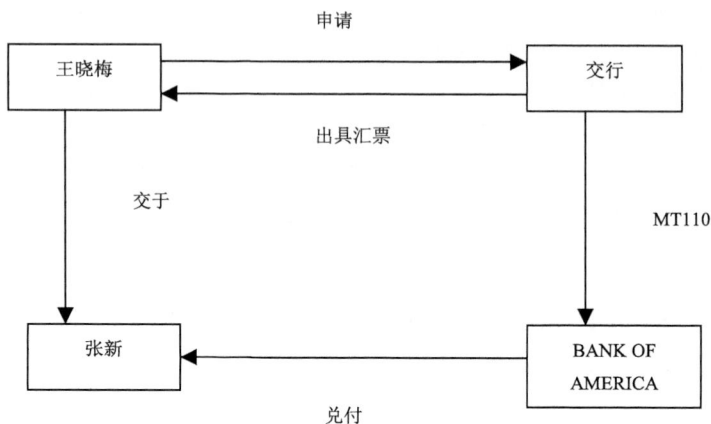

图 1.4 案例 1.3 的资金流程图

二、风险控制

票汇是汇出银行应汇款人的申请，代汇款人开立以另一家银行为付款人(付款行)的即期汇票，由汇款人自行寄送给或携带交与收款人，收款人凭此票向付款银行提示，要求解付票款的一种汇款方式。从此定义可以看出，在风险控制上，同样要求汇款人做到对汇款申请书的填写要准确完整，同时还需注意邮寄或携带的丢失风险。在实际业务中，因其使用灵活方便，具有可转让性且可以替代现金流通，因而是仅次于电汇的一种重要的汇款形式。

三、总结思考

相对于其他汇款方式，票汇无须支付电报费，收费相对较低。此外，汇票具有可转让性，并可通过寄送或汇款人自带出境方式传递，使用较为方便灵活。实际业务中，票汇多用于对私客户向国外支付报名费、学费等小额款项。

四、实训操练

练习 1.3

谢义因考试需要，2010 年 4 月 5 日向香港大学汇款 800 港币作为考试费。如果你是汇款行(假设交通银行)的经办人员，如何出具汇票？

请参照前文的案例编制下面的汇票，假设汇票号是 10062933，银行编号是
DD201000398。

BANK OF COMMUNICATIONS

DRAFT NO.
ISSUING OFFICE
REF   DATE
PAY TO THE ORDER OF   TO
THE SUM OF
DRAWN ON

参考答案：

BANK OF COMMUNICATIONS

DRAFT NO.   10062933
ISSUING OFFICE   JIANGSU PROVINCIAL BRANCH
REF   DD201000398   DATE 2010 APR. 05
PAY TO THE ORDER OF   TO   THE UNIVERSITY OF HONG KONG
THE SUM OF   HKD800.00   HK DOLLARS EIGHT HUNDRED ONLY
DRAWN ON   BANK OF COMMUNICATIONS HONG KONG BRANCH

练习 1.4

2010 年 3 月 7 日，王明因向张元借款 USD5000，需开具相应金额汇票偿还。
如果你是汇款行(假设交通银行)的经办人员，如何出具汇票？
请参照前文的案例编制下面的汇票，假设汇票号是 10062955，银行编号是
DD201000405。

BANK OF COMMUNICATIONS

DRAFT NO.
ISSUING OFFICE
REF   DATE
PAY TO THE ORDER OF   TO
THE SUM OF
DRAWN ON

参考答案：

BANK OF COMMUNICATIONS

DRAFT NO. 10062955
ISSUING OFFICE   JIANGSU PROVINCIAL BRANCH
REF   DD201000405   DATE 2010 MAR. 07
PAY TO THE ORDER OF   TO   THE ZHANG YUAN

THE SUM OF   USD5000.00   US DOLLARS FIVE THOUSAND ONLY
DRAWN ON   BANK OF COMMUNICATIONS NEW YORK BRANCH

第三节　信　汇

一、业务场景与操作

案例 1.4

客户李丽的女儿张佳在日本 KYOTO UNIVERSITY 学习法律。李丽于 2010 年 3 月 9 日来到交通银行欲将 5 000 000 日元作为生活费信汇给女儿，收款人银行为 BANK OF CHINA KYOTO BRANCH。

1. 银行柜面接单

交通银行汇款相关人员请李丽填具汇款申请书。

2. 客户填写汇款申请书

汇款人李丽应仔细看清银行所出具的汇款申请书的每一个栏位，并将业务场景中的汇款有关要素填写清楚。此时客户在填写汇款申请书时选择信汇。

银行业务编号 Bank Transac. Ref. No.	MT2010001	收电行/付款行 Receiver/Drawn on	
汇款币种及金额 Currency & Interbank Settlement Amount	JAPANESE YEN 5000000	金额大写 Amount in Words	日元伍佰万元整
汇款人名称及地址 Remitter's Name & Address	LILI 323 ZHUJIANG RD, NANJING, CHINA		

□对公　组织机构代码 Unit Code	□□□□□□□□	☒对私	个人身份证件号码 Individual ID No. □中国居民个人 Resident Individual □中国非居民个人 Non-Resident Individual	
收款银行之代理行名称及地址 Correspondent of Beneficiary's Bank Name &Address				
收款人开户银行名称及地址 Beneficiary's Bank Name & Address	收款人开户银行在其代理行账号 Bene's Bank A/C No. BANK OF CHINA KYOTO　P.O. BOX 10005, JAPAN			
收款人名称及地址 Beneficiary's Name & Address	ZHANGJIA P.O. BOX 258, HAIDE STREET, KYOTO, JAPAN			
汇款附言	只限 140 个字位		国内外费用承担 SHA	

收款人常驻国家(地区)名称及代码		日本		□□□		
交易 编码	□□□□□□	相应币种 及金额	JPY5000000.00		交易附言	cost of living
外汇局批件/备案表号			报 关 单 经 营 单位代码	□□□□□□□□□		

银行专用栏		申请人签章		银行签章	
购汇汇率		请按照贵行背页所列条款代办以上汇款并 进行申报			
等值人民币					
手续费					
电报费					
合计					
支付费用 方式	现金 支票 账户	申请人姓名：*LILI* 李丽 电话：45453333 日期：20100309		核准人签字 日期：20100309	
核印		经办		复核	

3. 信汇付款委托书

银行受理李丽的申请后开出如下信汇付款委托书(假设交通银行为汇款银行，汇款银行需填写信汇付款委托书)，该委托书与 SWIFT 报文不同之处主要在于，它不像 SWIFT 报文有固定的格式(MT103、MT202)，而是可以由李丽委托的银行自行决定格式，只要相关汇款要素明确显示，并由有权签字人签署即可。

交通银行股份有限公司

江苏省分行

Address: No.124 Zhongshan
Road(N), Nanjing, China
地址：中国南京市中山北路 124 号
Swift: COMMCNSHNJG

BANK OF COMMUNICATIONS CO., LTD.
Telex:34022
JIANGSU PROVINCIAL BRANCH
OUR REF MT2010001

To: BANK OF CHINA KYOTO BRANCH P. O. BOX 10005, JAPAN

MAIL TRANSFER

Beneficiary's Bank Name And Address: BANK OF CHINA KYOTO BRANCH, P. O. BOX 10005, JAPAN
Beneficiary's Name And Address: ZHANGJIA P.O. BOX 258, HAIDE STREET, KYOTO, JAPAN
Currency and Amount: JPY5000000.00   JAPANESE YEN FIVE MILLION ONLY
Remitter's Name And Address: LILI 323 ZHUJIANG RD, NANJING, CHINA
Remittance Information: COST OF LIVING
All bank charges if any are to be borne by

SHA   X
BEN
OUR

Name of Applicant: LILI

BANK'S SIGNATURE

AUTHORISED PERSONAL

DATE: 2010-3-9
Signature

图 1.5 为此案例的业务流程图。

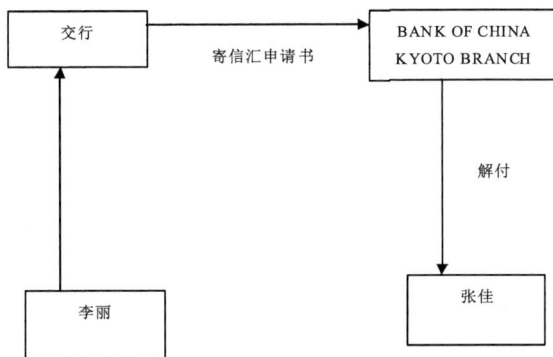

图 1.5　案例 1.4 的业务流程图

4.业务处理要点

信汇付款委托书是银行缮制，每个银行的格式可能不太一样，但以下的基本要素一般要体现在信汇付款委托书上：汇入行名称和地址(BANK OF CHINA KYOTO BRANCH, P. O. BOX 10005, JAPAN)、编号(OUR REF. MT2010001)、收款人(ZHANGJIA P. O. BOX 258, HAIDE STREET, KYOTO, JAPAN)、货币金额大小写(Currency and Amount: JPY5000000.00 JAPANESE YEN FIVE MILLION ONLY)、汇款人(LILI 323 ZHUJIANG RD, NANJING, CHINA)和附言(COST OF LIVING)。

如有不清楚的要素，银行会及时联系汇款人核实，以防产生风险。

二、风险控制

相对于电汇而言，信汇的唯一差别是汇出行不使用 SWIFT 方式，而是通过航空邮寄把信汇委托书邮寄给解付行，因此在对风险的控制上与电汇基本相同，对汇款申请书的填写同样要求做到准确完整。所不同的是，信汇是通过航邮至解付行，因此会有邮寄途中丢失的风险，并且还需考虑邮寄在途时间，另外还有不利于查询等缺点，因此现在较少采用。

三、总结思考

信汇与电汇的不同之处在于，信汇申请书是信汇付款委托书，其内容与电报委托书内容相同，只是汇出银行在信汇申请书上不加注密押，而以有权签字人签字代替。在办理信汇时，汇出银行出具由银行有权签字人员签发的银行信汇委托书，然后用信函寄往解付行，解付行凭此办理有关款项的解付手续。近年，由于通讯工具的大大改善，使得绝大多数银行已配备了诸如 SWIFT、TELEX 等一类的设备，银行的局域网(LAN)、远程网都有很大普及，因此，在实际业务中已经基本不采用这种方式。

四、实训操练

练习 1.5

2010 年 3 月 9 日，客户张海从日本 HIKITA CORP.进口原料进行深加工。张海于 2010 年 5 月 8 日来到汇款行(假设交通银行)欲将 300 000 日元作为预付款汇给客户 HIKITA CORP., 222 DOSAN RD, TOKYO，交通银行指示东京中行付款，受益人负担相关费用。

如果你是汇款行(假设交通银行)的经办人员，如何出具信汇委托书？

请参照前文的案例编制下面的信汇委托书，假设银行编号是 MT2010002。

交通银行股份有限公司

江苏省分行

Address: No.124 Zhongshan
Road(N), Nanjing, China
地址: 中国南京市中山北路 124 号
Swift: COMMCNSHNJG

BANK OF COMMUNICATIONS CO., LTD.
Telex:34022
JIANGSU PROVINCIAL BRANCH
OUR REF

MAIL TRANSFER

Beneficiary's Bank Name And Address:

Beneficiary's Name And Address:

Currency and Amount:

Remitter's Name And Address:

Remittance Information :

All bank charges if any are to be borne by

SHA

BEN   X

OUR

Name of Applicant:

BANK'S SIGNATURE

AUTHORISED PERSONAL

DATE

Signature

参考答案：

交通银行股份有限公司

江 苏 省 分 行

Address: No.124 Zhongshan
Road(N), Nanjing, China
地址：中国南京市中山北路 124 号
Swift: COMMCNSHNJG

BANK OF COMMUNICATIONS CO., LTD.
Telex:34022
JIANGSU PROVINCIAL BRANCH
OUR REF: MT2010002

MAIL TRANSFER

Beneficiary's Bank Name And Address: BANK OF CHINA TOKYO BRANCH, 514 SAMSTY RD, TOKYO

Beneficiary's Name And Address: HIKITA CORP. 222 DOSAN RD, TOKYO

Currency and Amount: JPY300000.00　　JAPANESE YEN THREE HUNDRED THOUSAND ONLY

Remitter's Name And Address: ZHANG HAI　323 ZHUJIANG RD, NANJING, CHINA

Remittance Information: IMPORT GOODS

All bank charges if any are to be borne by

SHA
BEN　X
OUR

Name of Applicant:　ZHANGHAI

BANK'S SIGNATURE
AUTHORISED PERSONAL
DATE: 2010-3-9
Signature 张海

第二章

托 收 业 务

学习目标：

了解托收业务的基本知识；知晓出口托收和进口代收的办理流程；掌握相关电文的发送；能够较熟练地处理各种类型的出口托收和进口代收相关业务。

第一节　出口托收业务

一、业务场景与操作

案例 2.1

2010 年 5 月 16 日，我国出口商 KOC CO., LTD.和进口商 GROVE NUTRITION LTD.签订合同出口货物 DORSAN 48 EC，双方在合同中约定采用即期付款托收方式(D/P SIGHT)结算货款，KOC CO., LTD.制作了汇票和发票，并将货物交船运公司出运后取得相关运输单据(如果需要保险，需要到保险公司办理相关手续取得保单，其他需要第三方出具的单据也需要到相关部门办理后取得)，然后携相关单据来托收银行(假设是交通银行)办理即期付款交单业务。

1. 交单委托书与交单

首先出口商 KOC CO., LTD.填写出口托收相关的交单委托书，详细列明进口代收银行名址，托收方式(是 D/P 还是 D/A，期限是即期还是远期)，交单的种类和份数，银行费用的承担方(一般是出口方)，收到货款的入账方式(原币还是结汇，入账账号)以及其他需要说明的事项。

客户交单委托书

致：交通银行江苏省分行国际业务部

　　向贵行递交下列出口单据(见附单据清单)，请贵行予以办理，(X)跟单托收(遵守现行的 URC522)

　　公司名称：KOC CO., LTD.　　　　　联系人：王小姐　电话：025-12345678

　　发票号码：21Z1134　　　　　　　　交单金额：USD13000.00

D/P SIGHT 交单

银行名称：MIDLAND BANK   U. K.

SUCURSAL: JUAN DE ARONA 893-SAN ISIDRO LONDON, UNITED KINGDOM

付款指示：请贵行收妥款项后，划入我司在：   (银行)

核销单号码：   账号：

汇票	2	一般地产证	
发票	3	普惠制地产证	
海关发票		出口许可证	
装箱单	3	保单	
提单	3	检验证明	
空运单		数量证明	
货物收据		质量证明	
船公司证明		副本单据	
装船通知			
受益人证明			

2. 出口商向托收行提示单据

1) 汇票

Drawn under _____COLLECTION_____

信用证或购买证第   号

L/C or A/P No. _____

日期   2010 年 5 月 16 日

Dated _____

按_____息_____付款 D/P SIGHT

Payable with interest @ _____% Per annum

号码   汇票金额   中国，   南京   年   月   日

No: __21Z1134__ Exchange for_____USD13000.00_____ Nanjing China_____

见票   日 后(本 汇 票 之 副 本 未 付)

At _____Sight of this __FIRST__ of Exchange (Second of exchange being unpaid)

pay to the order of __BANK OF COMMUNICATIONS CO., LTD., JIANGSU BRANCH__

或 其 指 定 人

金额

The sum of ____US DOLLARS THIRTEEN THOUSAND ONLY____

To   GROVE NUTRITION LTD.

64-68 AKEMAN STREET TRING

HERTFORDSHIRE HP23 6AF UK_____   __KOC CO., LTD.__

2) 发票

KOC CO., LTD.

25 Fortune Building No. 39 Hongwu Road, Nanjing, China

INVOICE

INVOICE NO. : 21Z1134	S/C NO. : 20100436	DATE OF INV: MAY 16, 2010
SOLD TO:	GROVE NUTRITION LTD. 64-68 AKEMAN STREET TRING HERTFORDSHIRE HP23 6AF UK	
FROM: SHANGHAI, CHINA	TO: FELIXSTOWE, UNITED KINGDOM	BY SEA
MARKS AND NO.	QUANTITIES AND DESCRIPTIONS	AMOUNT
N/M	DORSAN 48 EC 18800 MT USD0.6915/MT	FOB SHANGHAI TOTAL: USD13000.00
		SAY USD THIRTEEN THOUSAND ONLY
PAYMENT: D/P SIGHT		CERTIFICATE OF ORIGIN WE HEREBY CERTIFY
SHIPPER: KOC CO., LTD. REMARK: YOUR ORDER NO. : 756		THAT THE ABOVE MENTIONED GOODS ARE OF CHINA ORIGIN

SIGNATURE

3) 装箱单

装 箱 单

P A C K I N G   L I S T

发票号码:

Invoice No. : 21Z1134

合约号:

S/C No. : 10J0CW21Z-0056

日期:

DATE: 2010-05-16

品　名：DESCRIPTION

      DORSAN 48 EC

件　数：PACKAGES: 225 CARTONS

数　量：QUANTITY: 16000.00 LITRES

毛　重：GROSS WEIGHT:18800.00 KGS

净　重：NET WEIGHT: 17280.00 KGS

体　积：MEASUREMENT: 20.00 M3

唛头 MARKS

N/M

SIGNATURE

KOC CO., LTD.

Address: 25 Fortune Building No. 39 Hongwu Road, Nanjing, China

4) 提单

UNITED CONTAINER LINE		UCL 01615
as the Carrier	ORIGINAL	BILL OF LADING

and port to port shipment

SHIPPER (Complete Name/Street Address) KOC CO., LTD. Address: 25 Fortune Building No. 39 Hongwu road, Nanjing, China	MANIFEST NO.	BILL OF LADING NO .
		SHBFXT105038
	EXPORT REFERENCES DANNYZ SHAECA5028 MBI NO. : SHAEXT060438	
CONSIGNEE(Not Negotiable Unless consigned "To order") TO SHIPPERS ORDER	FORWARDING AGENT REFERENCES	
NOTIFY PARTY(Complete Name/Street Address) GROVE NUTRITION LTD. 64-68 AKEMAN STREET TRING HERTFORDSHIRE HP23 6AF, U. K.	ALSO NOTIFY, ROUTING & INSTRUCTIONS	
PRE-CARRIAGE BY(MODE) PLACE OF RECEIPT	FOR DELIVERY OF GOODS PLEASE APPLY TO: SBS WORLDWIDE LTD. SBS CARGO CENTRE,	
VESSEL/VOYAGE PORT OF LOADING EVER CONQUEST V 0566-057W SHANGHAI, CHINA PORT OF DISCHARGE FELIXSTOWE, U. K.	ANCHOR BOULEVARD, CROSSWAYS, DARTFORD, KENT DA2 6SB, UK Tel:+44 (0) 1322 424755 Fax:+44 (0) 1285592	

MARKS AND NUMBERS CONTAINER & SEAL, NUMBERS	PURCHASE ORDER NUMBER /ITEM NUMBER	NUMBER AND DESCRIPTION OF PACKAGES AND GOODS	GROSS WEIGHT	MEASURE
CCLU4236228/J856350/40 (PART OF)		(225 CARTONS 18800 KGS 20.000 CBM) CFS/CFS		

N/M		DORSAN 48 EC SHIPMENT EFFECTED BY CONTAINERIZED VESSEL	EVIDENCING	18800 KGS	20.00 M3

TOTAL IN WORDS:TWO HUNDRED AND TWENTY FIVE (225) CARTONS ONLY

FREIGHT/CHARGES, ITEM NO. RATE/RATE BASIS		PREPAID	COLLECT	DECLARATION OF VALUE IN EXCESS OF US$500 PER PACKAGE
				SEE REVERSE SIDE HEREOF CLAUSE
FREIGHT COLLECT			**AS ARRANGED**	**RECEIVED** by United Container line in apparent good order and condition unless other stated, the Goods as specified above for carriage by vessel and/or other modes of transport above. The Goods to be delivered at the above mentioned port of discharge or place of whichever applies. In accepting this Bill of Lading the Merchant(s) agree to be bound by stipulations,
	TOTAL FREIGHT			exceptions, terms and conditions on the front or back hereof, whether stamped, written or otherwise incorporated. In witness whereof three (3) original Bills of Lading have been signed, if
NUMBER OF ORIGINAL BILLS OF LADING **THREE (3)**		PLACE AND DATE OF ISSUE **SHANGHAI 2010.05.16**		not otherwise stated below all of this tenor and date. If required by Carrier, one original Bill of Lading duly endorsed must be surrendered in exchange for the or Delivery Order,
SHIPPED ON BOARD DATE **2010.05.16**				upon which the other(s) shall stand void. The contract evidenced by this Lading is governed by the laws of the Hong Kong Special Administrative Region. Any against the Carrier must be brought in the courts of the Hong Kong Special Administrative Region and no other court. **SBS CHINA LIMITED** **As Agents for Carrier**

3. 托收行寄单

托收行交通银行在审核单据无误后，缮制面函并向进口代收行邮寄单据及面函。2010年 5 月 16 日，托收行交通银行缮制以下面函连同以上单据寄往国外代收行。(假设银行编号是 OC201000065，且此笔业务通过账户行 WELLS FARGO BANK N. A. USA 来划拨资金。)

面函样本

交通银行股份有限公司
江苏省分行

Address: No.124 Zhongshan
Road(N), Nanjing, China
地址：中国南京市中山北路 124 号
Swift: COMMCNSHNJG

BANK OF COMMUNICATIONS CO., LTD.

JIANGSU PROVINCIAL BRANCH

REMITTANCE FOR COLLECTION

MAIL TO: MIDLAND BANK, UNITED KINGDOM
SUCURSAL: JUAN DE ARONA 893-SAN ISIDRO, LONDON, UNITED KINGDOM

ATTN: COLLECTION DEPT   DATE: 20100516
PLEASE ALWAYS QUOTE OUR NO. :   OC201000065

DRAWER: KOC CO., LTD.
DRAWEE: GROVE NUTRITION LTD.

WE ENCLOSE FOLLOWING DRAFT(S)/DOCUMENTS FOR COLLECTION:
DOCUMENTS INVOICE NO. : 21N1134
BILL AMOUNT: USD13000.00
TENOR: D/P SIGHT
INVOICE NUMBER：21Z1134
DRAFT   2/2
COMM. INV.   3/3
B/L   3/3
PKG LIST   3/3

TOTAL AMOUNT CLAIMED: USD13000.00
GENERAL INSTRUCTIONS:
1. THIS COLLECTION IS SUBJECT TO UNIFORM RULES FOR COLLECTIONS—ICC PUBLICATION NO. 522, 1995 REVISION.
2. PLEASE DELIVER THE DOCUMENTS AGAINST PAYMENT.
3. IN CASE OF A TIME BILL, PLEASE ADVISE US OF THE DATE OF MATURITY AFTER ACCEPTANCE.
4. ALL YOUR CHARGES ARE TO BE BORNE BY THE DRAWEE, WHICH CAN NOT BE WAIVED.
5. IF DISHONOUR, PLEASE DO NOT PROTEST, BUT ADVISE US OF NON-PAYMENT/NON-ACCEPTANCE GIVING DEFINITE REASONS.
AS TO THE PROCEEDS, PLEASE FOLLOW INSTRUCTIONS AS BELOW:
PLEASE COLLECT AND REMIT VIA CHIPS THE PROCEEDS USD13000.00 TO WELLS FARGO BANK, N. A. FORMERLY WACHOVIA BANK, NY, ABA NO. 0608 AT SIGHT/MATURITY FOR OUR H.O. SHANGHAI UID NO. 573455 FOR A/C NO. 27128383 WITH THEM UNDER YOUR/THEIR SWIFT/TELEX ADVISE TO US QUOTING OUR REFERENCE OC201000065.
THIS IS A COMPUTER GENERATED COVERING LETTER. MANUAL SIGNATURE NOT REQUIRED.

4. 代收行提示单据

代收行收到单据后根据交通银行指示向进口方提示付款交单,如进口方拒付,则代收行需要及时通知托收行(交通银行)转告出口商 KOC CO., LTD.,以便联系进口商 GROVE NUTRITION LTD.解决。

5. 业务处理要点

(1) 出口商 KOC CO., LTD.在与进口商 GROVE NUTRITION LTD.就该笔出口业务达成协议并同意采用托收方式收款后,缮制发票、汇票和装箱单,将货物交货运公司取得提单、空运单等运输单据,如需要保险还需同保险公司办理保险手续取得保单,如有需要,还需至相关机构办理手续取得质检证、产地证等托收所需单据,出口商需要保证此贸易的真实性且上面的单据能全面反映出贸易过程及合同的内容。

(2) 出口商在填写托收委托书时应注意,写明发票号码(21Z1134),金额(USD13000.00),进口代收银行(MIDLAND BANK SUCURSAL: JUAN DE ARONA 893-SAN ISIDRO LONDON, UNITED KINGDOM,需写明详细地址和国别,如未选择代收行,可要求银行代为选择,银行一般选择付款人所在地的银行代理行),托收方式(D/P)及付款期限(SIGHT),提交的单据种类和数量(汇票 2 份、发票 3 份、装箱单 3 份、提单 3 份),该笔出口业务负责人员联系方式(王小姐,电话 025-12345678)等相关事项后交予出口银行办理托收。

(3) 出口商在填制单据时还应该注意以下事项。

填制汇票时要注意大小写的正确性,如案例中的金额 USD13000.00 对应 US DOLLARS THIRTEEN THOUSAND ONLY,托收项下付款人是进口商,即 GROVE NUTRITION LTD., UK。

填制发票时应该注意,一般进口商填在左上角,商品描述应该完全反映出合同所出口的商品,如 DORSAN 48 EC,还应注意价格条款的完整,如 FOB SHANGHAI。如有更正,一定要盖章并小签。

提单应能够正确反映出合同的运输路线和整个货物的运输情况,如 SHIPPER 是 KOC CO., LTD.,把货物 DORSAN 48 EC 于 2010 年 5 月 16 日从 SHANGHAI 通过 EVER CONQUEST V 0566-057W 运往 FELIXSTOWE, U.K.,集装箱号及封号分别是 CCLU4236228/J856350,装 40 英寸的集装箱 EFFECTED BY CONTAINERIZED VESSEL,集装箱的交接是 CFS/CFS,运费是 FREIGHT COLLECT(注意和发票上的价格项匹配,现发票上是 FOB,因此提单上是 FREIGHT COLLECT,如果发票上是 CIF,则应与 FREIGHT PREPAID 项匹配)。这样提单已经从总体上反映出单据流和货物流的大概情况。再者,提单作为一个单独的单据来说,其各项要素和功能应该是明确的,如签发人身份、背书等,虽然对于托收业务,银行没有审核的责任,但对于出口商来说,还是应该从严把握,做到单据之间的一致性。

(4) 完整准确地向托收行提供代收行及进口企业名称和地址,如案例 2.1 中 MIDLAND

BANK SUCURSAL:JUAN DE ARONA 893-SAN ISIDRO LONDON, UNITED KINGDOM 项，明确注明银行是 MIDLAND BANK，城市是 LONDON，国别是 UNITED KINGDOM。单据中也注明了进口商名称(GROVE NUTRITION LTD.)和地址。因托收银行完全按照出口商的指示来处理托收业务，一般情况下，作为托收银行几乎无法、也不可能负责审核代收行的名称、地址等信息。因此如果出口商提供的代收行、进口商的名称或地址不完整、不正确，或邮寄地址错误，小则会延长收汇时间，增加风险，大则因地址错误导致单据反复转递，进而遗失，造成无法收汇。

此外，若代收银行和进口商不在一个国家，出口商一定要和进口商核实后才能交单给托收银行，上述案例中代收银行和进口商全在英国。

(5) 交单方式的风险以及防范。上述案例贸易双方签订的交单方式是 D/P SIGHT，即付款交单，这种方式的风险比承兑交单风险小，因为出口商仍然控制着货权。因此，对于初次做出口托收的出口商而言，或是面对新的进口商时，可以首先考虑此种交单方式。

图 2.1 为案例 2.1 的业务流程图。

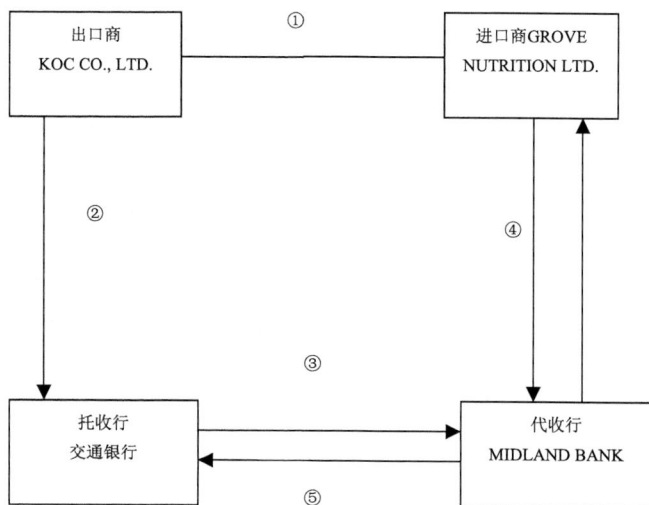

图 2.1　案例 2.1 的业务流程图

① 进出口双方签订合同并决定采用托收方式结算。

② 出口商备货并制单，以上述案例为例，交给银行汇票 2 份、发票 3 份、装箱单 3 份、提单 3 份，同时向托收行交单，要求办理托收业务。

③ 托收行接受委托，缮制银行面函和单据邮寄至进口方银行(代收行)交单。

④ 进口方银行(代收行 MIDLAND BANK)向进口商 GROVE NUTRITION LTD.提示单据，进口商根据付款条件付款。在进口商付款后，代收行 MIDLAND BANK 向进口商移交单据。

⑤ 托收行交通银行与代收行 MIDLAND BANK 之间进行清算。

二、风险控制

1. 交付单据

从此流程我们可以看出，托收这种国际贸易结算方式与汇款不同，因托收方式下出口商的全套单据是通过银行来转递的。进出口商承担的风险相对于汇款来说小一些，因为只有出口商发运货物后才能提交单据，只有进口商付款或者承兑后才能取得单据。但不论是哪种交单方式，总是出口商发货在先，收取货款在后，而出口商与托收行之间，托收行与代收行之间的关系，仅是委托和被委托，代理和被代理的关系，所以，出口货款能否收妥，何时收妥，银行是不负责的，出口商唯一依靠的是进口商的信誉，正因为如此，出口商更应注意风险的防范。以上述案例为例，前面我们已经从单据的角度进行了评价，在操作中还应注意后文提及的几方面风险。

2. 签订合同

从签订合同方面来看，出口商应根据对进口商的了解程度以及资信情况和经营作风来签订相关的贸易合同。同时还要注意合同金额与该进口商的能力是否匹配，从而对金额妥善掌握，这样才能为后续的贸易铺平道路。在实际业务中发生纠纷的一些大金额托收业务，很多就是对此疏忽所致，例如与一个小进口商签了金额达几百万美元的合同等。

此外，出口商应该注意，一旦签订了合同，则一定要严格按照合同规定办理出口，制作单据，以免造成收汇延误。

3. 商品价格

首先要随时把握出口商品在进口地的市场销售状态及行市趋势，同时对商品价格是否具有竞争力应该心中有数，一般应争取按 CIF 或 CIP 条件成交，由出口商办理货运保险，或投保出口信用险，在不采取 CIF 或 CIP 条件时，最好多加投保卖方利益险，当然还要根据个案考虑每一个合同的具体情况。在前文案例中，出口商采用的是 FOB 价格条款。实际业务中的纠纷常因价格变更引起。此外降价原因也可能是商品质量问题或商品行情有变等。

4. 进口国别的风险

托收业务中常常要考虑进口国别的风险。如案例 2.1 中，出口商要与英国进口商做生意，首先需了解英国的有关政策法令、贸易管制条例、外汇管制条例和商业惯例条例。因为在国际贸易结算处理中，单据往往带有明显的地区特点，如南亚、中东等地区就各不相同，尤其是在远期付款的情况下，许多地区或国家的处理方式各不相同，事先充分了解就可避免由于地区性问题影响安全迅速收汇从而造成损失。

5. 承兑交单

由于承兑交单只需进口商在汇票上办理承兑之后，即可取得商业单据，并凭以提取货物。所以，一般承兑交单方式只适用于远期汇票的托收。需提醒注意的是，由于只要进口商承兑后，银行便将单据释放，进口商便可取得货运单据并凭以提货，因此出口商将承担进口商到期不履行付款义务而产生的钱货两空的损失风险，尽管进口商承诺一定时期后交付汇票金额，但毕竟没有付款。对于出口商而言，一旦交了货物，就不能以物权单据来约束进口商付款，到期付不付款还是取决于进口企业的信用。一般来说，进口商一旦承兑汇票就要对债务负责，只要是比较讲信誉的进口商都会到期付款。但是也有一些资信不好的进口商，有的甚至存在欺诈行为。意图欺诈的进口商会在承兑后将货物取走，到期却拒绝付款，此时尽管出口商可凭付款人承兑的远期汇票依法起诉，但即便胜诉，进口商也不一定有能力赔偿全部货款和诉讼费用。因此在实际业务中，对于资信不是很好或不甚了解的新客户不宜采用承兑交单方式，有些出口商有时甚至要求代收行对进口企业已承兑的汇票进行保付加签，从而将商业信用转换成银行信用，大大提高收款的安全性。

6. 远期付款交单

交单方式中的远期付款交单与承兑交单相比，总体上，前者的风险要小一些。采用远期付款交单的方式，目的在于给进口商一段时间以准备或筹备资金，在到期付款之前，单据仍然由代收行掌握，以维护出口商的权益。但实际业务中，世界各国的处理方式不尽相同，有的仍视为即期，有的国家则按照 D/A 处理。尽管国际商会 URC522 重申 D/P 远期将被视为 D/P 方式，并明确双方当事人的责任，但它不具有法律的普遍约束力，通常不能逾越进口国国内法律规定。因此，建议出口商在采用 D/P 远期的结算方法时应该慎重，需考虑远期付款的期限与货物运抵目的地时间的匹配问题。如果运输时间较短，而国外代收行又坚持到期日付款赎单，常常会发生货到后，汇票期限还未到，进口商不能取单提货的情况，这样容易产生滞港费，甚至会面临对货物的存仓和保险风险。而有些国家(如中东地区)规定，货进公仓后 60 天内无人提取则容许公开拍卖，这对出口商来讲，会面临钱货两损。因此远期付款交单处理方式的不同，给贸易双方带来了更多不确定性，在选择这种方式时应慎重加以考虑。

三、往来电文

银行往来电文类型很多，且皆反映的是具体业务个案，在此简单介绍如下。

1. 催收电

以案例 2.1 为例来说明。如果托收行交通银行(SWIFT No.为 COMMCNSHNJG)2010 年

5月16日寄单给代收行MIDLAND BANK, UNITED KINGDOM(SWIFT No.为MIDLGB22)。之后,超过了合理时间还没有收汇,需发以下的催收电文。

　　MT499 电文

```
------------------------- Message Header -------------------------
Swift Output    : FIN 499 Free Format Message
Sender          : COMMCNSHNJG
Receiver        : MIDLGB22XXX
------------------------- Message Text -------------------------
    20 Transaction Reference Number
    OC201000065
    21 Related Reference
    NONREF  接收方业务编号
    79 Narrative
    ATTN: IMPORT BILLS DEPT
    RE OUR REF OC201000065 FOR USD13000.00   DATED 20100516
    DRAWER: KOC CO., LTD.
    DRAWEE: GROVE NUTRITION LTD.
    TENOR: AT SIGHT
    TO DATE, WE HAVE NOT RECEIVED THE PROCEEDS UNDER A/M REF
    OC201000065, PLS INVESTIGATE THE MATTER AND EFFECT PAYMENT ASAP.
    B. RGDS
```

2. 降价电

　　如进口商要求降价 USD3000(产生降价的原因在"风险控制"中已经阐述,这里不再重复),在进出口双方沟通后,交通银行根据出口商的授权发以下电文。

　　MT499 电文

```
------------------------- Message Header -------------------------
Swift Output    : FIN 499 Free Format Message
Sender          : COMMCNSHNJG
Receiver        : MIDLGB22XXX
------------------------- Message Text -------------------------
    20 Transaction Reference Number
```

OC201000065

21 Related Reference

NONREF

79 Narrative

ATTN: IMPORT BILLS DEPT

RE: OUR REF NO. OC201000065

FOR AMOUNT USD13000.00

DD 20100516

DRAWER: KOC CO., LTD.

DRAWEE: GROVE NUTRITION LTD.

AS PER DRAWER'S REQUEST, THE AMT OF A/M COLLECTION BE DECREASED FROM USD13000.00 TO USD10000.00 NOW, PLS UPDATE YR RECORD AND CONTACT THE DRAWEE MEANWHILE GIVE US YOUR CONFIRMATION ASAP.

B. RGDS

3. 电文的处理要点

在出口业务中代收行常发的电文有催付款电文，这一般是在托收业务超出收汇合理期时，银行主动提醒出口商注意并得到出口商授权而发。再者是降价电文，它是进出口商就降价问题达成一致后，由出口商给银行授权发出的电文。一般来说，不论何种电文，银行在发出前对整个业务都需进行全面的分析，对如何发，何时发，应和出口商做好沟通，避免日后产生纠纷。托收项下一般是发 MT499。如果不知道国外代收行的编号时，用 NON REF 来表示。

4. 电文的固定格式

TO: 代收银行

FM: 托收银行

ATTN:部门(如进口代收部门 IMPORT BILLS DEPT)

RE:引用托收的编号等

TEXT(具体内容)

B. RGDS(结尾用语)

四、总结思考

对于出口商来说，在对外签订合同时不能一味去迎合外商的要求而疏忽相关环节的警惕和防范。在使用业务术语时，尽量选择 D/A 和 D/P 这两种方式，因为在《托收统一规则》等国际惯例中都有详细规定，故进出口商和相关银行在国际贸易交往中很少就此发生争议。近几年在实际业务中，很多进出口商有时使用其他术语，例如目前比较流行的托收业务术语 CAD(也称交单付现)。由于目前《托收统一规则》并没有包括 CAD 这个术语，因此出口商很可能会承担术语解释不确定所带来的风险，这点在与进口商签订合同时应考虑周全。而实际业务中，一些银行的做法是比照 D/P 处理，在给代收行的指示中，还是采用 D/P 的条款(PLEASE DELIVER THE DOCUMENTS AGAINST PAYMENT)。

此外，在制作单据时，一是需做到单据和合同要求相符合，二是需做到单据能充分反映合同的内容。再者需注意合同的合理性和安全性，从而避免给业务的顺利完成带来不必要的风险。

对于托收行来说，在处理托收单据时，除按照出口商的指示办理外，还应注意到我国外汇管理政策和国际相关政策对业务的影响。如伊朗是受美国制裁的国家之一，因此在选择美元付款的账户行时就不应该选择美国的账户行，而应该选择代收行在美国以外地区的美元账户行。对于本案例而言，代收行在英国，出口商品是美元结算，托收行交行选择 WACHOVIA BANK, NA (NEW YORK INTERNATIONAL BRANCH)作为此业务的账户银行，因该银行在交行总行开有账户，可以直接划拨资金，因此会减少很多不必要的沟通时间，加快收汇速度。

五、实训操练

练习 2.1

2010 年 4 月 5 日，YUFAN TRADING LTD.向澳大利亚的 EMERGENCY CO., LTD. 出口商品 COAT，金额为 USD23000，指定 NATIONAL BANK OF AUSTRALIA, SYDNEY 为代收行，地址为 P.O. BOX 313 SYDNEY，期限为 D/A 60 DAYS AFTER B/L DATE(提单日期为 2010 年 4 月 2 日)。YUFAN TRADING LTD.人员携汇票 2 份，发票 3 份(发票号 T166)，装箱单 3 份，提单 3 份正本、3 份副本，来交通银行江苏省分行办理业务。如果你是银行经办人员，审核之后应如何制作托收面函呢?(假设交通银行选择 WELLS FARGO BANK, N. A. USA 作为账户行。)

交通银行股份有限公司
江苏省分行

Address: No.124 Zhongshan Road(N), Nanjing, China
地址：中国南京市中山北路 124 号
Swift: COMMCNSHNJG

BANK OF COMMUNICATIONS CO., LTD.

JIANGSU PROVINCIAL BRANCH

REMITTANCE FOR COLLECTION

MAIL TO:

DATE:

PLEASE ALWAYS QUOTE OUR NO. :

WE ENCLOSE FOLLOWING DRAFT(S)/DOCUMENTS FOR COLLECTION:

1ST 2ND DOCUMENTS INVOICE NO. :

BILL AMOUNT:

TENOR:

DOCS:

TOTAL AMOUNT CLAIMED:

GENERAL INSTRUCTIONS:

1. THIS COLLECTION IS SUBJECT TO UNIFORM RULES FOR COLLECTIONS—ICC PUBLICATION NO. 522, 1995 REVISION.

2. PLEASE DELIVER THE DOCUMENTS.

3. IN CASE OF A TIME BILL, PLEASE ADVISE US OF THE DATE OF MATURITY AFTER ACCEPTANCE.

4. ALL YOUR CHARGES ARE TO BE BORNE BY THE DRAWEE, WHICH CANNOT BE WAIVED.

5. IF DISHONOUR, PLEASE DO NOT PROTEST, BUT ADVISE US OF NON-PAYMENT/NON-ACCEPTANCE GIVING DEFINITE REASONS.

AS TO THE PROCEEDS, PLEASE FOLLOW INSTRUCTIONS AS BELOW:

PLEASE COLLECT AND REMIT VIA CHIPS THE PROCEEDS   TO   AT

WITH THEM UNDER YOUR/THEIR SWIFT/TELEX ADVISE TO US QUOTING OUR REFERENCE

THIS IS A COMPUTER GENERATED COVERING LETTER. MANUAL SIGNATURE NOT REQUIRED.

参考答案：

交通银行股份有限公司
江苏省分行

Address: No.124 Zhongshan Road(N), Nanjing, China
地址：中国南京市中山北路 124 号
Swift: COMMCNSHNJG

BANK OF COMMUNICATIONS CO., LTD.

JIANGSU PROVINCIAL BRANCH

REMITTANCE FOR COLLECTION

MAIL TO: ATIONAL BANK OF AUSTRALIA SYDNEY, P. O. BOX 313 SYDNEY, AUSTRALIA

DATE: 05 APR. 2010

PLEASE ALWAYS QUOTE OUR NO. :　OC201000XXX　流水号

DRAWER: YUFAN TRADING LTD.

DRAWEE: EMERGENCY CO., LTD.

WE ENCLOSE FOLLOWING DRAFT(S)/DOCUMENTS FOR COLLECTION:

1ST 2ND DOCUMENTS INVOICE NO. : T166

BILL AMOUNT: USD23000

TENOR: D/A 60 DAYS AFTER B/L DATE 02 APR. 2010, MATURITY 01 JUN. 2010

DOCS:

DRAFT	2/2
COMM. INV.	3/3
B/L	3/3
PKG LIST	3/3
B/L COPY	3/3

TOTAL AMOUNT CLAIMED: USD23000

GENERAL INSTRUCTIONS:

1. THIS COLLECTION IS SUBJECT TO UNIFORM RULES FOR COLLECTIONS－ICC PUBLICATION NO. 522, 1995 REVISION.

2. PLEASE DELIVER THE DOCUMENTS AGAINST ACCEPTANCE.

3. IN CASE OF A TIME BILL, PLEASE ADVISE US OF THE DATE OF MATURITY AFTER ACCEPTANCE.

4. ALL YOUR CHARGES ARE TO BE BORNE BY THE DRAWEE, WHICH CANNOT BE WAIVED.

5. IF DISHONOUR, PLEASE DO NOT PROTEST, BUT ADVISE US OF NON-PAYMENT/NON-ACCEPTANCE GIVING DEFINITE REASONS.

AS TO THE PROCEEDS, PLEASE FOLLOW INSTRUCTIONS AS BELOW:

PLEASE COLLECT AND REMIT VIA CHIPS THE PROCEEDS USD23000 TO WELLS FARGO BANK, N.A. FORMERLY WACHOVIA BANK, NY ABA NO. 0608 AT SIGHT/MATURITY FOR OUR H.O. SHANGHAI UID NO. 573455 FOR A/C NO. 27128383 WITH THEM UNDER YOUR/THEIR SWIFT/TELEX ADVISE TO US QUOTING OUR REFERENCE OC201000XXX.

THIS IS A COMPUTER GENERATED COVERING LETTER. MANUAL SIGNATURE NOT REQUIRED.

此案例交单方式是 D/A 远期。需提醒注意的是，若邮寄单据后，经查快邮记录知对方已收到单据，但未及时承兑，托收行需要发送催收电文，催代收行承兑。此时应如何填制电文呢？

MT499 电文

```
-------------------------- Message Header -----------------------
Swift Output    : FIN 499 Free Format Message
Sender          :
Receiver        :
-------------------------- Message Text -----------------------
    20 Transaction Reference Number


    21 Related Reference


    79 Narrative
    ATTN:
    RE
    DRAWER :
    DRAWEE :
    TENOR:


    B. RGDS
```

参考答案:

MT499 电文

------------------------ Message Header ------------------------
Swift Output   : FIN 499 Free Format Message
Sender   : COMMCNSHNJG
Receiver   : NATAUS33XXX
------------------------ Message Text ------------------------
   20 Transaction Reference Number
   OC201000XXXX
   21 Related Reference
   NON REF
   79 Narrative
   ATTN: IMPORT BILLS DEPT
   RE OUR REF OC201000XXX FOR USD23000.00 DATED 20100405
   DRAWER : YUFAN TRADING LTD.
   DRAWEE : EMERGENCY CO., LTD.
   TENOR: D/A 60 DAYS AFTER B/L DATE 02 APR. 2010, MATURITY 01 JUN. 2010
   THE COLLECTION OUR REF. OCXXXXXXX UNACCEPTABLE FOR A LONG TIME, PLS
   INVESTIGATE THE MATTER AND ACCEPT IT ASAP.
   B. RGDS

如果寄出不久，出口商要求降价至金额 USD3000 并授权托收行发降价电文，又应如何填制呢?

MT499 电文

------------------------ Message Header ------------------------
Swift Output   : FIN 499 Free Format Message
Sender   :
Receiver   :
------------------------ Message Text ------------------------
   20 Transaction Reference Number

   21 Related Reference

   79 Narrative

RE: OUR REF NO.

DRAWER:

DRAWEE:

TENOR:

B. RGDS

参考答案：

MT499 电文

-------------------------- Message Header ------------------------

Swift Output   : FIN 499 Free Format Message

Sender   : COMMCNSHNJG

Receiver   : NATAUS33XXX

-------------------------- Message Text ------------------------

20 Transaction Reference Number

OC201000XXX

21 Related Reference

NON REF

79 Narrative

RE: OUR REF NO. OC201000XXX

FOR AMOUNT USD23000.00

DATED 05 APR. 2010

DRAWER: YUFAN TRADING LTD.

DRAWEE: EMERGENCY CO., LTD.

TENOR: D/A 60 DAYS AFTER B/L DATE 02 APR. 2010, MATURITY 01 JUN. 2010

AS PER DRAWER'S REQUEST, THE AMT OF A/M COLLECTION BE CHANGED FROM USD23000.00 TO USD3000.00 NOW, PLS UPDATE YR RECORD AND CONTACT THE DRAWEE MEANWHILE GIVE US YOUR CONFIRMATION ASAP.

B. RGDS

假设经过上面的催承兑后，代收行来电做了承兑，且在联系进口商的同时，在承兑电文中对新金额做了确认，但是承兑付款日到期，货款没有收到。此时，托收行应该主动提醒出口商与进口商进行沟通，同时发电文催收付款。

MT499 电文

------------------------- Message Header -------------------------

Swift Output   : FIN 499 Free Format Message

Sender   :

Receiver   :

------------------------- Message Text -------------------------

20 Transaction Reference Number

21 Related Reference

79 Narrative

ATTN:

RE

DRAWER :

DRAWEE :

TENOR:

B. RGDS

参考答案：

MT499 电文

------------------------- Message Header -------------------------

Swift Output   : FIN 499 Free Format Message

Sender   : COMMCNSHNJG

Receiver   : NATAUS33XXX

------------------------- Message Text -------------------------

20 Transaction Reference Number

OC201000XXX

21 Related Reference

NONREF

79 Narrative

ATTN: IMPORT BILLS DEPT

RE OUR REF. OC201000XXX FOR USD3000.00 DATED 20100405

DRAWER: YUFAN TRADING LTD.

DRAWEE: EMERGENCY CO., LTD.

TENOR: D/A 60 DAYS AFTER B/L DATE 02 APR. 2010, MATURITY 01 JUN. 2010

TO DATE, WE HAVE NOT RECEIVED THE PROCEEDS UNDER A/M REF

OC201000XXX, PLS INVESTIGATE THE MATTER AND EFFECT PAYMENT ASAP.

B. RGDS

练习 2.2

2010 年 3 月 6 日，南京的 JIANGSU HOSO COMPANY 向德国的 GLOBAL HYGIENE PTY., LTD. 出口商品 GLOVE，金额为 EUR22688.00，指定 COMMERZBANK FRANKFURT 为代收行，地址为 P.O. BOX 234, FRANKFURT，期限为 D/P 60 DAYS AFTER B/L DATE(提单日期为 2010 年 3 月 3 日)。JIANGSU HOSO COMPANY 人员携汇票 2 份，发票 3 份(号码 FM147)，装箱单 3 份，提单 3 份正本、3 份副本，保单 3 份来交通银行江苏省分行办理业务。如果你是银行经办人员，审核之后应如何制作托收面函呢？

交通银行股份有限公司

江苏省分行

Address: No.124 Zhongshan
Road(N), Nanjing, China
地址：中国南京市中山北路 124 号
Swift: COMMCNSHNJG

BANK OF COMMUNICATIONS CO., LTD.

JIANGSU PROVINCIAL BRANCH

REMITTANCE FOR COLLECTION

MAIL TO:

DATE:

PLEASE ALWAYS QUOTE OUR NO. :

DRAWER:

DRAWEE:

WE ENCLOSE FOLLOWING DRAFT(S)/DOCUMENTS FOR COLLECTION:

1ST 2ND DOCUMENTS INVOICE NO. :

BILL AMOUNT:

TENOR:

DOCS:

TOTAL AMOUNT CLAIMED:

GENERAL INSTRUCTIONS:

1. THIS COLLECTION IS SUBJECT TO UNIFORM RULES FOR COLLECTIONS－ICC PUBLICATION NO. 522, 1995 REVISION.

2. PLEASE DELIVER THE DOCUMENTS

3. IN CASE OF A TIME BILL, PLEASE ADVISE US OF THE DATE OF MATURITY AFTER ACCEPTANCE.

4. ALL YOUR CHARGES ARE TO BE BORNE BY THE DRAWEE, WHICH CANNOT BE WAIVED.

5. IF DISHONOUR, PLEASE DO NOT PROTEST, BUT ADVISE US OF NON-PAYMENT/NON-ACCEPTANCE GIVING DEFINITE REASONS.

AS TO THE PROCEEDS, PLEASE FOLLOW INSTRUCTIONS AS BELOW:

PLEASE COLLECT AND REMIT VIA CHIPS THE PROCEEDS 　　TO 　此处填该币种(欧元)项下交通银行开有账户的银行(如 COMMDEFF)的名称、地址以及账号 　　　　AT 　　WITH THEM UNDER YOUR/THEIR SWIFT/TELEX ADVISE TO US QUOTING OUR REFERENCE

　 THIS IS A COMPUTER GENERATED COVERING LETTER. MANUAL SIGNATURE NOT REQUIRED.

参考答案：

交通银行股份有限公司
江苏省分行

Address: No.124 Zhongshan
Road(N), Nanjing, China
地址：中国南京市中山北路 124 号
Swift: COMMCNSHNJG

BANK OF COMMUNICATIONS CO., LTD.

JIANGSU PROVINCIAL BRANCH

REMITTANCE FOR COLLECTION

MAIL TO: COMMERZBANK FRANKFURT(代收行)，(地址为)P. O. BOX 234 FRANKFURT

DATE: 06 MAR. 2010

PLEASE ALWAYS QUOTE OUR NO.：　OC201000XXX　流水号

DRAWER: JIANGSU HOSO COMPANY

DRAWEE: GLOBAL HYGIENE PTY., LTD.

WE ENCLOSE FOLLOWING DRAFT(S)/DOCUMENTS FOR COLLECTION:

1ST 2ND DOCUMENTS INVOICE NO.: FM147

BILL AMOUNT: EUR22688.00

TENOR: D/P 60 DAYS AFTER B/L DATE 03 MAR. 2010, MATURITY 02 MAY 2010

DOCS:

DRAFT	2/2
COMM. INV.	3/3
B/L	3/3
PKG LIST	3/3
B/L COPY	3/3
INSURANCE POLICY	3/3

TOTAL AMOUNT CLAIMED: EUR22688.00

GENERAL INSTRUCTIONS:

1. THIS COLLECTION IS SUBJECT TO UNIFORM RULES FOR COLLECTIONS—ICC PUBLICATION NO. 522, 1995 REVISION.

2. PLEASE DELIVER THE DOCUMENTS AGAINST PAYMENT.

3. IN CASE OF A TIME BILL, PLEASE ADVISE US OF THE DATE OF MATURITY AFTER ACCEPTANCE.

4. ALL YOUR CHARGES ARE TO BE BORNE BY THE DRAWEE, WHICH CANNOT BE WAIVED.

5. IF DISHONOUR, PLEASE DO NOT PROTEST, BUT ADVISE US OF NON-PAYMENT/NON-ACCEPTANCE GIVING DEFINITE REASONS.

AS TO THE PROCEEDS, PLEASE FOLLOW INSTRUCTIONS AS BELOW:

PLEASE COLLECT AND REMIT VIA CHIPS THE PROCEEDS EUR22688.00 TO BANK OF COMMUNICATIONS CO., LTD., FRANKFURT BRANCH AT SIGHT/MATURITY FOR OUR H.O. SHANGHAI A/C NO. 94753260500268 WITH THEM UNDER YOUR/THEIR SWIFT/TELEX ADVISE TO US QUOTING OUR REFERENCE OC201000XXX.

THIS IS A COMPUTER GENERATED COVERING LETTER. MANUAL SIGNATURE NOT REQUIRED.

练习 2.3

2010 年 1 月 9 日，南京的 WIDE CO., LTD.向香港的 HANDS ORIGIN LTD.出口商品 SHIRT，金额为 HKD54635，指定 HSBC BANK LTD. HONG KONG 为代收行，地址为 20 GLOUCESTER ROAD, WAN CHAI, HONG KONG，期限为 D/P SIGHT。WIDE CO., LTD.人员携汇票 2 份，发票 3 份(号码 KK258)，装箱单 3 份，提单 3 份正本、3 份副本，产地证 1 份来交通银行江苏省分行办理业务。如果你是银行经办人员，审核之后应如何制作托收面函呢？

交通银行股份有限公司
江苏省分行

Address: No.124 Zhongshan Road(N), Nanjing, China
地址：中国南京市中山北路 124 号
Swift: COMMCNSHNJG

BANK OF COMMUNICATIONS CO., LTD.

JIANGSU PROVINCIAL BRANCH

REMITTANCE FOR COLLECTION

MAIL TO:

DATE:

PLEASE ALWAYS QUOTE OUR NO. :

DRAWER:

DRAWEE:

WE ENCLOSE FOLLOWING DRAFT(S)/DOCUMENTS FOR COLLECTION:

1ST 2ND DOCUMENTS INVOICE NO. :

BILL AMOUNT:

TENOR:

DOCS:

TOTAL AMOUNT CLAIMED:

GENERAL INSTRUCTIONS:

1. THIS COLLECTION IS SUBJECT TO UNIFORM RULES FOR COLLECTIONS—ICC PUBLICATION NO. 522, 1995 REVISION.

2. PLEASE DELIVER THE DOCUMENTS

3. IN CASE OF A TIME BILL, PLEASE ADVISE US OF THE DATE OF MATURITY AFTER ACCEPTANCE.

4. ALL YOUR CHARGES ARE TO BE BORNE BY THE DRAWEE, WHICH CANNOT BE WAIVED.

5. IF DISHONOUR, PLEASE DO NOT PROTEST, BUT ADVISE US OF NON-PAYMENT/NON-ACCEPTANCE GIVING DEFINITE REASONS.

AS TO THE PROCEEDS, PLEASE FOLLOW INSTRUCTIONS AS BELOW:

PLEASE COLLECT AND REMIT VIA CHIPS THE PROCEEDS   TO   此处填该币种(港币)项下交通银行开有账户的银行(如 COMMHKHH)的名称、地址以及账号   AT   WITH THEM UNDER YOUR/THEIR SWIFT/TELEX ADVISE TO US QUOTING OUR REFERENCE

THIS IS A COMPUTER GENERATED COVERING LETTER. MANUAL SIGNATURE NOT REQUIRED.

参考答案：

交通银行股份有限公司

江苏省分行

BANK OF COMMUNICATIONS CO., LTD.

JIANGSU PROVINCIAL BRANCH

Address: No.124 Zhongshan Road(N), Nanjing, China
地址：中国南京市中山北路 124 号
Swift: COMMCNSHNJG

REMITTANCE FOR COLLECTION

MAIL TO: HSBC BANK LTD., HONG KONG 20 GLOUCESTER ROAD, WAN CHAI, HONG KONG

DATE: 09 JAN. 2010

PLEASE ALWAYS QUOTE OUR NO. :   OC201000XXX   流水号

DRAWER: WIDE CO., LTD.

DRAWEE: HANDS ORIGIN LTD.

WE ENCLOSE FOLLOWING DRAFT(S)/DOCUMENTS FOR COLLECTION:

1ST 2ND DOCUMENTS INVOICE NO. : KK258

BILL AMOUNT: HKD54635.00

TENOR: D/P SIGHT

DOCS:

DRAFT	2/2
COMM. INV.	3/3
B/L	3/3
PKG LIST	3/3
B/L COPY	3/3
CERT OF ORIGIN	1/1

TOTAL AMOUNT CLAIMED: HKD54635.00

GENERAL INSTRUCTIONS:

1. THIS COLLECTION IS SUBJECT TO UNIFORM RULES FOR COLLECTIONS—ICC PUBLICATION NO. 522, 1995 REVISION.

2. PLEASE DELIVER THE DOCUMENTS AGAINST PAYMENT.

3. IN CASE OF A TIME BILL, PLEASE ADVISE US OF THE DATE OF MATURITY AFTER ACCEPTANCE.

4. ALL YOUR CHARGES ARE TO BE BORNE BY THE DRAWEE, WHICH CANNOT BE WAIVED.

5. IF DISHONOUR, PLEASE DO NOT PROTEST, BUT ADVISE US OF NON-PAYMENT/NON-ACCEPTANCE GIVING DEFINITE REASONS.

AS TO THE PROCEEDS, PLEASE FOLLOW INSTRUCTIONS AS BELOW:

PLEASE COLLECT AND REMIT VIA CHIPS THE PROCEEDS HKD54635.00 TO BANK OF COMMUNICATIONS CO., LTD., HONG KONG BRANCH AT SIGHT/MATURITY FOR OUR H.O. SHANGHAI A/C NO. 9475326 WITH THEM UNDER YOUR/THEIR SWIFT/TELEX ADVISE TO US QUOTING OUR REFERENCE OC201000XXX.

THIS IS A COMPUTER GENERATED COVERING LETTER. MANUAL SIGNATURE NOT REQUIRED.

第二节 进 口 代 收

一、业务场景与操作

案例 2.2

香港的滕锦公司 HONG KONG TENGJIN INTERNATIONAL COMPANY LIMITED 采用托收 D/P SIGHT 方式由港中行 BANK OF CHINA (HONG KONG) LIMITED 作为托收行，以交通银行南京分行为代收行，向南京埃特贸易有限公司(NANJING IRTEEL TRADE CO., LTD.)就出口货物收取款项 USD41609.38。

1. 代收行验收单据和指示

2010 年 7 月 3 日代收行交行在收到托收行港中行寄来的托收面函(如下)和单据后，经审查无误后打印"进口代收(到单)通知书"并附加主要单据复印件(主要单据一般为发票、运输单据和保单)，同时提示客户。在客户同意付款后，交行扣减客户账户款项，并按照托收行港中行付款指示对外付款，同时放单给客户提货。

如承兑，则在获得客户书面承兑后交行即可放单，待到期后客户再付款。如客户拒付，则及时通知托收行，按其指示处理单据。

托收面函：

BANK OF CHINA (HONG KONG) LIMITED, HONG KONG
REMITTANCE FOR COLLECTION

MAIL TO: BANK OF COMMUNICATINS JIANGSU PROVINCIAL BRANCH

ATTN:COLLECTION DEPT   DATE: 20100629

PLEASE ALWAYS QUOTE OUR NO.: 265B10EC006359

DRAWER: HONG KONG TENGJIN INTERNATIONAL CO., LTD.

DRAWEE: NANJING IRTEEL TRADE CO., LTD.

INVOICE NO.: IN-JTI100421

WE ENCLOSE FOLLOWING DRAFT(S)/DOCUMENTS FOR COLLECTION:

BILL AMOUNT: USD41609.38

TENOR: D/P AT SIGHT

DRAFT   2/2

COMM. INV.   4/4

QLY.CERT   2/2

WEIGHT LIST   2/2

TOTAL AMOUNT CLAIMED: USD41609.38

GENERAL INSTRUCTIONS:

1. THIS COLLECTION IS SUBJECT TO UNIFORM RULES FOR COLLECTIONS—ICC PUBLICATION NO. 522, 1995 REVISION.

2. PLEASE DELIVER THE DOCUMENTS AGAINST PAYMENT.

3. IN CASE OF A TIME BILL, PLEASE ADVISE US OF THE DATE OF MATURITY AFTER ACCEPTANCE.

4. ALL YOUR CHARGES ARE TO BE BORNE BY THE DRAWEE, WHICH CANNOT BE WAIVED.

5. IF DISHONOUR, PLEASE DO NOT PROTEST, BUT ADVISE US OF NON-PAYMENT/NON-ACCEPTANCE GIVING DEFINITE REASONS.

AS TO THE PROCEEDS, PLEASE FOLLOW INSTRUCTIONS AS BELOW:

PLEASE COLLECT AND REMIT VIA CHIPS THE PROCEEDS USD 41609.38 TO BKCHUS33XXX，FOR ACCOUNT 7201-1000101-006-001 AT MATURITY.

2. 代收行发通知

代收行交行根据托收行港中行寄来的托收面函和单据填制下面的进口代收(到单)通知书。假设交通银行业务编号为 IC201000022。

进口代收(到单)通知书

TO: (DRAWEE) NANJING IRTEEL TRADE CO., LTD.	DATE: 20100703 DOCUMENTS PMT REF.: IC201000022
REMITTING BANK'S REF. : 265B10EC006359	CONTRACT NO. : INVOICE NO.: IN-JTI100421
REMITTING BANK: BANK OF CHINA (HONG KONG) LIMITED, HONG KONG, BANK OF CHINA CENTER, FLOOR 19, OLYMPIAN CITY, 11 HOI FAI ROAD, WEST KOWLOON, HONG KONG	DRAWER: HONG KONG TENGJIN INTERNATIONAL COMPANY LIMITED

BILL AMOUNT: USD41609.38

REMITTING BANK CHARGES FOR DRAWEE: USD 0.00　　WAIVED(Y/N): N

INTEREST AMOUNT: USD 0.00　RATE 0.0000000 FROM　　TO:　　WAIVED(Y/N): N

TOTAL PAYMENT AMOUNT: USD 41609.38	OUR BANK CHARGES FOR DRAWEE: WAIVED(Y/N):N

DRAFT TENOR: D/P AT SIGHT　　　　　　　　　DUE DATE:

B/L DATE:　　　　　　　　　　　　　　　　DRAFT DATE: 20100503

WITH GUARANTEE(Y/N): N　　　　　　　　GUARANTEE NO. :

汇票(DRAFT)	发票 (COMM. INV.)	海关发票 (CUST. INV.)	提单(B/L)	空运单 (AWB)
2/2(1)	4/4(1)			
保险单 (INSUR POLICY/CERT)	装箱单 (PKG LIST)	重量单 (WEIGHT LIST)	质量单 (QLY. CERT)	数量单 (QTY. CERT)
		2/2(1)	2/2(1)	
产地证 (ORIGIN CERT)	受益人证明 (BENE. CERT)	装船通知 (SHIP. ADVICE)		

INFORMATION:

兹将上述全套托收单据附上，请贵公司认真审查并注意以下事项：

1. 我行将严格遵照国际商会 1995 年第 522 号出版物《托收统一规则》办理代收项下一切事宜。

2. 贵公司同意付款/承兑赎单时，请把所配核销单填好返回我行，并在来单通知书上注明是否承担银行费用/利息，加盖贵公司在我行的签章。

3. 若需要购汇付款，请先办好批汇手续，并把足额款项和银行费用(若有)调入我行。

4. 若拒付或要求退单，请书面通知我行并陈述理由。

5. 如发现所附单据中有不属于贵公司的内容，请速交于我行。电话：　　　　　　　联系人：

我公司已收到托收单据。现就有关事项回复如下：

对于 D/P 详细单据，我公司同意对外付款。

对于 D/A 项下单据，我公司同意对外承兑，请在到期日主动对外付款。

若到期日前，我公司对对外付款有异议，将另行发出不同意付款的书面通知。

对于下列费用和利息，我公司以其前面的方框中的符号 V 或 X 表示是否同意支付。V 表示同意；X 表示不同意。

[ ]你行的代收费用和电报费　　　　[ ]托收行的费用　　　　[ ]托收行指示收取的利息

该托收单据项下的货款，由我公司承担的银行费用及利息，请你行主动从我公司在你行的　　　　账户中扣付。

公司签章

2010 年 7 月 3 日

银行签章

3. 业务处理要点

对于进口代收(到单)通知书，要在审核港中行所寄的面函和单据之后正确地填制。填制时需注意以下几点。第一是对业务的描述，如发票号(INVOICE NO. : IN-JTI100421)、出口商(DRAWER: HONG KONG TENGJIN INTERNATIONAL CO., LTD.)、进口商(DRAWEE: NANJING IRTEEL TRADE CO., LTD.)、金额(BILL AMOUNT: USD41609.38 和 TOTAL PAYMENT AMOUNT: USD41609.38，如果不一致，应去电查询，是否里面含有电汇等情况)、单据份数和种类(DRAFT 2/2; COMM. INV. 4/4; QLY. CERT 2/2; WEIGHT LIST 2/2)。第二是付款方式(D/P AT SIGHT)，它决定了此笔业务如何付款，何时付款，因此千万需注意。第三是汇款路经的正确选择。因 BANK OF CHINA (HONG KONG) LIMITED, HONG KONG 是交通银行的账户行，因此对于此笔款项划拨，发电文 MT202 即可完成款项的支付；若是非账户行，则进口代收(到单)通知书还应该把相应的账户行注明，以方便付汇时使用。

图 2.2 为案例 2.2 的业务流程图。

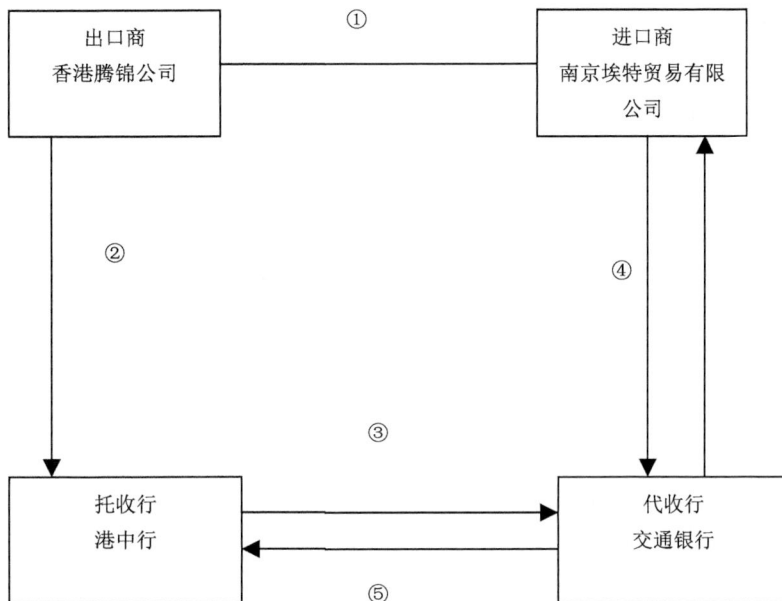

图 2.2 案例 2.2 的业务流程图

① 进出口双方签订合同并决定采用托收方式结算。

② 出口商香港腾锦公司(HONG KONG TENGJIN INTERNATIONAL COMPANY LIMITED)备货并制单(汇票 2 份、发票 4 份、重量单 2 份、质量单 2 份),同时向托收行港中行(BANK OF CHINA (HONG KONG) LIMITED)交单,要求办理托收业务。

③ 托收行港中行接受委托,缮制银行面函和单据邮寄至代收行交通银行交单。

④ 进口方银行(代收行交通银行)向进口商南京埃特贸易有限公司提示单据,进口商根据付款条件付款。在进口商付款后,代收行交通银行向进口商南京埃特贸易有限公司提交单据。

⑤ 代收行交通银行与托收行港中行之间进行清算。

二、风险控制

进口代收是出口托收业务的一个反向,进口代收和出口托收是一个业务过程的两个侧面,其风险点请参考前文出口托收部分,这里不再展开叙述。只需提醒注意:作为进口商,应按进口代收的规定处理业务,付款交单项下,应注意资金的落实,承兑交单项下注意承兑手续的完备;作为代收行,应注意对有关法律政策的掌握,如应严格按外管政策查验外管公布的《进口付汇核销黑名单》和《进口付汇登记分类表》(如有),确认进口商具有的相应付汇资格等。

三、往来电文

涉及此部分的银行往来电文类型很多，且皆反映的是具体业务个案。这里介绍进口代收项下最常用的电文。

1. 电文 MT410

代收行收到单据的当天向托收行发电文 MT410，告其已经收到寄送的单据。

MT410 电文

```
------------------------- Message Header -------------------------
Swift Output        : FIN 410 Acknowledgement
Sender              : COMMCNSHNJG
Receiver            : BKCHHKHHXXX(港中行)
------------------------- Message Text -------------------------
    20      Sending Bank's TRN
            IC201000022
    21      Related Reference
            265B10EC006359
    32B     Amount Acknowledged
            Currency        USD
            Amount          41609.38
```

就案例 2.2 而言，在付款方式 D/P AT SIGHT 项下，向账户行发电文 MT202，及时付款。(假设交通银行选择的账户行是 IRVTUS3NXXX，款项通过港中行的美元账户行 BKCHUS33XXX 进行划拨。)

MT202 电文

```
------------------------- Message Header -------------------------
Swift Output        : FIN 202 General Fin Inst Transfer
Sender              : COMMCNSHNJG
Receiver            : IRVTUS3NXXX
------------------------- Message Text -------------------------
    20 Transaction Reference Number
    IC201000022
    21 Related Reference
    265B10EC006359
```

32A Value Date, Currency Code, Amt

Date 100703

Currency USD

Amount 41609.38

53A Sender's Correspondent - BIC

BIC COMMCNSHXXX

57A Account With Institution - BIC

BIC BKCHUS33XXX

58A Beneficiary Institution - BIC

Party Identifier /7201-1000101-006-001

BIC BKCHHKHHXXX

72 Sender to Receiver Information

/BNF/IC201000022

2. 处理电文要点

注意在托收业务中，进口和出口是相反的。出口电文中 20 栏是出口托收行的编号，而在进口电文中是进口代收行的编号。如没有则注明 NON REF。

四、总结思考

对于该产品需时提示注意的是，由于承兑交单是出口商给予进口商的资金融通，代收行不负责承担进口商对汇票的到期付款，只是负责催促、通知有关信息，因此对出口商来说风险较大。

五、实训操练

练习 2.4

2010 年 1 月 11 日，代收行(假设是交通银行)收到 BANK EKONOMI RAHARJA PT. JAKARTA 寄来的托收全套单据及面函，其面函如下所示：

BANK EKONOMI RAHARJA PT. JAKARTA

REMITTANCE FOR COLLECTION

MAIL TO: BANK OF COMMUNICATIONS   JIANGSU PROVINCIAL BRANCH

ATTN: COLLECTION DEPT   DATE: 20100104

PLEASE ALWAYS QUOTE OUR NO. : OBCYOG100001

DRAWER: CV INDAROMA

DRAWEE: NANJING ANIMA CO., LTD.

INVOICE NO. : 0201/NRNP-2/0954

WE ENCLOSE FOLLOWING DRAFT(S)/DOCUMENTS FOR COLLECTION:

DOCUMENTS INVOICE NO. : 0201/NRNP-2/0954

BILL AMOUNT: USD82420.00

TENOR: D/ A 30 DAYS AFTER SIGHT

DRAFT	2/2
COMM. INV.	3/3
B/L	3/3
PKG LIST	3/3

TOTAL AMOUNT CLAIMED: USD82420.00

GENERAL INSTRUCTIONS:

1. THIS COLLECTION IS SUBJECT TO UNIFORM RULES FOR COLLECTIONS—ICC PUBLICATION NO. 522, 1995 REVISION.

2. PLEASE DELIVER THE DOCUMENTS AGAINST ACCEPTANCE.

3. IN CASE OF A TIME BILL, PLEASE ADVISE US OF THE DATE OF MATURITY AFTER ACCEPTANCE.

4. ALL YOUR CHARGES ARE TO BE BORNE BY THE DRAWEE, WHICH CANNOT BE WAIVED.

5. IF DISHONOUR, PLEASE DO NOT PROTEST, BUT ADVISE US OF NON-PAYMENT/NON-ACCEPTANCE GIVING DEFINITE REASONS.

AS TO THE PROCEEDS, PLEASE FOLLOW INSTRUCTIONS AS BELOW:

PLEASE COLLECT AND REMIT VIA CHIPS THE PROCEEDS USD 82420.00 TO MRMDUS33，FOR ACCOUNT 173142 AT MATURITY.

如果你是银行经办人员，审核全套单据及面函后，应如何填制进口代收(到单)通知书呢？假设银行编号是 IC201000011。

进口代收(到单)通知书

TO:(DRAWEE)	DATE:
	DOCUMENTS PMT REF. :
REMITTING BANK'S REF. :	CONTRACT NO. :
	INVOICE NO. :

REMITTING BANK:			DRAWER:	
BILL AMOUNT:				
REMITTING BANK CHARGES FOR DRAWEE: USD0.00			WAIVED(Y/N): N	
INTEREST AMOUNT: USD 0.00　RATE 0.0000000　FROM　TO:			WAIVED(Y/N): N	
TOTAL PAYMENT AMOUNT:			OUR　BANK　CHARGES　FOR　DRAWEE: WAIVED(Y/N):N	

DRAFT TENOR:　　　　　　　　　　　　　　DUE DATE:

B/L DATE:　　　　　　　　　　　　　　　　DRAFT DATE:

WITH GUARANTEE(Y/N):N　　　　　　　　GUARANTEE NO. :

汇票(DRAFT)	发票 (COMM. INV.)	海关发票 (CUST. INV.)	提单(B/L)	空运单(AWB)
保险单 (INSUR POLICY/CERT)	装箱单 (PKG LIST)	重量单 (WEIGHT LIST)	质量单 (QLY. CERT)	数量单 (QTY. CERT)
产地证 (ORIGIN CERT)	受益人证明 (BENE. CERT)	装船通知 (SHIP. ADVICE)		

INFORMATION:

兹将上述全套托收单据附上，请贵公司认真审查并注意以下事项：

1. 我行将严格遵照国际商会 1995 年第 522 号出版物《托收统一规则》办理代收项下一切事宜。

2. 贵公司同意付款/承兑赎单时，请把所配核销单填好返回我行，并在来单通知书上注明是否承担银行费用/利息，加盖贵公司在我行的签章。

3. 若需要购汇付款，请先办好批汇手续，并把足额款项和银行费用(若有)调入我行。

4. 若拒付或要求退单，请书面通知我行并陈述理由。

5. 如发现所附单据中有不属于贵公司的内容，请速交于我行。电话：　　　　　　　　联系人：

我公司已收到托收单据。现就有关事项回复如下：

对于 D/P 详细单据，我公司同意对外付款。

对于 D/A 项下单据，我公司同意对外承兑，请在到期日主动对外付款。

若到期日前，我公司对外付款有异议，将另行发出不同意付款的书面通知。

对于下列费用和利息，我公司以其前面的方框中的符号 V 或 X 表示是否同意支付。V 表示同意；X 表示不同意。

[ ]你行的代收费用和电报费　　　[ ]托收行的费用　　　[ ]托收行指示收取的利息

该托收单据项下的货款，由我公司承担的银行费用及利息，请你行主动从我公司在你行的　　　　账户中扣付。

公司签章

年　月　日

银行签章

参考答案:

进口代收(到单)通知书

TO:(DRAWEE) NANJING ANIMA CO., LTD.	DATE:20100111
	DOCUMENTS PMT REF. : IC201000011
REMITTING BANK'S REF. : OBCYOG100001	CONTRACT NO.:
	INVOICE NO.: 0201/NRNP-2/0954
REMITTING BANK: BANK EKONOMI RAHARJA PT. JAKARTA	DRAWER: CV INDAROMA

BILL AMOUNT: USD82420.00	
REMITTING BANK CHARGES FOR DRAWEE: USD0.00	WAIVED(Y/N): N
INTEREST AMOUNT: USD 0.00 RATE 0.0000000 FROM TO:	WAIVED(Y/N): N
TOTAL PAYMENT AMOUNT: USD82420.00	OUR BANK CHARGES FOR DRAWEE: WAIVED(Y/N): N

DRAFT TENOR: D/A 30 DAYS AFTER SIGHT   DUE DATE:

B/L DATE: DRAFT DATE: 20100108

WITH GUARANTEE(Y/N): N   GUARANTEE NO. :

汇票(DRAFT)	发票 (COMM. INV.)	海关发票 (CUST. INV.)	提单(B/L)	空运单(AWB)
2/2(1)	3/3(1)		3/3(1)	
保险单 (INSUR POLICY/CERT)	装箱单 (PKG LIST)	重量单 (WEIGHT LIST)	质量单 (QLY. CERT)	数量单 (QTY. CERT)
	3/3(1)			
产地证 (ORIGIN CERT)	受益人证明 (BENE. CERT)	装船通知 (SHIP. ADVICE)		

INFORMATION:

兹将上述全套托收单据附上,请贵公司认真审查并注意以下事项:

1. 我行将严格遵照国际商会 1995 年第 522 号出版物《托收统一规则》办理代收项下一切事宜。

2. 贵公司同意付款/承兑赎单时,请把所配核销单填好返回我行,并在来单通知书上注明是否承担银行费用/利息,加盖贵公司在我行的签章。

3. 若需要购汇付款,请先办好批汇手续,并把足额款项和银行费用(若有)调入我行。

4. 若拒付或要求退单,请书面通知我行并陈述理由。

5. 如发现所附单据中有不属于贵公司的内容,请速交于我行。电话: 联系人:

我公司已收到托收单据。现就有关事项回复如下：

对于 D/P 详细单据，我公司同意对外付款。

对于 D/A 项下单据，我公司同意对外承兑，请在到期日主动对外付款。

若到期日前，我公司对对外付款有异议，将另行发出不同意付款的书面通知。

对于下列费用和利息，我公司以其前面的方框中的符号 V 或 X 表示是否同意支付。V 表示同意；X 表示不同意。

[ ]你行的代收费用和电报费　　　 [ ]托收行的费用　　　 [ ]托收行指示收取的利息

该托收单据项下的货款，由我公司承担的银行费用及利息，请你行主动从我公司在你行的　　　 账户中扣付。

公司签章
2010 年 1 月 11 日

银行签章

由于此笔业务的付款方式是 D/ A 30 DAYS AFTER SIGHT，因此需向托收银行发电文告其承兑日期是 2010 年 2 月 10 日，请填制下列电文。假设交通银行编号是 IC201000011。

MT412 电文

```
------------------------- Message Header -------------------------
Swift Output     : FIN 412 Advice of Acceptance
Sender           :
Receiver         :
------------------------- Message Text -------------------------
    20      Sending Bank's TRN


    21      Related Reference


    32A      Mat Dt, Curr Code, Amt Accepted
            Date

            Currency

            Amount
    72      Sender to Receiver Information


            B. RGDS
```

参考答案：

MT412 电文

------------------------- Message Header -------------------------

Swift Output	: FIN 412 Advice of Acceptance
Sender	: COMMCNSHNJG
Receiver	: EKONIDJAXXX

------------------------- Message Text -------------------------

20　　Sending Bank's TRN

　　　IC201000011

21　　Related Reference

　　　OBCYOG100001

32A　 Mat Dt, Curr Code, Amt Accepted

　　　Date　　　　　　100210

　　　Currency　　　　USD

　　　Amount　　　　　82420

72　　Sender to Receiver Information

　　　PLS BE INFORMED THAT THE CAPTIONED

　　　DOCUMENTS ACCEPTED BY DRAWEE AND

　　　WE'LL URGE THE DRAWEE TO EFFECT

　　　PAYMENT ON MATURITY DATE.

　　　B. RGDS

付款到期日 2010 年 2 月 10 日发电文 MT202 划拨款项，请填制下列电文。相关账户行已经填好。(假设交通银行选择 MRMDUS33XXX 作为其账户行。)

MT202 电文

------------------------- Message Header -------------------------

Swift Output	: FIN 202 General Fin Inst Transfer
Sender	:
Receiver	:

------------------------- Message Text -------------------------

20　　Transaction Reference Number

21　　Related Reference

32A   Value Date, Currency Code, Amt

       Date

       Currency

       Amount

53A   Sender's Correspondent - BIC

       BIC   COMMCNSHXXX

57A   Account With Institution - BIC

       BIC   MRMDUS33XXX

58A   Beneficiary Institution - BIC

       Party Identifier /173142

       BIC   EKONIDJAXXX

72   Sender to Receiver Information

       /BNF/IC201000011

参考答案：

MT202 电文

-------------------------- Message Header -------------------------

Swift Output   : FIN 202 General Fin Inst Transfer

Sender   : COMMCNSHNJG

Receiver   : CITIUS33XXX

-------------------------- Message Text --------------------------

20   Transaction Reference Number

       IC201000011

21   Related Reference

       OBCYOG100001

32A   Value Date, Currency Code, Amt

       Date   100210

       Currency   USD

       Amount   82420

53A   Sender's Correspondent - BIC

       BIC   COMMCNSHXXX

57A   Account With Institution - BIC

       BIC   MRMDUS33XXX

58A   Beneficiary Institution - BIC

       Party Identifier /173142

BIC   EKONIDJAXXX

72 Sender to Receiver Information

/BNF/IC201000011

练习 2.5

2010 年 3 月 3 日，假设交通银行收到 BANK OF CHINA (HONG KONG) LIMITED, HONG KONG 发来的托收面函如下：

BANK OF CHINA (HONG KONG) LIMITED, HONG KONG
REMITTANCE FOR COLLECTION

MAIL TO: BANK OF COMMUNICATIONS JIANGSU PROVINCIAL BRANCH

ATTN: COLLECTION DEPT DATE: 20100302

PLEASE ALWAYS QUOTE OUR NO. : 265B10EC003207

DRAWER: HONG KONG TENGJIN INTERNATIONAL CO., LTD.

DRAWEE: NANJING IRTEEL TRADE CO., LTD.

INVOICE NO. : IN-JTI100214

WE ENCLOSE FOLLOWING DRAFT(S)/DOCUMENTS FOR COLLECTION:

DOCUMENTS INVOICE NO. : IN-JTI100214

BILL AMOUNT: USD6332781.91

TENOR: D/A 90 DAYS AFTER SIGHT

DRAFT	2/2
COMM. INV.	3/3
B/L	3/3
PKG LIST	3/3

TOTAL AMOUNT CLAIMED: USD6332781.91

GENERAL INSTRUCTIONS:

1. THIS COLLECTION IS SUBJECT TO UNIFORM RULES FOR COLLECTIONS—ICC PUBLICATION NO. 522, 1995 REVISION.

2. PLEASE DELIVER THE DOCUMENTS AGAINST ACCEPTANCE.

3. IN CASE OF A TIME BILL, PLEASE ADVISE US OF THE DATE OF MATURITY AFTER ACCEPTANCE.

4. ALL YOUR CHARGES ARE TO BE BORNE BY THE DRAWEE, WHICH CANNOT BE WAIVED.

5. IF DISHONOUR, PLEASE DO NOT PROTEST, BUT ADVISE US OF NON-PAYMENT/NON-ACCEPTANCE GIVING DEFINITE REASONS.

AS TO THE PROCEEDS, PLEASE FOLLOW INSTRUCTIONS AS BELOW:

PLEASE COLLECT AND REMIT VIA CHIPS THE PROCEEDS USD6332781.91 TO BKCHUS33XXX，FOR ACCOUNT 7201-1000101-006-001 AT MATURITY.

如果你是银行经办人员，审核全套单据及面函后，应如何填制进口代收(到单)通知书呢？假设银行编号是 IC201000066。

进口代收(到单)通知书

TO:(DRAWEE)	DATE:
	DOCUMENTS PMT REF. :
REMITTING BANK'S REF.:	CONTRACT NO. :
	INVOICE NO. :
REMITTING BANK:	DRAWER:
BILL AMOUNT:	
REMITTING BANK CHARGES FOR DRAWEE: USD 0.00 WAIVED(Y/N): N	
INTEREST AMOUNT: USD 0.00 RATE 0.0000000 FROM TO: WAIVED(Y/N): N	
TOTAL PAYMENT AMOUNT:	OUR BANK CHARGES FOR DRAWEE: WAIVED(Y/N):N
DRAFT TENOR: D/A	DUE DATE:
B/L DATE:	DRAFT DATE:
WITH GUARANTEE(Y/N): N	GUARANTEE NO.:

汇票(DRAFT)	发票 (COMM. INV.)	海关发票 (CUST. INV.)	提单(B/L)	空运单(AWB)
保险单 (INSUR POLICY/CERT)	装箱单 (PKG LIST)	重量单 (WEIGHT LIST)	质量单 (QLY. CERT)	数量单 (QTY. CERT)
产地证 (ORIGIN CERT)	受益人证明 (BENE. CERT)	装船通知 (SHIP. ADVICE)		

INFORMATION:

兹将上述全套托收单据附上，请贵公司认真审查并注意以下事项：

1. 我行将严格遵照国际商会 1995 年第 522 号出版物《托收统一规则》办理代收项下一切事宜。

2. 贵公司同意付款/承兑赎单时，请把所配核销单填好返回我行，并在来单通知书上注明是否承担银行费用/利息，加盖贵公司在我行的签章。

3. 若需要购汇付款，请先办好批汇手续，并把足额款项和银行费用(若有)调入我行。

4. 若拒付或要求退单，请书面通知我行并陈述理由。

5. 如发现所附单据中有不属于贵公司的内容，请速交于我行。电话：   联系人：

我公司已收到托收单据。现就有关事项回复如下：

对于 D/P 详细单据，我公司同意对外付款。

对于 D/A 项下单据，我公司同意对外承兑，请在到期日主动对外付款。

若到期日前，我公司对对外付款有异议，将另行发出不同意付款的书面通知。

对于下列费用和利息，我公司以其前面的方框中的符号 V 或 X 表示是否同意支付。V 表示同意；X 表示不同意。

[ ]你行的代收费用和电报费   [ ]托收行的费用   [ ]托收行指示收取的利息

该托收单据项下的货款，由我公司承担的银行费用及利息，请你行主动从我公司在你行的   账户中扣付。

公司签章

年   月   日

银行签章

参考答案：

进口代收(到单)通知书

TO:(DRAWEE) NANJING IRTEEL TRADE CO., LTD.	DATE: 20100303 DOCUMENTS PMT REF: IC201000066
REMITTING BANK'S REF. : 265B10EC003207	CONTRACT NO. : INVOICE NO. : IN-JTI100214
REMITTING BANK: BANK OF CHINA (HONG KONG) LIMITED, HONG KONG, BANK OF CHINA CENTER, FLOOR 19, OLYMPIAN CITY, 11 HOI FAI ROAD WEST KOWLOON, HONG KONG	DRAWER: HONG KONG TENGJIN INTERNATIONAL COMPANY LIMITED
BILL AMOUNT: USD6332781.91	
REMITTING BANK CHARGES FOR DRAWEE: USD 0.00	WAIVED(Y/N): N
INTEREST AMOUNT: USD 0.00 RATE 0.0000000 FROM	TO: WAIVED(Y/N): N
TOTAL PAYMENT AMOUNT: USD6332781.91	OUR BANK CHARGES FOR DRAWEE: WAIVED(Y/N): N

DRAFT TENOR: D/A 90 DAYS AFTER SIGHT   DUE DATE:

B/L DATE: DRAFT DATE: 20100301

WITH GUARANTEE(Y/N): N   GUARANTEE NO. :

汇票 (DRAFT)	发票 (COMM. INV.)	海关发票 (CUST. INV.)	提单(B/L)	空运单 (AWB)
2/2(1)	3/3(1)		3/3(1)	
保险单 (INSUR POLICY/CERT)	装箱单 (PKG LIST)	重量单 (WEIGHT LIST)	质量单 (QLY. CERT)	数量单 (QTY. CERT)
	3/3(1)			
产地证 (ORIGIN CERT)	受益人证明 (BENE. CERT)	装船通知 (SHIP. ADVICE)		

INFORMATION:

兹将上述全套托收单据附上，请贵公司认真审查并注意以下事项：

1. 我行将严格遵照国际商会 1995 年第 522 号出版物《托收统一规则》办理代收项下一切事宜。

2. 贵公司同意付款/承兑赎单时，请把所配核销单填好返回我行，并在来单通知书上注明是否承担银行费用/利息，加盖贵公司在我行的签章。

3. 若需要购汇付款，请先办好批汇手续，并把足额款项和银行费用(若有)调入我行。

4. 若拒付或要求退单，请书面通知我行并陈述理由。

5. 如发现所附单据中有不属于贵公司的内容，请速交于我行。电话：   联系人：

我公司已收到托收单据。现就有关事项回复如下：

对于 D/P 详细单据，我公司同意对外付款。

对于 D/A 项下单据，我公司同意对外承兑，请在到期日主动对外付款。

若到期日前，我公司对对外付款有异议，将另行发出不同意付款的书面通知。

对于下列费用和利息，我公司以其前面的方框中的符号 V 或 X 表示是否同意支付。V 表示同意；X 表示不同意。

[ ]你行的代收费用和电报费   [ ]托收行的费用   [ ]托收行指示收取的利息

该托收单据项下的货款，由我公司承担的银行费用及利息，请你行主动从我公司在你行的   账户中扣付。

公司签章

2010 年 3 月 3 日

银行签章

由于此笔业务的付款方式也是 D/A 90 DAYS AFTER SIGHT，因此需向托收银行 (SWIFT No.：BKCHHKHHXXX)发电文告其承兑日期是 2010 年 6 月 1 日，请填制下列电文。

MT412 电文

```
---------------------- Message Header ----------------------
Swift Output     : FIN 412 Advice of Acceptance
Sender           :
Receiver         :
---------------------- Message Text ----------------------
    20      Sending Bank's TRN

    21      Related Reference

    32A     Mat Dt, Curr Code, Amt Accepted
            Date
            Currency
            Amount
    72      Sender to Receiver Information

            B. RGDS
```

参考答案：

MT412 电文

```
---------------------- Message Header ----------------------
Swift Output     : FIN 412 Advice of Acceptance
Sender           : COMMCNSHNJG
Receiver         : BKCHHKHHXXX
---------------------- Message Text ----------------------
    20      Sending Bank's TRN
            IC201000066
    21      Related Reference
            265B10EC003207
    32A     Mat Dt, Curr Code, Amt Accepted
            Date              100601
            Currency          USD
```

Amount   6332781.91

72 Sender to Receiver Information

PLS BE INFORMED THAT THE CAPTIONED

DOCUMENTS ACCEPTED BY DRAWEE AND

WE'LL URGE THE DRAWEE TO EFFECT

PAYMENT ON MATURITY DATE.

B. RGDS

付款到期日 2010 年 6 月 1 日发电文 MT202 划拨款项，请填制下列电文。相关账户行已经填好。假设交通银行和香港中行皆在纽约中行(SWIFT No.：BKCHUS33XXX)开有账户。

MT202 电文

-------------------------- Message Header -------------------------

Swift Output   : FIN 202 General Fin Inst Transfer

Sender   :

Receiver   :

-------------------------- Message Text --------------------------

20 Transaction Reference Number

21 Related Reference

32A Value Date, Currency Code, Amt

Date

Currency

Amount

53A Sender's Correspondent - BIC

BIC   COMMCNSHXXX

58A Beneficiary Institution - BIC

Party Identifier /7201-1000101-006-001

BIC   BKCHHKHHXXX

72 Sender to Receiver Information

/BNF/IC201000066

参考答案:

MT202 电文

```
---------------------- Message Header -----------------------
Swift Output        : FIN 202 General Fin Inst Transfer
Sender              : COMMCNSHNJG
Receiver            : BKCHUS33XXX
------------------------ Message Text -----------------------
    20    Transaction Reference Number
          IC201000066
    21    Related Reference
          265B10EC003207
    32A   Value Date, Currency Code, Amt
          Date              100601
          Currency          USD
          Amount            6332701.91
    53A   Sender's Correspondent - BIC
          BIC               COMMCNSHXXX
    58A   Beneficiary Institution - BIC
          Party Identifier /7201-1000101-006-001
          BIC               BKCHHKHHXXX
    72    Sender to Receiver Information
          /BNF/IC201000066
          //LESS USD80 AS REIM. CHAR.(80 美元作为偿付费用扣除)
```

练习 2.6

2010 年 5 月 28 日,交通银行收到 BANK OF CHINA (FRANKFURT AM MAIN) LIMITED 寄来的全套单据和托收面函,请制作通知书及付款电。

BANK OF CHINA (FRANKFURT AM MAIN) LIMITED
REMITTANCE FOR COLLECTION

MAIL TO: BANK OF COMMUNICATIONS　　JIANGSU PROVINCIAL BRANCH
ATTN: COLLECTION DEPT　　DATE: 20100524
PLEASE ALWAYS QUOTE OUR NO. : 09DEJSY26SPECYZ2

DRAWER: SITEC EUROPA HANDELS GMBH

DRAWEE: CHINA INTERNATIONAL CO., LTD., NANJING BRANCH

INVOICE NO. : 10-033

WE ENCLOSE FOLLOWING DRAFT(S)/DOCUMENTS FOR COLLECTION:

BILL AMOUNT: EUR104,983.00

TENOR: D/P AT SIGHT

DRAFT	2/2
COMM. INV.	3/3
B/L	3/3
PKG LIST	3/3
CERT OF ORIGIN	3/3

TOTAL AMOUNT CLAIMED: EUR104,983.00

GENERAL INSTRUCTIONS:

1. THIS COLLECTION IS SUBJECT TO UNIFORM RULES FOR COLLECTIONS—ICC PUBLICATION NO. 522, 1995 REVISION.

2. PLEASE DELIVER THE DOCUMENTS AGAINST PAYMENT.

3. IN CASE OF A TIME BILL, PLEASE ADVISE US OF THE DATE OF MATURITY AFTER ACCEPTANCE.

4. ALL YOUR CHARGES ARE TO BE BORNE BY THE DRAWEE, WHICH CANNOT BE WAIVED.

5. IF DISHONOUR, PLEASE DO NOT PROTEST, BUT ADVISE US OF NON-PAYMENT/NON-ACCEPTANCE GIVING DEFINITE REASONS.

AS TO THE PROCEEDS, PLEASE FOLLOW INSTRUCTIONS AS BELOW:

PLEASE COLLECT AND REMIT VIA CHIPS THE PROCEEDS EUR104,983.00 TO BKCHDEFFXXX FOR ACCOUNT 0040040016 AT MATURITY.

如果你是银行经办人员，审核全套单据和面函后，应如何填制进口代收(到单)通知书呢？假设银行编号是 IC201000062。

进口代收(到单)通知书

TO:(DRAWEE)	DATE:
	DOCUMENTS PMT REF. :
REMITTING BANK'S REF. :	CONTRACT NO. :
	INVOICE NO. :

REMITTING BANK:		DRAWER:		
BILL AMOUNT:				
REMITTING BANK CHARGES FOR DRAWEE: USD 0.00			WAIVED(Y/N): N	
INTEREST AMOUNT: USD 0.00 RATE 0.0000000 FROM		TO:	WAIVED(Y/N): N	
TOTAL PAYMENT AMOUNT:		OUR BANK CHARGES FOR DRAWEE: WAIVED(Y/N):N		
DRAFT TENOR:		DUE DATE:		
B/L DATE:		DRAFT DATE:		
WITH GUARANTEE(Y/N):N		GUARANTEE NO.:		
汇票(DRAFT)	发票 (COMM. INV.)	海关发票 (CUST. INV.)	提单(B/L)	空运单(AWB)
保险单 (INSUR POLICY/CERT)	装箱单 (PKG LIST)	重量单 (WEIGHT LIST)	质量单 (QLY. CERT)	数量单 (QTY. CERT)
产地证 (ORIGIN CERT)	受益人证明 (BENE. CERT)	装船通知 (SHIP. ADVICE)		

INFORMATION:

兹将上述全套托收单据附上，请贵公司认真审查并注意以下事项：

1. 我行将严格遵照国际商会 1995 年第 522 号出版物《托收统一规则》办理代收项下一切事宜。

2. 贵公司同意付款/承兑赎单时，请把所配核销单填好返回我行，并在来单通知书上注明是否承担银行费用/利息，加盖贵公司在我行的签章。

3. 若需要购汇付款，请先办好批汇手续，并把足额款项和银行费用(若有)调入我行。

4. 若拒付或要求退单，请书面通知我行并陈述理由。

5. 如发现所附单据中有不属于贵公司的内容，请速交于我行。电话：　　　　　　　　联系人：

我公司已收到托收单据。现就有关事项回复如下：

对于 D/P 详细单据，我公司同意对外付款。

对于 D/A 项下单据，我公司同意对外承兑，请在到期日主动对外付款。

若到期日前，我公司对对外付款有异议，将另行发出不同意付款的书面通知。

对于下列费用和利息，我公司以其前面的方框中的符号 V 或 X 表示是否同意支付。V 表示同意；X 表示不同意。

[ ]你行的代收费用和电报费　　　[ ]托收行的费用　　　[ ]托收行指示收取的利息

该托收单据项下的货款，由我公司承担的银行费用及利息，请你行主动从我公司在你行的　　　　账户中扣付。

公司签章

年　月　日

银行签章

参考答案：

进口代收(到单)通知书

TO: (DRAWEE) CHINA INTERNATIONAL CO., LTD., NANJING BRANCH	DATE: 20100528
	DOCUMENTS PMT REF. :IC201000062
REMITTING BANK'S REF. : 09DEJSY26SPECYZ2	CONTRACT NO. :
	INVOICE NO. : 10-033
REMITTING BANK: BANK OF CHINA (FRANKFURT AM MAIN) LIMITED	DRAWER: SITEC EUROPA HANDELS GMBH
BILL AMOUNT: EUR104,983.00	
REMITTING BANK CHARGES FOR DRAWEE: USD 0.00　　WAIVED(Y/N): N	
INTEREST AMOUNT: USD 0.00　RATE 0.0000000 FROM　　TO:　　WAIVED(Y/N): N	
TOTAL PAYMENT AMOUNT: EUR104,983.00	OUR BANK CHARGES FOR DRAWEE: WAIVED(Y/N):N
DRAFT TENOR: D/P AT SIGHT	DUE DATE:
	DRAFT DATE: 20100524
WITH GUARANTEE(Y/N): N	GUARANTEE NO. :

汇票(DRAFT)	发票(COMM. INV.)	海关发票(CUST. INV.)	提单(B/L)	空运单(AWB)
2/2(1)	3/3(1)		3/3(1)	
保险单(INSUR POLICY/CERT)	装箱单(PKG LIST)	重量单(WEIGHT LIST)	质量单(QLY. CERT)	数量单(QTY. CERT)
	3/3(1)			
产地证(ORIGIN CERT)	受益人证明(BENE. CERT)	装船通知(SHIP. ADVICE)		
3/3				

INFORMATION:

兹将上述全套托收单据附上，请贵公司认真审查并注意以下事项：

1. 我行将严格遵照国际商会 1995 年第 522 号出版物《托收统一规则》办理代收项下一切事宜。

2. 贵公司同意付款/承兑赎单时，请把所配核销单填好返回我行，并在来单通知书上注明是否承担银行费用/利息，加盖贵公司在我行的签章。

3. 若需要购汇付款，请先办好批汇手续，并把足额款项和银行费用(若有)调入我行。

4. 若拒付或要求退单，请书面通知我行并陈述理由。

5. 如发现所附单据中有不属于贵公司的内容，请速交于我行。电话：   联系人：

我公司已收到托收单据。现就有关事项回复如下：

对于 D/P 详细单据，我公司同意对外付款。

对于 D/A 项下单据，我公司同意对外承兑，请在到期日主动对外付款。

若到期日前，我公司对对外付款有异议，将另行发出不同意付款的书面通知。

对于下列费用和利息，我公司以其前面的方框中的符号 V 或 X 表示是否同意支付。V 表示同意；X 表示不同意。

[ ]你行的代收费用和电报费   [ ]托收行的费用   [ ]托收行指示收取的利息

该托收单据项下的货款，由我公司承担的银行费用及利息，请你行主动从我公司在你行的   账户中扣付。

公司签章

2010 年 5 月 28 日

银行签章

向托收行(SWIFT No.：BKCHDEFFXXX)发电文 MT410，告其已经收到寄送的单据，请填制下列电文。

MT410 电文

```
---------------------------- Message Header -------------------------
Swift Output    : FIN 410 Acknowledgement
Sender          :
Receiver        :
---------------------------- Message Text ---------------------------
    20      Sending Bank's TRN

    21      Related Reference

    32B     Amount Acknowledged
            Currency
            Amount
```

参考答案：

MT410 电文

------------------------- Message Header -------------------------

Swift Output　　　: FIN 410 Acknowledgement

Sender　　　　: COMMCNSHNJG

Receiver　　　　: BKCHDEFFXXX

------------------------- Message Text -------------------------

20	Sending Bank's TRN
	IC201000062
21	Related Reference
	09DEJSY26SPECYZ2
32B	Amount Acknowledged
	Currency　　　EUR
	Amount　　　104,983.00

在付款方式 D/P AT SIGHT 项下，向账户行发电文 MT202，及时付款。账户行已经填好。

MT202 电文

------------------------- Message Header -------------------------

Swift Output　　　: FIN 202 General Fin Inst Transfer

Sender　　　　:

Receiver　　　　:

------------------------- Message Text -------------------------

20	Transaction Reference Number
21	Related Reference
32A	Value Date, Currency Code, Amt
	Date
	Currency
	Amount
53A	Sender's Correspondent - BIC
	BIC　　　　COMMCNSHXXX
58A	Beneficiary Institution - BIC
	BIC　　　　BKCHDEFFXXX

72   Sender to Receiver Information

/BNF/IC201000062

//CUSTOMER ACC: 0040040016

//IBAN: DE83514107000040040016

参考答案：

MT202 电文

------------------------- Message Header -----------------------

Swift Output   : FIN 202 General Fin Inst Transfer

Sender   : COMMCNSHNJG

Receiver   : MIDLGB22XXX

------------------------- Message Text ------------------------

20   Transaction Reference Number

IC201000062

21   Related Reference

09DEJSY26SPECYZ2

32A   Value Date, Currency Code, Amt

Date   100529

Currency   EUR

Amount   104,983.00

53A   Sender's Correspondent - BIC

BIC   COMMCNSHXXX

58A   Beneficiary Institution - BIC

BIC   BKCHDEFFXXX

72   Sender to Receiver Information

/BNF/IC201000062

//CUSTOMER ACC: 0040040016

//IBAN: DE83514107000040040016

第三章

出口信用证

学习目标：

　　了解和掌握出口信用证业务的流程并学会编写出口信用证通知书，根据信用证来缮制单据，编写出口 BP 面函以及业务中的相关电文；知晓如何控制出口信用证业务中的相关风险；掌握出口业务中每一个环节和步骤的要点。

第一节　出口方银行

一、业务场景与操作

案例 3.1

　　2010 年 8 月，出口商江苏 KOC CO., LTD.公司与进口商 ORIENTAL TRADING CO., LTD.公司签订了进口货物 4400 CARTONS MELON JAM 340 GMS X 24 TIN MALING BRAND 的贸易合同，金额为 USD26840.00，合同中约定以信用证方式结算。进口商通过银行 BANK OF AMERICA, LOS ANGELES 开出信用证。假设交通银行作为通知行于 2010 年 8 月 31 日收到此证。

1. 接收信用证

　　通知行通过 SWIFT 系统接收由开证行发来的信用证报文 SWIFT 700，并以通知行的身份向该信用证的受益人(出口商)通知这份信用证。

　　(1) 信用证 SWIFT 700

　　MT700 电文

```
-------------------------- Message Header -------------------------
Swift Output    : FIN 700 Acknowledgement
Sender          : BOFAUS6SXXX
Receiver        : COMMCNSHNJG
-------------------------- Message Text -------------------------
```

27 Sequence of Total:

NUMBER: 1

TOTAL: 1

TYPE: 700   BANK OF AMERICA, LOS ANGELES

40A Type of Documentary Credit : IRREVOCABLE

20 Letter of Credit Number: DES505606

31G Date of Issue: 20100831

40E Applicable Rules: UCP LATEST VERSION

31D Date and Place of Expiry: 20101030 CHINA

51D Applicant Bank: BANK OF AMERICA, LOS ANGELES

50 Applicant: ORIENTAL TRADING CO., LTD.

P.O. BOX 12345 CODE 55400 MA, U.S.A.

59 Beneficiary: KOC CO., LTD.

32B Currency Code, Amount: USD26,840.00

41D Available with...by... : ANY BANK BY NEGOTIATION

42C Drafts at: SIGHT

42D Drawee: BANK OF AMERICA, LOS ANGELES

43P Partial Shipments: NOT ALLOWED

43T Transhipment: NOT ALLOWED

44A Shipping on Board/Dispatch/Packing in Charge at/ from: NANJING

44B Transportation to: LOS ANGELES

44C Latest Date of Shipment: 20101015

45A Description of Goods or Services:

ABOUT 4400 CARTONS MELON JAM 340 GMS X 24 TIN MALING BRAND AT USD6.10 PER CARTON CFR LOS ANGELES INCOTERM 2000

46A Documents Required:

*FULL SET (AT LEAST THREE) ORIGINAL CLEAN SHIPPED ON BOARD BILLS OF LADING ISSUED TO ORDER BLANK ENDORSED NOTIFY PARTIES APPLICANT SHOWING FREIGHT PAYABLE AT DESTINATION AND BEARING THE NUMBER OF THIS CREDIT.

*PACKING LIST IN 3 COPIES.

*COMMERCIAL INVOICE IN 4 COPIES MANUAL SIGNED BY THE BENEFICIARY STATING THAT THE GOODS SHIPPED ARE IN ACCORDANCE WITH BENEFICIARIES PROFORMA INVOICE NO. HL050307 DATED 100802.

*INSURANCE POLICY ISSUED TO ORDER BLANK ENDORSED FOR 110% OF THE INVOICE VALUE COVERS ALL RISKS AND WAR RISKS IN TWO COPIES.

* CERTIFICATE OF ORIGIN IN 3 COPIES ISSUED BY AUTHORIZED INSTITUTION

SHOWING CHINESE ORIGIN OF THE GOODS.

47A Additional Instructions:

1. CHARTER PARTY B/L AND THIRD PARTY DOCUMENTS ARE ACCEPTABLE.

2. SHIPMENT PRIOR TO L/C ISSUING DATE IS ACCEPTABLE.

3. BOTH QUANTITY AND AMOUNT 10 PERCENT MORE OR LESS ARE ALLOWED.

71B Charges:

ALL BANKING CHARGES OUTSIDE THE OPENNING BANK ARE FOR BENEFICIARY'S ACCOUNT.

48 Period for Presentation:

DOCUMENTS MUST BE PRESENTED WITHIN 15 DAYS AFTER THE DATE OF ISSUANCE OF THE TRANSPORT DOCUMENTS BUT WITHIN THE VALIDITY OF THE CREDIT.

49 Confirmation Instructions:

WITHOUT

78 Instructions to the Paying/Accepting/Negotiating Bank:

1. ALL DOCUMENTS TO BE FORWARDED IN ONE COVER, UNLESS OTHERWISE STATED ABOVE.

2. DISCREPANT DOCUMENT FEE OF USD 50.00 OR EQUAL CURRENCY WILL BE DEDUCTED FROM DRAWING IF DOCUMENTS WITH DISCREPANCIES ARE ACCEPTED.

57A "Advising Through" Bank:

2. 信用证通知面函

交通银行作为通知行，在收到上述信用证以后，首先要对此证进行审核。在审核了此证的各项要素后，编制信用证通知面函，并在第一时间通知给出口商。假设该份信用证的银行编号是 LA201000218。信用证通知面函的填写格式如下：

ADVICE OF LETTER OF CREDIT

致(TO): KOC CO., LTD. NANJING, CHINA	我行编号(OUR REF. NO.):	LA201000218
	通知日期(DATE):	20100831
开证行 (ISSUING BANK): BANK OF AMERICA, LOS ANGELES	信用证号码(CREDIT NO.):	DES505606
	开证日期(ISSUING DATE):	20100831
	信用证金额(AMOUNT):	USD26840.00
转让行(TRANSFERRING BANK):		

转递行(TRANSMITTING BANK):

敬启者:

　　欣告贵司，我行从上述开证行/转让行/转递行收到一张以贵司为受益人的其真实性已经证实的电传/信函/SWIFT 开立的文件，敬请注意下列事项:

(Dear sirs:

We take a pleasure in notifying you that we have received an authenticated telex/mail/SWIFT L/C message in your favor from an opening bank/transferring bank/transmitting bank as follows and please note the following item(s):)

(•)不可撤销跟单信用证(An Irrevocable L/C)

(•)据信用证规定，我行通知费 USD30.0 由贵司承担。

As per stipulation of the L/C, our bank's advising commission USD30.0 is for your A/C.

(•)联系业务时，务请提供我行编号 LA201000218。

(When corresponding, please always mention our reference number: LA201000218.)

要项(Important)

　　如贵司发现该证中有任何条款难以接受，请径与开证申请人联系以便及时修改，避免单据提示时可能发生的问题。

　　(If you find terms and conditions which you are unable to comply with in this L/C, please directly contact applicant in order to make timely amendment and avoid any difficulties which may arise when documents are presented.)

3. 出口银行面函

　　出口银行(交通银行)将信用证通知给出口商后，出口商在信用证规定的交单期内向出口银行提交单据，出口银行在履行出口审单职责后，编制出口信用证业务面函，并连同单据按信用证要求寄往开证行或保兑行。面函格式如下(假设交通银行的业务编号是 BP201001203，账户行选择 WELLS FARGO BANK, N.A. U.S.A.):

交通银行股份有限公司

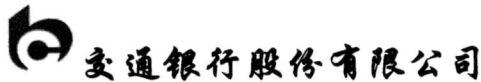

BANK OF COMMUNICATIONS CO., LTD. 江苏省分行

Swift: COMMCNSHNJG

DOCUMENTARY REMITTANCE

ORIGINAL

MAIL TO:

BANK OF AMERICA, LOS ANGELES 654 ANGELS ROAD, LOS ANGELES, U.S.A.

ATTN: L/C DEPT

DATE: 20101020

IN ALL CORRESPONDENCE PLS QUOTE OUR REF. NO. : BP201001203

WE ENCLOSE HEREWITH THE RELATIVE DOCUMENTS FOR PAYMENT PERTAINING TO THE

CREDIT MENTIONED BELOW.

CREDIT NO.: DES505606

ISSUED BY: BANK OF AMERICA, LOS ANGELES

APPL: ORIENTAL TRADING CO., LTD.

P.O. BOX 12345 CODE 55400 MA, U.S.A.

INVOICE NO. : 2010SDT001

1ST	2ND	DOCUMENTS	BILL AMOUNT: USD26840.00
2/2		DRAFT	TENOR: SIGHT
4/4		COMM. INV.	
3/3		B/L	
3/3		PKG LIST	
2/2		INSURANCE POLICY	
3/3		ORIGIN CERT	

PLEASE PAY/REMIT VIA CHIPS THE ABOVE TOTAL AMOUNT USD26840.00 TO WELLS FARGO BANK, N.A. FORMERLY WACHOVIA BANK, NY ABA NO. 0608 AT SIGHT/MATURITY FOR OUR H.O. SHANGHAI UID NO. 573455 FOR A/C NO. 27128383 WITH THEM UNDER YOUR/THEIR SWIFT/TELEX ADVISE TO US QUOTING OUR REFERENCE NO. BP BP201001203.

REMARKS:

X) THE BILL AMOUNT HAS BEEN ENDORSED ON THE REVERSE OF THE ORIGINAL L/C.

THIS TRANSACTION IS SUBJECT TO THE UNIFORM CUSTOMS AND PRACTICE FOR DOCUMENTARY CREDIT 2007 REVISION, ICC PUBLICATION NO. 600.

****THIS IS A COMPUTER GENERATED FORM AND REQUIRES NO SIGNATURE****

4. 业务流程图

图 3.1 为此案例的业务流程图。

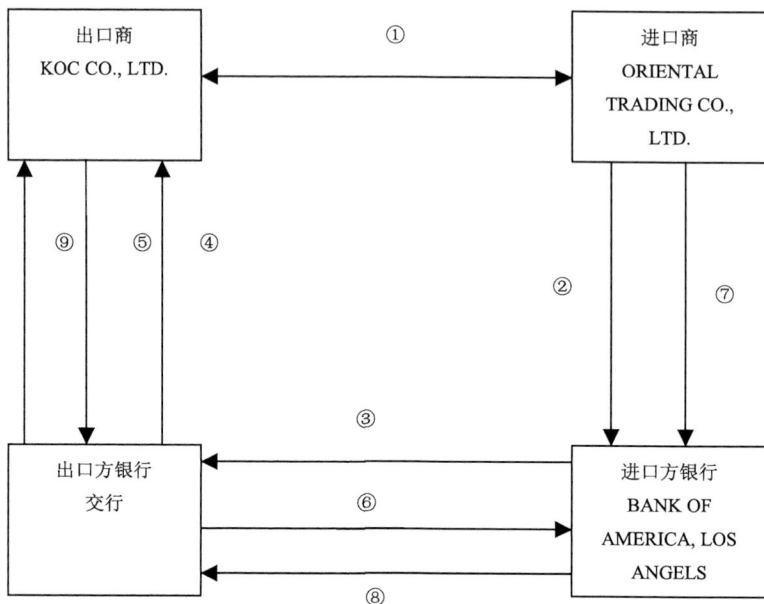

图 3.1　案例 3.1 的业务流程图。

① 进出口双方签订贸易合同。
② 进口商向进口方银行申请开证。
③ 开证银行开立信用证，通过交行通知给出口商。
④ 交行审核信用证后编制信用证通知书连同信用证交于出口商。
⑤ 出口商审核信用证后按规定准备好所需单据，提交交行。
⑥ 交行进行出口审单后编制 BP 面函连同单据按信用证要求寄给进口方银行。
⑦ 进口方银行审单后，单证一致则承担第一性付款责任，同时进口商赎单。
⑧ 进口方银行付款给交行，两行之间进行资金划拨。
⑨ 交行将款项按外管的相关规定结汇给出口商。

5. 银行往来电文

出口信用证业务中涉及的电文种类很多，这里主要介绍一下常见的电文格式。在编写电文时，原则是要让对方银行明白电文意思，语言以简洁明了为主。

1) 告收电文

信用证通知最常见的是告收电文，即开证行要求通知行在收到信用证后发电告知已经收悉此证。(案例 3.1 中的开证行 SWIFT No.为 BOFAUS6SXXX。)

MT730 电文

```
-------------------------- Message Header ------------------------
Swift Output     : FIN 730 Acknowledgement
Sender           : COMMCNSHNJG
Receiver         : BOFAUS6SXXX
-------------------------- Message Text --------------------------
    20     Sender's Reference
           LA201000218
    21     Receiver's Reference
           DES505606
    30     Date of Msg Being Acknowledged
           100831
    72     Sender to Receiver Information
           YR LC NO. DES505606 DD.100831 AMT USD26840.00
           BENE: KOC CO., LTD., NANJING, CHINA
           WE HAVE RECEIVED LC ON 100831.
```

2)　催款电文

在出口交单部分，如果寄出单据超出合理时间，即期未付款，远期未承兑，则出口方银行需发电文催促。案例中信用证是即期的，故电文如下：

MT799 电文

```
-------------------------- Message Header ------------------------
Swift Output     : FIN 799 Free Format Message
Sender           : COMMCNSHNJG
Receiver         : BOFAUS6SXXX
-------------------------- Message Text --------------------------
    20     Sender's Reference
           BP2010001203
    21     Receiver's Reference
           DES505606
    79     ATTN: L/C DEPT
           RE OUR DOCS UNDER YR L/C DES505606 FOR USD26840.00
           UP TO DATE, WE HAVE NOT RECEIVED THE PROCEEDS UNDER REF A/M, PLS
           INVESTIGATE THE MATTER AND EFFECT PAYMENT ASAP.
           B. RGDS
```

二、风险控制

出口银行在办理出口信用证业务中，要着重防范以下几个方面的风险。

1. 信用证的真实有效性

根据国外来证，通知行和出口商首先需对信用证进行审核。而在审核信用证时，银行和出口商的角度不同。银行审核的重点在于核实信用证表面的真实性，对于明显有问题的条款会在通知受益人时做提醒并沟通，促其接洽客户并同时联系开证行。通知行不管实际货物情况，对于贸易过程的审核，侧重于议付、收汇方面；对开证行资信及信用证条款的审查原则上是出口商的责任，尤其是对信用证条款的审查，主要应由出口商负责。因为信用证的主要条款是根据买卖合同设立的，出口商要审核信用证条款是否与合同一致，出口商侧重于交货、履约方面，其对信用证的审核有助于在信用证被接受前发现问题，并将问题解决于货物出运之前，为顺利出口和安全及时收汇铺平道路。通知行收到信用证后，首先审核是否是真实有效的信用证，此时需注意以下几个方面。

(1) SWIFT 信用证 MT700 报文是否有 SAC 字样，如系第一次打印应有 first copy 字样，信开信用证需核对签字是否相符。

(2) 检查信用证的付款保证是否有效。付款保证方面是否存在缺陷、是否是有生效条件的信用证、信用证密押是否相符、信用证简电或预先通知是否有详情后告的表述等。

(3) 明确信用证受益人以便及时通知。信用证上受益人名称和地址正确，可以方便通知银行及时递达通知。如果受益人名称不正确，则通知行需及时发电给开证银行查询，等确认后再做通知，但这样会给出口商制单时间上带来延迟。

(4) 检查装期的有关规定是否符合要求。逾信用证规定装期的运输单据将构成不符点，银行有权不付款。

(5) 检查信用证内容是否完整、不矛盾且逻辑上合理。如信用证价格条款是 CIF，但单据条款中没有提及保单，这时应去电开证行查询。

(6) 信用证的通知方式方面：一般信用证是通过出口商所在国家或地区的通知/保兑行通知给出口商的，这种方式的信用证通知比较安全。如果不是这样寄交的，遇到下列情况之一时应特别注意：如信用证是直接从海外寄给出口商的，那么应该小心查明它的来历；信用证是从本地某个地址寄出，要求出口商把货运单据寄往海外。对于上述情况，应该首先通过银行调查核实。

2. 信用证内容风险

信用证项下的履约风险应由受益人来控制，即能否做到单证相符，能否满足信用证规定的条件，都应该由受益人来控制。如果信用证条款受益人无法控制，无法通过自己的努力满足条款的要求，这种条款表面上看起来有其合理性，但实际上常常是申请人为受益人设下的陷阱，若出口商不能在审核信用证时发现，则极有可能钱货两空。例如实际业务中常见的软条款：信用证暂不生效，待签发了进口许可证后另行通知生效；或经申请人认货样后再通知生效；或等开证行生效电文后才生效；信用证只规定船只，装船日期及卸货港等须以申请人修改后的通知书为准等。如果接受此类条款，出口商正常处理信用证业务的主动权很大程度上掌握在对方手里，对安全收汇造成较大隐患。

转让信用证

转让信用证中常见此条款即转让行声明，转让证在国外原开证行付款后，再付款给第二受益人，这实际上将信用证付款方式转化成为托收方式，中间商可以名正言顺地将商品的市场风险转嫁给第二受益人。

3. 议付信用证的风险

1)　操作风险

在信用证业务中，对涉及的银行而言，审单所承担的操作风险主要在出口方银行(如议付行)和进口方银行(如开证行)。议付行在议付单据时，为了能向开证行安全索偿，必须合理小心地审核单据，保证单证一致，以避免开证行因单据不符点而提出拒付。银行审单时只审核单据表面有无不符点，而对任何单据的形式、完整性、准确性、真实性或法律效力等概不负责。

2)　单据语言风险

因在实际业务中常会因语言的使用问题带来不必要的拒付，根据国际标准银行实务做法，出口商出具的单据应使用信用证所使用的语言。如果信用证规定可以接受使用两种或两种以上语言的单据，指定银行在通知该信用证时，可限制单据使用语言的数量，作为对该信用证承担责任的条件，出口商出具的单据用信用证语言出具是一种期望而不是明确的要求。如果开证行要求单据用某一特定语言出具，信用证应该对此进行说明以便有据可依。本案例中的信用证未对单据语言作相应规定。

例如，信用证附加条款规定："所有单据必须用英语出具"，单据要求一份 CMR。拒付通知：CMR 没有用英语预先印制。这种实际业务中常见的问题如何处理，是否是不符？ICC 对此问题做了明确说明，该结论认为，"信用证'所有单据必须用英语出具'的要求与单据上表明与信用证条款及 UCP 的相关规定一致的内容相关"。故，只要该 CMR 单据的相关栏位的数据内容是英语，就没有不符。

三、总结思考

从出口银行的角度来理解"审单"的重要性，可以从"单证一致，单单一致"这个概念入手。

作为银行，审核信用证项下的单据是一项非常重要而细致的工作。我们知道开证行付款的条件是出口商(即受益人)提供的单据必须要与信用证条款相一致，只要提供的单据符合信用证条款，开证行就必须付款，如果单证不一致，开证行就可以拒绝付款。那么怎样才算单证相符呢，这就要凭审单人员的正确判断，他的责任非常重大，不仅要熟悉国际商会的有关惯例，如 UCP600，要了解银行内部的操作规范与政策、有关国家政府的各种规定和法规，同时还要遵守国际标准银行习惯，所以审单员不仅要熟悉业务，还要有一定的经验，才能在审单工作中应付自如，否则就可能由于疏忽，或不了解国际惯例而造成单证不符，给开证行以可乘之机，使得出口商或出口方银行蒙受损失。

再者，因为单证工作的复杂性，各国的法律制度不同，商业习惯不同，银行间对条款的理解和操作也有差异，因此，要由某一机构制定一些铁的规则，哪些不符点可拒付，哪些不符点不能拒付，几乎没有这种可能。在实际业务中，也存在"严格相符"和"实质相符"两种审核单据的态度。举一个简单的例子，单据中如果有拼写错误，能否拒付，在国外的法院中有两种不同的观点。一种观点认为："严格一致并不扩展到字母 i 上遗漏一点或字母 t 遗漏一横，或信用证或单据中明显的打字错误，因为信用证与单据所使用的语言可能有差异，以教条的甚至是一般化的方式来处理这个问题是行不通的。"美国某开证行因单据上将收件人 General Motor 的 G 写成 J 而拒付，议付行不服告之于法院，法院判定开证行不能拒付，因为稍有常识的人都不会因把 General Motor 的 G 写成 J 而将其视为另一家公司。但是，美国另一地区法院却持完全相反的意见。仅一处不符，包括对当事人姓名的误拼都足以成为开证行拒付信用证的借口。美国法院也曾以信用证上规定的被通知人 sofar，在提单上误拼为 sofan 而判定开证行可以拒付，这是因为 sofar 与 sofan 虽是一个字母之差，但可能是两个不同的人，因此如何审核单据应针对个案具体分析。

国际商会制订的统一惯例从制订开始到现在经历了多次的修改，但其精髓是不变的，那就是信用证应该是一种支付的工具，而不是阻碍支付的工具，银行开立信用证是为了付款，而不是从技术上找借口不付款，当然，银行也不能无视一些有充分理由拒付的不符点。因此从事审单工作的银行人员判定单据是否符合信用证的依据，首先或基本的仍然是信用证条款本身及其所适用的国际惯例，其次是人们公认的常理和常识，最后是是否符合逻辑。我们可以这样来理解"审单"二字，即出口审单的目的是保证收汇安全，进口审单的目的是为了在"单证一致，单单一致"的条件下，履行信用证下对出口商的义务。因此对审单员来说，熟悉相关的国际惯例及知识是十分重要的，为此可以参考"关于审核跟单信用证项下单据的国际标准银行实务"(ISBP681)。ISBP681 对单据中的共性问题做了详细的规定，它反映了有关审核单据的标准操作，当然不可能涉及审单时遇见的全部问题，因为任何完整的操作规定也代替不了审核者的合理判断。

审单与其说是一门科学，不如说是一门艺术。

四、实训操练

练习 3.1

假设交通银行于 2010 年 1 月 3 日收到开证行 METROPOLITAN BANK AND TRUST COMPANY, PHILIPPINES 开来的信用证，受益人为 ANJING XIAOCHEN TEXTILE CO., LTD.。信用证如下：

MT700 电文

```
------------------------- Message Header -------------------------
Swift Output    : FIN 700 Issue of a Documentary Credit
Sender          : MBTCPHMMXXX
Receiver        : COMMCNSHNJG
------------------------- Message Text -------------------------
```

27:     SEQUENCE OF TOTAL 总次序:

     1/1

40A: FORM OF DOCUMENTARY CREDIT:

     IRREVOCABLE

20:     DOCUMENTARY CREDIT NUMBER:

     004/LC/000020/03

31C: DATE OF ISSUE 开证日:

     100103

31D: DATE AND PLACE OF EXPIRY:

     100325 CHINA

50:     APPLICANT:

     POLLANDRE MANUFACTURING, INC.

     30 STO. ROSARIO STREET, KARUHATAN,

     VALENZUELA CITY, PHILIPPINES

59:     BENEFICIARY – NAME & ADDRESS:

     NANJING XIAOCHEN TEXTILE CO., LTD.

     101 BAIXIA ROAD, NANJING, CHINA

32B: CURRENCY CODE, AMOUNT:

     CURRENCY: USD (US DOLLAR)

     AMOUNT: #31620.00

41D: AVAILABLE WITH...BY...:

ANY BANK

42C: DRAFTS AT …:

30 DAYS AFTER SIGHT

42D: DRAWEE – NAME, ADDRESS:

ISSUING BANK

FOR FULL INVOICE VALUE

43P: PARTIAL SHIPMENTS:

NOT ALLOWED

43T: TRANSHIPMENT:

ALLOWED

44A: ON BOARD/DISP/TAKING CHARGE AT /FROM:

ANY PORT IN CHINA

44B: FOR TRANSPORTATION TO …:

MANILA, PHILIPPINES

44C: LATEST DATE OF SHIPMENT:

100304

45A: DESCRIPTION OF GOODS AND/OR SERVICE:

93000 PRINTED FABRIC

AS PER SALES CONFIRMATION NO. C X-021202A DATED DECEMBER 5, 2009 CIF MALINA

46A: DOCUMENTS REQUIRED:

1. FULL SET MARKED ORIGINAL(S) CLEAN ON BOARD OCEAN BILLS OF LADING PLUS 2 NON-NEGOTIABLE COPIES MARKED "FREIGHT PREPAID" MADE OUT TO ORDER OF METROPOLITAN BANK AND TRUST COMPANY AND NOTIFY APPLICANT.

2. SIGNED COMMERCIAL INVOICE IN TRIPLICATE.

3. PACKING LIST IN THREE COPIES.

4. BENEFICIARY'S CERTIFICATE THAT ONE FULL SET OF ADVANCE COPY OF NON-NEGOTIABLE SHIPPING DOCUMENTS HAS BEEN SENT DIRECTLY TO BUYER VIA COURIER.

47A: ADDITIONAL CONDITIONS:

ALL DOCUMENTS INCLUDING BILL OF LADING (B/L) MUST LEGIBLY CONTAIN THE L/C NUMBER PERTAINING TO THE SHIPMENT. DISCOUNT CHARGES AND/OR ACCEPTANCE COMMISSION IF ANY，ARE FOR BENEFICIARY'S ACCOUNT. SHIPPING LINES TO ACCEPT BANK GUARANTEE IN LIEU OF ORIGINAL SHIPPING DOCUMENTS. REMIT DOCUMENTS IN TWO LOTS BY DHL OR OTHER COURIER TO

METROPOLITAN BANK AND TRUST COMPANY

GRACE PARK CENTER, 446 RIZAL AVE. EXT. GRACE PARK

CALOOCAN CITY, PHILIPPINES

PLUS/MINUS 10 PERCENT ON QUANTITY AND VALUE ALLOWED.

71B:　CHARGES:

ALL BANK CHARGES OUTSIDE THE PHILIPPINES INCLUDING REIMBURSEMENT FEE ARE FOR BENEFICIARY'S ACCOUNT.

49:　CONFIRMATION INSTRUCTIONS:

WITHOUT

53D:　REIMBURSING BANK – NAME & ADDRESS　偿付行名称和地址如下:

METROPOLITAN BANK AND TRUST COMPANY, 1203 MARINE TOWER 1 PUDONG AVENUE, SHANGHAI, CHINA

78:　INST TO PAYG/ACCPTG/NEGOTG BANK:

CABLE ADVISE US AMOUNT AND DATE OF NEGOTIATION INDICATING THE PRINCIPAL AMOUNT AND BANK CHARGES (IN DETAILED) IF ANY. DISCREPANCY FEE OF USD50.00 (FOR DISCREPANT DOCUMENTS) PLUS ISSUING BANK'S COLLECTION CHARGES (FOR DOCUMENTS SENT ON COLLECTION/APPROVAL BASIS) WILL BE DEDUCTED FROM THE PROCEEDS OF ANY DRAWINGS. THESE CHARGES ARE FOR BENEFICIARY'S ACCOUNT EVEN IF THE L/C STIPULATES THAT ALL CHARGES ARE FOR THE APPLICANT'S ACCOUNT.

REMIT DOCUMENTS IN TWO LOTS BY DHL OR OTHER COURIER CERTIFYING THAT THE TERMS AND CONDITIONS OF THE CREDIT HAVE BEEN COMPLIED WITH. THE REIMBURSING BANK HOLDS SPECIAL REIMBURSEMENT INSTRUCTIONS TO THIS LETTER OF CREDIT.

57D:　'ADVISE THROUGH' BANK－NAME AND ADDR　通知行名称和地址如下:

BANK OF COMMUNICATIONS, NANJING BRANCH

124 NORTH ZHONGSHAN ROAD, NANJING, CHINA

72:　SENDER TO RECEIVER INFORMATION:

REIMBURSEMENT CLAIMS ARE SUBJECT TO ICC URR 525. WE HEREBY AUTHORIZE YOU TO HONOR REIMBURSEMENT CLAIMS FROM THE NEGOTIATING BANK PROVIDED ALL TERMS AND CONDITIONS ARE COMPLIED WITH.

交行作为通知银行，审核以上信用证之后，应填制以下信用证通知书：假设银行通知编号是 LA201000408，通知日期是 20100106，通知银行通知费是 USD30.00。

ADVICE OF LETTER OF CREDIT

致(TO):	我行编号(OUR REF NO.):	
	通知日期(DATE):	
开证行 (ISSUING BANK):	信用证号码(CREDIT NO.):	
	开证日期(ISSUING DATE):	
	信用证金额(AMOUNT):	

| 转让行(TRANSFERRING BANK): |
| 转递行(TRANSMITTING BANK): |

敬启者:

欣告贵司,我行从上述开证行/转让行/转递行收到一张以贵司为受益人的其真实性已经证实的电传/信函/SWIFT 开立的文件,敬请注意下列事项:

(Dear sirs:

We take a pleasure in notifying you that we have received an authenticated telex/mail/SWIFT L/C message in your favor from an opening bank/transferring bank/transmitting bank as follows and please note the following item(s):)

(·)不可撤销跟单信用证(An Irrevocable L/C)

(·)据信用证规定,我行通知费 　　　　由贵司承担。

As per stipulation of the L/C, our bank's advising commission 　　　　is for your A/C.

(·)联系业务时,务请提供我行编号

(When corresponding, please always mention our reference number: 　　　　)

要项(Important)

如贵司发现该证中有任何条款难以接受,请径与开证申请人联系以便及时修改,避免单据提示时可能发生的问题。

(If you find terms and conditions which you are unable to comply with in this L/C, please directly contact applicant in order to make timely amendment and avoid any difficulties which may arise when documents are presented.)

参考答案：

ADVICE OF LETTER OF CREDIT

致(TO): NANJING XIAOCHEN TEXTILE CO., LTD 101 BAIXIA ROAD, NANJING, CHINA	我行编号(OUR REF. NO.):	LA201000408
	通知日期(DATE):	20100106
开证行(ISSUING BANK): METROPOLITAN BANK AND TRUST COMPANY GRACE PARK CENTER, 446 RIZAL AVE. EXT. GRACE PARK, CALOOCAN CITY, PHILIPPINES	信用证号码(CREDIT NO.):	004/LC/000020/03
	开证日期(ISSUING DATE):	20100103
	信用证金额(AMOUNT):	USD31620.00
转让行(TRANSFERRING BANK):		
转递行(TRANSMITTING BANK):		

敬启者：

欣告贵司，我行从上述开证行/转让行/转递行收到一张以贵司为受益人的其真实性已经证实的电传/信函/SWIFT 开立的文件，敬请注意下列事项：

（Dear sirs:

We take a pleasure in notifying you that we have received an authenticated telex/mail/SWIFT L/C message in your favor from an opening bank/transferring bank/transmitting bank as follows and please note the following item(s):）

(•)不可撤销跟单信用证(An Irrevocable L/C)

(•)据信用证规定，我行通知费 USD30.0 由贵司承担。

As per stipulation of the L/C, our bank's advising commission USD30.0 is for your A/C.

(•)联系业务时，务请提供我行编号 LA201000408.

(When corresponding, please always mention our reference number: LA201000408.)

<table>
<tr><td>

要项(Important)

　　如贵司发现该证中有任何条款难以接受，请径与开证申请人联系以便及时修改，避免单据提示时可能发生的问题。

　　(If you find terms and conditions which you are unable to comply with in this L/C, please directly contact applicant in order to make timely amendment and avoid any difficulties which may arise when documents are presented.)
</td></tr>
</table>

　　2010 年 2 月 26 日，通知行收到此证的修改，延长有效期，最新日期为 2010 年 4 月 3 日。其他条款保持不变，修改如下：

　　MT707 电文

```
-------------------------- Message Header ------------------------
Swift Output    : FIN 707 Amendment to a Doc Credit
Sender          : MBTCPHMMXXX
Receiver        : COMMCNSHNJG
-------------------------- Message Text --------------------------
```

20: Sender's Reference:

　　004/LC/000020/03

21: Receiver's Reference:

　　NON REF

31C: Date of Issue:

　　100103

30: Date of Amendment:

　　100226

26E: Number of Amendment:

　　01

59: Beneficiary (before amndmt)—Nm & Add:

　　NANJING XIAOCHEN TEXTILE CO., LTD. NO. 101 BAI XIA ROAD, NANJING,

　　CHINA

31E: New Date of Expiry:

　　100403

44C: Latest Date of Shipment:

　　100304

79: Narrative:

　　EXTEND EXPIRY DATE AND LATEST DATE OF SHIPMENT TO

　　APRIL 03, 2010 AND MAR. 04, 2010.

　　ALL OTHER TERMS AND CONDITIONS REMAIN UNCHANGED.

假设你是通知银行交通银行的操作人员，审核以上信用证的第一次修改之后，请填制以下信用证修改通知书。假设银行通知编号是 LA201000408，修改通知日期是 2010 年 2 月 26 日，通知修改费用是 USD15.00。

ADVICE OF AMENDMENT OF LETTER OF CREDIT

致(TO):	我行编号(OUR REF. NO.):	
	通知日期(DATE):	
开证行(ISSUING BANK):	信用证号码(CREDIT NO.):	
	开证日期(ISSUING DATE):	
	信用证金额(AMOUNT):	
转让行(TRANSFERRING BANK):		
转递行(TRANSMITTING BANK):		

敬启者：
　　欣告贵司，我行从上述开证银行/转让银行/转递银行收到一张以贵司为受益人的其真实性已经证实的电传/信函/SWIFT/电报开立的信用证修改书，敬请注意下列事项：
(Dear sirs:
We take a pleasure in notifying you that we have received an authenticated telex /mail /SWIFT/cable L/C amendment message in your favor from A/M opening bank/transferring bank/transmitting bank as follows and please note the following item(s):)

(•)一张信用证修改书<第　　　次>(An amendment of the L/C)<No.　　　　　　>
(•)据信用证规定，我行修改费　　　由贵司承担。
As per stipulation of the L/C, our bank's amending commission　　　is for your A/C.
(•)根据国际商会 600 号出版物第十条规定，贵司只能全部地接受或者全部拒绝该修改内容，请务必在收到修改书后将正式书面意见(传真)回复我行。
(As per article 10 of the ICC Publication No. 600, you must alternatively opt for accepting or rejecting this amendment to same L/C, please reply to us<by fax> your formal view in writing.)
(•)联系业务时，务请提供我行编号
(When corresponding,please always mention our reference number:　　　　　　)

要项(Important)
　　如贵司发现该证中有任何条款难以接受，请径与开证申请人联系以便及时修改，避免单据提示时可能发生的问题。
　　(If you find terms and conditions which you are unable to comply with in this L/C, please directly contact applicant in order to make timely amendment and avoid any difficulties which may arise when documents are presented.)

参考答案：

ADVICE OF AMENDMENT OF LETTER OF CREDIT

致(TO): NANJING XIAOCHEN TEXTILE CO., LTD. 101 BAIXIA ROAD, NANJING, CHINA	我行编号(OUR REF. NO.):	LA201000408
	通知日期(DATE):	20100226
开证行(ISSUING BANK): METROPOLITAN BANK AND TRUST COMPANY GRACE PARK CENTER, 446 RIZAL AVE. EXT. GRACE PARK, CALOOCAN CITY, PHILIPPINES	信用证号码(CREDIT NO.):	004/LC/000020/03
	开证日期(ISSUING DATE):	20100103
	信用证金额(AMOUNT):	USD31620.00
转让行(TRANSFERRING BANK):		
转递行(TRANSMITTING BANK):		

敬启者：

　　欣告贵司，我行从上述开证银行/转让银行/转递银行收到一张以贵司为受益人的其真实性已经证实的电传/信函/SWIFT/电报开立的信用证修改书，敬请注意下列事项：

(Dear sirs:

We take a pleasure in notifying you that we have received an authenticated telex /mail /SWIFT/cable L/C amendment message in your favor from A/M opening bank/transferring bank/transmitting bank as follows and please note the following item(s):)

(•)一张信用证修改书<第 1 次>(An amendment of the L/C)<No.1>

(•)据信用证规定，我行修改费 USD15.0 由贵司承担。

As per stipulation of the L/C, our bank's amending commission USD15.0 is for your A/C.

(•)根据国际商会 600 号出版物第十条规定，贵司只能全部地接受或者全部拒绝该修改内容，请务必在收到修改书后将正式书面意见(传真)回复我行。

(As per article 10 of the ICC Publication No. 600, you must alternatively opt for accepting or rejecting this amendment to same L/C, please reply to us<by fax> your formal view in writing.)

(•)联系业务时，务请提供我行编号 LA201000408。

(When corresponding, please always mention our reference number: LA201000408.)

要项(Important)

如贵司发现该证中有任何条款难以接受，请径与开证申请人联系以便及时修改，避免单据提示时可能发生的问题。

(If you find terms and conditions which you are unable to comply with in this L/C, please directly contact applicant in order to make timely amendment and avoid any difficulties which may arise when documents are presented.)

如果开证行要求通知行发电告知其已经收到上述信用证，应如何填制电文？

MT730 告收电文

-------------------------- Message Header ------------------------

Swift Output   : FIN 730 Acknowledgement

Sender   :

Receiver   :

-------------------------- Message Text ---------------------------

   20   Sender's Reference

   21   Receiver's Reference

   30   Date of Msg Being Acknowledged

   72   Sender to Receiver Information

参考答案：

MT730 告收电文

-------------------------- Message Header ------------------------

Swift Output   : FIN 730 Acknowledgement

Sender   : COMMCNSHNJG

Receiver   : MBTCPHMMXXX

-------------------------- Message Text ---------------------------

   20   Sender's Reference

        LA201000408

21   Receiver's Reference

　　　004/LC/000020/03

30   Date of Msg Being Acknowledged

　　　100226

72   Sender to Receiver Information

　　　RE YR LC NO. 004/LC/000020/03

　　　DD.100103 AMT USD31620.00

　　　BENE: NANJING XIAOCHEN TEXTILE CO., LTD.

　　　WE HAVE RECEIVED LC ON 100226.

　　　还是以练习 3.1 的信用证为例，假设出口方银行是交行，在收到该证项下的单据进行审单后，如何制作面函呢？假设银行编号是 BP201002203，出单日期是 2010 年 3 月 3 日。账户行的选择参见"附录：账户行一览表"，假设交行选择美联银行作为账户行。

交通银行股份有限公司

Address: No.124 Zhongshan Road(N), Nanjing, China
地址：中国南京市中山北路 124 号
Swift: COMMCNSHNJG

BANK OF COMMUNICATIONS CO., LTD.
江苏省分行
JIANGSU PROVINCIAL BRANCH

DOCUMENTARY REMITTANCE

MAIL TO:

DATE:

IN ALL CORRESPONDENCE PLS QUOTE OUR REF. NO.

WE ENCLOSE HEREWITH THE RELATIVE DOCUMENTS FOR PAYMENT PERTAINING TO THE CREDIT MENTIONED BELOW.

CREDIT NO.:

ISSUED BY:

APPL:

INVOICE NO.:

1ST	2ND	DOCUMENTS	BILL AMOUNT:
			TENOR:

IN REIMBURSEMENT:

X) PLS ADVISE US OF THE DATE OF ACCEPTANCE AND MATURITY BY TESTED TELEX/SWIFT QUOTING OUR ABOVE REF NO.

X) AT MATURITY, WE WILL CLAIM REIMBURSEMENT FROM THE REIMBURSING BANK.

REMARKS:

X) THE BILL AMOUNT HAS BEEN ENDORSED ON THE REVERSE OF THE ORIGINAL L/C.

THIS TRANSACTION IS SUBJECT TO THE UNIFORM CUSTOMS AND PRACTICE FOR DOCUMENTARY CREDIT 2007 REVISION, ICC PUBLICATION NO. 600.

****THIS IS A COMPUTER GENERATED FORM AND REQUIRES NO SIGNATURE****

参考答案：

交通银行股份有限公司

Address: No.124 Zhongshan Road(N), Nanjing, China
地址：中国南京市中山北路 124 号
Swift: COMMCNSHNJG

BANK OF COMMUNICATIONS CO., LTD.
江苏省分行
JIANGSU PROVINCIAL BRANCH

DOCUMENTARY REMITTANCE

ORIGINAL

MAIL TO:

METROPOLITAN BANK AND TRUST COMPANY

GRACE PARK CENTER, 446 RIZAL AVE. EXT. GRACE PARK

CALOOCAN CITY, PHILIPPINES

ATTN: L/C DEPT

DATE: 20100303

IN ALL CORRESPONDENCE PLS QUOTE OUR REF. NO. BP201002203.

WE ENCLOSE HEREWITH THE RELATIVE DOCUMENTS FOR PAYMENT PERTAINING TO THE CREDIT MENTIONED BELOW.

CREDIT NO.: 004/LC/000020/03

ISSUED BY: METROPOLITAN BANK AND TRUST COMPANY, CALOOCAN CITY, PHILIPPINES

APPL: POLLANDRE MANUFACTURING，INC. 30 STO. ROSARIO STREET, KARUHATANVALENZUELA CITY, PHILIPPINES

INVOICE NO.: ED13445

1ST	2ND	DOCUMENTS	BILL AMOUNT: USD31620.00
1/2	1/2	DRAFT	TENOR: 30 DAYS AFTER SIGHT
2/3	1/3	COMM. INV.	
2/3	1/3	B/L	
2/3	1/3	PKG LIST	
1/2	1/2	B/L COPY	

IN REIMBURSEMENT:

X) PLS ADVISE US OF THE DATE OF ACCEPTANCE AND MATURITY BY TESTED TELEX/SWIFT QUOTING OUR ABOVE REF NO.

X) AT MATURITY, WE WILL CLAIM REIMBURSEMENT FROM THE REIMBURSING BANK.

REMARKS:

X) THE BILL AMOUNT HAS BEEN ENDORSED ON THE REVERSE OF THE ORIGINAL L/C.

THIS TRANSACTION IS SUBJECT TO THE UNIFORM CUSTOMS AND PRACTICE FOR DOCUMENTARY CREDIT 2007 REVISION, ICC PUBLICATION NO. 600.

****THIS IS A COMPUTER GENERATED FORM AND REQUIRES NO SIGNATURE****

请注意：因为信用证要求两次寄单，二次面函与一次内容相同，区别在于将一次上的 ORIGINAL 改为 DUPLICATE。

因是远期证，如果超出合理时间没有来承兑时，作为出口方银行需发电去催承兑，此时应如何填制电文？

催承兑 MT799 电文

-------------------------- Message Header --------------------------

Swift Output   : FIN 799 Free Format Message

Sender   :

Receiver   :

-------------------------- Message Text --------------------------

20 Sender's Reference

21 Receiver's Reference

79 ATTN:

参考答案：

催承兑 MT799 电文

-------------------------- Message Header ------------------------
Swift Output : FIN 799 Free Format Message
Sender : COMMCNSHNJG
Receiver : MBTCPHMMXXX
-------------------------- Message Text ----------------------------
20 Sender's Reference
BP201002203
21 Receiver's Reference
004/LC/000020/03
79 ATTN: IMPORT L/C DEPT
RE OUR DOCS UNDER YR L/C 004/LC/000020/03 FOR USD31620.00
OUR REF. BP201002203
TO DATE, WE HAVE NOT RECEIVED YR ACCEPTANCE UNDER REF A/M, PLS
INVESTIGATE THE MATTER AND GIVE US A REPLY ASAP.
B. RGDS

又因为此信用证是远期且有偿付行的，所以承兑到期日需向偿付行寄索偿联。请填制索偿面函。假设全额承兑，无扣费；交通银行选择 WELLS FARGO BANK, N.A. USA 作为账户行。

交通银行股份有限公司

Address: No.124 Zhongshan
Road(N), Nanjing, China
地址：中国南京市中山北路 124 号
Swift: COMMCNSHNJG

BANK OF COMMUNICATIONS CO., LTD.
江 苏 省 分 行
JIANGSU PROVINCIAL BRANCH

L/C REIMBURSEMENT CLAIM

OUR REFERENCE:

TO:

ATTN:

DATE:

DEAR SIRS,

DOCUMENTS OF THE L/C DESCRIBED HEREUNDER PRESENTED TO US.

WE ARE AUTHORIZED BY L/C INSTRUCTIONS TO CLAIM REIMBURSEMENT FROM YOUR GOOD BANK.

LETTER OF CREDIT NO. :   ISSUED DATE:

L/C ISSUING BANK :

PRINCIPAL AMOUNT:

TOTAL AMOUNT CLAIMED:

PLEASE PAY/REMIT VIA CHIPS THE ABOVE TOTAL AMOUNT   TO   UNDER YOUR/THEIR TELEX/SWIFT ADVICE TO US QUOTING OUR ABOVE REF. NO.

IF YOU DECIDE NOT TO HONOUR OUR CLAIM, PLEASE ADVISE US BY SWIFT OR TELEX WITHIN TWO WORKING DAYS UPON RECEIPT OF THIS LETTER.

SUBJECT TO UNIFORM RULES FOR BANK TO BANK REIMBURSEMENT UNDER LETTER OF CREDIT ICC PUBLICATION NO. 725.

参考答案：

交通银行股份有限公司

BANK OF COMMUNICATIONS CO., LTD.

Address: No.124 Zhongshan
Road(N), Nanjing, China
地址：中国南京市中山北路 124 号
Swift: COMMCNSHNJG

江苏省分行
JIANGSU PROVINCIAL BRANCH

L/C REIMBURSEMENT CLAIM

OUR REFERENCE: BP201002203

TO: METROPOLITAN BANK AND TRUST COMPANY, 1203 MARINE TOWER 1 PUDONG AVENUE, SHANGHAI, CHINA

ATTN: L/C REIMBURSEMENT DEPT

DATE: 20100306

DEAR SIRS,

DOCUMENTS OF THE L/C DESCRIBED HEREUNDER PRESENTED TO US.

WE ARE AUTHORIZED BY L/C INSTRUCTIONS TO CLAIM REIMBURSEMENT FROM YOUR GOOD BANK.

LETTER OF CREDIT NO.: 004/LC/000020/03   ISSUED DATE: 20100103

L/C ISSUING BANK: METROPOLITAN BANK AND TRUST COMPANY, CALOOCAN CITY, PHILIPPINES

PRINCIPAL AMOUNT: USD31620.00

TOTAL AMOUNT CLAIMED: USD31620.00

PLEASE PAY/REMIT VIA CHIPS THE ABOVE TOTAL AMOUNT USD31620.00 TO WELLS FARGO BANK, N.A. FORMERLY WACHOVIA BANK, NY ABA NO. 0608 AT SIGHT/MATURITY FOR OUR H.O. SHANGHAI UID NO. 573455 FOR A/C NO. 27128383 WITH THEM UNDER YOUR/THEIR SWIFT/TELEX ADVISE TO US QUOTING OUR REFERENCE NO. BP201002203.

IF YOU DECIDE NOT TO HONOUR OUR CLAIM, PLEASE ADVISE US BY SWIFT OR TELEX WITHIN TWO WORKING DAYS UPON RECEIPT OF THIS LETTER.

SUBJECT TO UNIFORM RULES FOR BANK TO BANK REIMBURSEMENT UNDER LETTER OF CREDIT ICC PUBLICATION NO. 725.

如果信用证没有规定不允许电索，那么作为出口方银行，为了提高出口收汇速度，可以不用寄送以上的索偿面函进行邮索，而是发 MT742 进行电索。请填制以下电文，账号已经填好。请注意：此案例中无开证行扣费，是全额索偿。若存在不符点，有扣费时，在 MT742

电文的 34B 栏中填明扣费后的金额。(偿付行 SWIFT No.为 MBTCCNSHXXX)

电索 MT742 电文

```
------------------------- Message Header -------------------------
Swift Output      : FIN 742 Reimbursement Claim
Sender            :
Receiver          :
------------------------- Message Text -------------------------
    20        Claiming Bank's Reference


    21        Documentary Credit Number


    31C       Date of Issue


    52A       Issuing Bank - BIC
              BIC
    32B       Principal Amount Claimed
              Currency
              Amount
    34B       Total Amount Claimed
              Currency
              Amount
    57A       Account With Bank - BIC
              BIC               PNBPUS3NNYC
    58A       Beneficiary Bank - BIC
              Party Identifier /27128383
              BIC               COMMCNSHXXX
```

参考答案:

电索 MT742 电文

```
------------------------- Message Header -------------------------
Swift Output      : FIN 742 Reimbursement Claim
Sender            : COMMCNSHNJG
Receiver          : MBTCCNSHXXX
------------------------- Message Text -------------------------
    20        Claiming Bank's Reference
              BP201002203
```

21	Documentary Credit Number

004/LC/000020/03

31C	Date of Issue

100103

52A	Issuing Bank - BIC
	BIC MBTCPHMMXXX

32B	Principal Amount Claimed
	Currency USD
	Amount 31620.00

34B	Total Amount Claimed
	Currency USD
	Amount 31620.00

57A	Account With Bank - BIC
	BIC PNBPUS3NNYC

58A	Beneficiary Bank - BIC
	Party Identifier /27128383
	BIC COMMCNSHXXX

再就该业务来看，开证行已经做了承兑，但付款到期日交通银行去偿付行索汇，对方却没有付款，交通银行在查询偿付行的同时需要发电文查询开证行。如果你是交通银行经办人员，此时应如何填制电文？

MT799 电文

```
-------------------------- Message Header ------------------------
Swift Output    : FIN 799 Free Format Message
Sender          :
Receiver        :
-------------------------- Message Text ------------------------
```

20	Sender's Reference

21	Receiver's Reference

79	ATTN:

参考答案：

MT799 电文

------------------------- Message Header -------------------------

Swift Output   : FIN 799 Free Format Message

Sender   : COMMCNSHNJG

Receiver   : MBTCPHMMXXX

------------------------- Message Text -------------------------

20	Sender's Reference	
	BP201002203	
21	Receiver's Reference	
	004/LC/000020/03	
79	ATTN: L/C DEPT	

        RE OUR DOCS UNDER YR L/C 004/LC/000020/03 FOR USD31620.00

        OUR REF BP201002203

        THOUGH THE MATURITY DATE IS PASSED AND TO DATE, WE HAVE NOT RECEIVED THE PROCEEDS UNDER A/M REF, PLS INVESTIGATE THE MATTER AND EFFECT PAYMENT ASAP.

        B. RGDS

练习 3.2

2010 年 5 月 4 日，假设交通银行收到 BANK OF KYOTO, KYOTO 银行开出的以下信用证，受益人是江苏 ABC COMPANY。如果交通银行来通知该信用证，应如何编制信用证通知书呢？假设交通银行的通知号是 LA201000537，通知费是 USD30.00。

MT700 电文

------------------------- Message Header -------------------------

Swift Output   : FIN 700 Issue of a Documentary Credit

Sender   : BOKFJPJZXXX

Receiver   : COMMCNSHNJG

------------------------- Message Text -------------------------

27: Sequence of Total:

    NUMBER: 1

    TOTAL: 1

    TYPE: 700

40A: Type of Documentary Credit: IRREVOCABLE

20: Letter of Credit Number:

100701

31G: Date of Issue:

20100503

40E: Applicable Rules: UCP LATEST VERSION

31D: Date and Place of Expiry:

20100630 CHINA

51D: Applicant Bank:

BOKFJPJZXXX

BANK OF KYOTO, KYOTO

50: Applicant:

AKURA CO., LTD.

P.O. BOX 123, KYOTO, JAPAN

59: Beneficiary:

ABC COMPANY, 111 ZHUJIANG RD, NANJING, CHINA

32B: Currency Code, Amount:

USD100,000.00 FOB NANJING

41D: Available with...by...:

ANY BANK BY NEGOTIATION

42C: Drafts at:

SIGHT

42D: Drawee:

BANK OF KYOTO, KYOTO

43P: Partial Shipments:

NOT ALLOWED

43T: Transhipment:

NOT ALLOWED

44A: Shipping on Board/Dispatch/Packing in Charge at/ from:

NANJING

44B: Transportation to:

TOKYO

44C: Latest Date of Shipment:

20100609

45A: Description of Goods or Services:

PLASMA TV 70 SETS

46A: Documents Required:

*FULL SET (AT LEAST THREE) ORIGINAL CLEAN SHIPPED ON BOARD BILLS OF LADING ISSUED TO ORDER BLANK ENDORSED NOTIFY APPLICANT SHOWING FREIGHT COLLECT AND BEARING THE NUMBER OF THIS CREDIT.

*PACKING LIST IN 3 COPIES.

*COMMERCIAL INVOICE IN 3 COPIES MANUAL SIGNED BY THE BENEFICIARY.

47A: Additional Instructions:

1. CHARTER PARTY B/L AND THIRD PARTY DOCUMENTS ARE ACCEPTABLE.

2. SHIPMENT PRIOR TO L/C ISSUING DATE IS ACCEPTABLE.

3. BOTH QUANTITY AND AMOUNT 10 PERCENT MORE OR LESS ARE ALLOWED.

71B: Charges:

ALL BANKING CHARGES OUTSIDE THE OPENNING BANK ARE FOR BENEFICIARY'S ACCOUNT.

48: Period for Presentation:

DOCUMENTS MUST BE PRESENTED WITHIN 21 DAYS AFTER THE DATE OF ISSUANCE OF THE TRANSPORT DOCUMENTS BUT WITHIN THE VALIDITY OF THE CREDIT.

49: Confirmation Instructions:

WITHOUT

78: Instructions to the Paying/Accepting/Negotiating Bank:

1. ALL DOCUMENTS TO BE FORWARDED TO BANK OF KYOTO, SUSAN RD 123, KYOTO, JAPAN IN ONE COVER, UNLESS OTHERWISE STATED ABOVE.

2. DISCREPANT DOCUMENT FEE OF USD 50.00 OR EQUAL CURRENCY WILL BE DEDUCTED FROM DRAWING IF DOCUMENTS WITH DISCREPANCIES ARE ACCEPTED.

ADVICE OF LETTER OF CREDIT

(TO):	我行编号(OUR REF. NO.):	
	通知日期(DATE):	
开证行 (ISSUING BANK):	信用证号码(CREDIT NO.):	
	开证日期(ISSUING DATE):	
	信用证金额(AMOUNT):	
转让行(TRANSFERRING BANK):		
转递行(TRANSMITTING BANK):		

敬启者：

　　欣告贵司，我行从上述开证行/转让行/转递行收到一张以贵司为受益人的其真实性已经证实的电传/信函/SWIFT 开立的文件，敬请注意下列事项：

(Dear sirs:

We take a pleasure in notifying you that we have received an authenticated telex/mail/SWIFT L/C message in your favor from an opening bank/transferring bank/transmitting bank as follows and please note the following item(s):)

(·)不可撤销跟单信用证(An Irrevocable L/C)

(·)据信用证规定，我行通知费　　　　　　　由贵司承担。

As per stipulation of the L/C, our bank's advising commission　　　　　　is for your A/C.

(·)联系业务时，务请提供我行编号

(When corresponding, please always mention our reference number:　　　　　)

要项(Important)

　　如贵司发现该证中有任何条款难以接受，请径与开证申请人联系以便及时修改，避免单据提示时可能发生的问题。

　　(If you find terms and conditions which you are unable to comply with in this L/C, please directly contact applicant in order to make timely amendment and avoid any difficulties which may arise when documents are presented.)

参考答案：

ADVICE OF LETTER OF CREDIT

致(TO): ABC COMPANY NANJING, CHINA	我行编号(OUR REF. NO.):	LA201000537
	通知日期(DATE):	20100504
开证行(ISSUING BANK): BANK OF KYOTO, KYOTO	信用证号码(CREDIT NO.):	100701
	开证日期(ISSUING DATE):	20100503
	信用证金额(AMOUNT):	USD100,000.00
转让行(TRANSFERRING BANK):		
转递行(TRANSMITTING BANK):		

敬启者：

　　欣告贵司，我行从上述开证行/转让行/转递行收到一张以贵司为受益人的其真实性已经证实的电传/信函/SWIFT 开立的文件，敬请注意下列事项：

（Dear sirs:

We take a pleasure in notifying you that we have received an authenticated telex/mail/SWIFT L/C message in your favor from an opening bank/transferring bank/transmitting bank as follows and please note the following item(s):)

(•)不可撤销跟单信用证(An Irrevocable L/C)

(•)据信用证规定，我行通知费 USD30.0 由贵司承担。

As per stipulation of the L/C, our bank's advising commission USD30.0 is for your A/C.

(•)联系业务时，务请提供我行编号 LA201000537。

(When corresponding, please always mention our reference number:LA201000537.)

要项(Important)

　　如贵司发现该证中有任何条款难以接受，请径与开证申请人联系以便及时修改，避免单据提示时可能发生的问题。

　　(If you find terms and conditions which you are unable to comply with in this L/C, please directly contact applicant in order to make timely amendment and avoid any difficulties which may arise when documents are presented.)

如果开证行要你回复告收情况，你应如何编制电文呢？
MT730 电文

```
------------------------- Message Header -------------------------
Swift Output    : FIN 730 Acknowledgement
Sender          :
Receiver        :
------------------------- Message Text -------------------------
    20      Sender's Reference

    21      Receiver's Reference
```

| 30 | Date of Msg Being Acknowledged |
| 72 | Sender to Receiver Information |

参考答案：

MT730 电文

------------------------- Message Header -------------------------

Swift Output　　: FIN 730 Acknowledgement

Sender　　　　 : COMMCNSHNJG

Receiver　　　 : BOKFJPJZXXXX

------------------------- Message Text -------------------------

20	Sender's Reference
	LA201000537
21	Receiver's Reference
	100701
30	Date of Msg Being Acknowledged
	100504
72	Sender to Receiver Information
	YR LC NO. 100701 DD.100503 AMT
	USD100,000.00
	BENE: ABC COMPANY, NANJING, CHINA
	WE HAVE RECEIVED LC ON 100504.

　　还是以练习 3.2 的信用证为例，假设你是出口方银行交通银行的经办人员，收到以上出口商交来的单据，经过审单后，如何编制出口面函呢？假设银行编号是 BP201001100，选择花旗银行作为账户行。请注意：该案例中，出口商交单时，多提交两份副本提单。对于附加单据，银行一般会询问出口商的处理意见，是退回还是随单据寄出，银行对多提交的单据不负责。此处，假设出口商要求随其他单据一起寄出。

交通银行股份有限公司
BANK OF COMMUNICATIONS CO., LTD.

Address: No.124 Zhongshan
Road(N), Nanjing, China
地址：中国南京市中山北路 124 号
Swift: COMMCNSHNJG

江苏省分行
JIANGSU PROVINCIAL BRANCH

DOCUMENTARY REMITTANCE

ORIGINAL

MAIL TO:

DATE:

IN ALL CORRESPONDENCE PLS QUOTE OUR REF. NO.

WE ENCLOSE HEREWITH THE RELATIVE DOCUMENTS FOR PAYMENT PERTAINING TO THE CREDIT MENTIONED BELOW.

CREDIT NO.:

ISSUED BY:

APPL:

INVOICE NO.:

1ST	2ND	DOCUMENTS	BILL AMOUNT:
			TENOR:

IN REIMBURSEMENT:

X) PLEASE PAY/REMIT VIA CHIPS THE ABOVE TOTAL AMOUNT　　　UNDER YOUR/THEIR TELEX/SWIFT ADVICE TO US QUOTING OUR ABOVE REF. NO.

REMARKS:

X) THE BILL AMOUNT HAS BEEN ENDORSED ON THE REVERSE OF THE ORIGINAL L/C.

THIS TRANSACTION IS SUBJECT TO THE UNIFORM CUSTOMS AND PRACTICE FOR DOCUMENTARY CREDIT 2007 REVISION, ICC PUBLICATION NO. 600.

****THIS IS A COMPUTER GENERATED FORM AND REQUIRES NO SIGNATURE****

参考答案：

交通银行股份有限公司

BANK OF COMMUNICATIONS CO., LTD.

江苏省分行

JIANGSU PROVINCIAL BRANCH

Address: No.124 Zhongshan
Road(N), Nanjing, China
地址：中国南京市中山北路 124 号
Swift: COMMCNSHNJG

DOCUMENTARY REMITTANCE

ORIGINAL

MAIL TO:

BANK OF KYOTO, SUSAN RD 123, KYOTO, JAPAN
ATTN: L/C DEPT

DATE: 20100606

IN ALL CORRESPONDENCE PLS QUOTE OUR REF. NO. BP201001100 .

WE ENCLOSE HEREWITH THE RELATIVE DOCUMENTS FOR PAYMENT PERTAINING TO THE CREDIT MENTIONED BELOW.

CREDIT NO.: 100701

ISSUED BY: BANK OF KYOTO, KYOTO

APPL: AKURA CO., LTD., P.O. BOX 123, KYOTO, JAPAN

INVOICE NO.: PX1001

1ST	2ND	DOCUMENTS	BILL AMOUNT: USD100,000.00
2/2		DRAFT	TENOR: SIGHT
3/3		COMM. INV.	
3/3		B/L	
2/2		COPY B/L	
3/3		PACKING LIST	

IN REIMBURSEMENT:

X) PLEASE PAY/REMIT VIA CHIPS THE ABOVE TOTAL AMOUNT USD100,000.00 TO CITIBANK N.A., ABA NO. FOR OUR SHANGHAI H.O. ACCOUNT UID 123456 FOR ACCOUNT NO. 36044455 WITH THEM AT SIGHT UNDER YOUR/THEIR TELEX/SWIFT ADVICE TO US QUOTING OUR ABOVE REF. NO. BP201001100.

REMARKS:

X) THE BILL AMOUNT HAS BEEN ENDORSED ON THE REVERSE OF THE ORIGINAL L/C.

THIS TRANSACTION IS SUBJECT TO THE UNIFORM CUSTOMS AND PRACTICE FOR DOCUMENTARY CREDIT 2007 REVISION, ICC PUBLICATION NO. 600.

****THIS IS A COMPUTER GENERATED FORM AND REQUIRES NO SIGNATURE****

练习 3.3

2010年6月9日，假设交通银行收到 JPMORGAN CHASE BANK 开出的证号为 MS2565 的信用证，受益人为江苏 ABC COMPANY。信用证如下所示。如果交通银行负责通知该信用证，应如何编制信用证通知书呢？假设交通银行的通知号是 LA201000648，通知费是 USD30.00。

MT700 电文

```
---------------------- Message Header ------------------------
Swift Output    : FIN 700 Issue of a Documentary Credit
Sender          : CHASUS33XXX
Receiver        : COMMCNSHNJG
----------------------- Message Text ---------------------------
```

27: Sequence of Total:

　　NUMBER: 1

　　TOTAL: 1

　　TYPE: 700

40A: Type of Documentary Credit: IRREVOCABLE

20: Letter of Credit Number:

MS2565

31G: Date of Issue:

20100608

40E: Applicable Rules: UCP LATEST VERSION

31D: Date and Place of Expiry:

20100830 CHINA

51D: Applicant Bank:

CHASUS33XXX

JPMORGAN CHASE BANK, NEW YORK

50: Applicant:

RAYTHEON COMPANY

CAMBRIDGE, MASSACHUSETTS, USA

59: Beneficiary:

ABC COMPANY, 111 ZHUJIANG RD, NANJING, CHINA

32B: Currency Code, Amount:

USD250,000.00

41D: Available with...by...:　JPMORGAN CHASE BANK, NEW YORK

BY DEFER PAYMENT

42P: Deferred Payment Details:

30 DAYS AFTER B/L DATE

43P: Partial Shipments:

ALLOWED

43T: Transhipment:

ALLOWED

44E: Port of Loading:

NANJING

44F: Port of Discharge:

NEW YORK

44C: Latest Date of Shipment:

20100809

45A: Description of Goods or Services:

MONO CELLS, CIF NEW YORK, AT USD50/PC 5000PCS

46A: Documents Required:

*COMMERCIAL INVOICE IN 3 COPIES MANUAL SIGNED BY THE BENEFICIARY.

*FULL SET (AT LEAST THREE) ORIGINAL CLEAN SHIPPED ON BOARD BILLS OF LADING
CONSIGNED TO APPLICANT AND NOTIFY APPLICANT SHOWING "FREIGHT PREPAID"
AND BEARING THE NUMBER OF THIS CREDIT.

*PACKING LIST IN 3 COPIES.

*INSURANCE POLICY/CERT IN DUPLICATE FOR 110 INVOICE AMT
 COVERING INSTITUTE CARGO CLAUSES(ALL RISKS)SHOWING CLAIM PAYABLE IN USA.

47A: Additional Instructions:

1. CHARTER PARTY B/L AND THIRD PARTY DOCUMENTS ARE ACCEPTABLE.

2. SHIPMENT PRIOR TO L/C ISSUING DATE IS ACCEPTABLE.

3. BOTH QUANTITY AND AMOUNT 10 PERCENT MORE OR LESS ARE ALLOWED.

71B: Charges:

ALL BANKING CHARGES OUTSIDE THE OPENNING BANK ARE FOR BENEFICIARY'S
ACCOUNT.

48: Period for Presentation:

DOCUMENTS MUST BE PRESENTED WITHIN 21 DAYS AFTER THE DATE OF ISSUANCE OF
THE TRANSPORT DOCUMENTS BUT WITHIN THE VALIDITY OF THE CREDIT.

49: Confirmation Instructions:

WITHOUT

78: Instructions to the Paying/Accepting/Negotiating Bank:

1. ALL DOCUMENTS TO BE FORWARDED TO JPMORGAN CHASE BANK, P.O. BOX 211, NEW YORK, USA IN ONE COVER, UNLESS OTHERWISE STATED ABOVE.

2. DISCREPANT DOCUMENT FEE OF USD 50.00 OR EQUAL CURRENCY WILL BE DEDUCTED FROM DRAWING IF DOCUMENTS WITH DISCREPANCIES ARE ACCEPTED.

ADVICE OF LETTER OF CREDIT

致(TO):	我行编号(OUR REF. NO.):	
	通知日期(DATE):	
开证行 (ISSUING BANK):	信用证号码(CREDIT NO.):	
	开证日期(ISSUING DATE)	
	信用证金额(AMOUNT):	

转让行(TRANSFERRING BANK):

转递行(TRANSMITTING BANK):

敬启者：

　　欣告贵司，我行从上述开证行/转让行/转递行收到一张以贵司为受益人的其真实性已经证实的电传/信函/SWIFT 开立的文件，敬请注意下列事项：

(Dear sirs:

We take a pleasure in notifying you that we have received an authenticated telex/mail/SWIFT L/C message in your favor from an opening bank/transferring bank/transmitting bank as follows and please note the following item(s):)

(•)不可撤销跟单信用证(An Irrevocable L/C)

(•)据信用证规定，我行通知费　　　　　　　由贵司承担。

As per stipulation of the L/C, our bank's advising commission　　　　is for your A/C.

(•)联系业务时，务请提供我行编号

(When corresponding, please always mention our reference number:　　　　　　　)

要项(Important)

　　如贵司发现该证中有任何条款难以接受，请径与开证申请人联系以便及时修改，避免单据提示时可能发生的问题。

　　(If you find terms and conditions which you are unable to comply with in this L/C, please directly contact applicant in order to make timely amendment and avoid any difficulties which may arise when documents are presented.)

参考答案：

ADVICE OF LETTER OF CREDIT

致(TO):	我行编号(OUR REF. NO.):	LA201000648
ABC COMPANY NANJING, CHINA	通知日期(DATE):	20100609
开证行(ISSUING BANK): JPMORGAN CHASE BANK, P.O. BOX 211, NEW YORK, USA	信用证号码(CREDIT NO.):	MS2565
	开证日期(ISSUING DATE):	20100608
	信用证金额(AMOUNT):	USD250,000.00
转让行(TRANSFERRING BANK):		
转递行(TRANSMITTING BANK):		

敬启者：

　　欣告贵司，我行从上述开证行/转让行/转递行收到一张以贵司为受益人的其真实性已经证实的电传/信函/SWIFT 开立的文件，敬请注意下列事项：

(Dear sirs:

We take a pleasure in notifying you that we have received an authenticated telex/mail/SWIFT L/C message in your favor from an opening bank/transferring bank/transmitting bank as follows and please note the following item(s):)

(•)不可撤销跟单信用证(An Irrevocable L/C)

(•)据信用证规定，我行通知费 USD30.0 由贵司承担。

As per stipulation of the L/C, our bank's advising commission USD30.0 is for your A/C.

(•)联系业务时，务请提供我行编号 LA201000648。

(When corresponding, please always mention our reference number: LA201000648.)

要项(Important)

　　如贵司发现该证中有任何条款难以接受，请径与开证申请人联系以便及时修改，避免单据提示时可能发生的问题。

　　(If you find terms and conditions which you are unable to comply with in this L/C, please directly contact applicant in order to make timely amendment and avoid any difficulties which may arise when documents are presented.)

如果开证行要你回复告收情况，应如何编制电文呢？

MT730 电文

```
---------------------- Message Header ----------------------
Swift Output    : FIN 730 Acknowledgement
Sender          :
Receiver        :
---------------------- Message Text ----------------------
    20    Sender's Reference


    21    Receiver's Reference


    30    Date of Msg Being Acknowledged


    72    Sender to Receiver Information
```

参考答案：

MT730 电文

```
---------------------- Message Header ----------------------
Swift Output    : FIN 730 Acknowledgement
Sender          : COMMCNSHNJG
Receiver        : CHASUS33XXX
---------------------- Message Text ----------------------
    20    Sender's Reference
          LA201000648
    21    Receiver's Reference
          MS2565
    30    Date of Msg Being Acknowledged
          100609
    72    Sender to Receiver Information
          YR LC NO. MS2565 DD.100608 AMT
          USD250,000.00
          BENE: ABC COMPANY, NANJING, CHINA
          WE HAVE RECEIVED LC ON 100609.
```

　　还是以练习 3.3 的信用证为例，假设你是出口方银行交通银行的经办人员，收到以上出口商交来的单据后，经过审单后，应如何编制出口面函呢？假设银行编号 BP201001230，选择花旗银行作为账户行。

交通银行股份有限公司

BANK OF COMMUNICATIONS CO., LTD.

Address: No.124 Zhongshan
Road(N), Nanjing, China
地址：中国南京市中山北路 124 号
Swift: COMMCNSHNJG

江苏省分行
JIANGSU PROVINCIAL BRANCH

DOCUMENTARY REMITTANCE

ORIGINAL

MAIL TO:

DATE:

IN ALL CORRESPONDENCE PLS QUOTE OUR REF. NO.

WE ENCLOSE HEREWITH THE RELATIVE DOCUMENTS FOR PAYMENT PERTAINING TO THE CREDIT MENTIONED BELOW.

CREDIT NO.:

ISSUED BY:

APPL:

INVOICE NO.:

1ST	2ND	DOCUMENTS	BILL AMOUNT:
			TENOR:

IN REIMBURSEMENT:

X) UPON MATURITY，PLEASE PAY/REMIT VIA CHIPS THE ABOVE TOTAL AMOUNT　　　　TO
　　WITH YOU UNDER YOUR/THEIR TELEX/SWIFT ADVICE TO US QUOTING OUR ABOVE REF. NO.

REMARKS:

X) THE BILL AMOUNT HAS BEEN ENDORSED ON THE REVERSE OF THE ORIGINAL L/C.

THIS TRANSACTION IS SUBJECT TO THE UNIFORM CUSTOMS AND PRACTICE FOR

DOCUMENTARY CREDIT 2007 REVISION, ICC PUBLICATION NO. 600.

****THIS IS A COMPUTER GENERATED FORM AND REQUIRES NO SIGNATURE****

参考答案：

交通银行股份有限公司

Address: No.124 Zhongshan Road(N), Nanjing, China
地址：中国南京市中山北路 124 号
Swift: COMMCNSHNJG

BANK OF COMMUNICATIONS CO., LTD.
江苏省分行
JIANGSU PROVINCIAL BRANCH

DOCUMENTARY REMITTANCE

ORIGINAL

MAIL TO:

JPMORGAN CHASE BANK, P.O. BOX 211, NEW YORK, USA
ATTN: L/C DEPT

DATE: 20100625

IN ALL CORRESPONDENCE PLS QUOTE OUR REF. NO. BP201001230.

WE ENCLOSE HEREWITH THE RELATIVE DOCUMENTS FOR PAYMENT PERTAINING TO THE CREDIT MENTIONED BELOW.

CREDIT NO.: MS2565

ISSUED BY: JPMORGAN CHASE BANK, P.O. BOX 211, NEW YORK, USA

APPL: RAYTHEON COMPANY, CAMBRIDGE, MASSACHUSETTS, USA

BENE：ABC COMPANY, 111 ZHUJIANG RD, NANJING, CHINA

INVOICE NO.: 100620

1ST	2ND	DOCUMENTS	BILL AMOUNT: USD250,000.00	
3/3		COMM. INV.	TENOR: 30 DAYS AFTER B/L DATE	
3/3		P/L	MATURITY 25 JULY 2010	
3/3		B/L		
2/2		B/L COPY		
2/2		INSURANCE POLICY		

IN REIMBURSEMENT:

X) UPON MATURITY, PLEASE PAY/REMIT VIA CHIPS THE ABOVE TOTAL AMOUNT USD250,000.00 TO CITIBANK N.A., ABA NO. FOR OUR SHANGHAI H.O. ACCOUNT UID 123456 FOR ACCOUNT NO. 36044455 WITH YOU UNDER YOUR/THEIR TELEX/SWIFT ADVICE TO US QUOTING OUR ABOVE REF. NO. BP201001230.

REMARKS:

X) THE BILL AMOUNT HAS BEEN ENDORSED ON THE REVERSE OF THE ORIGINAL L/C.

THIS TRANSACTION IS SUBJECT TO THE UNIFORM CUSTOMS AND PRACTICE FOR DOCUMENTARY CREDIT 2007 REVISION, ICC PUBLICATION NO. 600.

****THIS IS A COMPUTER GENERATED FORM AND REQUIRES NO SIGNATURE****

第二节 信用证受益人

一、业务场景与操作

我们还是以案例 3.1 中的信用证为例来说明。通知银行在通知此信用证后,出口商首先要审核信用证是否全面真实地对应双方签订的合同,信用证的条款是否合理完整。

在实际业务中,要严格按信用证的要求来准备单据。出口商向银行提示的单据必须符合信用证的要求,必须做到"单证一致,单单一致",唯有这样,出口商才能安全及时地收到货款。

1. 缮制单据

出口商收到信用证并出货后,就应着手准备缮制信用证所要求的单据。

1) 汇票(Draft)

凭 Drawn under **BANK OF AMERICA, LOS ANGELES** 信用证 L/C NO. **DES505606**

日期 Dated **20100831** 支取 Payable with interest @_____% 按_____息……付款

号码 NO. **2010SDT001** 汇票金额 Exchange for **USD26,840.00** 20101020

见票 _____SIGHT_____ 日后(本汇票之副本未付) 交付

AT _____ sight of this FIRST of Exchange(Second of Exchange being unpaid)

Pay to the order of _____BANK OF COMMUNICATIONS CO., LTD., JIANGSU BR._____ the sum of

_____US DOLLARS TWENTY SIX THOUSAND EIGHT HUNDRED AND FORTY ONLY_____

款已收讫 Value received _____.

此 致 **BANK OF AMERICA, LOS ANGELS** TO:

SIGNATURE(出口商签字和盖单) KOC CO., LTD.

汇票填制注意事项：

(1) 汇票的付款人名称、地址(BANK OF AMERICA, LOS ANGELS)是否正确。

(2) 汇票上金额的大小写必须一致：USD26,840.00＝US DOLLARS TWENTY SIX THOUSAND EIGHT HUNDRED AND FORTY ONLY。此外，汇票金额是否超出信用证金额，如信用证金额前有"大约"一词，可按10%的增减幅度掌握，此证没有涉及。

(3) Drawn under 后填写开证行(BANK OF AMERICA, LOS ANGELS)，日期填写开证日期(20100831)，号码为发票号码(2010SDT001)，汇票金额为索偿金额(USD26,840.00)，具体付款期限根据信用证要求填写(42C Drafts at: AT SIGHT)；Pay to the order of 后填写交行英文名称。

(4) 出票人(KOC CO., LTD.)和付款人(BANK OF AMERICA, LOS ANGELS)必须符合信用证规定。

(5) 币制名称 USD 应与信用证和发票相一致。

(6) 按需要进行背书。

(7) 汇票是否由出票人进行了签字。

(8) 汇票份数是否正确，如"只此一张"或"汇票一式两份，有第一联和第二联"。

2) 发票(Invoice)

ISSUER KOC CO., LTD. HUARONG MANSION NO.85, JIAQIAO, NANJING 210005, P.R. CHINA	商业发票 COMMERCIAL INVOICE	
TO ORIENTAL TRADING CO., LTD. P.O. BOX 12345 CODE 55400, MA, U.S.A.	**NO.** 2010SDT001	**DATE** SEP. 30, 2010
TRANSPORT DETAILS SHIPMENT FROM NANJING PORT TO LOS ANGELES PORT BY SEA	**S/C NO.** NEO2010/026	**L/C NO.** DES505606
	TERMS OF PAYMENT L/C AT SIGHT	

MARKS AND NUMBERS	NUMBER AND KIND OF PACKAGE; DESCRIPTION OF GOODS	QUANTITY	UNIT PRICE USD	AMOUNT
N/M	**CFR LOS ANGELES PORT, U.S.A. INCOTERM2000**			
	ABOUT 4400 CARTONS MELON JAM 340 GMS X 24 TIN MALING BRAND AT USD6.10 PER CARTON	4400 CARTONS	USD6.10	USD26,840.00
	TOTAL: **4400 CARTONS**			**USD26,840.00**

SAY TOTAL: USD TWENTY SIX THOUSAND EIGHT HUNDRED AND FORTY ONLY.

We hereby certify that the contents of invoice herein are true and correct.

KOC CO., LTD.

(受益人签字和盖单据章)

发票填制注意事项：

(1) 除非信用证中有特别规定，商业发票的抬头应为开证申请人，如本发票中抬头是 ORIENTAL TRADING CO., LTD, P.O. BOX 12345 CODE 55400, MA, U.S.A.。

(2) 发票中的货物描述必须与信用证规定相符，其他一切单据则可使用货物统称，但不得与信用证规定的货物描述有抵触。如本发票中 ABOUT 4400 CARTONS MELON JAM 340 GMS X 24 TIN MALING BRAND AT USD6.10 PER CARTON，若信用证品描中含有价格条款，则一定要加注。总之，发票货描需将信用证 45A 栏位有关本次出货的全部信息表述显示出来，而其他单据在货描栏位可以只显示统称。

(3) 除信用证另有规定外，发票金额不得超过信用证所允许的金额。如数量、金额均有"大约"，可按 10%的增减幅度掌握。

(4) 抬头人必须符合信用证规定；签发人必须是受益人 KOC CO., LTD., HUARONG MANSION NO. 85, JIAQIAO, NANJING 210005, P. R. CHINA。

(5) 商品的数量(4400 CARTONS)符合信用证的规定；单价 USD6.10(如有)符合信用证的规定。

(6) 信用证要求表明和证明的内容不得遗漏。

3) 装箱单(Packing List)

(假设毛重为 39494.00 KGS，净重为 35904.00 KGS，体积为 45.6 CBM。)

ISSUER KOC CO., LTD. HUARONG MANSION NO.85 JIAQIAO, NANJING 210005, P. R. CHINA	装箱单 PACKING LIST			
TO ORIENTAL TRADING CO., LTD. P.O. BOX 12345 CODE 55400, MA, U.S.A.				
	INVOICE NO. 2010SDT001		DATE SEP. 30, 2010	
MARKS AND NUMBERS	NUMBER AND KIND OF PACKAGE; DESCRIPTION OF GOODS	PACKAGE	G.W. KG	N.W. KG	MEAS. CBM
N/M	ABOUT 4400 CARTONS MELON JAM 340 GMS X 24 TIN MALING BRAND AT USD.6.10 PER CARTON	4400 CARTONS	39494.40	35904.00	45.60

TOTAL: 4400 CARTONS   39494.40 KGS 35904.00 KGS   45.60 CBM

SAY TOTAL: FOUR THOUSAND FOUR HUNDRED CARTONS ONLY.

(出口商签字和盖单据章)

装箱单填制注意事项：

关于装箱单，提醒受益人在制作单据时应该注意：其掌握的原则是均须先与信用证的条款进行核对，再与其他有关单据核对，以保证制作的内容与发票等其他单据和信用证一致。

4) 提单(Bill of Lading)

(假设船名及航次是 JINSHAN 115 V. 213。)

Shipper KOC CO., LTD. HUARONG MANSION NO.85, JIAQIAO, NANJING 210005, P. R. CHINA			BILL OF LADING			B/L No.:

Shipper KOC CO., LTD. HUARONG MANSION NO.85, JIAQIAO, NANJING 210005, P. R. CHINA	**COSCO** 中 国 远 洋 运 输 公 司 CHINA OCEAN SHIPPING COMPANY
Consignee TO ORDER	
Notify Party ORIENTAL TRADING CO., LTD. P.O. BOX 12345 CODE 55400, MA, U.S.A.	**ORIGINAL**

*Pre carriage by	*Place of Receipt	
Ocean Vessel Voy. No. JINSHAN 115 V. 213	Port of Loading NANJING	
Port of discharge LOS ANGELES	*Final destination	Freight payable at	Number of original Bs/L THREE

Marks and Numbers	Number and kind of packages;Description	Gross weight	Measurement m3
n/m	4400 CARTONS MELON JAM 340 GMS X 24 TIN MALING BRAND AT USD6.10 PER CARTON FREIGHT COLLECT L/C NUMBER: DES505606 ON BOARD　10 OCT. 2010	39494.40 KGS	45.6 CBM

TOTAL PACKAGES(IN WORDS)

Freight and charges

Place and date of issue

NANJING　　10 OCT. 2010

Signed for the Carrier
CHINA OCEAN SHIPPING COMPANY
船运公司负责人签字

*Applicable only when document used as a Through Bill of Lading.

提单填制注意事项：
(1)　提单的类型须符合信用证的规定。
(2)　起运地(NANJING)和目的地(LOS ANGELES)须符合信用证的规定。

(3) 装运日期/出单日期须符合信用证的规定。

(4) 收货人和被通知人(ORIENTAL TRADING CO., LTD., P.O. BOX 12345 CODE 55400, MA, U.S.A.)须符合信用证的规定。

(5) 商品名称(MELON JAM 340 GMS X 24 TIN MALING BRAND)可使用货物的统称，但不得与发票上货物说明的写法相抵触。

(6) 运费预付或运费到付须正确表明，此案例中是 FREIGHT COLLECT。

(7) 正副本份数应符合信用证的要求，案例中是 3。

(8) 包装件数(4400 CARTONS)须与其他单据相一致。

(9) 唛头(n/m)须与其他单据相一致。

(10) 全套正本都须盖妥承运人的印章及签发日期章；船运公司(CHINA OCEAN SHIPPING COMPANY)负责人签字。

(11) 应加背书的运输单据，须加背书。

5) 保单(Insurance Policy)

PICC 中国人民保险公司南京市分公司	
The People's Insurance Company of China Nanjing Branch	

总公司设于北京 Head Office Beijing	一九四九年创立 Established in 1949

货物运输保险单
CARGO TRANSPORTATION INSURANCE POLICY

发票号(INVOICE NO.) 2010SDT001 合同号(CONTRACT NO.)	保单号次 POLICY NO. FAAA9002

信用证号(L/C NO.) DES505606

被保险人: KOC CO., LTD.
Insured: HUARONG MANSION NO.85 JIAQIAO, NANJING 210005, P.R. CHINA

中国人民保险公司(以下简称本公司)根据被保险人的要求，由被保险人向本公司缴付约定的保险费，按照本保险单承保险别和背面所载条款与下列特款承保下述货物运输保险，特立本保险单。
THIS POLICY OF INSURANCE WITNESSES THAT THE PEOPLE'S INSURANCE COMPANY OF CHINA (HEREINAFTER CALLED "THE COMPANY") AT THE REQUEST OF THE INSURED AND IN CONSIDERATION OF THE AGREED PREMIUM PAID TO THE COMPANY BY THE INSURED, UNDERTAKES TO INSURE THE UNDERMENTIONED GOODS IN TRANSPORTATION SUBJECT TO THE CONDITIONS OF THIS POLICY AS PER THE CLAUSES PRINTED OVERLEAF AND OTHER SPECIAL CLAUSES ATTACHED HEREON.

标 记 MARKS & NOS	包装及数量 QUANTITY	保险货物项目 DESCRIPTION OF GOODS	保险金额 AMOUNT INSURED
N/M	4400 CARTONS	ABOUT 4400 CARTONS MELON JAM 340 GMS X 24 TIN MALING BRAND AT USD6.10 PER CARTON	USD29,524.00

总保险金额 TOTAL AMOUNT INSURED:	US DOLLARS TWENTY NINE THOUSAND FIVE HUNDRED AND TWENTY FOUR ONLY

保费：　　　　　　　　　　启运日期
PREMIUM:　AS ARRANGED　　DATE OF　　　　　装载运输工具：
　　　　　　　　　　COMMENCEMENT: 20011010　PER CONVEYANCE:　　JINSHAN 115 V. 213
自　　　　　　　　　　经　　　　　　　　　至
FROM:　NANJING　　　　　VIA:　　　　　　　TO:　LOS ANGELES

承保险别：
CONDITIONS:
　ALL RISKS AND WAR RISKS

所保货物，如发生保险单项下可能引起索赔的损失或损坏，应立即通知本公司下述代理人＿＿＿＿查勘。

如有索赔，应向本公司提交保单正本(本保险单共有＿＿＿＿＿＿＿份正本)及有关文件。如一份正本

已用于索赔，其余正本自动失效。

IN THE EVENT OF LOSS OR DAMAGE WHICH MAY RESULT IN A CLAIM UNDER THIS POLICY,
IMMEDIATE NOTICE MUST BE GIVEN TO THE＿＿＿＿＿＿＿COMPANY'S AGENT AS MENTIONED
HEREUNDER. CLAIMS, IF ANY, ONE OF THE ORIGINAL POLICY WHICH HAS BEEN ISSUED IN＿＿＿＿＿
ORIGINAL(S) TOGETHER WITH THE RELEVANT DOCUMENTS SHALL BE SURRENDERED TO THE
COMPANY. IF ONE OF THE ORIGINAL POLICY HAS BEEN ACCOMPLISHED, THE OTHERS TO BE
VOID.

中国人民保险公司南京市分公司
The People's Insurance Company of China
Nanjing Branch

赔款偿付地点
CLAIM PAYABLE AT　　LOS ANGELES

出单日期
ISSUING DATE　　　　20100914　　　　　　　　　Authorized Signature

地址(ADD)：中国南京石鼓路 225 号
电话(TEL)：(025)6521049
邮编(POST CODE)：210029
传真(FAX)：(025)4404593

保单填制注意事项：

(1) 保险单据必须在表面上看来是由保险公司、承保人或其代理人或代表出具并签署。

(2) 除信用证另有规定外，保险单必须提交正本。

(3) 除保险单据表明保险责任最迟于装运日起生效外，该单据的签发日期 14 SEP. 2010 不得迟于运输单据注明的装运日期 10 OCT. 2010。

(4) 保险单据必须按信用证使用的币种，并至少按信用证要求的金额出具。除信用证另有规定外，保险单据的投保金额不得低于发票上的货物金额。

(5) 信用证应规定所需投保险别及必要的附加险，无此规定的，保险单据应表明已投

保基本险。本案例投保 ALL RISKS AND WAR RISKS，需注意同一运输的同一险种的保险必须由同一保险单据表示，除非进行部分保险的多份保险单据通过百分比或其他方式明确反映每一保险人的保险价值，并且每一保险人将各自分别承担自己的责任份额，不受同一运输可能已经办理的其他保险的影响。

(6) 除信用证另有规定外，银行将接受标注有免赔率或免赔额约束的保险单据。此内容本案例没有提及。

(7) 保险单据必须按信用证要求的形式出具，并且在需要时经有权索偿人背书。本案例中 KOC CO., LTD.在保单后面做背书。

关于保单需提醒注意，若开证行要求出口商提交预约保单，在这种情况下，货物一旦装运，进口商把国外的装船通知告知保险公司，保单就生效了。信用证有此条款的目的就是确保进口商不会漏保。但实际业务中，一些进口商抱着侥幸心理，觉得发生海损的可能性不大，能不能不投保，省下这笔钱。问题是一旦船发生意外，后果不堪设想，所以投保是必须采取的措施之一，千万不能漏保。

6) 产地证(Certificate of Origin)

ORIGINAL

1. Exporter KOC CO., LTD. HUARONG MANSION NO. 85 JIAQIAO, NANJING 210005, P. R. CHINA			Certificate No. **CERTIFICATE OF ORIGIN OF** THE PEOPLE'S REPUBLIC OF CHINA		
2. Consignee ORIENTAL TRADING CO., LTD. P.O. BOX 12345 CODE 55400, MA, U.S.A.					
3. Means of transport and route SHIPMENT FROM NANJING PORT TO LOS ANGELES PORT BY SEA			5. For certifying authority use only		
4. Country / region of destination U.S.A.					
6. Marks and numbers	7. Number and kind of packages; description of goods	8. H.S. Code	9. Quantity	10. Number and date of invoices	
N/M	ABOUT 4400 CARTONS MELON JAM 340 GMS X 24 TIN MALING BRAND AT USD6.10 PER CARTON	2007.9910	4400 CARTONS	2010SDT001 SEP. 30, 2010	
SAY TOTAL: FOUR THOUSAND FOUR HUNDRED CARTONS ONLY. CERTIFICATE OF CHINESE ORIGIN ISSUED BY C.C.P.I.T. STATING THE NAME AND ADDRESS OF MANUFACTURER OR PRODUCERS AND STATING THAT GOODS EXPORTED ARE WHOLLY OF DOMESTIC ORIGIN.					

11. Declaration by the exporter	12. Certification
The undersigned hereby declares that the above details and statements are correct, that all the goods were produced in China and that they comply with the Rules of Origin of the People's Republic of China.	It is hereby certified that the declaration by the exporter is correct.
NANJING, CHINA SEP. 30, 2010	NANJING, CHINA SEP. 30, 2010
-------------------------------	-------------------------------
Place and date, signature and stamp of authorized signatory	Place and date, signature and stamp of certifying authority

原产地证明填制注意事项：

(1) 如信用证要求原产地证明，则提交经过签署并注明日期的货物原产地证明。

(2) 原产地证明必须由信用证规定的人出具。如果信用证要求原产地证明由出口商或厂商出具，则由商会出具的单据是可以接受的，只要该单据相应地注明受益人、出口商或厂商。如果信用证没有规定由谁来出具原产地证明，则由任何人包括受益人出具的单据都可接受。

(3) 原产地证明必须在表面上与发票的货物相关联。原产地证明中的货物描述可以使用与信用证规定不相矛盾的货物统称，或通过其他援引表明其与要求的单据中的货物相关联。

(4) 收货人的信息不得与运输单据中的收货人信息相矛盾。但是，如果信用证要求运输单据做成"凭指示"、"凭托运人指示"、"凭开证行指示"或"货发开证行"式抬头，则原产地证明可以显示信用证的申请人或信用证中具名的另外一人作为收货人。如果信用证已经转让，那么以第一受益人作为收货人也可接受。

2. 提示单据

出口商在完成单据的缮制后，需向出口银行提交单据。把握好交单的时间是出口信用证业务的一个重要环节， 即出口商要注意匹配好信用证效期、交单期与装船日期。

信用证的效期在国外到期时，必须提前一个邮程把单据交给指定银行。如装期和效期是同一天，即通常所称的"双到期"，在实际业务操作中，应将装期提前一定的时间(一般在效期前 10 天)，以便有合理的时间来制单结汇。一般情况下应该是装期加上交单期等于效期。

关于装期，应注意以下几点：能否在规定的装期内备妥有关货物并按期出运；如来证收到时装期太近，无法按期装运，应及时与进口商联系修改；实际装期与交单期相距时间是否太短；如果规定了分批出运的时间和数量，应注意能否办到，否则，任何一批未按期出运，以后各期即告失效。

信用证有规定的，应按规定向银行交单；没有规定的，不得迟于提单日期后 21 天。应充分考虑信用证中各种条款和实际出口业务链中下列事宜对交单期的影响：如内陆运输或集港运输所需时间；进行必要的检验如法定商检或客检所需的时间等。

关于运输条款的把握需注意，在所有单据中，最重要的单据就是代表货物所有权的单据。如果合同中规定了物权单据，那出口商一定要严格审查信用证是否与合同一样要求提交物权单据，如果信用证的运输条款未规定提交物权单据，或虽规定了物权单据，但未要求提交全套物权单据，则出口商一定要加以注意并及时联系。

二、风险控制

出口商的风险主要表现在制单、交货以及开证银行或保兑银行的资信等方面。

1. 贸易背景的真实性

1) 货物问题

对出口商而言，审核信用证是贸易能否顺利进行的第一步，也是控制风险的一方面。首先要注意货物的风险，即进口商是否愿意接受此货物，出口商需要考虑若提交的单据有不符点，进口商则可能会拒绝接受货物。另一方面，若贸易货物的市场价格有所下跌，进口商为了获得预期收益，很可能会迫使出口商降价处理。再者，如果货物被拒受后，滞留在海外港口，因此而产生的费用不断增加，那么出口商只能被逼采用直接谈判或法律仲裁方式来解决。而实际上，法律仲裁由于地区差异及适用法律选择问题而复杂化，会给出口商带来巨大的风险。此外出口商还要担心进口商逾期付款或不付款的风险。

信用证中还应注意检查货物是否允许分批出运。一般来说，除信用证另有规定外，货物是允许分批付运的。在实际业务中出口商需特别注意：如信用证中规定了每一批货物出运的确切时间，则必须严格照此办理，如不能办到，必须先联系对方改证。再者，注意检查货物是否允许转运。除信用证另有规定外，货物是允许转运的。

2) 商品价格

出口商应加强商品的价格分析，需特别关注进口商品的性质和进口商的从业经验，从而考察其对商品价格风险的判断能力。一般来说，进口商品价格不应过度偏离正常的国内外市场行情。价格过高，可能面临国内销售不畅、库存积压的风险，或遭受价格下跌的损失；价格过低，可能进口的是假冒伪劣商品，或者陷入国外出口商设置的陷阱。热门敏感商品容易带来市场价格风险。例如，20 世纪 80 年代，贸易商品主要集中在木材、三合板、造纸用木浆、钢材、食用油、白糖、化肥；90 年代又出现了诸如化工原料、化纤和成品油等商品。由于是热门的价格敏感商品，那么商品的价格波动也就很大，很难预测价格的升跌。若为即期付款，货到付款赎单，银行风险相对较小；而远期付款，进口商通常会以进口商品在其国内的销售款来偿付远期信用证项下货款。但是商品价格一旦下跌，销售不畅，到期资金不能收回，则会产生资金风险。

3)　进口商及进口国

国家风险与国际贸易结算方式有着密切联系，尤其对于出口商来讲，承担的国家风险较大，需要关注进口国相关的进口政策、海关监管的变化对贸易商品带来的影响。进口政策，如外管规定的变更等对贸易商品的准入或价格起伏往往产生重大的影响，特别要关注商品是否属于许可证商品、特许商品、国家限制进口或禁止进口的商品。

关注进口商有两个方面。一是关注其经营状况、财务情况、对风险的承受能力以及所开立信用证的业务背景等。一般来说，从业时间较长、经营规模较大的进口商具有更强的抗风险能力，因为其在业内实力较强、信誉很好，与出口商建立了多年良好的合作关系，更有可能在长期的经营中积累丰富的经验，形成广泛的购销网络和牢固的上下游客户关系。二是应充分关注其所经营业务的操作模式，如进口商的分销模式和销售渠道，是否有稳定而广泛的销售渠道以消化进口产品，是按需采购或以产定销的自营进口还是代理等。

2. 信用证的审核

一份不可撤销的信用证中如果有若干赋予开证申请人单方面可随时解除付款责任的条款，便使得表面上为不可撤销的信用证变成了实质上可撤销的信用证，这类条款对出口商是很不利的，也是无法做到单证一致的。

1)　信用证金额的审核

出口商需要检查信用证的金额和数量是否与合同规定相一致，要注意国际惯例对应数量增减的规定，5000 PCS 100% COTTON SHIRTS (5000 件全棉衬衫)由于数量单位是"件"，实际交货时只能是 5000 件，而不能有 5%的增减。 其次是价格条款是否符合合同规定。合同中规定是 FOB SHANGHAI AT USD50/PC，根据此价格条款，有关的运费和保险费由买方即开证人承担。如果信用证中的价格条款没有按合同的规定作上述表示，而是规定为 CIF NEW YORK AT USD50/PC，对此条款如不及时修改，那么受益人将承担有关的运费和保险费。

2)　信用证逻辑性

检查信用证中有无矛盾之处，例如：明明是空运，却要求提供海运提单；明明价格条款是 FOB，保险应由买方办理，而信用证中却要求提供保险单。

3. 单据可操作性

出口商在审证时应该明确知道自己能否提供或及时提供单据，尤其需注意一些特殊要求，例如：需要认证特别是使馆认证的单据；由其他机构或部门出具的有关文件，如出口许可证、运费收据、检验证明等。此外还需注意信用证中指定船龄、船籍、船公司或不准在某港口转船等条款。而对有疑问之处可以向通知行询问以得到银行的帮助，同时更应该与进口商联系，以明确信用证中的每一项条款。若出口商因自身的原因未能仔细审核信用证，且没按要求填写和完成所要求的单据，就可能造成进口商延期付款或拒绝付款，特别是在贸易条件对进口商不利的情况下，进口商可能就会以单据不符为凭拒付，以达到维护其自身利益的目的。

4. 不符点的处理

出口商的操作风险主要表现在因对国际惯例不熟悉、缺乏实践经验，忽视了单证方面关键环节的审核，同时在缮制单据上产生各种疏漏，从而造成单证不符、单单不符的情况，因此遭到开证行拒付的事例时有发生。

例如，出口商与巴西的进口商签订了一个出口货物的合同，并通过信用证来结算，但因为在货物加工时耽误了时间，使得提单过了信用证规定的装期，出口商自认为与进口商关系好，故向出口方提交单据时担保此不符点出单，开证行因此不符点拒付。此时，国际市场发生了变化，货物的价格下降了很多，又有另一家出口商以更低的价格给进口商供货，因此进口商不接受此不符点拒绝付款，从而造成货物滞留进口国码头，出口商不得不贱卖货物。由此可看出单证一致的重要性。

三、总结思考

信用证是一种银行的有条件的付款保证文件。用这种方式，出口商的收汇有保证。但能否取得货款，取决于开证行的资信和出口商所交的单据是否符合信用证的规定。对于开证行的资信，出口商可以通过通知行事先加以了解。如果开证行的资信确实有问题，可以要求进口商更换开证行或增开一家保兑行加以保兑。开证行的资信问题解决以后，出口商能否顺利收汇就完全取决于出口商所准备的单据，因为信用证纯粹是一种单据业务，因此在总结时，我们列举实际业务中常见的不符点供出口商参考，也请出口商在实际制单或准备单据时注意。

以下是信用证的常见不符点。

(1) Credit expired: Documents presented after expiry of credit
信用证过效期：单据提交迟于信用证效期。

(2) Late presentation
过交单期。

(3) Late shipment: Transport documents show a date after the latest date of shipment as shown on credit.

过装期：运输单据日期迟于信用证最迟装期。

(4) Port of loading/dispatch/taking in charge not as per the credit

起运港/起运地/接收地与信用证不符。

(5) Port of discharge/final destination not as per the credit

卸货港/最终目的地与信用证不符。

(6) Transport documents show an intended vessel/intended port of loading but on board notation does not additionally evidence actual port of loading and actual vessel.

运输单据上显示有预装船/预装货港，但装船批注上没有显示实际的装货港和船名。

(7) On board notation not dated

没有注明装船日。

(8) Full set of transport documents not presented as required by the credit

没有按信用证要求提供全套运输单据。

(9) Transport documents do not identify carrier and are not signed in accordance with the credit and / or UCP.

运输单据没有明确承运人或签发不符合信用证/国际惯例的要求。

(10) Bills of Lading not endorsed in blank(as stipulated by the credit)

提单没有空白背书(按信用证的要求)。

(11) The currency in the insurance is different from that of the credit.

保单的币种与信用证的币种不符 。

(12) The amount of insurance is insufficient/under insured.

保险金额超保/不足。

(13) The insurance policy/certificate is not endorsed.

保险单据/证明没有背书。

(14) The effective date for insurance is later than the date of shipment(or loading on board).

保单日期晚于船期。

(15) All the originals shown on the document as issued are not presented.

没有提交全套正本单据。

(16) Draft not signed by the beneficiary or draft signed but no indication of the name of the beneficiary

汇票非受益人签发或汇票虽签署但未显示受益人名称。

(17) Amount is in excess of the credit/over drawn.

金额超证。

(18) Words and figures on draft do not agree with each other.

汇票上金额大小写不符。

(19) Tenor of draft incorrectly shown (e.g. shows at sight instead of 60 days as required by the credit)

汇票期限不符(例如：显示即期而非信用证要求的 60 天远期)。

(20) Value of the invoice differs from that of draft.

发票金额与汇票金额不符。

(21) Value of the invoice exceeds the available balance of the L/C.

发票金额超过信用证有效金额。

(22) Marks and numbers on invoice inconsistent with those on transport docs(or other documents).

发票上的唛头和数字与运输单据(或其他单据)上的不符。

关于不符点的处理，银行在实际业务中，如果遇到国外开证行无理拒付，银行会据理力争，做到有理、有据、有节，决不能姑息迁就。但应如何交涉呢？处理时可视具体情况采取以下步骤。

(1) 论理。引经据典，摆事实、讲道理，以理服人。

(2) 上报。向对方的上一级主管反映，防止小鬼当道，并表示希望尽快解决。

(3) 讲情。希望对方采取合作的态度，从大局出发，从长远考虑，不要损害双方的感情，并表示遗憾。

(4) 外交。由代理行部门与对方的代理行部门联系。

(5) 通牒。表示不满，提出强烈抗议，并发出最后通牒。

(6) 通报国际商会、国际金融界及有关媒体。

(7) 法律诉讼。

四、实训操练

练习 3.4

如果你是出口商，收到练习 3.1 中的信用证及其修改后，应如何准备以下单据？假设船名航次是 SHENYAN V 115，装船日期是 2010 年 3 月 4 日，数量为 4400 箱，毛重为 39449.4千克，净重为 35904.00 千克，体积为 45.6 立方米。

信用证如下：

MT700 电文

------------------------- Message Header -----------------------

Swift Output　　　: FIN 700 Issue of a Documentary Credit

Sender　　　　　: MBTCPHMMXXX

Receiver　　　　: COMMCNSHNJG

------------------------- Message Text -----------------------

27: SEQUENCE OF TOTAL:

　　1/1

40A: FORM OF DOCUMENTARY CREDIT:

　　　IRREVOCABLE

20: DOCUMENTARY CREDIT NUMBER:

　　004/LC/000020/03

31C: DATE OF ISSUE 开证日:

　　　100103

31D: DATE AND PLACE OF EXPIRY:

　　　100325 CHINA

50: APPLICANT:

　　POLLANDRE MANUFACTURING, INC.

　　30 STO. ROSARIO STREET, KARUHATAN,

　　VALENZUELA CITY, PHILIPPINES

59: BENEFICIARY – NAME & ADDRESS:

　　NANJING XIAOCHEN TEXTILE CO., LTD.

　　101 BAIXIA ROAD NANJING CHINA

　　0086-25-2691025

32B: CURRENCY CODE, AMOUNT:

　　CURRENCY: USD (US DOLLAR)

　　AMOUNT: #31620.00

41D: AVAILABLE WITH…BY…: ANY BANK

42C: DRAFTS AT …:

　　　30 DAYS AFTER SIGHT

42D: DRAWEE – NAME, ADDRESS:

ISSUING BANK

FOR FULL INVOICE VALUE

43P: PARTIAL SHIPMENTS:

NOT ALLOWED

43T: TRANSHIPMENT:

ALLOWED

44A: ON BOARD/DISP/TAKING CHARGE AT / FROM:

ANY PORT IN CHINA

44B: FOR TRANSPORTATION TO …:

MANILA, PHILIPPINES

44C: LATEST DATE OF SHIPMENT:

100304

45A: DESCRIPTION OF GOODS & / OR SERVICE:

93000 PRINTED FABRIC

AS PER SALES CONFIRMATION NO. C X-021202A DATED DECEMBER 5, 2009 CIF

MALINA

46A: DOCUMENTS REQUIRED:

1. FULL SET MARKED ORIGINAL(S) CLEAN ON BOARD OCEAN BILLS OF LADING PLUS
   2 NON-NEGOTIABLE COPIES MARKED "FREIGHT PREPAID" MADE OUT TO ORDER
   OF METROPOLITAN BANK AND TRUST COMPANY AND NOTIFY APPLICANT.

2. SIGNED COMMERCIAL INVOICE IN TRIPLICATE.

3. PACKING LIST IN THREE COPIES.

4. BENEFICIARY'S CERTIFICATE THAT ONE FULL SET OF ADVANCE COPY OF
   NON-NEGOTIABLE SHIPPING DOCUMENTS HAS BEEN SENT DIRECTLY TO BUYER
   VIA COURIER.

47A: ADDITIONAL CONDITIONS:

ALL DOCUMENTS INCLUDING BILL OF LADING (B/L) MUST LEGIBLY CONTAIN THE
L/C NUMBER PERTAINING TO THE SHIPMENT. DISCOUNT CHARGES AND/OR
ACCEPTANCE COMMISSION IF ANY, ARE FOR BENEFICIARY'S ACCOUNT. SHIPPING
LINES TO ACCEPT BANK GUARANTEE IN LIEU OF ORIGINAL SHIPPING DOCUMENTS.
REMIT DOCUMENTS IN TWO LOTS BY DHL OR OTHER COURIER TO

METROPOLITAN BANK AND TRUST COMPANY

GRACE PARK CENTER, 446 RIZAL AVE. EXT. GRACE PARK

CALOOCAN CITY, PHILIPPINES

PLUS/MINUS 10 PERCENT ON QUANTITY AND VALUE ALLOWED.

71B: CHARGES:

ALL BANK CHARGES OUTSIDE THE PHILIPPINES INCLUDING REIMBURSEMENT FEE

ARE FOR BENEFICIARY'S ACCOUNT.

49: CONFIRMATION INSTRUCTIONS:

WITHOUT

53D: REIMBURSING BANK – NAME & ADDRESS　偿付行名称和地址:

METROPOLITAN BANK AND TRUST COMPANY, 1203 MARINE TOWER 1 PUDONG

AVENUE, SHANGHAI, CHINA

78: INST TO PAYG/ACCPTG/NEGOTG BANK:

CABLE ADVISE US AMOUNT AND DATE OF NEGOTIATION INDICATING THE

PRINCIPAL AMOUNT AND BANK CHARGES (IN DETAILED) IF ANY.

DISCREPANCY FEE OF USD50.00(FOR DISCREPANT DOCUMENTS) PLUS

ISSUING BANK'S COLLECTION CHARGES (FOR DOCUMENTS SENT ON

COLLECTION/APPROVAL BASIS) WILL BE DEDUCTED FROM THE PROCEEDS

OF ANY DRAWINGS. THESE CHARGES ARE FOR BENEFICIARY'S ACCOUNT

EVEN IF THE L/C STIPULATES THAT ALL CHARGES ARE FOR THE

APPLICANT'S ACCOUNT.

REMIT DOCUMENTS IN TWO LOTS BY DHL OR OTHER COURIER CERTIFYING

THAT THE TERMS AND CONDITIONS OF THE CREDIT HAVE BEEN COMPLIED

WITH. THE REIMBURSING BANK HOLDS SPECIAL REIMBURSEMENT

INSTRUCTIONS TO THIS LETTER OF CREDIT.

57D: 'ADVISE THROUGH' BANK–NAME & ADDR 通知行名称和地址:

BANK OF COMMUNICATIONS, NANJING BRANCH

124 NORTH ZHONGSHAN ROAD, NANJING, CHINA

72: SENDER TO RECEIVER INFORMATION:

REIMBURSEMENT CLAIMS ARE SUBJECT TO ICC URR 525. WE HEREBY AUTHORIZE YOU

TO HONOR REIMBURSEMENT CLAIMS FROM THE NEGOTIATING BANK PROVIDED ALL

TERMS AND CONDITIONS ARE COMPLIED WITH.

汇票

凭　　　　　　　　　　　　　　　　　　　　　　　　信用证
Drawn under .... L/C NO. ....

日期
Dated .... 支取 Payable with interest @........% 按........息........付款

号码　　　　　　汇票金额
NO. .... Exchange for ....

见票...........................日后(本汇票之副本未付)交付

　　　AT....................sight of this FIRST of Exchange(Second of Exchange being unpaid)

Pay to the order of .... the sum of

....

款已收讫
Value received ....

此致
TO: ....

商业发票

ISSUER	商业发票 COMMERCIAL INVOICE		
TO			
	NO.		DATE
TRANSPORT DETAILS	S/C NO.		L/C NO.
	TERMS OF PAYMENT		
MARKS AND NUMBERS	NUMBER AND KIND OF PACKAGE; DESCRIPTION OF GOODS	QUANTITY	UNIT PRICE AMOUNT USD
N/M			
TOTAL:			
We hereby certify that the contents of invoice herein are ture and correct.			
		(出口商签字和盖单据章)	

装箱单

ISSUER		装箱单 PACKING LIST			
TO		INVOICE NO.		DATE	
MARKS AND NUMBERS	NUMBER AND KIND OF PACKAGE; DESCRIPTION OF GOODS	PACKAGE	G.W.	N.W.	MEAS.
			KG		CBM
N/M					
TOTAL:					
SAY TOTAL:					

(出口商签字和盖单据章)

提单

Shipper		BILL OF LADING	B/L No.:
Consignee		COSCO	
Notify Party		中国远洋运输公司 CHINA OCEAN SHIPPING COMPANY	
*Pre carriage by	*Place of Receipt		
Ocean Vessel Voy. No.	Port of Loading		
		ORIGINAL	
Port of discharge	*Final destination	Freight payable at	Number of original Bs/L

Marks and Numbers	Number and kind of packages; Description	Gross weight	Measurement m3

TOTAL PACKAGES(IN WORDS)	
Freight and charges	
	Place and date of issue
	Signed for the Carrier **CHINA OCEAN SHIPPING COMPANY** 船运公司负责人签字

*Applicable only when document used as a Through Bill of Lading.

证明：

BENEFICIARY'S CERTIFICATE

NANJING XIAOCHEN TEXTILE CO., LTD.

张三

参考答案：

汇票

凭	METROPOLITAN BANK AND TRUST COMPANY,	信用证
Drawn under	PHILIPPINES	L/C NO. ____004/LC/000020/03____

日期
Dated ········20100103········　　支取 Payable with interest @ _____% 按_____息_____付款

号码　　　　　　汇票金额
NO. ····ED13445···　Exchange for ···USD31620.00····　20100303

见票····30 DAYS AFTER SIGHT····日后(本汇票之副本未付)交付

AT _____sight of this FIRST of Exchange(Second of Exchange being unpaid)

Pay to the order of ····BANK OF COMMUNICATIONS CO., LTD., JIANGSU BR.····　the sum of
····US DOLLARS THIRTY ONE THOUSAND SIX HUNDRED AND TWENTY ONLY····

款已收讫
Value received _____

此
致 ····METROPOLITAN BANK AND TRUST COMPANY, PHILIPPINES····
TO:

····SIGNATURE(出口商盖单和签字) NANJING XIAOCHEN TEXTILE CO., LTD.····

商业发票

ISSUER NANJING XIAOCHEN TEXTILE CO., LTD.	商业发票 COMMERCIAL INVOICE	
TO POLLANDRE MANUFACTURING, INC. 30 STO. ROSARIO STREET, KARUHATAN VALENZUELA CITY, PHILIPPINES	**NO.** ED13445	**DATE** 20100303
TRANSPORT DETAILS SHIPMENT FROM NANJING PORT TO MALINA PORT BY SEA	**S/C NO.** CX-021202A	**L/C NO.** 004/LC/000020/03
	TERMS OF PAYMENT L/C AT 30 DAYS AFTER SIGHT	

MARKS AND NUMBERS	NUMBER AND KIND OF PACKAGE; DESCRIPTION OF GOODS	QUANTITY	UNIT PRICE USD	AMOUNT
N/M	**CFR MALINA PORT**			
	93000 PRINTED FABRIC AS PER SALES CONFIRMATION NO. C X-021202A DATED DECEMBER 5, 2009	4400 CARTONS	USD7.186	USD31,620.00
	TOTAL: 4400 CARTONS			**USD31,620.00**

SAY TOTAL:USD THIRTY ONE THOUSAND SIX HUNDRED AND TWENTY ONLY.
We hereby certify that the contents of invoice herein are ture and correct.

NANJING XIAOCHEN TEXTILE CO., LTD. (出口商签字和盖单据章)

装箱单(假设毛重为 39449.40 KGS，净重为 35904.00 KGS，体积为 45.6 CBM)

ISSUER NANJING XIAOCHEN TEXTILE CO., LTD.		装箱单 PACKING LIST			
TO POLLANDRE MANUFACTURING, INC. 30 STO.ROSARIO STREET KARUHATAN VALENZUELA CITY , PHILIPPINES		**INVOICE NO.** ED13445		**DATE** 03 MAR. 2010	
MARKS AND NUMBERS	**NUMBER AND KIND OF PACKAGE; DESCRIPTION OF GOODS**	**PACKAGE**	**G.W.** KG	**N.W.**	**MEAS.** CBM
N/M	93000 PRINTED FABRIC AS PER SALES CONFIRMATION NO. C X-021202A	4400 CARTONS	39449.40	35904.00	45.60
	TOTAL:	**4400 CARTONS**	**39449.40 KGS**	**35904.00 KGS**	**45.60 CBM**

SAY TOTAL: FOUR THOUSAND FOUR HUNDRED CARTONS ONLY.

(出口商签字和盖单据章)

提单(假设船名及航次是 SHENYAN V 115)

Shipper NANJING XIAOCHEN TEXTILE CO., LTD.	**BILL OF LADING**	B/L No.:

Shipper NANJING XIAOCHEN TEXTILE CO., LTD.
Consignee TO ORDER OF METROPOLITAN BANK AND TRUST COMPANY
Notify Party POLLANDRE MANUFACTURING, INC. 30 STO. ROSARIO STREET, KARUHATAN VALENZUELA CITY, PHILIPPINES

COSCO

中 国 远 洋 运 输 公 司

CHINA OCEAN SHIPPING COMPANY

ORIGINAL

*Pre carriage by	*Place of Receipt
Ocean Vessel Voy. No. SHENYAN V 115	Port of Loading NANJING
Port of discharge MALINA	*Final destination

Freight payable at	Number of original Bs/L THREE

Marks and Numbers	Number and Kind of Packages; Description	Gross Weight	Measurement m3
	93000 PRINTED FABRIC AS PER SALES CONFIRMATION NO. C X-021202A DATED DECEMBER 5, 2009 ON BOARD 20100304	39449.40 KGS	45.6 CBM

TOTAL PACKAGES(IN WORDS)   FOUR THOUSAND FOUR HUNDRED CARTONS ONLY

Freight and charges

Place and date of issue
03 MAR. 2010, NANJING

Signed for the Carrier
CHINA OCEAN SHIPPING COMPANY
船运公司负责人签字

*Applicable only when document used as a Through Bill of Lading.

证明:

BENEFICIARY'S CERTIFICATE

DATE: 03 MAR. 2010

WE CERTIFY THAT ONE FULL SET OF ADVANCE COPY OF NON-NEGOTIABLE SHIPPING DOCUMENTS HAS BEEN SENT DIRECTLY TO BUYER VIA COURIER.

NANJING XIAOCHEN TEXTILE CO., LTD.
张三

练习 3.5

根据练习 3.2 中的信用证进行练习。如果你是出口商,应如何准备相关单据呢?假设毛重为 2500.00 KGS,净重为 2100.00 KGS,体积为 35.07 CBM,船名及航次是 JIHAIXIN V. 115。

信用证如下:

MT700 电文

-------------------------- Message Header -------------------------
Swift Output   : FIN 700 Issue of a Documentary Credit
Sender   : BOKFJPJZXXX
Receiver   : COMMCNSHNJG
-------------------------- Message Text -------------------------
27: Sequence of Total:

NUMBER: 1

TOTAL: 1

TYPE: 700

40A: Type of Documentary Credit: IRREVOCABLE

20: Letter of Credit Number:

100701

31G: Date of Issue:

20100503

40E: Applicable Rules: UCP LATEST VERSION

31D: Date and Place of Expiry:

20100630 CHINA

51D: Applicant Bank:

BOKFJPJZXXX

BANK OF KYOTO, KYOTO

50: Applicant:

AKURA CO., LTD.

P.O. BOX 123, KYOTO, JAPAN

59: Beneficiary:

ABC COMPANY, 111 ZHUJIANG RD, NANJING, CHINA

32B: Currency Code, Amount:

USD100,000.00 FOB NANJING

41D: Available with...by...:

ANY BANK BY NEGOTIATION

42C: Drafts at:

SIGHT

42D: Drawee:

BANK OF KYOTO, KYOTO

43P: Partial Shipments:

NOT ALLOWED

43T: Transhipment:

NOT ALLOWED

44A: Shipping on Board/Dispatch/Packing in Charge at/ from:

NANJING

44B: Transportation to:

TOKYO

44C: Latest Date of Shipment:

20100609

45A: Description of Goods or Services:

PLASMA TV 70 SETS

46A: Documents Required:

　*FULL SET (AT LEAST THREE) ORIGINAL CLEAN SHIPPED ON BOARD BILLS OF LADING ISSUED TO ORDER BLANK ENDORSED NOTIFY PARTIES APPLICANT SHOWING FREIGHT COLLECT AND BEARING THE NUMBER OF THIS CREDIT.

　*PACKING LIST IN 3 COPIES.

　*COMMERCIAL INVOICE IN 3 COPIES MANUAL SIGNED BY THE BENEFICIARY.

47A: Additional Instructions:

　1. CHARTER PARTY B/L AND THIRD PARTY DOCUMENTS ARE ACCEPTABLE.

　2. SHIPMENT PRIOR TO L/C ISSUING DATE IS ACCEPTABLE.

　3. BOTH QUANTITY AND AMOUNT 10 PERCENT MORE OR LESS ARE ALLOWED.

71B: Charges:

ALL BANKING CHARGES OUTSIDE THE OPENNING BANK ARE FOR BENEFICIARY'S ACCOUNT.

48: Period for Presentation:

DOCUMENTS MUST BE PRESENTED WITHIN 21 DAYS AFTER THE DATE OF ISSUANCE OF THE TRANSPORT DOCUMENTS BUT WITHIN THE VALIDITY OF THE CREDIT.

49: Confirmation Instructions:

WITHOUT

78: Instructions to the Paying/Accepting/Negotiating Bank:

1. ALL DOCUMENTS TO BE FORWARDED TO BANK OF KYOTO, SUSAN RD 123, KYOTO, JAPAN IN ONE COVER, UNLESS OTHERWISE STATED ABOVE.

2. DISCREPANT DOCUMENT FEE OF USD 50.00 OR EQUAL CURRENCY WILL BE DEDUCTED FROM DRAWING IF DOCUMENTS WITH DISCREPANCIES ARE ACCEPTED.

57A: "Advising Through" Bank:

汇票

凭		信用证	
Drawn under	-------------------------------------	L/C NO.	-----------------------

日期
Dated ------------------------------ 支取 Payable with interest @ ------% 按 ------息 ------付款

号码   汇票金额
NO. ---------------- Exchange for ---

见票 ------------------------ 日后(本汇票之副本未付)交付

AT ------------------------ sight of this FIRST of Exchange(Second of Exchange being unpaid)

Pay to the order of --- the sum of

款已收讫
Value received ---

此致
TO: ---

商业发票

ISSUER	商业发票 COMMERCIAL INVOICE		
TO			
	NO.		DATE
TRANSPORT DETAILS	S/C NO.		L/C NO.
	TERMS OF PAYMENT		

MARKS AND NUMBERS	NUMBER AND KIND OF PACKAGE; DESCRIPTION OF GOODS	QUANTITY	UNIT PRICE USD	AMOUNT
	TOTAL:			

We hereby certify that the contents of invoice herein are ture and correct.

(出口商签字和盖单据章)

装箱单

ISSUER	装箱单 PACKING LIST			
TO				
	INVOICE NO.		DATE	

MARKS AND NUMBERS	NUMBER AND KIND OF PACKAGE; DESCRIPTION OF GOODS	PACKAGE	G.W. KG	N.W.	MEAS. CBM
	TOTAL:				

(出口商签字和盖单据章)

提单

Shipper	BILL OF LADING	B/L No.:
Consignee	**COSCO** 中 国 远 洋 运 输 公 司 CHINA OCEAN SHIPPING COMPANY	
Notify Party		

*Pre carriage by	*Place of Receipt	
Ocean Vessel Voy. No.	Port of Loading	**ORIGINAL**
Port of discharge	*Final destination	Freight payable at	Number of original Bs/L

Marks and Numbers	Number and kind of packages; Description	Gross weight	Measurement m3

TOTAL PACKAGES(IN WORDS)

Freight and charges

Place and date of issue

Signed for the Carrier
CHINA OCEAN SHIPPING COMPANY
船运公司负责人签字

*Applicable only when document used as a Through Bill of Lading.

参考答案:

汇票

凭 Drawn under	BANK OF KYOTO, KYOTO	信用证 L/C NO. 100701

日期
Dated 20100503　　　　支取 Payable with interest @........%......按.......息....... 付款

号码　　　　　　　　汇票金额
NO. PX1001.　　Exchange for　　USD100000.00　　20100606

见票　　SIGHT　　日后(本汇票之副本未付)交付

AT _____ sight of this FIRST of Exchange(Second of Exchange being unpaid)

Pay to the order of　BANK OF COMMUNICATIONS CO., LTD., JIANGSU BR.　the sum of

US DOLLARS ONE HUNDRED THOUSAND ONLY

款已收讫
Value received

此致
TO:　　　　　BANK OF KYOTO, KYOTO

SIGNATURE(出口商签字和盖单) ABC COMPANY

商业发票

ISSUER ABC COMPANY, NANJING, CHINA	商业发票 COMMERCIAL INVOICE		
TO AKURA CO., LTD. P.O. BOX 123, KYOTO, JAPAN			
	NO. PX1001		DATE 20100605
TRANSPORT DETAILS SHIPMENT FROM NANJING PORT TO TOKYO PORT BY SEA	S/C NO. NEO2010/026		L/C NO. 100701
	TERMS OF PAYMENT L/C AT SIGHT		

MARKS AND NUMBERS	NUMBER AND KIND OF PACKAGE; DESCRIPTION OF GOODS	QUANTITY	UNIT PRICE USD	AMOUNT
N/M				
	PLASMA TV	70 SETS	USD1428.57	FOB NANJING USD100,000.00
	TOTAL:	70 SETS		USD100,000.00

SAY TOTAL:USD ONE HUNDRED THOUSAND ONLY.
We hereby certify that the contents of invoice herein are true and correct.

ABC COMPANY

(出口商签字和盖单据章)

装箱单(假设毛重为2500.00 KGS，净重为2100.00 KGS，体积为35.07 CBM)

ISSUER

ABC COMPANY, NANJING, CHINA

TO

AKURA CO., LTD.
P.O. BOX 123, KYOTO, JAPAN

装箱单

PACKING LIST

INVOICE NO.	DATE
PX1001	05 JUN. 2010

MARKS AND NUMBERS	NUMBER AND KIND OF PACKAGE; DESCRIPTION OF GOODS	PACKAGE	G.W. KG	N.W. KG	MEAS. CBM
N/M	PLASMA TV	70 SETS	2500.00	2100.00	35.07
	TOTAL:	70 SETS	2500.00 KGS	2100.00 KGS	35.07 CBM

SAY TOTAL: SEVENTY SETS ONLY.

(出口商签字和盖单据章)

提单

Shipper ABC COMPANY, NANJING, CHINA		B/L No.:
Consignee TO ORDER		**BILL OF LADING**
Notify Party AKURA CO., LTD., KYOTO, JAPAN		**COSCO** 中 国 远 洋 运 输 公 司 CHINA OCEAN SHIPPING COMPANY
*Pre carriage by	*Place of Receipt	

Ocean Vessel Voy. No. JIHAIXIN V. 115	Port of Loading NANJING	**ORIGINAL**	
Port of discharge TOKYO	*Final destination	Freight payable at	Number of original Bs/L THREE

Marks and Numbers	Number and kind of packages; Description	Gross weight	Measurement m3
	PLASMA TV 70 SETS FREIGHT COLLECT ON BOARD 20100604	2500.00 KGS	35.07 CBM

TOTAL PACKAGES (IN WORDS)

Freight and charges

	Place and date of issue 4 JUNE 2010, NANJING
	Signed for the Carrier CHINA OCEAN SHIPPING COMPANY 船运公司负责人签字

*Applicable only when document used as a Through Bill of Lading.

练习 3.6

根据练习 3.3 中的信用证进行练习。如果你是出口商，应如何准备相关单据呢？假设毛重为 200.00 KGS，净重为 150.00 KGS，体积为 5.00 CBM，船名及航次是 JINHE V. 230。

信用证如下：

MT700 电文

```
------------------------- Message Header -----------------------
Swift Output      : FIN 700 Issue of a Documentary Credit
Sender            : CHASUS33XXX
Receiver          : COMMCNSHNJG
------------------------- Message Text -----------------------
```

27: Sequence of Total

NUMBER: 1

TOTAL: 1

TYPE: 700

40A: Type of Documentary Credit: IRREVOCABLE

20: Letter of Credit Number:

MS2565

31G: Date of Issue:

20100608

40E: Applicable Rules: UCP LATEST VERSION

31D: Date and Place of Expiry:

20100830 CHINA

51D: Applicant Bank:

CHASUS33XXX

JPMORGAN CHASE BANK, NEW YORK

50: Applicant:

RAYTHEON COMPANY

CAMBRIDGE, MASSACHUSETTS, USA

59: Beneficiary:

ABC COMPANY, 111 ZHUJIANG RD, NANJING, CHINA

32B: Currency Code, Amount:

USD250,000.00

41D: Available with...by...: JPMORGAN CHASE BANK, NEW YORK

BY DEFER PAYMENT

42P: Deferred Payment Details:

30 DAYS AFTER B/L DATE

43P: Partial Shipments:

ALLOWED

43T: Transhipment:

ALLOWED

44E: Port of Loading:

NANJING

44F: Port of Discharge:

NEW YORK

44C: Latest Date of Shipment:

20100809

45A: Description of Goods or Services:

MONO CELLS CIF NEW YORK 5000 PCS AT USD50/PC

46A: Documents Required:

　*COMMERCIAL INVOICE IN 3 COPIES MANUAL SIGNED BY THE BENEFICIARY.

　*FULL SET (AT LEAST THREE) ORIGINAL CLEAN SHIPPED ON BOARD BILLS OF
　LADING CONSIGNED TO APPLICANT AND NOTIFY APPLICANT SHOWING
　"FREIGHT PREPAID" AND BEARING THE NUMBER OF THIS CREDIT.

　*PACKING LIST IN 3 COPIES.

　*INSURANCE POLICY/CERT IN DUPLICATE FOR 110 INVOICE AMT
　COVERING INSTITUTE CARGO CLAUSES(ALL RISKS)SHOWING CLAIM
　PAYABLE IN USA.

47A: Additional Instructions:

　1. CHARTER PARTY B/L AND THIRD PARTY DOCUMENTS ARE ACCEPTABLE.

　2. SHIPMENT PRIOR TO L/C ISSUING DATE IS ACCEPTABLE.

　3. BOTH QUANTITY AND AMOUNT 10 PERCENT MORE OR LESS ARE ALLOWED.

71B: Charges:

ALL BANKING CHARGES OUTSIDE THE OPENNING BANK ARE FOR
BENEFICIARY'S ACCOUNT.

48: Period for Presentation:

DOCUMENTS MUST BE PRESENTED WITHIN 21 DAYS AFTER THE DATE OF
ISSUANCE OF THE TRANSPORT DOCUMENTS BUT WITHIN THE VALIDITY OF
THE CREDIT.

49: Confirmation Instructions:

WITHOUT

78: Instructions to the Paying/Accepting/Negotiating Bank:

　　1. ALL DOCUMENTS TO BE FORWARDED TO JPMORGAN CHASE BANK,
　　P.O. BOX 211, NEW YORK, USA IN ONE COVER, UNLESS OTHERWISE STATED
　　ABOVE.

　　2. DISCREPANT DOCUMENT FEE OF USD 50.00 OR EQUAL CURRENCY WILL BE
　　DEDUCTED FROM DRAWING IF DOCUMENTS WITH DISCREPANCIES ARE
　　ACCEPTED.

57A: "Advising Through" Bank:

商业发票

ISSUER					
TO		商业发票 COMMERCIAL INVOICE			
		NO.		DATE	
TRANSPORT DETAILS		S/C NO.		L/C NO.	
		TERMS OF PAYMENT			
MARKS AND NUMBERS	NUMBER AND KIND OF PACKAGE; DESCRIPTION OF GOODS	QUANTITY	UNIT PRICE USD	AMOUNT	
	TOTAL:				
We hereby certify that the contents of invoice herein are true and correct.					
			(出口商签字和盖单据章)		

装箱单

ISSUER					
TO		装箱单 PACKING LIST			
		INVOICE NO.		DATE	
MARKS AND NUMBERS	NUMBER AND KIND OF PACKAGE; DESCRIPTION OF GOODS	PACKAGE	G.W. KG	N.W.	MEAS. CBM
	TOTAL:				
			(出口商签字和盖单据章)		

提单

Shipper	BILL OF LADING		B/L No.:

BILL OF LADING

B/L No.:

Shipper	
Consignee	
Notify Party	

COSCO

中 国 远 洋 运 输 公 司

CHINA OCEAN SHIPPING COMPANY

*Pre carriage by	*Place of Receipt
Ocean Vessel Voy. No.	Port of Loading

ORIGINAL

Port of discharge	*Final destination	Freight payable at	Number of original Bs/L

Marks and Numbers	Number and kind of packages; Description	Gross weight	Measurement m3

TOTAL PACKAGES(IN WORDS)

Freight and charges

Place and date of issue

Signed for the Carrier

CHINA OCEAN SHIPPING COMPANY

船运公司负责人签字

*Applicable only when document used as a Through Bill of Lading.

保单

PICC 中国人民保险公司南京市分公司

The People's Insurance Company of China Nanjing Branch

总公司设于北京   一九四九年创立

Head Office Beijing   Established in 1949

货物运输保险单

CARGO TRANSPORTATION INSURANCE POLICY

发票号(INVOICE NO.)   保单号次

合同号(CONTRACT NO.)   POLICY NO.

信用证号(L/C NO.)

被保险人:

Insured:

中国人民保险公司(以下简称本公司)根据被保险人的要求，由被保险人向本公司缴付约定的保险费，按照本保险单承保险别和背面所载条款与下列特款承保下述货物运输保险，特立本保险单。

THIS POLICY OF INSURANCE WITNESSES THAT THE PEOPLE'S INSURANCE COMPANY OF CHINA (HEREINAFTER CALLED "THE COMPANY")AT THE REQUEST OF THE INSURED AND IN CONSIDERATION OF THE AGREED PREMIUM PAID TO THE COMPANY BY THE INSURED, UNDERTAKES TO INSURE THE UNDERMENTIONED GOODS IN TRANSPORTATION SUBJECT TO THE CONDITIONS OF THIS POLICY AS PER THE CLAUSES PRINTED OVERLEAF AND OTHER SPECIAL CLAUSES ATTACHED HEREON.

标 记 MARKS & NOS	包装及数量 QUANTITY	保险货物项目 DESCRIPTION OF GOODS	保险金额 AMOUNT INSURED

总保险金额

TOTAL AMOUNT

INSURED: _____

保费   AS   启运日期
DATE OF   装载运输工具
PER

PREMIUM: ARRANGED   COMMENCEMENT: _____ CONVEYANCE: _____

自   经   至

FROM: _____ VIA: _____ TO: _____

承保险别：

CONDITIONS:

所保货物，如发生保险单项下可能引起索赔的损失或损坏，应立即通知本公司下述代理人_____查勘。如有索赔，应向本公司提交保单正本(本保险单共有_____份正本)及有关文件。如一份正本已用于索赔，其余正本自动失效。

IN THE EVENT OF LOSS OR DAMAGE WHICH MAY RESULT IN A CLAIM UNDER THIS POLICY, IMMEDIATE NOTICE MUST BE GIVEN TO_____THE COMPANY'S AGENT AS MENTIONED HEREUNDER. CLAIMS, IF ANY, ONE OF THE ORIGINAL POLICY WHICH HAS BEEN ISSUED IN_____ORIGINAL(S) TOGETHER WITH THE RELEVANT DOCUMENTS SHALL BE SURRENDERED TO THE COMPANY. IF ONE OF THE ORIGINAL POLICY HAS BEEN ACCOMPLISHED, THE OTHERS TO BE VOID.

赔款偿付地点

CLAIM PAYABLE AT_____

出单日期

ISSUING DATE_____

中国人民保险公司南京市分公司

The People's Insurance Company of China

Nanjing Branch

Authorized Signature

| 地址(ADD)：中国南京石鼓路 225 号 | 电话(TEL): (025)6521049 |
| 邮编(POST CODE): 210029 | 传真(FAX): (025)4404593 |

参考答案：

商业发票

ISSUER ABC COMPANY, NANJING, CHINA	商业发票 COMMERCIAL INVOICE	
TO RAYTHEON COMPANY CAMBRIDGE, MASSACHUSETTS, USA		
	NO. 100620	**DATE** 20100620
TRANSPORT DETAILS SHIPMENT FROM NANJING PORT TO NEW YORK PORT BY SEA	**S/C NO.**	**L/C NO.** MS2565
	TERMS OF PAYMENT L/C AT 30 DAYS AFTER B/L DATE	

MARKS AND NUMBERS	NUMBER AND KIND OF PACKAGE; DESCRIPTION OF GOODS	QUANTITY	UNIT PRICE	AMOUNT
			USD	
N/M	CIF NEW YORK			
	MONO CELLS 5000 PCS CIF NEW YORK	5000 PCS	USD50.00	USD250,000.00
	TOTAL:	5000 PCS		USD250,000.00

SAY TOTAL: USD TWO HUNDRED FIFTY THOUSAND ONLY.
We hereby certify that the contents of invoice herein are true and correct.

ABC COMPANY

(出口商签字和盖单据章)

装箱单

ISSUER ABC COMPANY, NANJING, CHINA	装箱单 PACKING LIST			
TO RAYTHEON COMPANY CAMBRIDGE, MASSACHUSETTS, USA	INVOICE NO.		DATE	
	100620		20 JUN. 2010	

MARKS AND NUMBERS	NUMBER AND KIND OF PACKAGE; DESCRIPTION OF GOODS	PACKAGE	G.W.	N.W.	MEAS.
			KG		CBM
N/M	MONO CELLS	5000 PCS	200.00	150.00	5.00
	TOTAL:	5000 PCS	200.00 KGS	150.00 KGS	5.00 CBM

SAY TOTAL: FIVE THOUSANDS PCS ONLY.

ABC COMPANY
(出口商签字和盖单据章)

提单

Shipper ABC COMPANY, NANJING, CHINA		BILL OF LADING	B/L No.:
Consignee RAYTHEON COMPANY CAMBRIDGE, MASSACHUSETTS,USA		**COSCO** 中 国 远 洋 运 输 公 司 CHINA OCEAN SHIPPING COMPANY	
Notify Party RAYTHEON COMPANY CAMBRIDGE, MASSACHUSETTS, USA			
*Pre carriage by	*Place of Receipt	**ORIGINAL**	
Ocean Vessel Voy. No. JINHE V. 230	Port of Loading NANJING		
Port of discharge NEW YORK	*Final destination	Freight payable at	Number of original Bs/L THREE
Marks and Numbers	Number and kind of packages; Description	Gross weight	Measurement m3
N/M	MONO CELLS 5000 PCS FREIGHT PREPAID ON BOARD 20100620	200.00 KGS	5.00 CBM
TOTAL PACKAGES(IN WORDS)	FIVE THOUSAND PIECES		
Freight and charges		Place and date of issue 20 JUN. 2010, NANJING	
		Signed for the Carrier CHINA OCEAN SHIPPING COMPANY 船运公司负责人签字	

*Applicable only when document used as a Through Bill of Lading.

保单

PICC 中国人民保险公司南京市分公司
The People's Insurance Company of China Nanjing Branch

总公司设于北京　　　　　　　　一九四九年创立

Head Office Beijing　　　　　　　Established in 1949

货物运输保险单
CARGO TRANSPORTATION INSURANCE POLICY

发票号(INVOICE NO.)　　　100620　　　　　　　　　保单号次

合同号(CONTRACT NO.)　　　　　　　　　　　POLICY NO.　　FAAA9002

信用证号(L/C NO.)　　MS2565

被保险人：
Insured:　　ABC COMPANY, 111 ZHUJIANG RD, NANJING, CHINA

中国人民保险公司(以下简称本公司)根据被保险人的要求，由被保险人向本公司缴付约定的保险费，按照本保险单承保险别和背面所载条款与下列特款承保下述货物运输保险，特立本保险单。

THIS POLICY OF INSURANCE WITNESSES THAT THE PEOPLE'S INSURANCE COMPANY OF CHINA (HEREINAFTER CALLED "THE COMPANY") AT THE REQUEST OF THE INSURED AND IN CONSIDERATION OF THE AGREED PREMIUM PAID TO THE COMPANY BY THE INSURED, UNDERTAKES TO INSURE THE UNDERMENTIONED GOODS IN TRANSPORTATION SUBJECT TO THE CONDITIONS OF THIS POLICY AS PER THE CLAUSES PRINTED OVERLEAF AND OTHER SPECIAL CLAUSES ATTACHED HEREON.

标　记 MARKS & NOS	包装及数量 QUANTITY	保险货物项目 DESCRIPTION OF GOODS	保险金额 AMOUNT INSURED
N/M	5000 PCS	MONO CELLS　5000 PCS	USD275000.00

总保险金额
TOTAL AMOUNT INSURED: US DOLLARS TWO HUNDRED SEVENTY FIVE THOUSAND ONLY

		启运日期	装载运输工具
保费　　AS		DATE OF	PER
PREMIUM: ARRANGED		COMMENCEMENT: 20100620	CONVEYANCE:　JINHE V. 230
自	经		至
FROM:　NANJING	VIA:		TO:　NEW YORK

承保险别：

CONDITIONS:

 INSTITUTE CARGO CLAUSES(ALL RISKS)

所保货物，如发生保险单项下可能引起索赔的损失或损坏，应立即通知本公司下述代理人＿＿＿＿＿＿查勘。如有索赔，应向本公司提交保单正本(本保险单共有＿＿＿＿＿＿＿＿＿份正本)及有关文件。如一份正本已用于索赔，其余正本自动失效。

IN THE EVENT OF LOSS OR DAMAGE WHICH MAY RESULT IN A CLAIM UNDER THIS POLICY, IMMEDIATE NOTICE MUST BE GIVEN TO＿＿＿＿＿＿＿＿＿＿THE COMPANY'S AGENT AS MENTIONED HEREUNDER. CLAIMS, IF ANY, ONE OF THE ORIGINAL POLICY WHICH HAS BEEN ISSUED IN＿＿＿＿＿＿ORIGINAL(S) TOGETHER WITH THE RELEVANT DOCUMENTS SHALL BE SURRENDERED TO THE COMPANY. IF ONE OF THE ORIGINAL POLICY HAS BEEN ACCOMPLISHED, THE OTHERS TO BE VOID.

中国人民保险公司南京市分公司

The People's Insurance Company of China

Nanjing Branch

赔款偿付地点

CLAIM PAYABLE AT ＿＿＿NEW YORK＿＿＿

出单日期

ISSUING DATE ＿＿＿20100619＿＿＿

Authorized Signature

地址(ADD)：中国南京石鼓路 225 号　　　　　　　　电话(TEL): (025)6521049

邮编(POST CODE): 210029　　　　　　　　　　　　传真(FAX): (025)4404593

进口信用证

学习目标：

　　了解并掌握进口信用证业务的流程并学会开立进口信用证，根据国外银行发来的出口议付面函编写信用证来单付汇通知书以及业务中的相关电文；知晓如何控制进口信用证业务中的风险；掌握进口业务中的每一个环节和步骤。

第一节　进口商申请开立信用证

一、业务场景与操作

案例 4.1

　　2010 年 4 月 1 日，中国进口商 ABC 公司和德国出口商 ALLEN CO., LTD.签订合同，约定采用 L/C 方式支付进口货物 US UPLAND BALED COTTON，金额为 236 994.50 美元，期限为 B/L 后 90 天。进口商 ABC 公司根据下面所签订的贸易合同，填制进口开证申请书递行开证(假设交通银行是开证行)。

Contract

No.: 30850

Date:

Sellers: ALLEN CO., LTD.

Address: P.O. BOX 3254, GERMANY

Postal Code:

Tel:　　　　　　　　　　Fax:

Buyers: ABC CO.

Address:

Postal Code:

Tel:　　　　　　　　　　Fax:

The seller agrees to sell and the buyer agrees to buy the under-mentioned goods on the terms and conditions stated below.

1. Article No.:

2. Description & Specification:

US UPLAND BALED COTTON

3. Quantity:

4. Unit Price : USD107.50 PER LB CIF ZHANGJIAGANG, CHINA

5. Total Amount: USD236,994.50 CIF ZHANGJIAGANG, CHINA

With ___10___ % more or less both in amount and quantity allowed at the seller's option.

6. Country of Origin and Manufacturer:

7. Packing:

8. Shipping Marks:

9. Time of Shipment: BEFORE 20100531   Date and Place of Expire: 20100921   GERMANY

10. Port of Loading: MAIN GERMANY PORT

11. Port of Destination: ZHANGJIAGANG

12. Insurance: To be effected by buyers for 110% of full invoice value covering _____ up to _____ only.

13. Payment:

By irrevocable L/C to be available BY 90 DAYS AFTER B/L DATE draft to reach the sellers before ___/___/_____ and to remain valid for negotiation in China until 15 days after the aforesaid time of shipment. The L/C must specify that transhipment and partial shipments are allowed.

14. Documents:

1) Signed commercial invoice in 2 original and 1 copy indicating L/C No. and Contract No. 30850.

2) Full set of clean ON BOARD ocean bill of lading made out to order of shipper and blank endorsed marked "freight prepaid" notifying the applicant with full name and address.

3) Insurance policy in 2 copies for 110 % of the invoice value showing claims payable in China in currency of the draft, blank endorsed, covering all risks and war risks.

4) Packing list in 1 original 3 copies indicating total gross weight and net weight and total number of bales.

5) Certificate of origin in 1 original and 1 copy attested by Chamber of Commerce in Germany.

15. Force Majeure:

Either party shall not be held responsible for failure or delay to perform all or any part of this agreement due to flood, fire, earthquake, draught, war or any other events which could not be predicted, controlled, avoided or overcome by the relative party. However, the party affected by the event of Force Majeure shall inform the other party of its occurrence in writing as soon as possible and thereafter send a certificate of the event issued by the relevant authorities to the other party within 15 days after its occurrence.

16. Arbitration:

All disputes arising from the execution of this agreement shall be settled through friendly consultations. In case no settlement can be reached, the case in dispute shall then be submitted to the Foreign Trade Arbitration Commission of the China Council for the Promotion of International Trade for Arbitration in accordance with its Provisional Rules of Procedure. The decision made by this commission shall be regarded as final and binding upon both parties. Arbitration fees shall be borne by the losing party, unless otherwise awarded.

17. Remarks:

Sellers: ALLEN CO., LTD., P.O. BOX 3254, GERMANY   Buyers: ABC 公司

Signature: Signature:

进口开证申请书样本

IRREVOCABLE DOCUMENTARY CREDIT APPLICATION

TO: **BANK OF COMMUNICATIONS**   DATE: 20100512

BENEFICIARY (FULL NAME AND ADDRESS): ALLEN CO., LTD., P.O. BOX 3254, GERMANY	L/C NO.: EX-CARD NO.: CONTRACT NO.: 30850
	DATE AND PLACE OF EXPIRY OF THE CREDIT: 100921 GERMANY

PARTIAL SHIPMENTS [X]ALLOWED ☐NOT ALLOWED	TRANSSHIPMENT [X]ALLOWED ☐NOT ALLOWED	☐BY AIRMAIL ☐WITH BRIEF ADVICE BY TELETRANSMISSION ☐BY EXPRESS DELIVERY ☐BY TELETRANSMISSION(WHICH SHALL BE THE OPERATIVE INSTRUMENT)
LOADING ON BOARD / DISPATCH / TAKING IN CHARGE AT / FROM: MAIN GERMANY PORT NOT LATER THAN: 100531 FOR TRANSPORTATION TO: ZHANGJIAGANG		AMOUNT (BOTH IN FIGURES AND WORDS): USD236,994.50 SAY US DOLLARS TWO HUNDRED THIRTY SIX THOUSAND NINE HUNDRED NINETY FOUR POINT FIFTY ONLY
DESCRIPTION OF GOODS: US UPLAND BALED COTTON UNIT PRICE: USD107.50 PER LB CIF ZHANGJIAGANG, CHINA TOTAL AMOUNT: USD236,994.50 CIF ZHANGJIAGANG, CHINA ORIGIN: GERMANY PACKING:		CREDIT AVAILABLE WITH ☐ BY SIGHT PAYMENT [X] BY ACCEPTANCE ☐ BY NEGOTIATION ☐ BY DEFERRED PAYMENT AT AGAINST THE DOCUMENTS DETAILED HEREIN ☐ AND BENEFICIARY'S DRAFT FOR % OF THE INVOICE VALUE AT ON
		☐ FOB ☐ CFR [X] CIF ☐ OR OTHER TERMS

DOCUMENTS REQUIRED: (MARKED WITH X)

1. (X) SIGNED COMMERCIAL INVOICE IN 2 ORIGINAL AND 1 COPY INDICATING L/C NO., CONTRACT NO. 30850.

2. (X) FULL SET OF CLEAN ON BOARD OCEAN BILLS OF LADING MADE OUT TO ORDER OF SHIPPER AND BLANK ENDORSED, MARKED "FREIGHT ( ) TO COLLECT / (X) PREPAID"

NOTIFYING THE APPLICANT WITH FULL NAME AND ADDRESS.

3. ( ) AIR WAYBILLS SHOWING "FREIGHT ( ) TO COLLECT / ( ) PREPAID" ( ) INDICATING FREIGHT AMOUNT AND CONSIGNED TO _____.

4. ( ) MEMORANDUM ISSUED BY _____ CONSIGNED TO _____ .

5. (X) INSURANCE POLICY / CERTIFICATE IN 2 COPIES FOR 110% OF THE INVOICE VALUE SHOWING CLAIMS PAYABLE IN CHINA IN CURRENCY OF THE DRAFT, BLANK ENDORSED, COVERING ( ) OCEAN MARINE TRANSPORTATION/ ( ) AIR TRANSPORTATION / ( ) OVER LAND TRANSPORTATION FOR ( ) ALL RISKS, ( ) WAR RISKS.

6. (X) PACKING LIST IN 1 ORIGINAL AND 3 COPIES INDICATING TOTAL GROSS WEIGHT, TOTAL NET WEIGHT AND TOTAL NUMBER OF BALES.

7. ( ) CERTIFICATE OF QUANTITY / WEIGHT IN ___ COPIES ISSUED BY AN INDEPENDENT SURVEYOR AT THE LOADING PORT, INDICATING THE ACTUAL SURVEYED QUANTITY / WEIGHT OF SHIPPED GOODS AS WELL AS THE PACKING CONDITION.

8. ( ) CERTIFICATE OF QUALITY IN ___ COPIES ISSUED BY ( ) MANUFACTURER / ( ) PUBLIC RECOGNIZED SURVEYOR / ( )

9. ( ) BENEFICIARY'S CERTIFIED COPY OF FAX DISPATCHED TO THE ACCOUNTEE WITH _____ DAYS AFTER SHIPMENT ADVISING ( ) NAME OF VESSEL / ( ) DATE, QUANTITY, WEIGHT AND VALUE OF SHIPMENT.

10. ( ) BENEFICIARY'S CERTIFICATE CERTIFYING THAT EXTRA COPIES OF THE DOCUMENTS HAVE BEEN DISPATCHED ACCORDING TO THE CONTRACT TERMS.

11. ( ) SHIPPING COMPANY'S CERTIFICATE ATTESTING THAT THE CARRYING VESSEL IS CHARTERED OR BOOKED BY ACCOUNTEE OR THEIR SHIPPING AGENTS:

12. (X) OTHER DOCUMENTS, IF ANY:

  A)X CERTIFICATE OF ORIGIN IN 1 ORIGINAL AND 1 COPY ATTESTED BY
     CHAMBER OF COMMERCE IN GERMANY.

  B) CERTIFICATE OF HEALTH IN ___ COPIES ISSUED BY AUTHORIZED INSTITUTION.

ADDITIONAL INSTRUCTIONS:

1. (X) ALL BANKING CHARGES OUTSIDE THE OPENING BANK ARE FOR BENEFICIARY'S ACCOUNT.

2. (X) DOCUMENTS MUST BE PRESENTED WITH 21 DAYS AFTER THE DATE OF ISSUANCE OF THE TRANSPORT DOCUMENTS BUT WITHIN THE VALIDITY OF THIS CREDIT.

3. ( ) THIRD PARTY AS SHIPPER IS NOT ACCEPTABLE. SHORT FORM / BLANK BACK B/L IS NOT ACCEPTABLE.

4. (X) BOTH QUANTITY AND AMOUNT 10 % MORE OR LESS ARE ALLOWED.

5. ( ) PREPAID FREIGHT DRAWN IN EXCESS OF L/C AMOUNT IS ACCEPTABLE AGAINST PRESENTATION OF ORIGINAL CHARGES VOUCHER ISSUED BY SHIPPING CO. / AIR LINE OR ITS AGENT.

6. ( ) ALL DOCUMENTS TO BE FORWARDED IN ONE COVER, UNLESS OTHERWISE STATED ABOVE.

7. (　) OTHER TERMS, IF ANY:

ONE EXTRA COPY OF COMMERCIAL INVOICE, TRANSPORT DOCUMENT, INSURANCE DOCUMENT (IF ANY) TO BE PRESENTED TO US FOR OUR FILE, OTHERWISE USD10.00(OR EQUIVALENT) WILL BE DEDUCTED FROM THE PROCEEDS.

ADVISING BANK: NOSCDEFFXXX

ACCOUNT NO.:

WITH_____BANK OF COMMUNICATIONS, CO., LTD., JIANGSU BR. (NAME OF BANK)

TRANSACTED BY:

APPLICANT:_____(NAME, SIGNATURE OF AUTHORIZED PERSON)

TELEPHONE NO.:

(WITH SEAL)　　ABC COMPANY

进口开证申请书背面保证条款

开证申请人声明

交通银行：

我公司已办妥一切进口手续，现请贵行按我公司申请书内容开出不可撤销跟单信用证。我公司声明如下：

一、我公司同意贵行依照国际商会第 600 号出版物《跟单信用证统一惯例》办理该信用证项下一切事宜，并同意承担由此产生的一切责任。

二、我公司保证按时向贵行支付该证项下的货款、手续、利息及一切费用等所需的外汇和人民币资金。

三、我公司保证在贵行单到通知书中规定的期限之内通知贵行办理对外付款/承兑，否则贵行可以认为我公司已接受单据，同意付款/承兑。

四、我公司保证在单证表面相符的条件下办理有关付款/承兑手续，如因单证有不符之处而拒绝付款/承兑，我公司保证在贵行单到通知书规定的日期之前将全套单据如数退还贵行并附书面拒绝理由，由贵行按国际惯例确定能否对外拒付。如贵行确定我公司所提拒付理由不成立，或虽然拒付理由成立，但我公司未能退还全套单据，贵行有权主动办理对外付款/承兑，并从我公司账户中扣款。

五、该信用证及其项下业务往来中如因邮、电传递发生遗失、延误、错漏，贵行当不负责。

六、该信用证如需修改，由我公司向贵行提出书面申请，由贵行根据具体情况确定能否办理修改。我公司确认所有修改当由信用证受益人接受时才能生效。

七、我公司在收到贵行开出的信用证、修改副本后，保证及时与原申请书核对，如有不符之处，保证在接到副本之日起，两个工作日内通知贵行。如未通知，当视为正确无误。

八、如因申请书字迹不清或词意含混而引起的一切后果由我公司负责。

(签字盖章)

填写开证申请书的要点：

(1) DATE(申请开证日期)。在申请书右上角填写实际申请日期。

(2) TO(致)。银行印制的申请书上事先都会印就开证银行的名称、地址，银行的 SWIFT CODE、TELEX NO.等也可同时显示。

(3) PLEASE ISSUE ON OUR BEHALF AND/OR FOR OUR ACCOUNT THE FOLLOWING IRREVOCABLE LETTER OF CREDIT(请开列以下不可撤销信用证)。如果信用证是保兑或可转让的，应在此加注有关字样。开证方式多为电开(BY SWIFT，以前使用的 TELEX(电传)开证方式现在已经基本被淘汰)，也可以是信开或简电开立。

(4) L/C NO.(信用证号码)。此栏由银行填写。

(5) APPLICANT(申请人)。填写申请人的全称及详细地址，有的要求注明联系电话、传真号码等。

(6) BENEFICIARY(受益人)。填写受益人的全称及详细地址。

(7) ADVISING BANK(通知行)。国外通知行由开证行指定，如果进出口商在订立合同时，坚持指定通知行，可供开证行在选择通知行时作参考。

(8) AMOUNT(信用证金额)。需分别用数字和文字两种形式表示，并且表明币制。如果允许有一定比率的上下浮动，在信用证中须明示。

(9) DATE AND PLACE OF EXPIRY(到期日期和地点)。填写信用证的有效期及到期地点。

(10) PARTIAL SHIPMENT(分批装运)和 TRANSSHIPMENT(转运)。根据合同的实际规定选择。

(11) LOADING IN CHARGE、FOR TRANSPORTATION TO、NOT LATER THAN(装运地/港、目的地/港的名称，最迟装运日期)。按实际填写，如允许有转运地/港，也应清楚标明。

(12) CREDIT AVAILABLE WITH/BY(付款方式)。在所提供的即期、承兑、议付和延期付款四种信用证有效兑付方式中选择与合同要求一致的类型。

(13) BENEFICIARY'S DRAFT(汇票要求)。金额应根据合同规定填写为：发票金额的一定百分比；发票金额的 100%(全部货款都用信用证支付)；如部分信用证、部分托收时按信用证下的金额比例填写。付款期限可根据实际填写即期或远期，如属后者必须填写具体的天数。信用证条件下的付款人通常是开证行，也可能是开证行指定的另外一家银行。

(14) DOCUMENTS REQUIRED(单据条款)。各银行提供的申请书中已印就的单据条款通常为十几条，从上至下一般为发票、运输单据(提单、空运单、铁路运输单据及运输备忘录等)、保险单、装箱单、质量证书、装运通知和受益人证明等，另外还有 OTHER DOCUMENTS，IF ANY(其他单据) 栏，如要求提交超过上述所列范围的单据就可以在此栏填写。例如，有的合同要求 CERTIFICATE OF NO SOLID WOOD PACKING MATERIAL(无实木包装材料证明)、CERTIFICATE OF FREE SALE(自由销售证明书)、

CERTIFICATE OF CONFORMITY(合格证明书)等。申请人填制这部分内容时应依据合同规定，不能随意增加或减少。选中某单据后对该单据的具体要求(如一式几份、要否签字、正副本的份数、单据中应标明的内容等)也应如实填写，如申请书印制好的要求不完整应在其后予以补足。

(15) DESCRIPTION OF GOODS(商品描述)。所有内容(品名、规格、包装、单价、唛头)都必须与合同内容相一致，价格条款里附带"AS PER INCOTERMS 2000"、数量条款中规定"MORE OR LESS"或"ABOUT"、使用某种特定包装物等特殊要求必须清楚列明。

(16) ADDITIONAL INSTRUCTIONS(附加指示)。该栏通常体现为以下一些条款。

- ALL DOCUMENTS MUST INDICATE CONTRACT NUMBER(所有单据加列合同号码)。

- ALL BANKING CHARGES OUTSIDE THE OPENING BANK ARE FOR BENEFICIARY'S ACCOUNT(所有开证行以外的银行费用由受益人承担)。

- BOTH QUANTITY AND AMOUNT FOR EACH ITEM % MORE OR LESS ALLOWED(每项数量与金额允许 %增减)。

- THIRD PARTY AS SHIPPER IS NOT ACCEPTABLE(第三方作为托运人是不能接受的)。

- DOCUMENTS MUST BE PRESENTED WITHIN xxx DAYS AFTER THE DATE OF ISSUANCE OF THE TRANSPORT DOCUMENTS BUT WITHIN THE VALIDITY OF THIS CREDIT(单据必须在提单日后 xxx 天送达银行并且不超过信用证有效期)。

- SHORT FORM/BLANK BACK/CLAUSED/CHARTER PARTY B/L IS UNACCEPTABLE(银行不接受略式/不清洁/租船提单)。

- ALL DOCUMENTS TO BE FORWARDED IN ONE COVER，UNLESS OTHERWISE STATED ABOVE(除非有相反规定，所有单据应一次提交)。

- PREPAID FREIGHT DRAWN IN EXCESS OF L/C AMOUNT IS ACCEPTABLE AGAINST PRESENTATION OF ORIGINAL CHARGES VOUCHER ISSUED BY SHIPPING CO./AIR LINE OR ITS AGENT(银行接受凭船公司/航空公司或其代理人签发的正本运费收据索要超过信用证金额的预付运费)。

- DOCUMENT ISSUED PRIOR TO THE DATE OF ISSUANCE OF CREDIT NOT ACCEPTABLE(不接受早于开证日出具的单据)。

如需要已印就的上述条款，可在条款前打"X"，对合同涉及但未印就的条款还可以做补充填写。

(17) NAME，SIGNATURE OF AUTHORISED PERSON，TEL. NO.，FAX，ACCOUNT NO.(授权人名称、签字、电话、传真、账号等内容)。

二、风险控制

由于信用证是一项独立于合同以外的业务，进口商在向开证行申请开立信用证时，应注意防范和控制风险。

1. 细审合同条款

信用证一经开出就独立于合同之外，但合同是双方履约的合约和开证基础，应仔细审核合同每一条款。开立信用证时单据条款要严格遵守开证申请书内容，做到条款清晰完整，具可操作性，能表达贸易合同的内容，将所要求的条款全部单据化。实际业务中对于一些有地区特色的单据尤其需要加以明确，如南亚及中东地区的船证明，确保没有自相矛盾或不合理的信用证条款。否则，进口商按照贸易合同付款后，不一定能够从出口商那里保质保量地收到所定购的货物，或者没有获得价格最低和最优惠的条件，包括资金融通。

2. 斟酌信用证条款

(1) 信用证的货描及单据要求简单，无具体的货物描述，出现问题时不能拒付货款。

(2) 信用证条款是否规定拒付条款。信用证中规定拒付条款是对进口商的保护，是防止出口商商业欺诈的手段之一。若单证一致，银行在规定时间内必须付款，进口商只能在对外付汇后向出口商和船公司提出索赔要求，加大了获得赔偿的难度和工作量。

(3) 对于进口商来说，根据其贸易情况，可以尽量多采用远期方式结算。这样，如出口方无货可交，进口商也无需付款。出口方交单后如货物有品质问题，买方也有足够的时间取证以申请一项法院禁令，同时也可迫使出口商主动降价，这也不失为防范风险的手段。

3. 紧盯货物防欺诈

进口商与出口商签约后，应及时调查货物航程与行踪，随时掌握船舶的情况，确认提单是否真实、货物是否存在。

4. 选择开证行

进口商应尽量选择信誉好的大银行作为开证行，这样可避免很多风险(提供出口商的资信调查、信用证条款把关等)。银行一旦发现问题，会及早与进口商沟通，把未来预期产生的损失程度降到最低。因此，选择信誉好、管理严格的大银行作为开证行是进口商防范风险的又一重要措施。

三、总结思考

从进口业务实质上来讲，要想真正防范信用证的风险，关键还是要看进出口双方的资信。在信用证这种以银行信用为基础的结算方式中，进口商的信用风险常常转而由银行承担。进口商得到合格单据并不一定得到单据所记载的货物，如果出口商经营道德欠佳，那么进口商可能在不知情的情况下对空头提单付款赎单，落得钱货两空。在此情况下，即使进口商可凭合同向出口商索赔，但蓄意行骗的出口商可能已不知去向。对此，进口商应提高警惕，落实交易的各个关键环节，掌握市场信息，利用进口银行以更有效的方式，推动国际贸易的正常开展，维护良好的国际经济秩序。

再者，需要理解信用证这种结算工具，如对信用证独立抽象性原则的局限性的理解。在进出口业务中，买卖双方签订进出口贸易合同后，进口商依照合同规定对外开立不可撤销的跟单信用证，出口商在信用证规定的最晚装期内装运货物，并通过交单行/议付行提交单据给开证行。根据国际惯例，银行只对单据表面真实性负责，不对货物负责，银行审单的原则是"单单一致、单证一致"，即信用证的独立抽象性原则。在此原则下进口商面临的风险有：①出口商故意递交假单据。如果签约后出口商不守信用，存在商业欺诈行为，就有可能发生实际并未装运货物，递交伪造单据的情况，而开证银行审单后，在确认单证相符的情况下就会对外付款给出口商，出口商在取得货款后不再出现或无法联系，进口商付款赎单后，凭提单不能提取货物而造成货款两空。因开证行和议付行均不负赔偿之责，保险公司也不承担货物未上船的索赔，因此进口商的损失很难挽回。②出口商提供真单据，但货物品质不合格。跟单信用证方式下，银行处理的是单据而不是货物。因此信用证并不能确保实际所装运的货物就是买卖合同中规定的货物。

最后，从事进口业务的人员应不断学习以提高自身的业务水平。在日常的业务操作中，注意提高自身业务素质，增强风险防范意识。许多的贸易欺诈是可以通过进口商的适度谨慎而避免的。对于信用证条款和所需单证的识别和防范，在很大程度上也取决于进口商的素质，只有具备相当程度的经贸和法律知识、丰富的实践经验和强烈的风险意识，才足以扼制与信用证结算有关的欺诈活动。因此，认真学习并掌握 UCP600、ISBP 等国际惯例并在实践中灵活运用，是降低信用证业务风险的关键。

四、实训操练

练习 4.1

2010 年 8 月 23 日，进口商 HK MACHINE COMPANY 与出口商 ICA CO., LTD., CHICAGO, U.S.A.签订了如下的贸易合同，选择信用证方式结算。进口商去开证行(假设是交通银行)开立信用证时，应如何填制进口开证申请书呢？请根据以下贸易合同来填制。

Contract

Contract No.: ZETG01

Date:

Sellers:　ICA CO., LTD., CHICAGO, U.S.A.

Address:　　　　　　　　　　Postal Code:

Tel: 123456　　　　　　　　　Fax:

Buyers: HK MACHINE COMPANY

Address:　　　　　　　　　　Postal Code:

Tel:　　　　　　　　　　　　Fax:

The seller agrees to sell and the buyer agrees to buy the under-mentioned goods on the terms and conditions stated below.

1. Article No.:

2. Description & Specification:

ELECTRONIC TUBE

ORIGIN: USA

3. Quantity:

4. Unit Price: USD200 PER TUBE

5. Total Amount: USD40,000.00 FOB SHANGHAI, CHINA

With 　10　% more or less both in amount and quantity allowed at the seller's option.

6. Country of Origin and Manufacturer: USA, ICA CO., LTD., CHICAGO, U.S.A.

7. Packing:

8. Shipping Marks:

9. Time of Shipment: BEFORE 20100923　　Date and Place of Expire: 20101201　U.S.A.

10. Port of Loading: MAIN USA PORT

11. Port of Destination: SHANGHAI, CHINA

12. Insurance: To be effected by buyers for 110% of full invoice value covering ___ RISK up to _____ only.

13. Payment Terms: SIGHT

By confirmed, irrevocable, transferable and divisible L/C to be available by sight draft to reach the sellers before ___/___/_____ and to remain valid for negotiation in China until 15 days after the aforesaid time of shipment. The L/C must specify that transshipment and partial shipments are allowed.

14. Documents:

+ SIGNED COMMERCIAL INVOICE IN 2 ORIGINALS AND 1 COPY INDICATING

 L/C NO. AND CONTRACT NO.

+ FULL SET OF CLEAN ON BOARD OCEAN BILLS OF LADING CONSIGNED TO APPLICANT,

 MARKED "FREIGHT TO COLLECT" NOTIFYING THE APPLICANT

 WITH FULL NAME AND ADDRESS.

+ PACKING LIST / WEIGHT MEMO IN 1 ORIGINAL AND 3 COPIES INDICATING TOTAL GROSS WEIGHT, TOTAL NET WEIGHT AND TOTAL NUMBER OF CARTONS.

15. Terms of Shipment: CFR SHANGHAI

16. Quality/Quantity Discrepancy and Claim:

17. Force Majeure:

Either party shall not be held responsible for failure or delay to perform all or any part of this agreement due to flood, fire, earthquake, draught, war or any other events which could not be predicted, controlled, avoided or overcome by the relative party. However, the party affected by the event of Force Majeure shall inform the other party of its occurrence in writing as soon as possible and thereafter send a certificate of the event issued by the relevant authorities to the other party within 15 days after its occurrence.

18. Arbitration:

All disputes arising from the execution of this agreement shall be settled through friendly consultations. In case no settlement can be reached, the case in dispute shall then be submitted to the Foreign Trade Arbitration Commission of the China Council for the Promotion of International Trade for Arbitration in accordance with its Provisional Rules of Procedure. The decision made by this commission shall be regarded as final and binding upon both parties. Arbitration fees shall be borne by the losing party, unless otherwise awarded.

19. Remarks:

Sellers:

ICA CO., LTD., CHICAGO   Buyers: HK MACHINE COMPANY

Signature: Signature:

IRREVOCABLE DOCUMENTARY CREDIT APPLICATION

TO: **BANK OF COMMUNICATIONS**   DATE:

BENEFICIARY (FULL NAME AND ADDRESS):		L/C NO.:
		EX-CARD NO.:
		CONTRACT NO.:
		DATE AND PLACE OF EXPIRY OF THE CREDIT
PARTIAL SHIPMENTS ☐ALLOWED ☐NOT ALLOWED	TRANSSHIPMENT ☐ALLOWED ☐NOT ALLOWED	☐BY AIRMAIL ☐WITH BRIEF ADVICE BY TELETRANSMISSION ☐BY EXPRESS DELIVERY ☐BY TELETRANSMISSION(WHICH SHALL BE THE OPERATIVE INSTRUMENT)
LOADING ON BOARD / DISPATCH / TAKING IN CHARGE AT / FROM: NOT LATER THAN: FOR TRANSPORTATION TO:		AMOUNT (BOTH IN FIGURES AND WORDS):

DESCRIPTION OF GOODS:	CREDIT AVAILABLE WITH
	☐ BY SIGHT PAYMENT
	☐ BY ACCEPTANCE
	☐ BY NEGOTIATION
	☐ BY DEFERRED PAYMENT AT
PACKING:	AGAINST THE DOCUMENTS DETAILED HEREIN
	☐ AND BENEFICIARY'S DRAFT FOR % OF THE INVOICE VALUE
	AT
	ON
	☐ FOB ☐ CFR ☐CIF
	☐ OR OTHER TERMS

DOCUMENTS REQUIRED: (MARKED WITH X)

1 .( ) SIGNED COMMERCIAL INVOICE IN_____ORIGINAL AND_____COPY INDICATING L/C NO. AND CONTRACT NO. ZETG01.

2. ( ) FULL SET OF CLEAN ON BOARD OCEAN BILLS OF LADING CONSIGNED TO APPLICANT, MARKED "FREIGHT (X) TO COLLECT / ( ) PREPAID" NOTIFYING THE APPLICANT WITH FULL NAME AND ADDRESS.

3. ( ) AIR WAYBILLS SHOWING "FREIGHT ( ) TO COLLECT / ( ) PREPAID "( ) INDICATING FREIGHT AMOUNT AND CONSIGNED TO _____ .

4. ( ) MEMORANDUM ISSUED BY _____ CONSIGNED TO _____.

5. ( ) INSURANCE POLICY / CERTIFICATE IN_____COPIES FOR _____ % OF THE INVOICE VALUE SHOWING CLAIMS PAYABLE IN CHINA IN CURRENCY OF THE DRAFT, BLANK ENDORSED, COVERING ( ) OCEAN MARINE TRANSPORTATION / ( ) AIR TRANSPORTATION / ( ) OVER LAND TRANSPORTATION FOR( ) ALL RISKS ( ), WAR RISKS.

6. ( ) PACKING LIST/WEIGHT MEMO IN_____ORIGINAL AND_____COPIES INDICATING TOTAL GROSS WEIGHT, TOTAL NET WEIGHT AND TOTAL NUMBER OF CARTONS.

7. ( ) CERTIFICATE OF QUANTITY / WEIGHT IN __ COPIES ISSUED BY AN INDEPENDENT SURVEYOR AT THE LOADING PORT, INDICATING THE ACTUAL SURVEYED QUANTITY / WEIGHT OF SHIPPED GOODS AS WELL AS THE PACKING CONDITION.

8. ( ) CERTIFICATE OF QUALITY IN _____ COPIES ISSUED BY ( ) MANUFACTURER / ( ) PUBLIC RECOGNIZED SURVEYOR / ( )

9. ( ) BENEFICIARY'S CERTIFIED COPY OF FAX DISPATCHED TO THE ACCOUNTEE WITH __

DAYS AFTER SHIPMENT ADVISING ( ) NAME OF VESSEL / ( ) DATE, QUANTITY, WEIGHT AND VALUE OF SHIPMENT.

10. ( ) BENEFICIARY'S CERTIFICATE CERTIFYING THAT EXTRA COPIES OF THE DOCUMENTS HAVE BEEN DISPATCHED ACCORDING TO THE CONTRACT TERMS.

11. ( ) SHIPPING COMPANY'S CERTIFICATE ATTESTING THAT THE CARRYING VESSEL IS CHARTERED OR BOOKED BY ACCOUNTEE OR THEIR SHIPPING AGENTS:

12. ( ) OTHER DOCUMENTS, IF ANY:

  A) CERTIFICATE OF ORIGIN IN ___ ORIGINAL AND___COPY ATTESTED BY

      CHAMBER OF COMMERCE IN U.S.A.

  B) CERTIFICATE OF HEALTH IN ___ COPIES ISSUED BY AUTHORIZED INSTITUTION.

ADDITIONAL INSTRUCTIONS:

1. ( ) ALL BANKING CHARGES OUTSIDE THE OPENING BANK ARE FOR BENEFICIARY'S ACCOUNT.

2. ( ) DOCUMENTS MUST BE PRESENTED WITH____DAYS AFTER THE DATE OF ISSUANCE OF THE TRANSPORT DOCUMENTS BUT WITHIN THE VALIDITY OF THIS CREDIT.

3. ( ) THIRD PARTY AS SHIPPER IS NOT ACCEPTABLE. SHORT FORM / BLANK BACK B/L IS NOT ACCEPTABLE.

4. ( ) BOTH QUANTITY AND AMOUNT_____% MORE OR LESS ARE ALLOWED.

5. ( ) PREPAID FREIGHT DRAWN IN EXCESS OF L/C AMOUNT IS ACCEPTABLE AGAINST PRESENTATION OF ORIGINAL CHARGES VOUCHER ISSUED BY SHIPPING CO. / AIR LINE OR ITS AGENT.

6. ( ) ALL DOCUMENTS TO BE FORWARDED IN ONE COVER, UNLESS OTHERWISE STATED ABOVE.

( ) OTHER DOCUMENTS, IF ANY:

ADDITIONAL INSTRUCTIONS:

1. ( ) ALL BANKING CHARGES OUTSIDE THE OPENING BANK ARE FOR BENEFICIARY'S ACCOUNT.

2. ( ) DOCUMENTS MUST BE PRESENTED WITH ____ DAYS AFTER THE DATE OF ISSUANCE OF THE TRANSPORT DOCUMENTS BUT WITHIN THE VALIDITY OF THIS CREDIT.

3. ( ) THIRD PARTY AS SHIPPER IS NOT ACCEPTABLE. SHORT FORM / BLANK BACK B/L IS NOT ACCEPTABLE.

4. ( ) BOTH QUANTITY AND AMOUNT___% MORE OR LESS ARE ALLOWED.

5. ( ) PREPAID FREIGHT DRAWN IN EXCESS OF L/C AMOUNT IS ACCEPTABLE AGAINST PRESENTATION OF ORIGINAL CHARGES VOUCHER ISSUED BY SHIPPING CO. / AIR LINE OR ITS AGENT.

6. ( ) ALL DOCUMENTS TO BE FORWARDED IN ONE COVER, UNLESS OTHERWISE STATED ABOVE.

7. ( ) OTHER TERMS, IF ANY:

ADVISING BANK:

ACCOUNT NO.:

WITH <u>BANK OF COMMUNICATIONS CO., LTD., JIANGSU BR.</u>　　　　(NAME OF BANK)

TRANSACTED BY:

APPLICANT:　　　　　　　　　　(NAME, SIGNATURE OF AUTHORIZED PERSON)

TELEPHONE NO.:

(WITH SEAL)

参考答案:

IRREVOCABLE DOCUMENTARY CREDIT APPLICATION

TO: **BANK OF COMMUNICATIONS**　　　　　　　DATE: 20100823

BENEFICIARY (FULL NAME AND ADDRESS):		L/C NO.:
		EX-CARD NO.:
ICA CO., LTD., CHICAGO, U.S.A.		CONTRACT NO.: ZETG01
		DATE AND PLACE OF EXPIRY OF THE CREDIT: 20101201　U.S.A.
PARTIAL SHIPMENTS ☒ALLOWED ☐NOT ALLOWED	TRANSSHIPMENT ☒ALLOWED ☐NOT ALLOWED	☐BY AIRMAIL ☐WITH BRIEF ADVICE BY TELETRANSMISSION ☐BY EXPRESS DELIVERY ☐BY TELETRANSMISSION(WHICH SHALL BE THE OPERATIVE INSTRUMENT)
LOADING ON BOARD / DISPATCH / TAKING IN CHARGE AT / FROM: MAIN USA PORT NOT LATER THAN: 100923 FOR TRANSPORTATION TO: SHANGHAI		AMOUNT (BOTH IN FIGURES AND WORDS): USD40,000.00 CFR SHANGHAI SAY US DOLLARS FORTY THOUSAND ONLY

DESCRIPTION OF GOODS: ELECTRONIC TUBE UNIT PRICE: USD 200 PER TUBE TOTAL AMOUNT: USD40,000.00 CFR SHANGHAI, CHINA ORIGIN: U.S.A. PACKING:	CREDIT AVAILABLE WITH ☐ BY SIGHT PAYMENT ☐ BY ACCEPTANCE ☒ BY NEGOTIATION ☐ BY DEFERRED PAYMENT AT AGAINST THE DOCUMENTS DETAILED HEREIN ☐ AND BENEFICIARY'S DRAFT FOR % OF THE INVOICE VALUE AT ON
	☐ FOB ☒ CFR ☐ CIF ☐ OR OTHER TERMS

DOCUMENTS REQUIRED: (MARKED WITH X)

1 .(X) SIGNED COMMERCIAL INVOICE IN__2__ORIGINAL AND__1__COPY INDICATING L/C NO. AND CONTRACT NO. ZETG01.

2. (X) FULL SET OF CLEAN ON BOARD OCEAN BILLS OF LADING CONSIGNED TO APPLICANT, MARKED "FREIGHT (X) TO COLLECT / ( ) PREPAID" NOTIFYING THE APPLICANT WITH FULL NAME AND ADDRESS.

3. ( ) AIR WAYBILLS SHOWING "FREIGHT ( ) TO COLLECT / ( ) PREPAID "( ) INDICATING FREIGHT AMOUNT AND CONSIGNED TO _____ .

4. ( ) MEMORANDUM ISSUED BY _____ CONSIGNED TO _____.

5. ( ) INSURANCE POLICY / CERTIFICATE IN_____COPIES FOR _____ % OF THE INVOICE VALUE SHOWING CLAIMS PAYABLE IN CHINA IN CURRENCY OF THE DRAFT, BLANK ENDORSED, COVERING ( ) OCEAN MARINE TRANSPORTATION / ( ) AIR TRANSPORTATION / ( ) OVER LAND TRANSPORTATION FOR( ) ALL RISKS ( ), WAR RISKS.

6. (X) PACKING LIST/WEIGHT MEMO IN _1_ ORIGINAL AND_3_ COPIES INDICATING TOTAL GROSS WEIGHT, TOTAL NET WEIGHT AND TOTAL NUMBER OF CARTONS.

7. ( ) CERTIFICATE OF QUANTITY / WEIGHT IN __ COPIES ISSUED BY AN INDEPENDENT SURVEYOR AT THE LOADING PORT, INDICATING THE ACTUAL SURVEYED QUANTITY / WEIGHT OF SHIPPED GOODS AS WELL AS THE PACKING CONDITION.

8. ( ) CERTIFICATE OF QUALITY IN ____ COPIES ISSUED BY ( ) MANUFACTURER / ( ) PUBLIC RECOGNIZED SURVEYOR / ( )

9. ( ) BENEFICIARY'S CERTIFIED COPY OF FAX DISPATCHED TO THE ACCOUNTEE WITH _ DAYS AFTER SHIPMENT ADVISING ( ) NAME OF VESSEL / ( ) DATE, QUANTITY, WEIGHT AND VALUE OF SHIPMENT.

10. ( ) BENEFICIARY'S CERTIFICATE CERTIFYING THAT EXTRA COPIES OF THE DOCUMENTS HAVE BEEN DISPATCHED ACCORDING TO THE CONTRACT TERMS.

11. ( ) SHIPPING COMPANY'S CERTIFICATE ATTESTING THAT THE CARRYING VESSEL IS CHARTERED OR BOOKED BY ACCOUNTEE OR THEIR SHIPPING AGENTS:

12. ( ) OTHER DOCUMENTS, IF ANY:

  A) CERTIFICATE OF ORIGIN IN ___ ORIGINAL AND___COPY ATTESTED BY

    CHAMBER OF COMMERCE IN U.S.A.

  B) CERTIFICATE OF HEALTH IN ___ COPIES ISSUED BY AUTHORIZED INSTITUTION.

ADDITIONAL INSTRUCTIONS:

1. (X) ALL BANKING CHARGES OUTSIDE THE OPENING BANK ARE FOR BENEFICIARY'S ACCOUNT.

2. (X) DOCUMENTS MUST BE PRESENTED WITH__7__DAYS AFTER THE DATE OF ISSUANCE OF THE TRANSPORT DOCUMENTS BUT WITHIN THE VALIDITY OF THIS CREDIT.

3. ( ) THIRD PARTY AS SHIPPER IS NOT ACCEPTABLE. SHORT FORM / BLANK BACK B/L IS NOT ACCEPTABLE.

4. (X) BOTH QUANTITY AND AMOUNT__10 %__ MORE OR LESS ARE ALLOWED.

5. ( ) PREPAID FREIGHT DRAWN IN EXCESS OF L/C AMOUNT IS ACCEPTABLE AGAINST PRESENTATION OF ORIGINAL CHARGES VOUCHER ISSUED BY SHIPPING CO. / AIR LINE OR ITS AGENT.

6. ( ) ALL DOCUMENTS TO BE FORWARDED IN ONE COVER, UNLESS OTHERWISE STATED ABOVE.

7. ( ) OTHER TERMS, IF ANY:

ADVISING BANK:　BKCHUS33XXX

ACCOUNT NO.:

WITH___BANK OF COMMUNICATIONS CO,. LTD., JIANGSU BR.___ (NAME OF BANK)

TRANSACTED BY:

APPLICANT: _____ (NAME, SIGNATURE OF AUTHORIZED PERSON)

TELEPHONE NO.:

(WITH SEAL)　HK MACHINE COMPANY

练习 4.2

2010 年 4 月 1 日，进口商 YUFAN CORPORATION 与出口商 KOWA COMPANY LTD., TOKYO 签订了如下的贸易合同，选择以信用证方式来支付。进口商去开证行(假设是交通银行)开立信用证时，应如何填制进口开证申请书呢？请根据以下贸易合同来填制进口开证申请书。

Contract

Contract No.: 050020

Date :

Sellers: KOWA COMPANY LTD., TOKYO

Address: Postal Code:

Tel: 123456   Fax:

Buyers: YUFAN CORPORATION

Address: NO.112

ZHONGSHAN SOUTH ROAD, JIANGNING

DEVELOPMENT ZONE, NANJING, 211100, P.R.C.

Postal Code:

Tel: Fax:

The seller agrees to sell and the buyer agrees to buy the under-mentioned goods on the terms and conditions stated below.

1. Article No.:

2. Description & Specification:

IODINE PRILLS (99.8PCT)

UNIT PRICE: USD29,700.00/MT FCA SHANGHAI WAIGAOQIAO BONDED

WAREHOUSE, CHINA

QUANTITY:

ORIGIN: CHILE/SQM

3. Quantity: 10.7744 MTS

4. Unit Price: USD29,700.00/MT

5. Total Amount: USD320,000.00 FCA SHANGHAI WAIGAOQIAO BONDED WAREHOUSE, CHINA

With _____% more or less both in amount and quantity allowed at the seller's option.

6. Country of Origin and Manufacturer: CHILE

7. Packing:

8. Shipping Marks:

9. Time of Shipment: BEFORE 20100415　　Date and Place of Expire: 20100715 JAPAN

10. Port of Loading: SHANGHAI WAIGAOQIAO BONDED WAREHOUSE, CHINA

11. Port of Destination: SHANGHAI, CHINA

12. Insurance: To be effected by buyers for 110% of full invoice value covering ___ up to _____ only.

13. Payment: 60 DAYS AFTER DELIVERY ORDER DATE

By confirmed, irrevocable, transferable and divisible L/C to be available by sight draft to reach the sellers before ___/___/_____ and to remain valid for negotiation in China until 15 days after the aforesaid time of shipment. The L/C must specify that transshipment and partial shipments are allowed.

14. Documents:

+SIGNED COMMERCIAL INVOICE IN 2 ORIGINALS AND 2 COPIES
　INDICATING L/C NO. AND CONTRACT NO. 050020.

+PACKING LIST/WEIGHT MEMO IN 3 COPIES ISSUED BY MANUFACTURER.

+CERTIFICATE OF ANALYSIS IN 3 COPIES ISSUED BY MANUFACTURER.

+CERTIFICATE OF ORIGIN IN 3 COPIES ISSUED BY MANUFACTURER.

　+DELIVERY ORDER IN 1 ORIGINAL ISSUED BY SQM EUROPE N.V. DATED NOT LATER THAN
　APR.15, 2010.

15. Terms of Shipment: FCA

16. Quality/Quantity Discrepancy and Claim:

17. Force Majeure:

Either party shall not be held responsible for failure or delay to perform all or any part of this agreement due to flood, fire, earthquake, draught, war or any other events which could not be predicted, controlled, avoided or overcome by the relative party. However, the party affected by the event of Force Majeure shall inform the other party of its occurrence in writing as soon as possible and thereafter send a certificate of the event issued by the relevant authorities to the other party within 15 days after its occurrence.

18. Arbitration:

All disputes arising from the execution of this agreement shall be settled through friendly consultations. In case no settlement can be reached, the case in dispute shall then be submitted to the Foreign Trade Arbitration Commission of the China Council for the Promotion of International Trade for Arbitration in accordance with its Provisional Rules of Procedure. The decision made by this commission shall be regarded as final and binding upon both parties. Arbitration fees shall be borne by the losing party, unless otherwise awarded.

19. Remarks:

Sellers: KOWA COMPANY LTD., TOKYO　　　Buyers: YUFAN CORPORATION

Signature:　　　　　　　　　　　　　　　Signature:

IRREVOCABLE DOCUMENTARY CREDIT APPLICATION

TO： **BANK OF COMMUNICATIONS**   DATE:

BENEFICIARY (FULL NAME AND ADDRESS):		L/C NO.: EX-CARD NO.: CONTRACT NO.:
		DATE AND PLACE OF EXPIRY OF THE CREDIT
PARTIAL SHIPMENTS ☐ALLOWED ☐NOT ALLOWED	TRANSSHIPMENT ☐ALLOWED ☐NOT ALLOWED	☐BY AIRMAIL ☐WITH BRIEF ADVICE BY TELETRANSMISSION ☐BY EXPRESS DELIVERY ☐BY TELETRANSMISSION(WHICH SHALL BE THE OPERATIVE INSTRUMENT)
LOADING ON BOARD / DISPATCH / TAKING IN CHARGE AT / FROM: NOT LATER THAN: FOR TRANSPORTATION TO:		AMOUNT (BOTH IN FIGURES AND WORDS)：
DESCRIPTION OF GOODS: PACKING:		CREDIT AVAILABLE WITH ☐ BY SIGHT PAYMENT ☐ BY ACCEPTANCE ☐ BY NEGOTIATION ☐ BY DEFERRED PAYMENT AT AGAINST THE DOCUMENTS DETAILED HEREIN ☐ AND BENEFICIARY'S DRAFT FOR % OF THE INVOICE VALUE AT ON
		☐ FOB ☐ CFR ☐CIF ☐ OR OTHER TERMS
DOCUMENTS REQUIRED: 		

( ) OTHER DOCUMENTS, IF ANY:

ADDITIONAL INSTRUCTIONS: (MARKED WITH X)

1. ( ) ALL BANKING CHARGES OUTSIDE THE OPENING BANK ARE FOR BENEFICIARY'S ACCOUNT.

2. ( ) DOCUMENTS MUST BE PRESENTED WITH___DAYS AFTER THE DATE OF ISSUANCE OF THE TRANSPORT DOCUMENTS BUT WITHIN THE VALIDITY OF THIS CREDIT.

3. ( ) THIRD PARTY AS SHIPPER IS NOT ACCEPTABLE. SHORT FORM / BLANK BACK B/L IS NOT ACCEPTABLE.

4. ( ) BOTH QUANTITY AND AMOUNT___% MORE OR LESS ARE ALLOWED.

5. ( ) PREPAID FREIGHT DRAWN IN EXCESS OF L/C AMOUNT IS ACCEPTABLE AGAINST PRESENTATION OF ORIGINAL CHARGES VOUCHER ISSUED BY SHIPPING CO. / AIR LINE OR ITS AGENT.

6. ( ) ALL DOCUMENTS TO BE FORWARDED IN ONE COVER, UNLESS OTHERWISE STATED ABOVE.

7. ( ) OTHER TERMS, IF ANY:

ADVISING BANK:

ACCOUNT NO.:

WITH _____ BANK OF COMMUNICATIONS CO., LTD. JIANGSU BR. (NAME OF BANK)

TRANSACTED BY:

APPLICANT: _____ (NAME, SIGNATURE OF AUTHORIZED PERSON)

TELEPHONE NO.:

(WITH SEAL) YUFAN CORPORATION

参考答案：

IRREVOCABLE DOCUMENTARY CREDIT APPLICATION

TO：**BANK OF COMMUNICATIONS**　　　　　　　　　DATE: 20100401

BENEFICIARY (FULL NAME AND ADDRESS): KOWA COMPANY LTD., TOKYO BRANCH	L/C NO.: EX-CARD NO.: CONTRACT NO.: 050020
	DATE AND PLACE OF EXPIRY OF THE CREDIT: 100715　JAPAN

PARTIAL SHIPMENTS ☒ALLOWED ☐NOT ALLOWED	TRANSSHIPMENT ☒ALLOWED ☐NOT ALLOWED	☐BY AIRMAIL ☐WITH BRIEF ADVICE BY TELETRANSMISSION ☐BY EXPRESS DELIVERY ☐BY TELETRANSMISSION(WHICH SHALL BE THE OPERATIVE INSTRUMENT)
LOADING ON BOARD / DISPATCH / TAKING IN CHARGE AT / FROM: SHANGHAI WAIGAOQIAO BONDED WAREHOUSE, CHINA NOT LATER THAN: 100415 FOR TRANSPORTATION TO: SHANGHAI, CHINA		AMOUNT (BOTH IN FIGURES AND WORDS): USD320,000.00 SAY US DOLLARS THREE HUNDRED TWENTY THOUSAND ONLY
DESCRIPTION OF GOODS: IODINE PRILLS (99.8PCT) UNIT PRICE: USD29,700.00/MT FCA SHANGHAI WAIGAOQIAO BONDED WAREHOUSE, CHINA QUANTITY: 10.7744 MTS TOTAL AMOUNT:USD320,000.00 FCA SHANGHAI WAIGAOQIAO BONDED WAREHOUSE, CHINA PACKING: IN 50.00 KGS FIBRE DRUM ORIGIN: CHILE/SQM PACKING:		CREDIT AVAILABLE WITH ☐ BY SIGHT PAYMENT ☐ BY ACCEPTANCE ☒ BY NEGOTIATION 60 DAYS AFTER DELIVERY ORDER DATE ☐ BY DEFERRED PAYMENT AT AGAINST THE DOCUMENTS DETAILED HEREIN ☐ AND BENEFICIARY'S DRAFT FOR % OF THE INVOICE VALUE AT ON
		☐ FOB ☐ CFR ☐CIF ☒ OR OTHER TERMS FCA

DOCUMENTS REQUIRED:

+SIGNED COMMERCIAL INVOICE IN 2 ORIGINALS AND 2 COPIES INDICATING L/C NO. AND CONTRACT NO. 050020.

+PACKING LIST/WEIGHT MEMO IN 3 COPIES ISSUED BY MANUFACTURER.

+CERTIFICATE OF ANALYSIS IN 3 COPIES ISSUED BY MANUFACTURER.

+CERTIFICATE OF ORIGIN IN 3 COPIES ISSUED BY MANUFACTURER.

+DELIVERY ORDER IN 1 ORIGINAL ISSUED BY SQM EUROPE N.V. DATED NOT LATER THAN APR.15, 2010.

(   ) OTHER DOCUMENTS, IF ANY:

ADDITIONAL INSTRUCTIONS:

1. (X) ALL BANKING CHARGES OUTSIDE THE OPENING BANK ARE FOR BENEFICIARY'S ACCOUNT.

2. (X) DOCUMENTS MUST BE PRESENTED WITH___21___DAYS AFTER THE DATE OF ISSUANCE OF THE TRANSPORT DOCUMENTS BUT WITHIN THE VALIDITY OF THIS CREDIT.

3. ( ) THIRD PARTY AS SHIPPER IS NOT ACCEPTABLE. SHORT FORM / BLANK BACK B/L IS NOT ACCEPTABLE.

4. (X) BOTH QUANTITY AND AMOUNT 10 % MORE OR LESS ARE ALLOWED.

5. ( ) PREPAID FREIGHT DRAWN IN EXCESS OF L/C AMOUNT IS ACCEPTABLE AGAINST PRESENTATION OF ORIGINAL CHARGES VOUCHER ISSUED BY SHIPPING CO. / AIR LINE OR ITS AGENT.

6. ( ) ALL DOCUMENTS TO BE FORWARDED IN ONE COVER, UNLESS OTHERWISE STATED ABOVE.

7. ( ) OTHER TERMS, IF ANY:

ADVISING BANK:

ACCOUNT NO.:

WITH _____BANK OF COMMUNICATIONS CO., LTD., JIANGSU BR._____ (NAME OF BANK)

TRANSACTED BY:

APPLICANT: (NAME, SIGNATURE OF AUTHORIZED PERSON)

TELEPHONE NO.:

(WITH SEAL) YUFAN CORPORATION

第二节 开证行开证

一、业务场景与操作

开立信用证

开证行一旦收到开证的详尽指示，有责任尽快开证。但开证行在开证前必须仔细审查开证申请书的内容，如申请书上有自相矛盾或不符合国际惯例的条款，必须与进口商联系进行修改。同时必须严格按照申请人的指示行事，在审核无误并确认企业符合外管局有关进口付汇分类管理后，通过以下电开的方式(SWIFT)开立信用证，并通过出口商所在地的相关代理行(通知行)将信用证及时通知受益人。以案例4.1为背景，开出如下信用证。

信用证样本

MT700 电文

```
-------------------------- Message Header --------------------------
Swift Output     : FIN 700 Issue of a Documentary Credit
Sender           : COMMCNSHNJG
Receiver         : NOSCDEFFXXX
-------------------------- Message Text --------------------------
```

27	Sequence of Total	
	Number	1
	Total	1
40A	Form of Documentary Credit	
	IRREVOCABLE	
20	Documentary Credit Number	
	LC201000928	
31C	Date of Issue	
	100512	
40E	Applicable Rules	
	UCP LATEST VERSION	
31D	Date and Place of Expiry	
	Date	100921
	Place	GERMANY
50	Applicant	
	ABC COMPANY, NANJING, CHINA	
59	Beneficiary – Name & Address	
	ALLEN CO., LTD., P.O. BOX 3254, GERMANY	
32B	Currency Code, Amount	
	Currency	USD
	Amount	236,994.50
39A	Percentage Credit Amt Tolerance	
	Tolerance 1	10
	Tolerance 2	10
41D	Available With...By... – Name & Address	

ANY BANK IN GERMANY

Code　　　　　BY NEGOTIATION

42C　Drafts at...

AT 90 DAYS AFTER B/L DATE FOR

100.0PCT INVOICE VALUE

42A　Drawee - BIC

BIC　　　　　COMMCNSHNJG

43P　Partial Shipments

ALLOWED

43T　Transshipment

ALLOWED

44E　Port of Loading/Airport of Dep.

MAIN PORTS IN GERMANY

44F　Port of Discharge

ZHANGJIAGANG, CHINA

44C　Latest Date of Shipment

100531

45A　Description of Goods &/or Services

US UPLAND BALED COTTON

UNIT PRICE: USD107.50 PER LB CIF ZHANGJIAGANG, CHINA

TOTAL AMOUNT: USD236,994.50 CIF ZHANGJIAGANG, CHINA

ORIGIN: GERMANY

46A　Documents Required

+SIGNED COMMERCIAL INVOICE IN 2 ORIGINALS AND 1 COPY INDICATING

L/C NO. AND CONTRACT NO. 30850.

+FULL SET (3/3 ORIGINALS AND 3 COPIES) OF CLEAN ON BOARD OCEAN

BILLS OF LADING MADE OUT TO ORDER OF SHIPPER AND ENDORSED IN

BLANK MARKED 'FREIGHT PREPAID' NOTIFYING THE APPLICANT WITH FULL

NAME AND ADDRESS.

+INSURANCE POLICY/CERTIFICATE IN DUPLICATE FOR 110PCT OF THE

INVOICE VALUE, SHOWING CLAIMS IF ANY PAYABLE IN CHINA, IN

CURRENCY OF THE DRAFT , BLANK ENDORSED, COVERING OCEAN MARINE

TRANSPORTATION ALL RISKS AND WAR RISK.

+PACKING LIST / WEIGHT MEMO IN 1 ORIGINAL AND 3 COPIES

INDICATING TOTAL GROSS WEIGHT, TOTAL NET WEIGHT AND TOTAL NUMBER
OF BALES.

+CERTIFICATE OF ORIGIN IN 1 ORIGINAL AND 1 COPY ATTESTED BY
CHAMBER OF COMMERCE IN GERMANY.

47A   Additional Conditions

+BOTH CREDIT AMOUNT AND QUANTITY 10PCT MORE OR LESS ARE ALLOWED.

+DOCUMENTS TO BE PRESENTED TO THE PLACE OF EXPIRATION WITHIN   21
DAYS AFTER THE SHIPMENT DATE BUT WITHIN THE VALIDITY OF THIS
CREDIT.

+A DISCREPANCY FEE OF USD80.00(OR EQUIVALENT) PAYABLE BY
BENEFICIARY SHALL BE DEDUCTED FROM THE PROCEEDS FOR EACH
PRESENTATION OF DISCREPANT DOCUMENTS UNDER THIS DOCUMENTARY
CREDIT.

+ALL BANKING CHARGES OUTSIDE THE ISSUING BANK ARE FOR ACCOUNT OF
BENEFICIARY. NOTWITHSTANDING THE ABOVE, COSTS RELATING TO
REIMBURSEMENT/PAYMENT ARE ALSO FOR ACCOUNT OF BENEFICIARY AND
WILL BE DEDUCTED FROM PROCEEDS UPON PAYMENT.

+ONE EXTRA COPY OF COMMERCIAL INVOICE, TRANSPORT DOCUMENT,
INSURANCE DOCUMENT (IF ANY) TO BE PRESENTED TO US FOR OUR
FILE, OTHERWISE USD10.00 (OR EQUIVALENT) WILL BE DEDUCTED FROM THE PROCEEDS.

+THE PRESENTING BANK'S SWIFT CODE MUST BE SHOWN ON THE BANKING
SCHEDULE.

+ALL DOCUMENTS TO BE DISPATCHED TO ISSUING BANK IN ONE LOT BY
FIRST AVAILABLE AIRMAIL THROUGH BANK. ISSUING BANK ADDRESS: BANK
OF COMMUNICATIONS CO., LTD., JIANGSU PROVINCIAL BRANCH,
11F. NO. 124 NORTH ZHONGSHAN ROAD, NANJING, JIANGSU, CHINA
SWIFT: COMMCNSHNJG

48   Period for Presentation

DOCUMENTS TO BE PRESENTED
WITHIN 21 DAYS AFTER
THE DATE OF SHIPMENT BUT WITHIN
THE VALIDITY OF THE CREDIT.

49   Confirmation Instructions

WITHOUT

78　Instr to Payg/Accptg/Negotg Bank

UPON RECEIPT OF THE DOCUMENTS AND DRAFTS IN STRICT COMPLIANCE
WITH THE TERMS AND CONDITIONS OF THIS CREDIT, WE SHALL ACCEPT THE
DRAFTS AND REIMBURSE THE PRESENTING BANK AS INSTRUCTED AT
MATURITY.
THIS IS THE OPERATIVE CREDIT INSTRUMENT AND NO AIRMAIL
CONFIRMATION WILL FOLLOW.

二、风险控制

1. 细审合同条款

UCP600 规定，在单证严格相符的情况下，信用证的开证行必须承担第一性的付款责任，因此开证行在开证时应仔细斟酌合同的每一条款。

2. 进口商的资信

在开立信用证时，可以根据对进口商的了解，慎重考虑信贷额度的结构，使得信贷额度的金额、期限、币种等都与相应的进口贸易相联系，以确保信贷额度的正常使用。从这个角度来说，开证行首先需要对申请人的经营资格、资信和实力，贸易背景的真实性，进口物品的合法性等审核把关。完备开证申请手续，明晰开证行在将开立的信用证中所承担的责任和义务，同时也告知进口商其责任和义务。对增额、期限延长等增大开证银行风险的修改，尤其需要落实相应的风险控制措施。

3. 信用证条款

开证行在开立信用证条款时，要注意信用证的货描及单据要求应明确，单据之间不应有矛盾，以免之后因此不明确而带来不符点的争议。

4. 远期信用证

远期信用证既是国际贸易结算方式，也是出口商及其银行对进口商的一种融通资金的方式。但是，由于远期信用证项下付款时间较长，国家风险、资信风险、市场风险等诸多不确定因素不易预测，且银行一旦进行了承兑，所承担的责任将由信用证项下单证一致付款转变为对票据的无条件付款责任，风险程度进一步提高。再者，若开立远期信用证进口热门敏感商品，由于该类产品的价格波动较大，且变动趋势相对较难预测，应尽量缩短销售周期，以减少由于价格波动而造成的销售不确定性。因此开立远期信用证虽然不失为防范风险的手段，但还是应该十分注意对贸易的把握。

5. 修改信用证

银行在对信用证修改申请全面审核后，如发现问题，应及时处理。对于影响安全收汇，难以接受或做到的信用证条款，必须要求进口商进行修改。修改时应注意凡是需要修改的内容，应做到一次性向进口商提出，避免多次修改信用证的情况。

严格按照国际惯例处理进口来单，避免卷入贸易纠纷。

三、总结思考

就信用证本身特性来说，信用证是一份独立自足性文件，其独立于基础合同，因此，开证行一经开出信用证，开证行即对信用证承担第一性付款责任。只要受益人提交单证相符的单据，开证行就必须付款。银行的第一性付款责任并不因为进口商即开证申请人发生无力或无意愿偿付货款的情况而解除。在此意义上，开证银行承担着进口商的信用风险，因此，银行对于风险的控制一般多侧重于开证授信条件、放单条件和付款资金的落实、货权的掌握等。银行应加强对开证个案本身的分析研究，强化事后监控，以便控制进口信用证新增被动垫款的发生，防范进口信用证业务风险。

就进口商来说，其对进出口贸易业务的分析及掌控也是进口商自己经营水平及能力的体现。进口贸易项目所产生的现金流量，是进口开证还款的第一来源，也是银行进口开证风险分析的基础和着力点，因此，开证行同样应该分析与关注以下几个方面的内容。

(1) 分析进口商品是否属于许可证商品、国家限制进口或禁止进口商品等，而且该进口商品是否属于进口商的主营产品，进口商的历史经营情况如何，是否有足够的经验和能力进口和销售该种商品。如果涉及炒作商品的进口时，开证银行一定要慎重地进行风险分析，对于那些赌博式进口贸易项目，不应给其开证。

(2) 分析付款期限。对于即期信用证，要注意进口商的资金准备是否与出口方银行所寄单据的时间相匹配。对于远期信用证来说，则要测算进口商品的合理周转期。远期信用证的付款期限原则上不应超过合理周转期。

(3) 分析进口商品价格，一般不应过度偏离正常的国内外市场行情。如果价格过高，可能面临国内销售不畅、库存积压的风险或者遭受价格下跌的损失；而价格过低，进口的商品则有可能会是假冒伪劣商品，或者堕入国外出口商精心设置的欺诈陷阱中。

四、实训操练

练习 4.3

假设交通银行收到进口开证申请人 ABC COMPANY, NANJING, CHINA 提交的以下进口开证申请书，在落实开证相关条件后，应如何发送 MT700 电文呢？假设银行编号是 LC201000928。

IRREVOCABLE DOCUMENTARY CREDIT APPLICATION

TO：**BANK OF COMMUNICATIONS**　　　　　　DATE: 20100512

BENEFICIARY (FULL NAME AND ADDRESS): ALLEN CO., LTD., P.O. BOX 3254, GERMANY	L/C NO.: EX-CARD NO.: CONTRACT NO.:
	DATE AND PLACE OF EXPIRY OF THE CREDIT: 100621 GERMANY
PARTIAL SHIPMENTS ☒ALLOWED ☐NOT ALLOWED 　　TRANSSHIPMENT ☒ALLOWED ☐NOT ALLOWED	☐BY AIRMAIL ☐WITH BRIEF ADVICE BY TELETRANSMISSION ☐BY EXPRESS DELIVERY ☐BY TELETRANSMISSION(WHICH SHALL BE THE OPERATIVE INSTRUMENT)
LOADING ON BOARD / DISPATCH / TAKING IN CHARGE AT / FROM: MAIN GERMANY PORT NOT LATER THAN: 100531 FOR TRANSPORTATION TO: ZHANGJIAGANG	AMOUNT (BOTH IN FIGURES AND WORDS): USD236,994.50 SAY US DOLLARS TWO HUNDRED THIRTY SIX THOUSAND NINE HUNDRED AND NINETY FOUR POINT FIFTY ONLY
DESCRIPTION OF GOODS: US UPLAND BALED COTTON UNIT PRICE: USD107.50 PER LB CIF ZHANGJIAGANG, CHINA TOTAL AMOUNT: USD236,994.50 CIF ZHANGJIAGANG,CHINA ORIGIN: GERMANY PACKING:	CREDIT AVAILABLE WITH ☐BY SIGHT PAYMENT ☐BY ACCEPTANCE ☒BY NEGOTIATION 90 DAYS AFTER B/L DATE ☐BY DEFERRED PAYMENT AT AGAINST THE DOCUMENTS DETAILED HEREIN ☐AND BENEFICIARY'S DRAFT FOR　　% OF THE INVOICE VALUE AT ON
	☐ FOB　　☐ CFR　　☒ CIF ☐ OR OTHER TERMS

DOCUMENTS REQUIRED: (MARKED WITH X)

1 .(X) SIGNED COMMERCIAL INVOICE IN 2 ORIGINALS AND 1 COPY INDICATING L/C NO. AND CONTRACT NO. 30850.

2. (X) FULL SET OF CLEAN ON BOARD OCEAN BILLS OF LADING MADE OUT TO ORDER OF SHIPPER AND BLANK ENDORSED, MARKED "FREIGHT ( ) TO COLLECT / (X) PREPAID" NOTIFYING THE APPLICANT WITH FULL NAME AND ADDRESS.

3. ( ) AIR WAYBILLS SHOWING "FREIGHT ( ) TO COLLECT / ( ) PREPAID" ( )INDICATING FREIGHT AMOUNT AND CONSIGNED TO _____ .

4. ( ) MEMORANDUM ISSUED BY _____ CONSIGNED TO _____ .

5. (X) INSURANCE POLICY / CERTIFICATE IN 2 COPIES FOR 110 % OF THE INVOICE VALUE SHOWING CLAIMS PAYABLE IN CHINA IN CURRENCY OF THE DRAFT, BLANK ENDORSED, COVERING (X) OCEAN MARINE TRANSPORTATION / ( ) AIR TRANSPORTATION / ( ) OVER LAND TRANSPORTATION FOR (X) ALL RISKS (X) WAR RISKS.

6. (X) PACKING LIST IN 1 ORIGINAL AND 3 COPIES INDICATING TOTAL GROSS WEIGHT, TOTAL NET WEIGHT AND TOTAL NUMBER OF BALES.

7. ( ) CERTIFICATE OF QUANTITY / WEIGHT IN___COPIES ISSUED BY AN INDEPENDENT SURVEYOR AT THE LOADING PORT, INDICATING THE ACTUAL SURVEYED QUANTITY / WEIGHT OF SHIPPED GOODS AS WELL AS THE PACKING CONDITION.

8. ( ) CERTIFICATE OF QUALITY IN___COPIES ISSUED BY ( ) MANUFACTURER / ( ) PUBLIC RECOGNIZED SURVEYOR / ( )

9. ( ) BENEFICIARY'S CERTIFIED COPY OF FAX DISPATCHED TO THE ACCOUNTEE WITH _____ DAYS AFTER SHIPMENT ADVISING ( ) NAME OF VESSEL / ( ) DATE, QUANTITY, WEIGHT AND VALUE OF SHIPMENT.

10. ( ) BENEFICIARY'S CERTIFICATE CERTIFYING THAT EXTRA COPIES OF THE DOCUMENTS HAVE BEEN DISPATCHED ACCORDING TO THE CONTRACT TERMS.

11. ( ) SHIPPING COMPANY'S CERTIFICATE ATTESTING THAT THE CARRYING VESSEL IS CHARTERED OR BOOKED BY ACCOUNTEE OR THEIR SHIPPING AGENTS: _____.

12. (X) OTHER DOCUMENTS, IF ANY:

  A)X CERTIFICATE OF ORIGIN IN 1 ORIGINAL AND 1 COPY ATTESTED BY

  CHAMBER OF COMMERCE IN GERMANY.

  B) CERTIFICATE OF HEALTH IN ____COPIES ISSUED BY AUTHORIZED INSTITUTION.

ADDITIONAL INSTRUCTIONS:

1. (X) ALL BANKING CHARGES OUTSIDE THE OPENING BANK ARE FOR BENEFICIARY'S ACCOUNT.

2. (X) DOCUMENTS MUST BE PRESENTED WITH 21 DAYS AFTER THE DATE OF ISSUANCE OF THE TRANSPORT DOCUMENTS BUT WITHIN THE VALIDITY OF THIS CREDIT.

3. ( ) THIRD PARTY AS SHIPPER IS NOT ACCEPTABLE. SHORT FORM / BLANK BACK B/L IS NOT ACCEPTABLE.

4. (X) BOTH QUANTITY AND AMOUNT 5 % MORE OR LESS ARE ALLOWED.

5. ( ) PREPAID FREIGHT DRAWN IN EXCESS OF L/C AMOUNT IS ACCEPTABLE AGAINST PRESENTATION OF ORIGINAL CHARGES VOUCHER ISSUED BY SHIPPING CO. / AIR LINE OR ITS AGENT.

6. (X) ALL DOCUMENTS TO BE FORWARDED IN ONE COVER, UNLESS OTHERWISE STATED ABOVE.

7. ( ) OTHER TERMS, IF ANY:

ONE EXTRA COPY OF COMMERCIAL INVOICE, TRANSPORT DOCUMENT, INSURANCE DOCUMENT (IF ANY) TO BE PRESENTED TO US FOR OUR FILE, OTHERWISE USD10.00(OR EQUIVALENT) WILL BE DEDUCTED FROM THE PROCEEDS.

ADVISING BANK: NOSCUS33XXX

ACCOUNT NO.:

WITH _____ BANK OF COMMUNICATIONS CO., LTD., JIANGSU BR.   (NAME OF BANK) ___

TRANSACTED BY:

APPLICANT: _____   (NAME, SIGNATURE OF AUTHORIZED PERSON)

TELEPHONE NO.:

(WITH SEAL)   ABC COMPANY

MT700 电文

```
------------------------- Message Header -------------------------
Swift Output    : FIN 700 Issue of a Documentary Credit
Sender          :
Receiver        :
------------------------- Message Text -------------------------
```

27	Sequence of Total
	Number
	Total
40A	Form of Documentary Credit
20	Documentary Credit Number

31C   Date of Issue

40E   Applicable Rules

31D   Date and Place of Expiry

Date

Place

50   Applicant

59   Beneficiary – Name & Address

Name And Address

32B   Currency Code, Amount

Currency   Amount

39A   Percentage Credit Amt Tolerance

Tolerance 1

Tolerance 2

41D   Available With...By... –Name&Address

Name And Address

Code

42C   Drafts at...

AT

42A   Drawee - BIC

BIC

43P   Partial Shipments

43T   Transshipment

44E   Port of Loading/Airport of Dep.

44F   Port of Discharge/Airport of Dest.

44C   Latest Date of Shipment

45A   Description of Goods &/or Services

46A	Documents Required
47A	Additional Conditions
48	Period for Presentation
49	Confirmation Instructions
78	Instr to Payg/Accptg/Negotg Bank

参考答案：

MT700 电文

```
--------------------------- Message Header ------------------------
Swift Output      : FIN 700 Issue of a Documentary Credit
Sender            : COMMCNSHNJG
Receiver          : NOSCDEFFXXX
--------------------------- Message Text ---------------------------
```

27	Sequence of Total	
	Number	1
	Total	1
40A	Form of Documentary Credit	
	IRREVOCABLE	
20	Documentary Credit Number	
	LC201000928	
31C	Date of Issue	
	100512	
40E	Applicable Rules	
	UCP LATEST VERSION	
31D	Date and Place of Expiry	

	Date	100621
	Place	GERMANY
50	Applicant	
	ABC COMPANY, NANJING, CHINA	
59	Beneficiary – Name & Address	
	Name And Address	ALLEN CO., LTD., P.O. BOX
		3254, GERMANY
32B	Currency Code, Amount	
	Currency	USD
	Amount	236,994.50
39A	Percentage Credit Amt Tolerance	
	Tolerance 1	05
	Tolerance 2	05
41D	Available With...By... – Name & Address	
	Name And Address	ANY BANK IN USA
	Code	BY NEGOTIATION
42C	Drafts at...	
	AT 90 DAYS AFTER B/L DATE FOR	
	100.0PCT INVOICE VALUE	
42A	Drawee - BIC	
	BIC	COMMCNSHNJG
43P	Partial Shipments	
	ALLOWED	
43T	Transshipment	
	ALLOWED	
44E	Port of Loading/Airport of Dep.	
	MAIN PORTS IN GERMANY	
44F	Port of Discharge	
	ZHANGJIAGANG, CHINA	
44C	Latest Date of Shipment	
	100531	
45A	Description of Goods &/or Services	

US UPLAND BALED COTTON

UNIT PRICE: USD 107.50 PER LB CIF ZHANGJIAGANG, CHINA

TOTAL AMOUNT: USD236,994.50 CIF ZHANGJIAGANG,CHINA

ORIGIN: GERMANY

46A　Documents Required

+SIGNED COMMERCIAL INVOICE IN 2 ORIGINALS AND 1 COPY INDICATING
L/C NO. AND CONTRACT NO. 30850.

+FULL SET (3/3 ORIGINALS AND 3 COPIES) CLEAN ON BOARD OCEAN
BILLS OF LADING MADE OUT TO ORDER OF SHIPPER AND ENDORSED IN
BLANK MARKED 'FREIGHT PREPAID' NOTIFYING THE APPLICANT WITH FULL
NAME AND ADDRESS.

+INSURANCE POLICY/CERTIFICATE IN DUPLICATE FOR 110PCT OF THE
INVOICE VALUE, SHOWING CLAIMS IF ANY PAYABLE IN CHINA, IN
CURRENCY OF THE DRAFT , BLANK ENDORSED, COVERING OCEAN MARINE
TRANSPORTATION ALL RISKS AND WAR RISK.

+PACKING LIST / WEIGHT MEMO IN 1 ORIGINAL AND 3 COPIES
INDICATING TOTAL GROSS WEIGHT, TOTAL NET WEIGHT AND TOTAL NUMBER
OF BALES.

+CERTIFICATE OF ORIGIN IN 1 ORIGINAL AND 1 COPY ATTESTED BY
CHAMBER OF COMMERCE IN GERMANY.

47A　Additional Conditions

+BOTH CREDIT AMOUNT AND QUANTITY 5 PCT MORE OR LESS ARE ALLOWED.

+DOCUMENTS TO BE PRESENTED TO THE PLACE OF EXPIRATION WITHIN　21
DAYS AFTER THE SHIPMENT DATE BUT WITHIN THE VALIDITY OF THIS
CREDIT.

+A DISCREPANCY FEE OF USD80.00(OR EQUIVALENT) PAYABLE BY
BENEFICIARY SHALL BE DEDUCTED FROM THE PROCEEDS FOR EACH
PRESENTATION OF DISCREPANT DOCUMENTS UNDER THIS DOCUMENTARY
CREDIT.

+ALL BANKING CHARGES OUTSIDE THE ISSUING BANK ARE FOR ACCOUNT OF
BENEFICIARY. NOTWITHSTANDING THE ABOVE, COSTS RELATING TO
REIMBURSEMENT/PAYMENT ARE ALSO FOR ACCOUNT OF BENEFICIARY AND

WILL BE DEDUCTED FROM PROCEEDS UPON PAYMENT.

+ONE EXTRA COPY OF COMMERCIAL INVOICE, TRANSPORT DOCUMENT,

INSURANCE DOCUMENT (IF ANY) TO BE PRESENTED TO US FOR OUR

FILE, OTHERWISE USD10.00(OR EQUIVALENT) WILL BE DEDUCTED FROM THE

PROCEEDS.

+THE PRESENTING BANK'S SWIFT CODE MUST BE SHOWN ON THE BANKING

SCHEDULE.

+ALL DOCUMENTS TO BE DISPATCHED TO ISSUING BANK IN ONE LOT BY

FIRST AVAILABLE AIRMAIL THROUGH BANK. ISSUING BANK ADDRESS:BANK

OF COMMUNICATIONS CO.,LTD., JIANGSU PROVINCIAL BRANCH,

11F. NO. 124 NORTH ZHONGSHAN ROAD, NANJING, JIANGSU, CHINA

SWIFT: COMMCNSHNJG

48	Period for Presentation	

DOCUMENTS TO BE PRESENTED

WITHIN 21 DAYS AFTER

THE DATE OF SHIPMENT BUT WITHIN

THE VALIDITY OF THE CREDIT.

49   Confirmation Instructions

WITHOUT

78   Instr to Payg/Accptg/Negotg Bank

UPON RECEIPT OF THE DOCUMENTS AND DRAFTS IN STRICT COMPLIANCE

WITH THE TERMS AND CONDITIONS OF THIS CREDIT, WE SHALL ACCEPT THE

DRAFTS AND REIMBURSE THE PRESENTING BANK AS INSTRUCTED AT

MATURITY.

THIS IS THE OPERATIVE CREDIT INSTRUMENT AND NO AIRMAIL

CONFIRMATION WILL FOLLOW.

练习 4.4

EFG 公司与新加坡 AGILENT TECHNOLOGIES SINGAPORE(SALES)PTE LTD. 签订合同，约定采用 L/C 方式进口货物 AGILENT 1200 HPLC SYSTEM，金额为 USD94000，期限为即期。进口开证申请书如下。假设你是进口方银行交通银行的经办人员，请编写 MT700 电文。假设银行编号是 LC201000929。

IRREVOCABLE DOCUMENTARY CREDIT APPLICATION

TO: **BANK OF COMMUNICATIONS**   DATE: 20100507

BENEFICIARY (FULL NAME AND ADDRESS): AGILENT TECHNOLOGIES SINGAPORE(SALES) PTE LTD.	L/C NO.: EX-CARD NO.: CONTRACT NO.:
	DATE AND PLACE OF EXPIRY OF THE CREDIT: 100831 SINGAPORE

PARTIAL SHIPMENTS ☐ALLOWED ☒NOT ALLOWED	TRANSSHIPMENT ☒ALLOWED ☐NOT ALLOWED	☐BY AIRMAIL ☐WITH BRIEF ADVICE BY TELETRANSMISSION ☐BY EXPRESS DELIVERY
LOADING ON BOARD / DISPATCH / TAKING IN CHARGE AT / FROM: SINGAPORE AIRPORT NOT LATER THAN: 100709 FOR TRANSPORTATION TO: NANJING AIRPORT		☐ BY TELETRANSMISSION(WHICH SHALL BE THE OPERATIVE INSTRUMENT)
		AMOUNT (BOTH IN FIGURES AND WORDS): USD94,000.00 SAY US DOLLARS NINETY FOUR THOUSAND ONLY

DESCRIPTION OF GOODS: COMMODITY: AGILENT 1200 HPLC SYSTEM QUANTITY: 2 SETS UNIT PRICE: USD 47,000.00/SET FOB SINGAPORE AIRPORT, SINGAPORE TOTAL AMOUNT: USD 94,000.00 FOB SINGAPORE AIRPORT, SINGAPORE PACKING:	CREDIT AVAILABLE WITH ☒ BY SIGHT PAYMENT ☐ BY ACCEPTANCE ☐ BY NEGOTIATION ☐ BY DEFERRED PAYMENT AT AGAINST THE DOCUMENTS DETAILED HEREIN ☐ AND BENEFICIARY'S DRAFT FOR % OF THE INVOICE VALUE AT ON
	☒ FOB ☐ CFR ☐CIF ☐ OR OTHER TERMS

DOCUMENTS REQUIRED: (MARKED WITH X)

1. (X) SIGNED COMMERCIAL INVOICE IN QUINTUPLICATE INDICATING L/C NO., CONTRACT NO. 20100412/CTTQ, AND SHIPPING MARK.

2. ( ) FULL SET OF CLEAN ON BOARD OCEAN BILLS OF LADING MADE OUT TO ORDER OF SHIPPER AND BLANK ENDORSED, MARKED "FREIGHT ( ) TO COLLECT / (X) PREPAID" NOTIFYING THE APPLICANT WITH FULL NAME AND ADDRESS.

3. (X) AIR WAYBILLS SHOWING "FREIGHT (X) TO COLLECT / ( ) PREPAID" ( ) INDICATING FREIGHT AMOUNT AND CONSIGNED TO APPLICANT.

4. ( ) MEMORANDUM ISSUED BY _____ CONSIGNED TO _____.

5. ( ) INSURANCE POLICY / CERTIFICATE IN___COPIES FOR ____% OF THE INVOICE VALUE SHOWING CLAIMS PAYABLE IN CHINA IN CURRENCY OF THE DRAFT, BLANK ENDORSED, COVERING ( ) OCEAN MARINE TRANSPORTATION / ( ) AIR TRANSPORTATION / ( ) OVER LAND TRANSPORTATION FOR ( ) ALL RISKS, ( ) WAR RISKS.

6. (X) PACKING LIST IN DUPLICATE INDICATING QUANTITY/GROSS AND NET WEIGHT OF EACH PACKAGE AND PACKING CONDITIONS.

7. ( ) CERTIFICATE OF QUANTITY / WEIGHT IN___COPIES ISSUED BY AN INDEPENDENT SURVEYOR AT THE LOADING PORT, INDICATING THE ACTUAL SURVEYED QUANTITY / WEIGHT OF SHIPPED GOODS AS WELL AS THE PACKING CONDITION.

8. ( ) CERTIFICATE OF QUALITY IN___ COPIES ISSUED BY ( ) MANUFACTURER / ( ) PUBLIC RECOGNIZED SURVEYOR / ( )

9. (X) BENEFICIARY'S CERTIFIED COPY OF FAX DISPATCHED TO THE APPLICANT WITH 24 HOURS AFTER SHIPMENT ADVISING (X) NAME OF VESSEL / (X) DATE, QUANTITY, WEIGHT AND VALUE OF SHIPMENT.

10. ( ) BENEFICIARY'S CERTIFICATE CERTIFYING THAT EXTRA COPIES OF THE DOCUMENTS HAVE BEEN DISPATCHED ACCORDING TO THE CONTRACT TERMS.

11. ( ) SHIPPING COMPANY'S CERTIFICATE ATTESTING THAT THE CARRYING VESSEL IS CHARTERED OR BOOKED BY ACCOUNTEE OR THEIR SHIPPING AGENTS: _____。

12. ( ) OTHER DOCUMENTS, IF ANY:

A)

B)

ADDITIONAL INSTRUCTIONS:

1. (X) ALL BANKING CHARGES OUTSIDE THE OPENING BANK ARE FOR BENEFICIARY'S ACCOUNT.

2. (X) DOCUMENTS MUST BE PRESENTED WITH 21 DAYS AFTER THE DATE OF ISSUANCE OF THE TRANSPORT DOCUMENTS BUT WITHIN THE VALIDITY OF THIS CREDIT.

3. ( ) THIRD PARTY AS SHIPPER IS NOT ACCEPTABLE. SHORT FORM / BLANK BACK B/L IS NOT ACCEPTABLE.

4. (X) BOTH QUANTITY AND AMOUNT 5 % MORE OR LESS ARE ALLOWED.

5.( ) PREPAID FREIGHT DRAWN IN EXCESS OF L/C AMOUNT IS ACCEPTABLE AGAINST PRESENTATION OF ORIGINAL CHARGES VOUCHER ISSUED BY SHIPPING CO. / AIR LINE OR ITS AGENT.

6. ( ) ALL DOCUMENTS TO BE FORWARDED IN ONE COVER, UNLESS OTHERWISE STATED ABOVE.

7. ( ) OTHER TERMS, IF ANY:

+THIRD PARTY AS SHIPPER IS NOT ACCEPTABLE.

+SHORT FORM/BLANK BACK B/L IS NOT ACCEPTABLE.

+ON DECK SHIPMENT IS NOT ALLOWED.

ADVISING BANK: CHASSGSGXXX

ACCOUNT NO.:

WITH _____ BANK OF COMMUNICATIONS CO., LTD., JIANGSU BR. _____ (NAME OF BANK)

TRANSACTED BY:

APPLICANT: _____ (NAME, SIGNATURE OF AUTHORIZED PERSON)

TELEPHONE NO.:

(WITH SEAL)   EFG COMPANY

MT700 电文

---------------------------- Message Header ------------------------

Swift Output   : FIN 700 Issue of a Documentary Credit

Sender   :

Receiver   :

---------------------------- Message Text ---------------------------

27	Sequence of Total
	Number
	Total

40A   Form of Documentary Credit

20   Documentary Credit Number

31C   Date of Issue

40E   Applicable Rules

31D   Date and Place of Expiry

50   Applicant

59   Beneficiary – Name & Address

32B   Currency Code, Amount

39A   Percentage Credit Amt Tolerance

Tolerance 1

Tolerance 2

41D   Available With...By... – Name & Address

42C   Drafts at...

42A   Drawee – BIC

43P   Partial Shipments

43T   Transshipment

44E   Port of Loading/Airport of Dep.

44F   Port of Discharge/Airport of Dest.

44C   Latest Date of Shipment

45A   Description of Goods &/or Services

46A   Documents Required

47A   Additional Conditions

48   Period for Presentation

49   Confirmation Instructions

78   Instr to Payg/Accptg/Negotg Bank

72   Sender to Receiver Information

参考答案：

MT700 电文

```
------------------------ Message Header ------------------------
Swift Output    : FIN 700 Issue of a Documentary Credit
Sender          : COMMCNSHNJG
Receiver        : CHASSGSGXXX
------------------------ Message Text ------------------------
```

27	Sequence of Total		
	Number	1	
	Total	1	
40A	Form of Documentary Credit		
	IRREVOCABLE		
20	Documentary Credit Number		
	LC201000929		
31C	Date of Issue		
	100507		
40E	Applicable Rules		
	UCP LATEST VERSION		
31D	Date and Place of Expiry		
	Date	100831	
	Place	SINGAPORE	
50	Applicant		
	EFG COMPANY		
59	Beneficiary – Name & Address		
	AGILENT TECHNOLOGIES		
	SINGAPORE(SALES)PTE, LTD.		
32B	Currency Code, Amount		
	Currency	USD	
	Amount	94,000.00	
39A	Percentage Credit Amt Tolerance		
	Tolerance 1	5	
	Tolerance 2	5	
41D	Available With...By... – Name & Addess		
	ANY BANK IN SINGAPORE		

Code   BY PAYMENT

42C   Drafts at...

AT SIGHT FOR 100.0PCT INVOICE VALUE

42A   Drawee - BIC

BIC   COMMCNSHNJG

43P   Partial Shipments

NOT ALLOWED

43T   Transshipment

ALLOWED

44E   Port of Loading/Airport of Dep.

SINGAPORE AIRPORT

44F   Port of Discharge/Airport of Dest.

NANJING AIRPORT, CHINA

44C   Latest Date of Shipment

100709

45A   Description of Goods &/or Services

COMMODITY: AGILENT 1200 HPLC SYSTEM

QUANTITY: 2 SETS

UNIT PRICE: USD47,000.00/SET FOB SINGAPORE AIRPORT, SINGAPORE

TOTAL AMOUNT: USD94,000.00 FOB SINGAPORE AIRPORT, SINGAPORE

46A   Documents Required

+SIGNED COMMERCIAL INVOICE IN QUINTUPLICATE INDICATING CONTRACT NO. 20100412/CTTQ AND L/C NO., AND SHIPPING MARK.

+ORIGINAL AIR WAYBILL SHOWING 'FREIGHT TO COLLECT' CONSIGNED TO APPLICANT INDICATING FREIGHT AMOUNT.

+PACKING LIST/WEIGHT LIST IN DUPLICATE INDICATING QUANTITY/GROSS AND NET WEIGHT OF EACH PACKAGE AND PACKING CONDITIONS.

+ BENEFICIARY'S CERTIFIED COPY OF FAX DISPATCHED TO THE APPLICANT WITH 24 HOURS AFTER SHIPMENT ADVISING NAME OF VESSEL, DATE, QUANTITY, WEIGHT AND VALUE OF SHIPMENT.

47A   Additional Conditions

+5PCT MORE OR LESS OF THE QUANTITY AND AMOUNT ARE ALLOWED.

+APPLICANT'S ADD: NO. 9 HUI'OU ROAD, NANJING ECONOMIC AND TECHNOLOGICAL DEVELOPMENT ZONE, NANJING, 210038

TEL:+86-25-85801888 FAX:+86-25-85803122.

+BENEFICIARY'S TEL: 8008100712   FAX: 8008100717

+THIRD PARTY AS SHIPPER IS NOT ACCEPTABLE.

+SHORT FORM/BLANK BACK B/L IS NOT ACCEPTABLE.

+ON DECK SHIPMENT IS NOT ALLOWED.

+A DISCREPANCY FEE OF USD80.00(OR EQUIVALENT) PAYABLE BY BENEFICIARY SHALL BE DEDUCTED FROM THE PROCEEDS FOR EACH PRESENTATION OF DISCREPANT DOCUMENTS UNDER THIS DOCUMENTARY CREDIT.

+ALL BANKING CHARGES OUTSIDE THE ISSUING BANK ARE FOR ACCOUNT OF BENEFICIARY. NOTWITHSTANDING THE ABOVE, COSTS RELATING TO REIMBURSEMENT/PAYMENT ARE ALSO FOR ACCOUNT OF BENEFICIARY AND WILL BE DEDUCTED FROM PROCEEDS UPON PAYMENT.

+THE PRESENTING BANK'S SWIFT CODE MUST BE SHOWN ON THE BANKING SCHEDULE.

+ALL DOCUMENTS TO BE DISPATCHED TO ISSUING BANK IN ONE LOT BY FIRST AVAILABLE AIRMAIL THROUGH BANK. ISSUING BANK ADDRESS: BANK OF COMMUNICATIONS CO., LTD., JIANGSU PROVINCIAL BRANCH, SWIFT: COMMCNSHNJG

48   Period for Presentation

DOCUMENTS TO BE PRESENTED

WITHIN 21 DAYS AFTER

THE DATE OF SHIPMENT BUT WITHIN

THE VALIDITY OF THE CREDIT.

49   Confirmation Instructions

WITHOUT

78   Instr to Payg/Accptg/Negotg Bank

UPON RECEIPT OF THE DOCUMENTS AND DRAFT(S) IN STRICT COMPLIANCE WITH THE TERMS AND CONDITIONS OF THIS CREDIT, WE SHALL REIMBURSE THE NEGOTIATING BANK AS INSTRUCTED.

THIS IS THE OPERATIVE CREDIT INSTRUMENT AND NO AIRMAIL CONFIRMATION WILL FOLLOW.

72   Sender to Receiver Information

ATTN:TRANSACTION EXCHANGE CENTER

练习 4.5

南京的 HK MACHINE COMPANY 公司和 ICA CO., LTD., CHICAGO, U.S.A.签订合同，约定采用 L/C 方式进口货物 ELECTRONIC TUBE，金额为 USD40000，期限为 SIGHT。假设你是开证行交通银行的经办人员，收到下面的进口开证申请书，在落实开证相关条件后，如何发送 MT700 电文呢？假设银行编号是 LC2010001039。

IRREVOCABLE DOCUMENTARY CREDIT APPLICATION

TO：**BANK OF COMMUNICATIONS**   DATE: 20100612

BENEFICIARY (FULL NAME AND ADDRESS): ICA CO., LTD., CHICAGO, U.S.A.	L/C NO.: EX-CARD NO.: CONTRACT NO.: 30850
	DATE AND PLACE OF EXPIRY OF THE CREDIT: 101201 U.S.A.
PARTIAL SHIPMENTS TRANSSHIPMENT ☒ALLOWED ☒ALLOWED ☐NOT ALLOWED ☐NOT ALLOWED	☐BY AIRMAIL ☐WITH BRIEF ADVICE BY TELETRANSMISSION ☐BY EXPRESS DELIVERY
LOADING ON BOARD / DISPATCH / TAKING IN CHARGE AT / FROM: MAIN USA PORT	☐BY TELETRANSMISSION(WHICH SHALL BE THE OPERATIVE INSTRUMENT)
NOT LATER THAN: 100923 FOR TRANSPORTATION TO: SHANGHAI	AMOUNT (BOTH IN FIGURES AND WORDS): USD40,000.00 SAY US DOLLARS FORTY THOUSAND ONLY
DESCRIPTION OF GOODS: ELECTRONIC TUBE UNIT PRICE: USD 200 PER TUBE CFR SHANGHAI TOTAL AMOUNT: USD40,000.00 CFR SHANGHAI ORIGIN: U.S.A. PACKING:	CREDIT AVAILABLE WITH ☐ BY SIGHT PAYMENT ☐ BY ACCEPTANCE ☒ BY NEGOTIATION ☐ BY DEFERRED PAYMENT AT AGAINST THE DOCUMENTS DETAILED HEREIN ☐ AND BENEFICIARY'S DRAFT FOR % OF THE INVOICE VALUE AT ON
	☐ FOB ☒ CFR ☐CIF ☐ OR OTHER TERMS

DOCUMENTS REQUIRED: (MARKED WITH X)

1 .(X) SIGNED COMMERCIAL INVOICE IN 2 ORIGINALS AND 1 COPY INDICATING L/C NO.

2. (X) FULL SET OF CLEAN ON BOARD OCEAN BILLS OF LADING CONSIGNED TO APPLICANT, MARKED "FREIGHT (X) TO COLLECT / ( ) PREPAID" NOTIFYING THE APPLICANT WITH FULL NAME AND ADDRESS.

3. ( ) AIR WAYBILLS SHOWING "FREIGHT ( ) TO COLLECT / ( ) PREPAID" ( ) INDICATING FREIGHT AMOUNT AND CONSIGNED TO_____.

4. ( ) MEMORANDUM ISSUED BY _____CONSIGNED TO_____.

5. ( ) INSURANCE POLICY / CERTIFICATE IN _____ COPIES FOR _____% OF THE INVOICE VALUE SHOWING CLAIMS PAYABLE IN CHINA IN CURRENCY OF THE DRAFT, BLANK ENDORSED, COVERING ( ) OCEAN MARINE TRANSPORTATION / ( ) AIR TRANSPORTATION / ( ) OVER LAND TRANSPORTATION FOR ( ) ALL RISKS, ( ) WAR RISKS.

6. (X) PACKING LIST IN 1 ORIGINAL AND 3 COPIES INDICATING TOTAL GROSS WEIGHT, TOTAL NET WEIGHT AND TOTAL NUMBER OF CARTONS.

7. ( ) CERTIFICATE OF QUANTITY / WEIGHT IN__COPIES ISSUED BY AN INDEPENDENT SURVEYOR AT THE LOADING PORT, INDICATING THE ACTUAL SURVEYED QUANTITY / WEIGHT OF SHIPPED GOODS AS WELL AS THE PACKING CONDITION.

8. ( ) CERTIFICATE OF QUALITY IN ____ COPIES ISSUED BY ( ) MANUFACTURER / ( ) PUBLIC RECOGNIZED SURVEYOR / ( )

9. ( ) BENEFICIARY'S CERTIFIED COPY OF FAX DISPATCHED TO THE ACCOUNTEE WITH_____ DAYS AFTER SHIPMENT ADVISING ( ) NAME OF VESSEL / ( ) DATE, QUANTITY, WEIGHT AND VALUE OF SHIPMENT.

10. ( ) BENEFICIARY'S CERTIFICATE CERTIFYING THAT EXTRA COPIES OF THE DOCUMENTS HAVE BEEN DISPATCHED ACCORDING TO THE CONTRACT TERMS.

11. ( ) SHIPPING COMPANY'S CERTIFICATE ATTESTING THAT THE CARRYING VESSEL IS CHARTERED OR BOOKED BY ACCOUNTEE OR THEIR SHIPPING AGENTS:_____ .

12. ( ) OTHER DOCUMENTS, IF ANY:

  A) CERTIFICATE OF ORIGIN IN _____ ORIGINAL AND _____ COPY ATTESTED BY
   CHAMBER OF COMMERCE IN USA.

  B) CERTIFICATE OF HEALTH IN_____COPIES ISSUED BY AUTHORIZED INSTITUTION.

ADDITIONAL INSTRUCTIONS:

1. (X) ALL BANKING CHARGES OUTSIDE THE OPENING BANK ARE FOR BENEFICIARY'S ACCOUNT.

2. (X) DOCUMENTS MUST BE PRESENTED WITH 7 DAYS AFTER THE DATE OF ISSUANCE OF THE TRANSPORT DOCUMENTS BUT WITHIN THE VALIDITY OF THIS CREDIT.

3. ( ) THIRD PARTY AS SHIPPER IS NOT ACCEPTABLE. SHORT FORM / BLANK BACK B/L IS NOT ACCEPTABLE.

4. (X) BOTH QUANTITY AND AMOUNT 10 % MORE OR LESS ARE ALLOWED.

5. ( ) PREPAID FREIGHT DRAWN IN EXCESS OF L/C AMOUNT IS ACCEPTABLE AGAINST PRESENTATION OF ORIGINAL CHARGES VOUCHER ISSUED BY SHIPPING CO. / AIR LINE OR ITS AGENT.

6. ( ) ALL DOCUMENTS TO BE FORWARDED IN ONE COVER, UNLESS OTHERWISE STATED ABOVE.

7. ( ) OTHER TERMS, IF ANY:

ADVISING BANK:　BKCHUS33XXX

ACCOUNT NO.:

WITH _____ BANK OF COMMUNICATIONS CO., LTD., JIANGSU BR. _____ (NAME OF BANK) ___

TRANSACTED BY:

APPLICANT: _____ (NAME, SIGNATURE OF AUTHORIZED PERSON)

TELEPHONE NO.:

(WITH SEAL)　HK MACHINE COMPANY

MT700 电文

```
-------------------------- Message Header ------------------------

Swift Output    : FIN 700 Issue of a Documentary Credit
Sender        :
Receiver      :
-------------------------- Message Text ------------------------
    27    Sequence of Total
          Number
          Total
    40A   Form of Documentary Credit


    20    Documentary Credit Number


    31C   Date of Issue
```

40E　　Applicable Rules

31D　　Date and Place of Expiry
　　　　Date
　　　　Place

50　　　Applicant

59　　　Beneficiary － Name & Address

32B　　Currency Code, Amount
　　　　Currency
　　　　Amount

39A　　Percentage Credit Amt Tolerance
　　　　Tolerance 1
　　　　Tolerance 2

41D　　Available With...By... – Name & Address
　　　　Name And Address
　　　　Code

43P　　Partial Shipments

43T　　Transshipment

44E　　Port of Loading/Airport of Dep.

44F　　Port of Discharge/Airport of Dest.

44C　　Latest Date of Shipment

45A　　Description of Goods &/or Services

46A　　Documents Required

47A	Additional Conditions

48	Period for Presentation

49	Confirmation Instructions

78	Instr to Payg/Accptg/Negotg Bank

参考答案：

MT700 电文

-------------------------- Message Header --------------------------

Swift Output : FIN 700 Issue of a Documentary Credit

Sender : COMMCNSHNJG

Receiver : SCBLUS33XXX

-------------------------- Message Text --------------------------

27 Sequence of Total

Number 1

Total 1

40A Form of Documentary Credit

IRREVOCABLE

20 Documentary Credit Number

LC2010001039

31C Date of Issue

100612

40E Applicable Rules

UCP LATEST VERSION

31D Date and Place of Expiry

Date 100930

Place U.S.A.

50 Applicant

HK MACHINE COMPANY

59   Beneficiary – Name & Address

ICA CO., LTD., CHICAGO, U.S.A.

32B   Currency Code, Amount

Currency   USD

Amount   40,000.00

39A   Percentage Credit Amt Tolerance

Tolerance 1   10

Tolerance 2   10

41D   Available With...By... – Name& Address

Name And Address   ANY BANK IN USA

Code   BY NEGOTIATION

43P   Partial Shipments

ALLOWED

43T   Transshipment

ALLOWED

44E   Port of Loading/Airport of Dep.

MAIN PORTS IN U.S.A.

44F   Port of Discharge/Airport of Dest.

SHANGHAI, CHINA

44C   Latest Date of Shipment

100923

45A   Description of Goods &/or Services

ELECTRONIC TUBE

UNIT PRICE: USD 200 PER TUBE CFR SHANGHAI, CHINA

TOTAL AMOUNT: USD40,000.00 CFR SHANGHAI, CHINA

ORIGIN: U.S.A.

46A   Documents Required

+SIGNED COMMERCIAL INVOICE IN 2 ORIGINALS AND 1 COPY INDICATING
L/C NO.

+ FULL SET OF CLEAN ON BOARD OCEAN BILLS OF LADING CONSIGNED TO
APPLICANT,   MARKED "FREIGHT TO COLLECT" NOTIFYING THE APPLICANT.

+PACKING LIST / WEIGHT MEMO IN 1 ORIGINAL AND 3 COPIES

INDICATING TOTAL GROSS WEIGHT, TOTAL NET WEIGHT AND TOTAL NUMBER OF CARTONS.

47A Additional Conditions

+BOTH CREDIT AMOUNT AND QUANTITY 10PCT MORE OR LESS ARE ALLOWED.

+A DISCREPANCY FEE OF USD80.00(OR EQUIVALENT) PAYABLE BY BENEFICIARY SHALL BE DEDUCTED FROM THE PROCEEDS FOR EACH PRESENTATION OF DISCREPANT DOCUMENTS UNDER THIS DOCUMENTARY CREDIT.

+ALL BANKING CHARGES OUTSIDE THE ISSUING BANK ARE FOR ACCOUNT OF BENEFICIARY. NOTWITHSTANDING THE ABOVE, COSTS RELATING TO REIMBURSEMENT/PAYMENT ARE ALSO FOR ACCOUNT OF BENEFICIARY AND WILL BE DEDUCTED FROM PROCEEDS UPON PAYMENT.

+THE PRESENTING BANK'S SWIFT CODE MUST BE SHOWN ON THE BANKING SCHEDULE.

+ALL DOCUMENTS TO BE DISPATCHED TO ISSUING BANK IN ONE LOT BY FIRST AVAILABLE AIRMAIL THROUGH BANK. ISSUING BANK ADDRESS:BANK OF COMMUNICATIONS CO., LTD., JIANGSU PROVINCIAL BRANCH, SWIFT:COMMCNSHNJG

48 Period for Presentation

DOCUMENTS TO BE PRESENTED

WITHIN 7 DAYS AFTER

THE DATE OF SHIPMENT BUT WITHIN

THE VALIDITY OF THE CREDIT.

49 Confirmation Instructions

WITHOUT

78 Instr to Payg/Accptg/Negotg Bank

UPON RECEIPT OF THE DOCUMENTS AND DRAFTS IN STRICT COMPLIANCE WITH THE TERMS AND CONDITIONS OF THIS CREDIT, WE SHALL ACCEPT THE DRAFTS AND REIMBURSE THE PRESENTING BANK AS INSTRUCTED AT MATURITY.

THIS IS THE OPERATIVE CREDIT INSTRUMENT AND NO AIRMAIL CONFIRMATION WILL FOLLOW.

2010 年 6 月 14 日，在开证银行开出信用证后，进口商又要求修改信用证的装效期。下面是进口商提交的进口信用证开证补充协议。

进口信用证开证补充协议

协议编号   年   第   号

甲方(开证银行)：交通银行江苏省分行

乙方(开证申请人)：HK MACHINE COMPANY

开证申请人(以下称乙方)因进口业务需要申请开证银行(以下称甲方)开立信用证。甲方根据乙方申请已开立信用证(编号：LC2010001039)，后乙方因客户要求需将该信用证：

1. 效期___2010 年 9 月 30 日___改为___2010 年 10 月 30 日___；

2. 装期___2010 年 9 月 23 日___改为___2010 年 9 月 30 日___；

故甲方按乙方要求将该信用证进行修改。现经甲、乙双方平等协商，达成以下协议。

一、本协议就该信用证修改部分所产生的甲、乙双方的权利义务按原协议的规定处理。

二、本协议作为原协议的补充协议，具有同等的法律效力。甲、乙双方均应遵守。

本协议一式___两___份，签约方各执一份，副本数备查。

甲方(公章)   乙方(公章)

法定代表人(或授权代理人)   法定代表人(或授权代理人)

经办人   经办人

                                                    合同签订日期：2010 年 6 月 14 日

                                                    合同签订地：江苏省南京市

交行收到此申请，在落实了相关开证条件后，如何编写电文 MT707？

MT707 电文

```
------------------------- Message Header -------------------------
Swift Output    : FIN 707 Amendment to a Doc Credit
Sender          :
Receiver        :
------------------------- Message Text -------------------------


    20      Sender's Reference


    21      Receiver's Reference


    31C     Date of Issue
```

30	Date of Amendment

26E	Number of Amendment

59	Beneficiary (before amndmt)-Nm & Add
	Name And Address

31E	New Date of Expiry

44C	Latest Date of Shipment

79	Narrative

参考答案:

MT707 电文

```
------------------------- Message Header -------------------------
Swift Output    : FIN 707Amendment to a Doc Credit
Sender          : COMMCNSHNJG
Receiver        : SCBLUS33XXX
------------------------- Message Text -------------------------
    20      Sender's Reference
            LC2010001039
    21      Receiver's Reference
            UNKNOWN
    31C     Date of Issue
            100612
    30      Date of Amendment
            100614
    26E     Number of Amendment
            02
    59      Beneficiary (before amndmt)-Nm & Add
            Name And Address    ICA CO., LTD., CHICAGO, U.S.A.
    31E     New Date of Expiry
            101030
```

44C　　Latest Date of Shipment

100930

79　　Narrative

ADDITIONAL CONDITIONS:

ALL OTHER TERMS AND CONDITIONS OF THE L/C REMAIN

UNALTERED. PLS ADVISE THE AMENDMENT TO

BENEFICIARY.

REGARDS(IMPORT DEPT.)

练习 4.6

南京的 YUFAN CORPORATION 和 KOWA COMPANY LTD., TOKYO BRANCH 签订合同，约定采用 L/C 方式进口货物 IODINE PRILLS (99.8PCT)，金额为 USD320000.00，期限为 60 DAYS AFTER DELIVERY ORDER DATE。开证行交通银行收到下面的进口开证申请书，在落实开证相关条件后，如何发送 MT700 电文呢？假设银行编号是 LC201000678。

IRREVOCABLE DOCUMENTARY CREDIT APPLICATION

TO: **BANK OF COMMUNICATIONS**　　　　　　　DATE: 20100329

BENEFICIARY (FULL NAME AND ADDRESS): KOWA COMPANY LTD., TOKYO BRANCH		L/C NO.: EX-CARD NO.: CONTRACT NO.:
		DATE AND PLACE OF EXPIRY OF THE CREDIT: 100715　JAPAN
PARTIAL SHIPMENTS ☒ALLOWED ☐NOT ALLOWED	TRANSSHIPMENT ☒ALLOWED ☐NOT ALLOWED	☐BY AIRMAIL ☐WITH BRIEF ADVICE BY TELETRANSMISSION ☐BY EXPRESS DELIVERY ☐BY TELETRANSMISSION(WHICH SHALL BE THE OPERATIVE INSTRUMENT)
LOADING ON BOARD / DISPATCH / TAKING IN CHARGE AT / FROM: SHANGHAI WAIGAOQIAO BONDED WAREHOUSE, CHINA NOT LATER THAN: 100415 FOR TRANSPORTATION TO: SHANGHAI, CHINA		AMOUNT (BOTH IN FIGURES AND WORDS): USD320,000.00 SAY US DOLLARS THREE HUNDRED TWENTY THOUSAND ONLY

DESCRIPTION OF GOODS: IODINE PRILLS (99.8PCT) UNIT PRICE:USD29,700.00/MT FCA SHANGHAI WAIGAOQIAO BONDED WAREHOUSE, CHINA QUANTITY: 10.7744 MTS TOTAL AMOUNT:USD320,000.00 FCA SHANGHAI WAIGAOQIAO BONDED WAREHOUSE, CHINA PACKING: IN 50.00 KGS FIBRE DRUM ORIGIN: CHILE/SQM	CREDIT AVAILABLE WITH ☐ BY SIGHT PAYMENT ☐ BY ACCEPTANCE ☒ BY NEGOTIATION 60 DAYS AFTER DELIVERY ORDER DATE ☐ BY DEFERRED PAYMENT AT AGAINST THE DOCUMENTS DETAILED HEREIN ☐ AND BENEFICIARY'S DRAFT FOR % OF THE INVOICE VALUE AT ON
PACKING:	☐ FOB ☐ CFR ☐CIF ☒ OR OTHER TERMS FCA

DOCUMENTS REQUIRED:

+SIGNED COMMERCIAL INVOICE IN 2 ORIGINALS AND 2 COPIES INDICATING L/C NO. AND CONTRACT NO. 050020.

+PACKING LIST/WEIGHT MEMO IN 3 COPIES ISSUED BY MANUFACTURER.

+CERTIFICATE OF ANALYSIS IN 3 COPIES ISSUED BY MANUFACTURER.

+CERTIFICATE OF ORIGIN IN 3 COPIES ISSUED BY MANUFACTURER.

+DELIVERY ORDER IN 1 ORIGINAL ISSUED BY SQM EUROPE N.V. DATED NOT LATER THAN APR. 15, 2010.

( ) OTHER DOCUMENTS, IF ANY:

ADDITIONAL INSTRUCTIONS: (MARKED WITH X)

1. (X) ALL BANKING CHARGES OUTSIDE THE OPENING BANK ARE FOR BENEFICIARY'S ACCOUNT.

2. (X) DOCUMENTS MUST BE PRESENTED WITH 21 DAYS AFTER THE DATE OF ISSUANCE OF THE TRANSPORT DOCUMENTS BUT WITHIN THE VALIDITY OF THIS CREDIT.

3. ( ) THIRD PARTY AS SHIPPER IS NOT ACCEPTABLE. SHORT FORM / BLANK BACK B/L IS NOT ACCEPTABLE.

4. (X) BOTH QUANTITY AND AMOUNT 10 % MORE OR LESS ARE ALLOWED.

5. ( ) PREPAID FREIGHT DRAWN IN EXCESS OF L/C AMOUNT IS ACCEPTABLE AGAINST PRESENTATION OF ORIGINAL CHARGES VOUCHER ISSUED BY SHIPPING CO. / AIR LINE OR ITS AGENT.

6. (　) ALL DOCUMENTS TO BE FORWARDED IN ONE COVER, UNLESS OTHERWISE STATED ABOVE.

7. (　) OTHER TERMS, IF ANY:

ADVISING BANK:　SMBCJPJTXXX

ACCOUNT NO.:

WITH _____ BANK OF COMMUNICATIONS CO., LTD., JIANGSU BR. ____ (NAME OF BANK) ____

TRANSACTED BY:

APPLICANT: _____ (NAME, SIGNATURE OF AUTHORIZED PERSON)

TELEPHONE NO.:

(WITH SEAL)　YUFAN CORPORATION

MT700 电文

```
-------------------------- Message Header ------------------------
Swift Output     : FIN 700 Issue of a Documentary Credit
Sender           :
Receiver         :
-------------------------- Message Text ----------------------------
    27     Sequence of Total
           Number
           Total
    40A    Form of Documentary Credit

    20     Documentary Credit Number

    31C    Date of Issue

    40E    Applicable Rules

    31D    Date and Place of Expiry
           Date
           Place
    50     Applicant
```

59   Beneficiary – Name & Address

32B   Currency Code, Amount
      Currency
      Amount

39A   Percentage Credit Amt Tolerance
      Tolerance 1
      Tolerance 2

41D   Available With...By... – Name & Addr
      Name And Address
      Code

42C   Drafts at...

42A   Drawee - BIC
      BIC

43P   Partial Shipments

43T   Transshipment

44A   Pl of Tking in Chrg / of Rceipt

44B   Pl of Final Dest / of Delivery

44C   Latest Date of Shipment

45A   Description of Goods &/or Services

46A   Documents Required

47A	Additional Conditions

48	Period for Presentation

49	Confirmation Instructions

78	Instr to Payg/Accptg/Negotg Bank

参考答案：

MT700 电文

-------------------------- Message Header ------------------------

Swift Output : FIN 700 Issue of a Documentary Credit

Sender : COMMCNSHNJG

Receiver : SMBCJPJTXXX

-------------------------- Message Text ------------------------

27	Sequence of Total	
	Number	1
	Total	1
40A	Form of Documentary Credit	
	IRREVOCABLE	
20	Documentary Credit Number	
	LC201000678	
31C	Date of Issue	
	100329	
40E	Applicable Rules	
	UCP LATEST VERSION	
31D	Date and Place of Expiry	
	Date	100715
	Place	JAPAN
50	Applicant	

YUFAN CORPORATION

NO. 112 ZHONGSHAN SOUTH ROAD, JIANGNING

DEVELOPMENT ZONE, NANJING, 211100, P.R.C.

59   Beneficiary – Name & Address

      Name And Address   KOWA COMPANY LTD., TOKYO BRANCH

                            (ADDRESS SEE FIELD 47A)

32B   Currency Code, Amount

      Currency   USD

      Amount   320,000.00

39A   Percentage Credit Amt Tolerance

      Tolerance 1   10

      Tolerance 2   10

41D   Available With...By... – Name & Address

      Name And Address   ANY BANK IN JAPAN

      Code   BY NEGOTIATION

42C   Drafts at...

      60 DAYS AFTER DELIVERY ORDER DATE

      FOR 100PCT INVOICE VALUE

42A   Drawee - BIC

      BIC   COMMCNSHNJG

43P   Partial Shipments

      ALLOWED

43T   Transshipment

      ALLOWED

44A   Pl of Tking in Chrg / of Rceipt

      SHANGHAI WAIGAOQIAO BONDED WAREHOUSE, CHINA

44B   Pl of Final Dest / of Delivery

      SHANGHAI, CHINA

44C   Latest Date of Shipment

      100415

45A   Description of Goods &/or Services

      COMMODITY: IODINE PRILLS (99.8PCT)

      UNIT PRICE: USD29,700.00/MT FCA SHANGHAI WAIGAOQIAO BONDED

      WAREHOUSE, CHINA

      QUANTITY: 10.7744 MTS

      TOTAL AMOUNT:USD320,000.00 FCA SHANGHAI WAIGAOQIAO BONDED

      WAREHOUSE, CHINA

PACKING: IN 50.00 KGS FIBRE DRUM

ORIGIN: CHILE/SQM

46A   Documents Required

+SIGNED COMMERCIAL INVOICE IN 2 ORIGINALS AND 2 COPIES
INDICATING L/C NO. AND CONTRACT NO. 050020.

+PACKING LIST/WEIGHT MEMO IN 3 COPIES ISSUED BY MANUFACTURER.

+CERTIFICATE OF ANALYSIS IN 3 COPIES ISSUED BY MANUFACTURER.

+CERTIFICATE OF ORIGIN IN 3 COPIES ISSUED BY MANUFACTURER.

+DELIVERY ORDER IN 1 ORIGINAL ISSUED BY SQM EUROPE N.V. DATED
NOT LATER THAN APR. 15, 2010.

47A   Additional Conditions

+APPLICANT'S TEL: 86-25-52782933   FAX:86-25-52782926

+BENEFICIARY'S ADD:

BLDG.6F 4-10, 3-CHOME, NIHONBASHI-HONCHO, CHUO-KU, TOKYO
103-0023, JAPAN

+BOTH CREDIT AMOUNT AND QUANTITY 10PCT MORE OR LESS ARE ALLOWED.

+A DISCREPANCY FEE OF USD80.00(OR EQUIVALENT) PAYABLE BY
BENEFICIARY SHALL BE DEDUCTED FROM THE PROCEEDS FOR EACH
PRESENTATION OF DISCREPANT DOCUMENTS UNDER THIS DOCUMENTARY
CREDIT.

+THE PRESENTING BANK'S SWIFT CODE MUST BE SHOWN ON THE BANKING
SCHEDULE.

+ALL BANKING CHARGES OUTSIDE CHINA ARE FOR ACCOUNT OF
BENEFICIARY. NOTWITHSTANDING THE ABOVE, COSTS RELATING TO
REIMBURSEMENT/PAYMENT ARE ALSO FOR ACCOUNT OF BENEFICIARY AND
WILL BE DEDUCTED FROM PROCEEDS UPON PAYMENT.

+ALL DOCUMENTS TO BE DISPATCHED TO ISSUING BANK IN ONE LOT BY FIRST
AVAILABLE AIRMAIL THROUGH BANK. ISSUING BANK ADDRESS: BANK OF
COMMUNICATIONS CO., LTD., JIANGSU PROVINCIAL BRANCH, SWIFT: COMMCNSHNJG

48   Period for Presentation

DOCUMENTS TO BE PRESENTED WITHIN

21 DAYS FROM THE DATE OF DELIVERY

ORDER BUT WITHIN THE VALIDITY OF THE CREDIT.

49   Confirmation Instructions

WITHOUT

78　Instr to Payg/Accptg/Negotg Bank

UPON RECEIPT OF THE DOCUMENTS AND DRAFTS IN STRICT COMPLIANCE WITH THE TERMS AND CONDITIONS OF THIS CREDIT, WE SHALL ACCEPT THE DRAFTS AND REIMBURSE THE PRESENTING BANK AS INSTRUCTED AT MATURITY.

THIS IS THE OPERATIVE CREDIT INSTRUMENT AND NO AIRMAIL CONFIRMATION WILL FOLLOW.

第三节　开证行付汇

一、业务场景与操作

1. 进口来单

当开证行开出信用证后，正常情况下会在该信用证的效期内收到出口方银行寄交的索汇面函、单据等。开证行需在收单后五个工作日内及时审核单据，确定其表面与信用证条款是否相符。当开证行对即期付款信用证的单据审核无误后，即从进口商账户收取款项对外付款，对外付款时严格按照寄单行的付汇指示付款。开证行应严格按照国际惯例处理进口来单，避免卷入贸易纠纷。

开证行对外付款电文是 MT799/756 和 MT202。开证行付款后将出具信用证来单付汇通知书并连同单据一起交给进口商。对于远期信用证，开证行应向出口方银行发出到期付款承兑电，并于到期日从进口商账户收取款项支付给出口方银行。

下面是案例 4.1 中的出口方银行(BANK OF NOVA SCOTIA，SWIFT No.为 NOSCDEFF)的索汇面函。

DOCUMENTARY REMITTANCE

BANK OF NOVA SCOTIA

SWIFT: NOSCDEFF

ORIGINAL

MAIL TO:

BANK OF COMMUNICATIONS, JIANGSU PROVINCIAL BRANCH NO. 124 NORTH ZHONGSHAN ROAD ATTN: L/C DEPT.

DATE: 20100610

IN ALL CORRESPONDENCE PLS QUOTE OUR REF. NO. 2132/18135.

WE ENCLOSE HEREWITH THE RELATIVE DOCUMENTS FOR PAYMENT PERTAINING TO THE CREDIT MENTIONED BELOW.

CREDIT NO.: LC201000928

ISSUED BY: BANK OF COMMUNICATIONS, JIANGSU PROVINCIAL BRANCH

APPL: ABC COMPANY, NANJING, CHINA

BENE: ALLEN CO., LTD., P.O. BOX 3254, GERMANY

INVOICE NO.: 20100001

1ST	2ND	DOCUMENTS	BILL AMOUNT: USD236,994.50	
2/2		DRAFT	TENOR: 90 DAYS AFTER B/L DATE	
3/3		COMM. INV.	MATURITY:20100901	
3/3		B/L		
4/4		PKG LIST		
2/2		INSURANCE POLICY		
2/2		ORIGIN CERT		
3/3		B/L COPY		
1/1		BANK COPY		

PLEASE PAY/REMIT VIA CHIPS THE ABOVE TOTAL AMOUNT USD236994.50 TO BANK OF NOVA SCOTIA, NEW YORK FOR CREDIT ACCOUNT NO. 12345678 WITH THEM AT MATURITY   UNDER YOUR/THEIR TELEX/SWIFT ADVICE TO US QUOTING OUR ABOVE REF. NO. 2132/18135.

REMARKS:

X)THE BILL AMOUNT HAS BEEN ENDORSED ON THE REVERSE OF THE ORIGINAL L/C.

THIS TRANSACTION IS SUBJECT TO THE UNIFORM CUSTOMS AND PRACTICE FOR DOCUMENTARY CREDIT 2007 REVISION, ICC PUBLICATION NO. 600.

2. 来单付汇

　　开证行交行在审核单证一致后，要对外发送承兑电文，因为案例 4.1 中的信用证是远期信用证。在对外发送承兑电文的同时，还要出具信用证来单付汇通知书，连同单据一起交给进口商做承兑。下面是信用证来单付汇通知书。

信用证来单付汇通知书

致：ABC COMPANY　　　　　　我行付款编号：LP201001173

进口合同号：30850

寄单行：BANK OF NOVA SCOTIA, GERMANY　来单金额：USD236994.50

付款期限：90 DAYS AFTER B/L DATE

信用证号码：LC201000928

寄单行编号：2132/18135 最后付款/承兑日期：20100901

兹将上述信用证项下的全套单据附上，请贵公司认真审核并注意以下事项：

【√】按照信用证条款和国际商会 UCP600 规定，如贵公司审核单据认为存在不符点，决定拒付/拒绝承兑，请务必于两个工作日内以书面形式(加盖公司章)通知我行，并将全套单据退回我行。如我行根据国际惯例审核不符点不成立，或贵公司未能及时将全套单据退回我行，贵公司仍须承担到期付款/承兑责任，我行将按期对外付款/承兑，并有权主动从贵公司账户中扣款。如我行未在两个工作日内接到贵公司的任何书面通知，将视同贵公司同意付款/承兑，我行将按期对外付款/承兑，并有权主动从贵公司账户扣款，由此造成的一切损失由贵公司承担。

【 】按照信用证条款和国际商会 UCP600 规定，我行审核单据时发现下列所示不符点(此不符点陈列即代表开证申请书中所提不符点通知书，我行不再发通知)。请贵公司于两个工作日内决定是否接受不符点，并以书面形式(加盖贵公司章)通知我行。如贵公司接受不符点，我行将按期对外付款/承兑，并有权主动从贵公司账户中扣款；如贵公司不接受不符点，需将全套单据退回我行，由我行对外拒付/拒绝承兑。如我行未在两个工作日内接到贵公司的任何书面通知，将视为贵公司不接受所有不符点，由我行对外拒付/拒绝承兑，由此造成的一切损失由贵公司承担。

【√】根据国家外汇管理局有关外汇付汇核销的规定，我行已从国外来单中抽取提单、发票副本各一份。

【√】如果已接受该笔来单的电提不符点，不得拒付。

【√】如果已办理该来单项下提单背书/提货担保，不得拒付。

汇票(DRAFT)	2/2*1
发票(COMM. INV.)	3/3*1
提单(B/L)	3/3*1
B/L COPY	3/3*1
装箱单(PKG LIST)	4/4*1
保险单(INSUR POLICY/CERT)	2/2*1
产地证(ORIGIN CERT.)	2/2*1
BANK COPY	1*1

不符点提示： 无

如发现所附单据中有不属于贵公司的内容，请速与江苏省分行国际部联系，

电话号码　　　　　　联系人

银行签章

进口商回复：

我公司已收到全套单据并对其进行了审核，现就有关事项答复如下：

1. 我公司同意对外承兑/付款。

2. 远期单据到期时，请于到期日主动对外付款，我公司不再另行通知。

3. 该单据项下货款及银行费用，请你主动从我公司在你行的_____账户中扣付。

日期：　　　　年　　月　　日

3. 到期付款

开证行在信用证规定的付款日对外进行付款，所发的报文是 MT799 和 MT202。一个完整的进口业务流程就此完成。

图 4.1 为案例 4.1 的业务流程图。

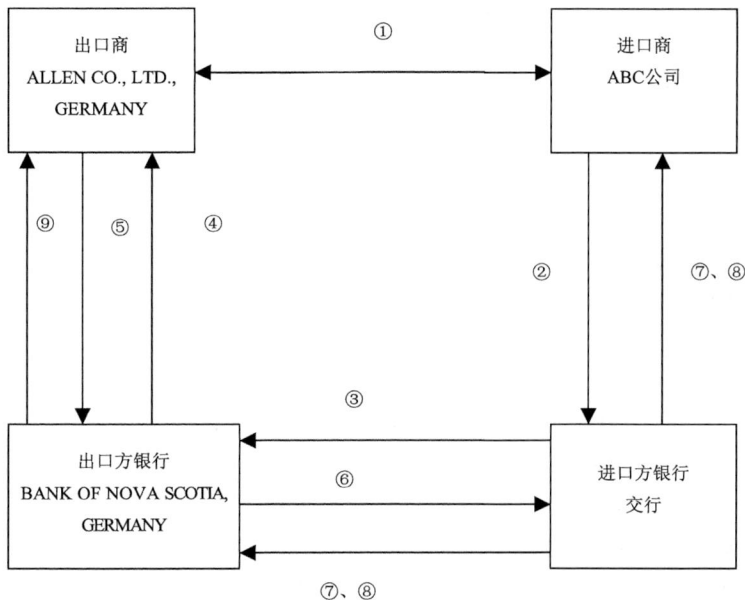

图 4.1　案例 4.1 的业务流程图

① 进口商 ABC 公司和出口商德国 ALLEN CO., LTD.签订贸易合同，约定采用 L/C 支付方式。
② 进口商向交行申请开立信用证。
③ 交行按有关规定审核并落实相关资金，手续齐备后向出口方银行 BANK OF NOVA SCOTIA, GERMANY 发送 MT700 电文。
④ 出口方银行通知此证。
⑤ 出口商交单据给出口方银行审核。(不一定是通知行，符合 L/C 要求即可。)
⑥ 出口方银行审核单据后寄送单据和出口银行索汇面函给进口方银行。
⑦ 即期信用证项下，交行审核单据一致后，付款给出口交单银行，之后出具信用证来单付汇通知书连同单据给进口商，同时扣减进口商在银行的款项。
⑧ 在远期信用证项下，交行审核单据一致后，发电文给出口交单银行，告知承兑到期日。之后，出具信用证来单付汇通知书连同单据给进口商做承兑。到期后，交行付款给出口交单银行，之后扣减进口商在银行的款项。
⑨ 出口交单银行收到头寸后，付款给出口商。

4. 电文处理

按进口业务流程来看，分为以下几种情况，以案例 4.1 为例说明。

(1) 如果是远期信用证，即案例中所示 90 DAYS AFTER B/L DATE 20100531，则开证行收到出口方银行提交的单据并审核后，如果单证一致，应该发承兑电文。承兑电文格式如下：

MT799 电文

```
------------------------- Message Header -------------------------
Swift Output    : FIN 799 Free Format Message
Sender          : COMMCNSHNJG
Receiver        : NOSCDEFFXXX
------------------------- Message Text -------------------------

    20      Transaction Reference Number
            LP201001173
    21      Related Reference
            2132/18135
    79      Narrative
            PLS BE ADVISED THAT YOUR A/M DOCUMENTS DD
            20100611 DRAWN UNDER OUR L/C NO.
            LC201000928 ARE ACCEPTED DUE ON 20100901.
            WE WILL EFFECT PAYMENT FOR USD236,994.50 AT
            MATURITY DATE AS PER YOUR INSTRUCTIONS SHOWN
            ON YOUR COVERING LETTER AND OUR CHARGES
            TOTALLY FOR USD140.00 INCLUDING USD60.00 AS
            TELECOMM CHARGE AND USD80.00 AS REIMBURSING
            CHARGE WILL BE DEDUCTED FROM PROCEEDS.
```

(2) 开证行收到出口方银行提交的单据并审核后，如果单证一致，开证行对外承兑，电文见(1)，付款到期时，开证行应立即对外付款。付款电文格式如下。

请注意：若信用证为即期，则不存在承兑环节，在 5 个工作日内，若单证一致，及时对外付款，若不一致，则对外拒付。

MT799 电文

```
------------------------- Message Header -------------------------
Swift Output    : FIN 799 Free Format Message
Sender          : COMMCNSHNJG
Receiver        : NOSCDEFFXXX
------------------------- Message Text -------------------------
```

20　Transaction Reference Number
LP201001173
21　Related Reference
2132/18135
79　Narrative
PLEASE BE ADVISED THAT WE HAVE
EFFECTED PAYMENT FOR USD236,994.50
VALUE DATE 20100604 THROUGH
CITIUS33 AS PER YOUR INSTRUCTIONS.

MT202 付款电文

------------------------- Message Header -------------------------
Swift Output　　　　: FIN 202 General Fin Inst Transfer
Sender　　　　　　: COMMCNSHNJG
Receiver　　　　　: NOSCUS33XXX
------------------------- Message Text -------------------------

20　Transaction Reference Number
LP201001173
21　Related Reference
2132/18135
32A　Value Date, Currency Code, Amt
Date　　　　　100604
Currency　　　USD
Amount　　　　236,854.50
53A　Sender's Correspondent – BIC
BIC　　　　　COMMCNSHXXX
58A　Beneficiary Institution – BIC
Party Identifier　/12345678
BIC　　　　　NOSCDEFF
72　Sender to Receiver Information
/BNF/LC201000928
//LESS USD60 AS TELE. CHAR. AND
//USD80 AS REIM. CHAR.

（备注：USD60 是交行电报费，USD80 是手续费，相关银行费用在对外付款时扣除。）

二、风险控制

开证行拒付的风险

对于开证银行来讲，拒付掌握的原则是以事实为依据，以国际惯例为准则，独立审单，并根据单据表面是否相符做出付款、承兑或拒付的决定。要注意对已承兑信用证的拒付问题，这里有一个关于禁付令的例子。如案例 4.1 中是远期证，如果出口商欺诈证据确凿，法院下达了禁付令，但开证行已经对远期信用证项下的汇票做了承兑，出口商已经凭开证行的承兑办理贴现，这时对已承兑远期信用证项下货物进行冻结就损害了无辜第三者的利益。此时，对银行来说，该欺诈并不构成冻结信用证的充分条件。在有限制的欺诈例外原则中，对此点阐明得很清楚，即在明显存在受益人欺诈的情况下，能不能冻结信用证项下货款，还要看是否存在善意的第三人，如果有善意的第三人，则不能冻结信用证项下货款。而对进口商而言，如果真的货款冻结了，则应认真处理冻结项下货款，不能以信用证项下付款的冻结作为逼迫出口商履行合同的筹码，使得信用证项下票据责任成为一种极不严肃的事情，也损害了法律执行的严肃性。

无论是即期还是远期证，如果审核单据有不符点，则需发 MT734 拒付电文免除开证行或保兑行(如有)第一性的付款责任，同时联系进口商。若进口商同意接受不符点，则可对外付款并发付款电文。

开证行发 MT734 拒付电文时应注意：当开证行或保兑行(如有)决定拒绝时，必须明确表明拒绝，同时在电文内容中必须一次性将所有不符点全部列出并对单据如何处理做出说明。

(1) 银行持有单据等候提示人进一步指示；或
(2) 开证行持有单据直至收到申请人通知弃权并同意接受该弃权，或在同意接受弃权前从提示人处收到进一步指示；或
(3) 银行退回单据；或
(4) 银行按照先前从提示人处收到的指示行事。

MT734 拒付电文的格式如下：

```
------------------------- Message Header -------------------------
Swift Output        : FIN 734 Advice of Refusal
Sender              :
Receiver            :
------------------------- Message Text -------------------------
20    Sender's TRN
```

21　　Presenting Bank's Reference

32A　　Date and Amount of Utilization

　　　Date

　　　Currency

　　　Amount

72　　Sender to Receiver Information

77J　　Discrepancies

77B　　Disposal of Documents

三、总结思考

近年来，许多银行的进口信用证被动垫款的数额急剧增加，外汇不良资产比例不断提高，严重制约了其国际业务的持续稳定发展。信用证被动垫款的大量增加，除了与金融危机及我国总体外贸形势不景气等客观因素有关外，还与银行对进口开证业务风险分析的薄弱及风险防范的滞后有关系。

开证行除上述拒付风险外，还应注意处理流程上的风险。银行员工在处理业务中的每一个环节时都应该按相关的规章制度进行，在这里提醒以下几点。

(1) 仔细审查开证申请书，如申请书上有自相矛盾或不符合国际惯例的条款，必须与进口商联系做修改。

(2) 严格按照国际惯例处理进口来单，避免卷入贸易纠纷。

(3) 对外付款时严格按照寄单行的付汇指示付款。

(4) 处理背对背信用证业务时，应该特别注意把子证与母证的关系衔接好，避免两证脱节，加大子证的开证风险。

四、实训操练

练习 4.7

EFG 公司与新加坡 AGILENT TECHNOLOGIES SINGAPORE(SALES)PTE LTD. 签订合同，约定采用 L/C 方式进口货物 AGILENT 1200 HPLC SYSTEM，金额为 USD94000，期限为即期。进口方银行交通银行电开信用证 MT700 如下。信用证编号是 LC201000929，选择新加坡 CHASSGSGXXX 为通知行。

MT700 电文

```
------------------------ Message Header ------------------------
Swift Output     : FIN 700 Issue of a Documentary Credit
Sender           : COMMCNSHNJG
Receiver         : CHASSGSGXXX
------------------------ Message Text ------------------------
```

27	Sequence of Total	
	Number	1
	Total	1

40A	Form of Documentary Credit
	IRREVOCABLE

20	Documentary Credit Number
	LC201000929

31C	Date of Issue
	100507

40E	Applicable Rules
	UCP LATEST VERSION

31D	Date and Place of Expiry	
	Date	100831
	Place	SINGAPORE

50	Applicant
	EFG COMPANY, NANJING

59	Beneficiary – Name & Address	
	Name And Address	AGILENT TECHNOLOGIES SINGAPORE(SALES)PTE LTD. ADDRESS: NO.1, YISHUN AVE 7, SINGAPORE, 768923

32B	Currency Code, Amount	
	Currency	USD
	Amount	94,000.00

41D	Available With...By... – Name&Addr	
	Name And Address	ANY BANK IN SINGAPORE
	Code	BY PAYEMNT

42C	Drafts at...

AT SIGHT FOR 100.0PCT INVOICE VALUE

42A　Drawee - BIC

　　　BIC　　　　　　　　COMMCNSHNJG

43P　Partial Shipments

　　　NOT ALLOWED

43T　Transshipment

　　　ALLOWED

44E　Port of Loading/Airport of Dep.

　　　SINGAPORE AIRPORT

44F　Port of Dischrge/Airport of Dest.

　　　NANJING AIRPORT, CHINA

44C　Latest Date of Shipment

　　　100709

45A　Description of Goods &/or Services

　　　COMMODITY: AGILENT 1200 HPLC SYSTEM

　　　QUANTITY: 2 SETS

　　　UNIT PRICE: USD 47,000.00/SET FCA SINGAPORE AIRPORT, SINGAPORE

　　　TOTAL AMOUNT: USD 94,000.00 FCA SINGAPORE AIRPORT, SINGAPORE

46A　Documents Required

　　　+SIGNED COMMERCIAL INVOICE IN QUINTUPLICATE INDICATING CONTRACT
　　　NO. 20100412/CTTQ, L/C NO., AND SHIPPING MARK.

　　　+ORIGINAL AIR WAYBILL SHOWING 'FREIGHT TO COLLECT' CONSIGNED TO
　　　APPLICANT INDICATING FREIGHT AMOUNT.

　　　+PACKING LIST/WEIGHT LIST IN DUPLICATE INDICATING QUANTITY/GROSS AND
　　　NET WEIGHT OF EACH PACKAGE AND PACKING CONDITIONS.

　　　+ BENEFICIARY'S CERTIFIED COPY OF FAX DISPATCHED TO THE APPLICANT
　　　WITH 24 HOURS AFTER SHIPMENT ADVISING NAME OF VESSEL, DATE,
　　　QUANTITY, WEIGHT AND VALUE OF SHIPMENT.

47A　Additional Conditions

　　　+APPLICANT'S ADD: NO.9 HUI'OU ROAD, NANJING ECONOMIC AND
　　　TECHNOLOGICAL DEVELOPMENT ZONE, NANJING, 210038

　　　+THIRD PARTY AS SHIPPER IS NOT ACCEPTABLE.

　　　+SHORT FORM/BLANK BACK B/L IS NOT ACCEPTABLE.

　　　+ON DECK SHIPMENT IS NOT ALLOWED.

+A DISCREPANCY FEE OF USD80.00(OR EQUIVALENT) PAYABLE BY BENEFICIARY SHALL BE DEDUCTED FROM THE PROCEEDS FOR EACH PRESENTATION OF DISCREPANT DOCUMENTS UNDER THIS DOCUMENTARY CREDIT.

+ALL BANKING CHARGES OUTSIDE THE ISSUING BANK ARE FOR ACCOUNT OF BENEFICIARY. NOTWITHSTANDING THE ABOVE, COSTS RELATING TO REIMBURSEMENT/PAYMENT ARE ALSO FOR ACCOUNT OF BENEFICIARY AND WILL BE DEDUCTED FROM PROCEEDS UPON PAYMENT.

+THE PRESENTING BANK'S SWIFT CODE MUST BE SHOWN ON THE BANKING SCHEDULE.

+ALL DOCUMENTS TO BE DISPATCHED TO ISSUING BANK IN ONE LOT BY FIRST AVAILABLE AIRMAIL THROUGH BANK. ISSUING BANK ADDRESS: BANK OF COMMUNICATIONS CO., LTD., JIANGSU PROVINCIAL BRANCH, SWIFT: COMMCNSHNJG

48   Period for Presentation

DOCUMENTS TO BE PRESENTED

WITHIN 21 DAYS AFTER

THE DATE OF SHIPMENT BUT WITHIN

THE VALIDITY OF THE CREDIT.

49   Confirmation Instructions

WITHOUT

78   Instr to Payg/Accptg/Negotg Bank

UPON RECEIPT OF THE DOCUMENTS AND DRAFT(S) IN STRICT COMPLIANCE WITH THE TERMS AND CONDITIONS OF THIS CREDIT, WE SHALL REIMBURSE THE NEGOTIATING BANK AS INSTRUCTED.

THIS IS THE OPERATIVE CREDIT INSTRUMENT AND NO AIRMAIL CONFIRMATION WILL FOLLOW.

72   Sender to Receiver Information

ATTN: TRANSACTION EXCHANGE CENTER

在开出上述信用证后，开证行收到出口方银行(SWIFT No.为 CHASSGSG)寄交的索汇面函、单据等。开证行及时核对，证实单据表面与信用证条款相符后，向出口方银行发出到期付款电。假设银行编号是 LP201001386。

出口方银行面函

DOCUMENTARY REMITTANCE
CHASE BANK OF SINGAPORE

SWIFT: CHASSGSG   ORIGINAL

MAIL TO:

| BANK OF COMMUNICATIONS, JIANGSU PROVINCIAL BRANCH |
| NO.124 NORTH ZHONGSHAN ROAD |
| ATTN: L/C DEPT. |

DATE: 20100718

IN ALL CORRESPONDENCE PLS QUOTE OUR REF. NO. 6910194126.

WE ENCLOSE HEREWITH THE RELATIVE DOCUMENTS FOR PAYMENT PERTAINING TO THE CREDIT MENTIONED BELOW.

CREDIT NO.: LC201000929

ISSUED BY: BANK OF COMMUNICATIONS, JIANGSU PROVINCIAL BRANCH

APPL: EFG COMPANY, NANJING, CHINA

BENE: AGILENT TECHNOLOGIES SINGAPORE(SALES)PTE LTD.

INVOICE NO.: 20100001

1ST	2ND	DOCUMENTS	BILL AMOUNT: USD94,000.00
2/2		DRAFT	TENOR: SIGHT
5/5		COMM. INV.	
1/1		AWB	
2/2		PKG LIST	
1/1		FAX COPY	

PLEASE PAY/REMIT VIA CHIPS THE ABOVE TOTAL AMOUNT USD94,000.00 TO CHASE BANK, NEW YORK FOR CREDIT ACCOUNT NO. 10991581 WITH THEM AT SIGHT UNDER YOUR/THEIR TELEX/SWIFT ADVICE TO US QUOTING OUR ABOVE REF. NO. 6910194126.

REMARKS:

X)THE BILL AMOUNT HAS BEEN ENDORSED ON THE REVERSE OF THE ORIGINAL L/C.

THIS TRANSACTION IS SUBJECT TO THE UNIFORM CUSTOMS AND PRACTICE FOR DOCUMENTARY CREDIT 2007 REVISION, ICC PUBLICATION NO. 600.

请编写付款电文。账户行的选择参见附录(假设银行费用是 USD40 AS TELE. CHAR. AND USD80 AS REIM. CHAR，账户行选择美国大通银行 CHASUS33XXX)。

MT202 电文

-------------------------- Message Header --------------------------

Swift Output   : FIN 202 General Fin Inst Transfer

Sender   :

Receiver   :

-------------------------- Message Text --------------------------

    20   Transaction Reference Number

    21   Related Reference

    32A   Value Date, Currency Code, Amt

            Date

            Currency

            Amount

    53A   Sender's Correspondent - BIC

            BIC

    58A   Beneficiary Institution - BIC

    72   Sender to Receiver Information

MT799 电文

-------------------------- Message Header --------------------------

Swift Output   : FIN 799 Free Format Message

Sender   :

Receiver   : CHASSGSGXXX

-------------------------- Message Text --------------------------

    20   Transaction Reference Number

    21   Related Reference

    79   Narrative

参考答案：

MT202 电文

```
------------------------- Message Header -------------------------
Swift Output    : FIN 202 General Fin Inst Transfer
Sender          : COMMCNSHNJG
Receiver        : CHASUS33XXX
------------------------- Message Text -------------------------
```

20	Transaction Reference Number		
	LP201001386		
21	Related Reference		
	6910194126		
32A	Value Date, Currency Code, Amt		
	Date	100726	
	Currency	USD	
	Amount	93,880.00	
53A	Sender's Correspondent - BIC		
	BIC	COMMCNSHXXX	
58A	Beneficiary Institution - BIC		
	Party Identifier	/10991581	
	BIC	CHASSGSGXXX	
72	Sender to Receiver Information		
	/BNF/LC201000929		
	//LESS USD40 AS TELE. CHAR. AND		
	//USD80 AS REIM. CHAR.		

MT799 电文

```
------------------------- Message Header -------------------------
Swift Output    : FIN 799 Free Format Message
Sender          : COMMCNSHNJG
Receiver        : CHASSGSGXXX
------------------------- Message Text -------------------------
```

20	Transaction Reference Number
	LP201001386

21   Related Reference
      6910194126
79   Narrative
      PLEASE BE ADVISED THAT WE HAVE
      EFFECTED PAYMENT FOR USD93,880
      VALUE DATE 2010/7/23 THROUGH
      CHASUS33 AS PER YOUR INSTRUCTIONS.

同时请填写给进口商的信用证来单付汇通知书。假设银行编号是 LP201001386。

信用证来单付汇通知书

致：   我行付款编号：

进口合同号：

寄单行：   来单金额：

付款期限：

信用证号码：   远期到期日期：

寄单行编号：   最后付款/承兑日期：

　　兹将上述信用证项下的全套单据附上，请贵公司认真审核并注意以下事项：

　　【　】按照信用证条款和国际商会 UCP600 规定，如贵公司审核单据认为存在不符点，决定拒付/拒绝承兑，请务必于两个工作日内以书面形式(加盖公司章)通知我行，并将全套单据退回我行。如我行根据国际惯例审核不符点不成立，或贵公司未能及时将全套单据退回我行，贵公司仍须承担到期付款/承兑责任，我行将按期对外付款/承兑，并有权主动从贵公司账户中扣款。如我行未在两个工作日内接到贵公司的任何书面通知，将视同贵公司同意付款/承兑，我行将按期对外付款/承兑，并有权主动从贵公司账户扣款，由此造成的一切损失由贵公司承担。

　　【　】按照信用证条款和国际商会 UCP600 规定，我行审核单据时发现下列所示不符点(此不符点陈列即代表开证申请书中所提不符点通知书，我行不再发通知)。请贵公司于两个工作日内决定是否接受不符点，并以书面形式(加盖贵公司章)通知我行。如贵公司接受不符点，我行将按期对外付款/承兑，并有权主动从贵公司账户中扣款；如贵公司不接受不符点，需将全套单据退回我行，由我行对外拒付/拒绝承兑。如我行未在两个工作日内接到贵公司的任何书面通知，将视为贵公司不接受所有不符点，由我行对外拒付/拒绝承兑，由此造成的一切损失由贵公司承担。

　　【　】根据国家外汇管理局有关外汇付汇核销的规定，我行已从国外来单中抽取提单、发票副本各一份。

　　【　】如果已接受该笔来单的电提不符点，不得拒付。

　　【　】如果已办理该来单项下提单背书/提货担保，不得拒付。

汇票(DRAFT)
发票(COMM. INV.)
空运单(AIR WAYBILL)
装箱单(PKG LIST)
传真　(COPY OF FAX)

进口商回复:
我公司已收到全套单据并对其进行了审核,现就有关事项答复如下:
1. 我公司同意对外承兑/付款。
2. 远期单据到期时,请于到期日主动对外付款,我公司不再另行通知。
3. 该单据项下货款及银行费用,请你主动从我公司在你行的_____账户中扣付。

日期:　　　年　月　日

_____

公司签章

参考答案:

信用证来单付汇通知书

致:南京 EFG 公司　我行付款编号:LP201001386
进口合同号:20100412/CTTQ
寄单行:CHASE BANK OF SINGAPORE　来单金额:USD94000.00
付款期限:AT SIGHT
信用证号码:LC201000929　　　　　　　远期到期日期:
寄单行编号:6910194126　　　　　　　最后付款/承兑日期:20100723

兹将上述信用证项下的全套单据附上,请贵公司认真审核并注意以下事项:

【√】按照信用证条款和国际商会 UCP600 规定,如贵公司审核单据认为存在不符点,决定拒付/拒绝承兑,请务必于两个工作日内以书面形式(加盖公司章)通知我行,并将全套单据退回我行。如我行根据国际惯例审核不符点不成立,或贵公司未能及时将全套单据退回我行,贵公司仍须承担到期付款/承兑责任,我行将按期对外付款/承兑,并有权主动从贵公司账户中扣款。如我行未在两个工作日内接到贵公司的任何书面通知,将视同贵公司同意付款/承兑,我行将按期对外付款/承兑,并有权主动从贵公司账户扣款,由此造成的一切损失由贵公司承担。

【　】按照信用证条款和国际商会 UCP600 规定,我行审核单据时发现下列所示不符点(此不符点陈列即代表开证申请书中所提不符点通知书,我行不再发通知)。请贵公司于两个工作日内决定是否接受不符点,并以书面形式(加盖贵公司章)通知我行。如贵公司接受不符点,我行将按期对外付款/承兑,并有权主动从贵公司账户中扣款;如贵公司不接受不符点,需将全套单据退回我行,由我行对外拒付/拒绝承兑。如我行未在两个工作日内接到贵公司的任何书面通知,将视为贵公司不接受所有不符点,由我行对外拒付

/拒绝承兑，由此造成的一切损失由贵公司承担。

【√】根据国家外汇管理局有关外汇付汇核销的规定，我行已从国外来单中抽取提单、发票副本各一份。

【√】如果已接受该笔来单的电提不符点，不得拒付。

【√】如果已办理该来单项下提单背书/提货担保，不得拒付。

汇票(DRAFT)	2/2*1
发票(COMM. INV.)	5/5*1
空运单(AIR WAYBILL)	1/1*1
装箱单(PKG LIST)	2/2*1
传真 (COPY OF FAX)	1/1*1

进口商回复：

我公司已收到全套单据并对其进行了审核，现就有关事项答复如下：

1. 我公司同意对外承兑/付款。

2. 远期单据到期时，请于到期日主动对外付款，我公司不再另行通知。

3. 该单据项下货款及银行费用，请你主动从我公司在你行的_____账户中扣付。

日期：　　　年　　月　　日
　　　　　　　————————
　　　　　　　公司签章

练习 4.8

南京的 HK MACHINE COMPANY 和 ICA CO., LTD., CHICAGO, U.S.A.签订合同，约定采用 L/C 方式进口货物 ELECTRONIC TUBE，金额为 USD40000，期限为 SIGHT。开证行交通银行在落实开证相关条件后，电开信用证 MT700 如下。假设银行编号是 LC2010001039。

MT700 电文

```
------------------------- Message Header -------------------------
Swift Output    : FIN 700 Issue of a Documentary Credit
Sender          : COMMCNSHNJG
Receiver        : SCBLUS33XXX
------------------------- Message Text -------------------------
   27      Sequence of Total
```

	Number	1
	Total	1

40A Form of Documentary Credit
IRREVOCABLE

20 Documentary Credit Number
LC2010001039

31C Date of Issue
100612

40E Applicable Rules
UCP LATEST VERSION

31D Date and Place of Expiry
Date　　　　　100930
Place　　　　　U.S.A.

50 Applicant
HK MACHINE COMPANY

59 Beneficiary—Name & Address
Name And Address　ICA CO., LTD., CHICAGO, U.S.A.

32B Currency Code, Amount
Currency　　　　USD
Amount　　　　　40,000.00

39A Percentage Credit Amt Tolerance
Tolerance 1　　　10
Tolerance 2　　　10

41D Available With...By... - Name & Address
Name And Address　ANY BANK IN USA
Code　　　　　　　BY NEGOTIATION

43P Partial Shipments
ALLOWED

43T Transshipment
ALLOWED

44E Port of Loading/Airport of Dep.
MAIN PORTS IN U.S.A.

44F Port of Discharge/Airport of Dest.
SHANGHAI, CHINA

44C Latest Date of Shipment

100923

45A   Description of Goods &/or Services

ELECTRONIC TUBE

UNIT PRICE: USD 200 PER TUBE CFR SHANGHAI, CHINA

TOTAL AMOUNT: USD40,000.00 CFR SHANGHAI, CHINA

ORIGIN: U.S.A.

46A   Documents Required

+SIGNED COMMERCIAL INVOICE IN 2 ORIGINALS AND 1 COPY INDICATING

L/C NO. AND CONTRACT NO. 30850.

+ FULL SET OF CLEAN ON BOARD OCEAN BILLS OF LADING CONSIGNED TO

APPLICANT, MARKED "FREIGHT TO COLLECT" NOTIFYING THE APPLICANT.

+PACKING LIST / WEIGHT MEMO IN 1 ORIGINAL AND 3 COPIES

INDICATING TOTAL GROSS WEIGHT, TOTAL NET WEIGHT AND TOTAL NUMBER

OF CARTONS.

47A   Additional Conditions

+BOTH CREDIT AMOUNT AND QUANTITY 10PCT MORE OR LESS ARE ALLOWED.

+A DISCREPANCY FEE OF USD80.00(OR EQUIVALENT) PAYABLE BY

BENEFICIARY SHALL BE DEDUCTED FROM THE PROCEEDS FOR EACH

PRESENTATION OF DISCREPANT DOCUMENTS UNDER THIS DOCUMENTARY

CREDIT.

+ALL BANKING CHARGES OUTSIDE THE ISSUING BANK ARE FOR ACCOUNT OF

BENEFICIARY. NOTWITHSTANDING THE ABOVE, COSTS RELATING TO

REIMBURSEMENT/PAYMENT ARE ALSO FOR ACCOUNT OF BENEFICIARY AND

WILL BE DEDUCTED FROM PROCEEDS UPON PAYMENT.

+THE PRESENTING BANK'S SWIFT CODE MUST BE SHOWN ON THE BANKING

SCHEDULE.

+ALL DOCUMENTS TO BE DISPATCHED TO ISSUING BANK IN ONE LOT BY

FIRST AVAILABLE AIRMAIL THROUGH BANK. ISSUING BANK ADDRESS:BANK

OF COMMUNICATIONS CO., LTD., JIANGSU PROVINCIAL BRANCH,

11F. NO. 124 NORTH ZHONGSHAN ROAD, NANJING, JIANGSU, SWIFT: COMMCNSHNJG

48   Period for Presentation

DOCUMENTS TO BE PRESENTED

WITHIN 7 DAYS AFTER

THE DATE OF SHIPMENT BUT WITHIN

THE VALIDITY OF THE CREDIT.

49   Confirmation Instructions

      WITHOUT

78   Instr to Payg/Accptg/Negotg Bank

      UPON RECEIPT OF THE DOCUMENTS AND DRAFTS IN STRICT COMPLIANCE
      WITH THE TERMS AND CONDITIONS OF THIS CREDIT, WE SHALL ACCEPT THE
      DRAFTS AND REIMBURSE THE PRESENTING BANK AS INSTRUCTED AT
      MATURITY.
      THIS IS THE OPERATIVE CREDIT INSTRUMENT AND NO AIRMAIL
      CONFIRMATION WILL FOLLOW.

之后进口商又要求修改信用证的装效期，开证行又电开 MT707 修改。

MT707 电文

-------------------------- Message Header --------------------------

Swift Output   : FIN 707 Amendment to a Doc Credit
Sender   : COMMCNSHNJG
Receiver   : SCBLUS33XXX

-------------------------- Message Text --------------------------

20   Sender's Reference
      LC2010001039

21   Receiver's Reference
      UNKNOWN

31C   Date of Issue
      100612

30   Date of Amendment
      100614

26E   Number of Amendment
      01

59   Beneficiary (before amndmt)-Nm & Add
      Name And Address   ICA CO., LTD., CHICAGO, U.S.A.

31E   New Date of Expiry
      101030

44C   Latest Date of Shipment
      101020

79   Narrative

ADDITIONAL CONDITIONS:

ALL OTHER TERMS AND CONDITIONS OF THE L/C REMAIN

UNALTERED. PLS ADVISE THE AMENDMENT TO

BENEFICIARY.

REGARDS(IMPORT DEPT.)

上述信用证及修改开出后，开证行收到出口方银行 STANDARD CHARTERED BANK, NEW YORK 寄交的索汇面函、单据等，及时核对并确认单据表面与信用证条款相符后，向出口方银行发出到期付款电。账户行的选择参见附录(假设银行编号是 LP201001284，银行相关费用是 USD60 AS TELE. CHAR. AND USD80 AS REIM. CHAR.)。

出口方银行 STANDARD CHARTERED BANK, NEW YORK 寄交的索汇面函如下。

DOCUMENTARY REMITTANCE

STANDARD CHARTERED BANK NEW YORK

SWIFT: SCBLUS33   ORIGINAL

MAIL TO:

BANK OF COMMUNICATIONS, JIANGSU PROVINCIAL BRANCH
NO.124 NORTH ZHONGSHAN ROAD
ATTN: L/C DEPT.

DATE: 20100810

IN ALL CORRESPONDENCE PLS QUOTE OUR REF. NO. 0580.

WE ENCLOSE HEREWITH THE RELATIVE DOCUMENTS FOR PAYMENT PERTAINING TO THE CREDIT MENTIONED BELOW.

CREDIT NO.: LC2010001039

ISSUED BY: BANK OF COMMUNICATIONS, JIANGSU PROVINCIAL BRANCH

APPL: HK MACHINE COMPANY, NANJING, CHINA

BENE: ICA CO., LTD., CHICAGO, U.S.A.

INVOICE NO.: 34445

1ST	2ND	DOCUMENTS	BILL AMOUNT: USD40,000.00
3/3		COMM. INV.	TENOR: SIGHT
3/3		B/L	
4/4		PKG LIST	
3/3		B/L COPY	

PLEASE PAY/REMIT VIA CHIPS THE ABOVE TOTAL AMOUNT USD40,000.00 TO BANK OF CHINA, NEW YORK FOR CREDIT ACCOUNT NO. 112233 WITH THEM AT SIGHT UNDER YOUR/THEIR TELEX/SWIFT ADVICE TO US QUOTING OUR ABOVE REF. NO. 0580.

REMARKS:

X)THE BILL AMOUNT HAS BEEN ENDORSED ON THE REVERSE OF THE ORIGINAL L/C.

THIS TRANSACTION IS SUBJECT TO THE UNIFORM CUSTOMS AND PRACTICE FOR DOCUMENTARY CREDIT 2007 REVISION, ICC PUBLICATION NO. 600.

USD80 AS REIM. CHAR.

通知付款电文 MT799

------------------------- Message Header -------------------------

Swift Output	: FIN 799 Free Format Message
Sender	:
Receiver	:

------------------------- Message Text -------------------------

20　　Transaction Reference Number

21　　Related Reference

79　　Narrative

付款电文 MT202

------------------------- Message Header -------------------------

Swift Output	: FIN 202 General Fin Inst Transfer
Sender	:
Receiver	:

------------------------- Message Text -------------------------

20　　Transaction Reference Number

21　　Related Reference

32A　　Value Date, Currency Code, Amt

　　　Date

　　　Currency

Amount

53A   Sender's Correspondent BIC

BIC

58A   Beneficiary Institution - BIC

Party Identifier /

BIC

72   Sender to Receiver Information

参考答案:

通知付款电文 MT799

```
------------------------- Message Header -------------------------
Swift Output    : FIN 799 Free Format Message
Sender          : COMMCNSHNJG
Receiver        : SCBLUS33XXX
------------------------- Message Text -------------------------
    20    Transaction Reference Number
          LP201001284
    21    Related Reference
          0580
    79    Narrative
          PLEASE BE ADVISED THAT WE HAVE
          EFFECTED PAYMENT FOR USD40,000.00
          VALUE DATE 2010/08/14 THROUGH
          BKCHUS33 AS PER YOUR INSTRUCTIONS.
```

付款电文 MT202

```
------------------------- Message Header -------------------------
Swift Output    : FIN 202 General Fin Inst Transfer
Sender          : COMMCNSHNJG
Receiver        : BKCHUS33XXX
------------------------- Message Text -------------------------

    20    Transaction Reference Number
          LP201001284
```

| 21 | Related Reference |
| | 0580 |

32A　Value Date, Currency Code, Amt
　　Date　　　　　　　100815
　　Currency　　　　　USD
　　Amount　　　　　　39,860.00

53A　Sender's Correspondent - BIC
　　BIC　　　　　　　COMMCNSHXXX

58A　Beneficiary Institution - BIC
　　Party Identifier /112233
　　BIC　　　　　　　SCBLUS33XXX

72　Sender to Receiver Information
　　/BNF/LC2010001039
　　//LESS USD60 AS TELE. CHAR. AND
　　//USD80 AS REIM. CHAR.

　　交行同时出具信用证来单付汇通知书，连同单据一起交给进口商办理付款。请编写给进口商的信用证来单付汇通知书。假设银行编号是 LP201001284。

信用证来单付汇通知书

致：　　　　　　我行付款编号：
进口合同号：
寄单行：　　　　来单金额：
付款期限：
信用证号码：
寄单行编号：　　最后付款/承兑日期：

　　兹将上述信用证项下的全套单据附上，请贵公司认真审核并注意以下事项：

　　【　】按照信用证条款和国际商会 UCP600 规定，如贵公司审核单据认为存在不符点，决定拒付/拒绝承兑，请务必于两个工作日内以书面形式(加盖公司章)通知我行，并将全套单据退回我行。如我行根据国际惯例审核不符点不成立，或贵公司未能及时将全套单据退回我行，贵公司仍须承担到期付款/承兑责任，我行将按期对外付款/承兑，并有权主动从贵公司账户中扣款。如我行未在两个工作日内接到贵公司的任何书面通知，将视同贵公司同意付款/承兑，我行将按期对外付款/承兑，并有权主动从贵公司账户扣款，由此造成的一切损失由贵公司承担。

　　【　】按照信用证条款和国际商会 UCP600 规定，我行审核单据时发现下列所示不符点(此不符点陈列即代表开证申请书中所提不符点通知书，我行不再发通知)。请贵公司于两个工作日内决定是否接受不符点,并以书面形式(加盖贵公司章)通知我行。如贵公司接受不符点,我行将按期对外付款/承兑,并有权主动从贵公司账户中扣款;如贵公司不接受不符点,需将全套单据退回我行,由我行对外拒付/拒绝承兑。如我行未在两个工作日内接到贵公司的任何书面通知,将视为贵公司不接受所有不符点,由我行对外拒付/拒绝承兑,由此造成的一切损失由贵公司承担。

【 】根据国家外汇管理局有关外汇付汇核销的规定,我行已从国外来单中抽取提单、发票副本各一份。

【 】如果已接受该笔来单的电提不符点,不得拒付。

【 】如果已办理该来单项下提单背书/提货担保,不得拒付。

发票(COMM. INV.)

提单(B/L)

B/L COPY

装箱单(PKG LIST)

不符点提示: 无

如发现所附单据中有不属于贵公司的内容,请速与江苏省分行国际部联系,

电话号码   联系人

银行签章

进口商回复:

我公司已收到全套单据并对其进行了审核,现就有关事项答复如下:

1. 我公司同意对外承兑/付款。

2. 远期单据到期时,请于到期日主动对外付款,我公司不再另行通知。

3. 该单据项下货款及银行费用,请你主动从我公司在你行的_____账户中扣付。

日期: 年   月   日
_____

公司签章

参考答案:

信用证来单付汇通知书

致: HK MACHINE COMPANY   我行付款编号:LP201001284

进口合同号:30850

寄单行:STANDARD CHARTERED BANK, NEW YORK 来单金额:USD40000.00

付款期限:SIGHT

信用证号码:LC2010001039

寄单行编号：0580   最后付款/承兑日期：20100815

兹将上述信用证项下的全套单据附上，请贵公司认真审核并注意以下事项：

【√】按照信用证条款和国际商会 UCP600 规定，如贵公司审核单据认为存在不符点，决定拒付/拒绝承兑，请务必于两个工作日内以书面形式(加盖公司章)通知我行，并将全套单据退回我行。如我行根据国际惯例审核不符点不成立，或贵公司未能及时将全套单据退回我行，贵公司仍须承担到期付款/承兑责任，我行将按期对外付款/承兑，并有权主动从贵公司账户中扣款。如我行未在两个工作日内接到贵公司的任何书面通知，将视同贵公司同意付款/承兑，我行将按期对外付款/承兑，并有权主动从贵公司账户扣款，由此造成的一切损失由贵公司承担。

【　】按照信用证条款和国际商会 UCP600 规定，我行审核单据时发现下列所示不符点(此不符点陈列即代表开证申请书中所提不符点通知书，我行不再发通知)。请贵公司于两个工作日内决定是否接受不符点，并以书面形式(加盖贵公司章)通知我行。如贵公司接受不符点，我行将按期对外付款/承兑，并有权主动从贵公司账户中扣款；如贵公司不接受不符点，需将全套单据退回我行，由我行对外拒付/拒绝承兑。如我行未在两个工作日内接到贵公司的任何书面通知，将视为贵公司不接受所有不符点，由我行对外拒付/拒绝承兑，由此造成的一切损失由贵公司承担。

【√】根据国家外汇管理局有关外汇付汇核销的规定，我行已从国外来单中抽取提单、发票副本各一份。

【√】如果已接受该笔来单的电提不符点，不得拒付。

【√】如果已办理该来单项下提单背书/提货担保，不得拒付。

发票(COMM. INV.)   3/3*1

提单(B/L)   3/3*1

B/L COPY   3/3*1

装箱单(PKG LIST)   4/4*1

不符点提示：无

进口商回复：

我公司已收到全套单据并对其进行了审核，现就有关事项答复如下：

1. 我公司同意对外承兑/付款。

2. 远期单据到期时，请于到期日主动对外付款，我公司不再另行通知。

3. 该单据项下货款及银行费用，请你主动从我公司在你行的_____账户中扣付。

日期：　　年　月　日
　　　　　　　　　　　　　　　————————
公司签章

练习 4.9

南京的 YUFAN CORPORATION 和 KOWA COMPANY LTD., TOKYO BRANCH 签订合同，约定采用 L/C 方式进口货物 IODINE PRILLS (99.8PCT)，金额为 USD320000.00，期限为 60 DAYS AFTER DELIVERY ORDER DATE。开证行交通银行在落实开证相关条件后，电开以下信用证。假设银行编号是 LC201000678。

MT700 电文

```
------------------------ Message Header ------------------------
Swift Output      : FIN 700 Issue of a Documentary Credit
Sender            : COMMCNSHNJG
Receiver          : SMBCJPJTXXX
------------------------- Message Text -------------------------
```

27	Sequence of Total	
	Number	1
	Total	1
40A	Form of Documentary Credit	
	IRREVOCABLE	
20	Documentary Credit Number	
	LC201000678	
31C	Date of Issue	
	100329	
40E	Applicable Rules	
	UCP LATEST VERSION	
31D	Date and Place of Expiry	
	Date	100506
	Place	JAPAN
50	Applicant	
	YUFAN CORPORATION NO.112	
	ZHONGSHAN SOUTH ROAD, JIANGNING	
	DEVELOPMENT	
	ZONE, NANJING, 211100, P.R.C.	
59	Beneficiary - Name & Address	
	Name and Address KOWA COMPANY LTD., TOKYO BRANCH	
	(ADDRESS SEE FIELD 47A)	
32B	Currency Code, Amount	

Currency   USD

Amount   320,000.00

41D   Available With...By... – Name & Address

Name And Address   ANY BANK IN JAPAN

Code   BY NEGOTIATION

42C   Drafts at...

60 DAYS AFTER DELIVERY ORDER DATE

FOR 100PCT INVOICE VALUE

42A   Drawee - BIC

BIC   COMMCNSHNJG

43P   Partial Shipments

ALLOWED

43T   Transshipment

ALLOWED

44A   Pl of Tking in Chrg / of Rceipt

SHANGHAI WAIGAOQIAO BONDED WAREHOUSE, CHINA

44B   Pl of Final Dest / of Delivery

SHANGHAI, CHINA

44C   Latest Date of Shipment

100415

45A   Description of Goods &/or Services

COMMODITY: IODINE PRILLS (99.8PCT)

UNIT PRICE: USD29,700.00/MT FCA SHANGHAI WAIGAOQIAO BONDED

WAREHOUSE, CHINA

QUANTITY: 10.7744 MTS

TOTAL AMOUNT: USD320,000.00 FCA SHANGHAI WAIGAOQIAO BONDED

WAREHOUSE, CHINA

PACKING: IN 50.00 KGS FIBRE DRUM

ORIGIN: CHILE/SQM

46A   Documents Required

+SIGNED COMMERCIAL INVOICE IN 2 ORIGINALS AND 2 COPIES

INDICATING L/C NO. AND CONTRACT NO. 050020.

+PACKING LIST/WEIGHT MEMO IN 3 COPIES ISSUED BY MANUFACTURER.

+CERTIFICATE OF ANALYSIS IN 3 COPIES ISSUED BY MANUFACTURER.

+CERTIFICATE OF ORIGIN IN 3 COPIES ISSUED BY MANUFACTURER.

+DELIVERY ORDER IN 1 ORIGINAL ISSUED BY SQM EUROPE N.V. DATED NOT LATER THAN APR.15, 2010.

47A　　Additional Conditions

+APPLICANT'S TEL: 86-25-52782933　FAX:86-25-52782926

+BENEFICIARY'S ADD:

BLDG. 6F 4-10, 3-CHOME, NIHONBASHI-HONCHO, CHUO-KU, TOKYO 103-0023, JAPAN

+A DISCREPANCY FEE OF USD80.00(OR EQUIVALENT) PAYABLE BY BENEFICIARY SHALL BE DEDUCTED FROM THE PROCEEDS FOR EACH PRESENTATION OF DISCREPANT DOCUMENTS UNDER THIS DOCUMENTARY CREDIT.

+THE PRESENTING BANK'S SWIFT CODE MUST BE SHOWN ON THE BANKING SCHEDULE.

+ALL BANKING CHARGES OUTSIDE CHINA ARE FOR ACCOUNT OF BENEFICIARY. NOTWITHSTANDING THE ABOVE, COSTS RELATING TO REIMBURSEMENT/PAYMENT ARE ALSO FOR ACCOUNT OF BENEFICIARY AND WILL BE DEDUCTED FROM PROCEEDS UPON PAYMENT.

+ALL DOCUMENTS TO BE DISPATCHED TO ISSUING BANK IN ONE LOT BY FIRST AVAILABLE AIRMAIL THROUGH BANK. ISSUING BANK ADDRESS:BANK OF COMMUNICATIONS CO., LTD., JIANGSU PROVINCIAL BRANCH, SWIFT:COMMCNSHNJG

48　　Period for Presentation

DOCUMENTS TO BE PRESENTED WITHIN

21 DAYS FROM THE DATE OF DELIVERY

ORDER BUT WITHIN THE VALIDITY OF THE CREDIT.

49　　Confirmation Instructions

WITHOUT

78　　Instr to Payg/Accptg/Negotg Bank

UPON RECEIPT OF THE DOCUMENTS AND DRAFTS IN STRICT COMPLIANCE WITH THE TERMS AND CONDITIONS OF THIS CREDIT, WE SHALL ACCEPT THE DRAFTS AND REIMBURSE THE PRESENTING BANK AS INSTRUCTED AT MATURITY.

THIS IS THE OPERATIVE CREDIT INSTRUMENT AND NO AIRMAIL CONFIRMATION WILL FOLLOW.

在开出上述信用证后，开证行收到出口方银行 Sumitomo Mitsui Banking Corporation, Tokyo 寄交的索汇面函、单据等。

出口方银行索汇面函如下：

DOCUMENTARY REMITTANCE

SUMITOMO MITSUI BANKING CORPORATION, TOKYO

SWIFT：SMBCJPJT

ORIGINAL

MAIL TO:

BANK OF COMMUNICATIONS, JIANGSU PROVINCIAL BRANCH

NO.124 NORTH ZHONGSHAN ROAD

ATTN: L/C DEPT.

DATE: 20100425

IN ALL CORRESPONDENCE PLS QUOTE OUR REF. NO. MS0430.

WE ENCLOSE HEREWITH THE RELATIVE DOCUMENTS FOR PAYMENT PERTAINING TO THE CREDIT MENTIONED BELOW.

CREDIT NO.: LC201000678

ISSUED BY: BANK OF COMMUNICATIONS, JIANGSU PROVINCIAL BRANCH

APPL: YUFAN CORPORATION

　　　　NO. 112 ZHONGSHAN SOUTH ROAD, JIANGNING

　　　　DEVELOPMENT ZONE, NANJING, 211100, P.R.C.

BENE: KOWA COMPANY LTD., TOKYO BRANCH

INVOICE NO.: QA224

1ST	2ND	DOCUMENTS	BILL AMOUNT: USD320,000.00
2/2		DRAFT	TENOR: 60 DAYS AFTER DELIVERY
4/4		COMM. INV.	ORDER DATE
3/3		CERT OF ANALYSIS	
3/3		PKG LIST	
3/3		CERT OF ORIGIN	
1/1		DELIVERY ORDER	

PLEASE PAY/REMIT VIA CHIPS THE ABOVE TOTAL AMOUNT USD 320,000.00 TO CITIBANK, NEW YORK FOR CREDIT ACCOUNT NO. 223344 WITH THEM AT SIGHT UNDER YOUR/THEIR TELEX/SWIFT ADVICE TO US QUOTING OUR ABOVE REF. NO. MS0430.

REMARKS:

X)THE BILL AMOUNT HAS BEEN ENDORSED ON THE REVERSE OF THE ORIGINAL L/C.

THIS TRANSACTION IS SUBJECT TO THE UNIFORM CUSTOMS AND PRACTICE FOR DOCUMENTARY CREDIT 2007 REVISION, ICC PUBLICATION NO. 600.

开证行及时审核单据表面与信用证条款是否相符。当发现单据中有不符点时，便向出口方银行发出拒付电文。请编写拒付电文。假设银行的编号是 LP201000949。

拒付电文 MT734

```
------------------------- Message Header -------------------------
Swift Output        : FIN 734 Advice of Refusal
Sender              :
Receiver            :
------------------------- Message Text -------------------------
    20      Sender's TRN

    21      Presenting Bank's Reference

    32A     Date and Amount of Utilization
            Date
            Currency
            Amount
    72      Sender to Receiver Information

    77J     Discrepancies

    77B     Disposal of Documents

            .
```

参考答案:

拒付电文 MT734

```
------------------------- Message Header -------------------------
Swift Output        : FIN 734 Advice of Refusal
Sender              : COMMCNSHNJG
Receiver            : SMBCJPJTXXX
------------------------- Message Text -------------------------
    20      Sender's TRN
            LC201000678
    21      Presenting Bank's Reference
```

MS0430

32A	Date and Amount of Utilization

Date   100425

Currency   USD

Amount   320,000.00

72   Sender to Receiver Information

LP201000949

77J   Discrepancies

1. CONTRACT NO. ON DELIVERY ORDER IS 05020 I/O 050020.

2. L/C ISSUING DATE ON CERTIFICATE OF ANALYSIS IS 06.05.2010 I/O 29.03.2010.

77B   Disposal of Documents

HOLDING YOUR DOCUMENTS PENDING

YOUR INSTRUCTIONS.

　　开证行交行在对外发出拒付电后，又将此不符点通告进口商。而进口商因为急需此货物，便书面同意接受不符点到期付款。交行因此出具了一份信用证来单付汇通知书，并连同单据一起交给进口商，要求进口商对这笔远期付款做书面承兑，同时交行给 SUMITOMO MITSUI BANKING CORPORATION, TOKYO 发出承兑电文。

　　请填写这份承兑电文，假设银行编号是 LP201000949。

承兑电文 MT799

```
------------------------- Message Header -------------------------
Swift Output    : FIN 799 Free Format Message
Sender          :
Receiver        :
------------------------- Message Text -------------------------
```

20   Transaction Reference Number

21   Related Reference

79   Narrative

参考答案：

承兑电文 MT799

```
------------------------- Message Header -------------------------
Swift Output    : FIN 799 Free Format Message
Sender          : COMMCNSHNJG
Receiver        : SMBCJPJTXXX
------------------------- Message Text -------------------------
```

20	Transaction Reference Number
	LP201000949
21	Related Reference
	MS0430
79	Narrative

PLS BE ADVISED THAT YOUR A/M DOCUMENTS DD
20100425 DRAWN UNDER OUR L/C NO.
LC201000678 ARE ACCEPTED DUE ON 20100531.
WE WILL EFFECT PAYMENT FOR USD320,000.00 AT
MATURITY DATE AS PER YOUR INSTRUCTIONS SHOWN
ON YOUR COVERING LETTER AND OUR CHARGES
TOTALLY FOR USD240.00 INCLUDING USD80.00 AS
TELECOMM CHARGE AND USD80.00 AS REIMBURSING
CHARGE, AND USD80.00 AS DISC. FEE WILL BE DEDUCTED
FROM PROCEEDS.
B. RGDS

同时请填写信用证来单付汇通知书。

信用证来单付汇通知书

致：   银行付款编号：

寄单行：   来单金额：

付款期限：

信用证号码：   远期到期日期：

寄单行编号：   最后付款/承兑日期：

划款帐号：   来单日期： 核销单编号：

利息金额：USD 0.0 国外银行费用：USD 0.0 付款总金额：

兹将上述信用证项下的全套单据附上，请贵公司认真审核并注意以下事项：

【 】按照信用证条款和国际商会 UCP600 规定，如贵公司审核单据认为存在不符点，决定拒付/拒绝承兑，请务必于两个工作日内以书面形式(加盖公司章)通知我行，并将全套单据退回我行。如我行根据国际惯例审核不符点不成立，或贵公司未能及时将全套单据退回我行，贵公司仍须承担到期付款/承兑责任，我行将按期对外付款/承兑，并有权主动从贵公司账户中扣款。如我行未在两个工作日内接到贵公司的任何书面通知，将视同贵公司同意付款/承兑，我行将按期对外付款/承兑，并有权主动从贵公司账户扣款，由此造成的一切损失由贵公司承担。

【 】按照信用证条款和国际商会 UCP600 规定，我行审核单据时发现下列所示不符点(此不符点陈列即代表开证申请书中所提不符点通知书，我行不再发通知)。请贵公司于两个工作日内决定是否接受不符点，并以书面形式(加盖贵公司章)通知我行。如贵公司接受不符点，我行将按期对外付款/承兑，并有权主动从贵公司账户中扣款；如贵公司不接受不符点，需将全套单据退回我行，由我行对外拒付/拒绝承兑。如我行未在两个工作日内接到贵公司的任何书面通知，将视为贵公司不接受所有不符点，由我行对外拒付/拒绝承兑，由此造成的一切损失由贵公司承担。

【　】根据国家外汇管理局有关外汇付汇核销的规定，我行已从国外来单中抽取提单、发票副本各一份。

【　】如果已接受该笔来单的电提不符点，不得拒付。

【　】如果已办理该来单项下提单背书/提货担保，不得拒付。

汇票(DRAFT)

发票(COMM. INV.)

CERT OF ANALYSIS

装箱单(PKG LIST)

产地证(CERT OF ORIGIN)

DELIVERY ORDER

不符点提示：

进口商回复：

我公司已收到全套单据并对其进行了审核，现就有关事项答复如下：

1. 我公司同意对外承兑/付款。

2. 远期单据到期时，请于到期日主动对外付款，我公司不再另行通知。

3. 该单据项下货款及银行费用，请你主动从我公司在你行的＿＿＿＿＿账户中扣付。

日期：　　　年　　月　　日
　　　　　―――――――――

公司签章

参考答案：

信用证来单付汇通知书

致：YUFAN CORPORATION, NANJING　　　　　　　我行付款编号：LP201000949

寄单行：SUMITOMO MITSUI BANKING CORPORATION, TOKYO　来单金额：USD320000.00

付款期限：60 DAYS AFTER DELIVERY ORDER DATE

信用证号码：LC201000678　远期到期日期：20100531

寄单行编号：MS0430

划款帐号：N/A　来单日期：20100430　核销单编号：123456

利息金额：USD 0.0 国外银行费用：USD 0.0 付款总金额：USD 320000.00

兹将上述信用证项下的全套单据附上，请贵公司认真审核并注意以下事项：

【　】按照信用证条款和国际商会 UCP600 规定，如贵公司审核单据认为存在不符点，决定拒付/拒绝承兑，请务必于两个工作日内以书面形式(加盖公司章)通知我行，并将全套单据退回我行。如我行根据国际惯例审核不符点不成立，或贵公司未能及时将全套单据退回我行，贵公司仍须承担到期付款/承兑责任，我行将按期对外付款/承兑，并有权主动从贵公司账户中扣款。如我行未在两个工作日内接到贵公司的任何书面通知，将视同贵公司同意付款/承兑，我行将按期对外付款/承兑，并有权主动从贵公司账户扣款，由此造成的一切损失由贵公司承担。

【√】按照信用证条款和国际商会 UCP600 规定，我行审核单据时发现下列所示不符点(此不符点陈列即代表开证申请书中所提不符点通知书，我行不再发通知)。请贵公司于两个工作日内决定是否接受不符点，并以书面形式(加盖贵公司章)通知我行。如贵公司接受不符点，我行将按期对外付款/承兑，并有权主动从贵公司账户中扣款；如贵公司不接受不符点，需将全套单据退回我行，由我行对外拒付/拒绝承兑。如我行未在两个工作日内接到贵公司的任何书面通知，将视为贵公司不接受所有不符点，由我行对外拒付/拒绝承兑，由此造成的一切损失由贵公司承担。

【√】根据国家外汇管理局有关外汇付汇核销的规定，我行已从国外来单中抽取提单、发票副本各一份。

【√】如果已接受该笔来单的电提不符点，不得拒付。

【√】如果已办理该来单项下提单背书/提货担保，不得拒付。

汇票(DRAFT)	2/2*1
发票(COMM. INV.)	4/4*1
CERT OF ANALYSIS	3/3*1
装箱单(PKG LIST)	3/3*1
产地证(CERT. OF ORIGIN)	3/3*1
DELIVERY ORDER	1/1*1

不符点提示：

1. CONTRACT NO. ON DELIVERY ORDER IS 05020 I/O 050020.

2. L/C ISSUING DATE ON CERTIFICATE OF ANALYSIS IS 06.05.2010 I/O 29.03.2010.

进口商回复：

我公司已收到全套单据并对其进行了审核，现就有关事项答复如下：

1. 我公司同意对外承兑/付款。

2. 远期单据到期时，请于到期日主动对外付款，我公司不再另行通知。

3. 该单据项下货款及银行费用，请你主动从我公司在你行的_____账户中扣付。

日期：　　　年　　月　　日

　　　　　　————————

　　　　　　公司签章

　　开证行交行付款到期后对出口方银行付款。请编写相关付款电文及通知电文。假设银行相关费用为 USD80 AS TELE. CHAR. AND USD80 AS REIM. CHAR. AND USD80 AS DISC. FEE。如果 CITIBANK, NEW YORK(CITIUS33)是开证行的账户行，则开证行可以直接通过其付款。

付款电文 MT799

```
------------------------ Message Header ------------------------
Swift Output    : FIN 799 Free Format Message
Sender          :
Receiver        :
------------------------ Message Text ------------------------
    20    Transaction Reference Number


    21    Related Reference


    79    Narrative
```

MT 202 电文

```
------------------------ Message Header ------------------------
Swift Output    : FIN 202 General Fin Inst Transfer
Sender          :
Receiver        :
------------------------ Message Text ------------------------
    20    Transaction Reference Number


    21    Related Reference


    32A   Value Date, Currency Code, Amt
          Date
          Currency
          Amount
    53A   Sender's Correspondent - BIC
          BIC
    58A   Beneficiary Institution - BIC
```

72   Sender to Receiver Information

参考答案：

MT799 付款电文

-------------------------- Message Header ------------------------

Swift Output   : FIN 799 Free Format Message

Sender   : COMMCNSHNJG

Receiver   : SMBCJPJTXXX

-------------------------- Message Text ------------------------

20   Transaction Reference Number

       LP201000949

21   Related Reference

       MS0430

79   Narrative

       PLEASE BE ADVISED THAT WE HAVE

       EFFECTED PAYMENT FOR USD319760

       VALUE DATE 20100531 THROUGH

       CITIUS33 AS PER YOUR INSTRUCTIONS.

MT 202 电文

-------------------------- Message Header ------------------------

Swift Output   : FIN 202 General Fin Inst Transfer

Sender   : COMMCNSHNJG

Receiver   : CITIUS33XXX

-------------------------- Message Text ------------------------

20   Transaction Reference Number

       LP201000949

21   Related Reference

       MS0430

32A   Value Date, Currency Code, Amt

       Date   100531

       Currency   USD

       Amount   319,760.00

53A   Sender's Correspondent - BIC
       BIC   COMMCNSHXXX
58A   Beneficiary Institution - BIC
       Party Identifier /223344
       BIC   SMBCJPJTXXX
72   Sender to Receiver Information
       /BNF/LC201000678
       //LESS USD80 AS TELE. CHAR. AND
       //USD80 AS REIM. CHAR. AND
       //USD80 AS DISC. FEE.

保函与备用信用证

学习目标：

了解和掌握出口保函的业务流程，学会填制银行的通知面函；了解和掌握进口开立备用信用证的业务流程并学会根据开证申请书填制 MT760 等电文；知晓如何控制出口保函的通知和进口开立备用信用证中的相关风险。

第一节 出口保函的通知业务

一、业务场景与操作

案例 5.1

2009 年 1 月 10 日，交通银行作为通知银行收到由德国银行(SWIFT No.: DEUTDE3BXXX) 开来的 MT760 保函电文。

```
------------------------ Message Header ------------------------
Swift Output    : FIN 760 Guarantee/Standby Letter Credit
Sender          : DEUTDE3BXXX
Receiver        : COMMCNSHNJG
------------------------ Message Text ------------------------
27 Sequence of Total
    Number 1
    Total 1
20 Transaction Reference Number
    123456
23 Further Identification
    ISSUE
30 Date
    090107
40C Applicable Rules
```

Type NONE

77C Details of Guarantee

ATTN.:

BANK OF COMMUNICATION

CO., LTD., JIANGSU, CHINA

TRANSFER TO:

NANJING QINGTIAN CO., LTD.

NANJING, CHINA

ADVANCE PAYMENT GUARANTEE NO.3300900493

WE HAVE BEEN INFORMED THAT A CONTRACT HAS BEEN SIGNED BETWEEN

NANJING QINGTIAN CO., LTD. AND PLUEMAT MASCHINENBAU

VERTRIEBSGESELLSCHAFT M.B.H., DR. MAX-ILGNER-STRASSE

19, 32339 ESPELKAMP, F.R. GERMANY,

HEREINAFTER CALLED "PRINCIPAL", UNDER REF. NO. PLB 10 03 004 FOR

"ONE SET OF AUTOMATIC FORM-FILL-SEAL PRODUCTION LINE FFS 892HS

MACH.-NO. 2157, DETAILS AS PER APPENDIX I SCOPE OF SUPPLY AND

TECHNICAL SPECIFICATION" AT A TOTAL PRICE OF EUR150,000.00

AND THAT THE UNDERLYING CONTRACT STIPULATES THAT AN ADVANCE

PAYMENT IN THE AMOUNT OF 10 PERCENT OF THE TOTAL PRICE BE

EFFECTED AGAINST AN ADVANCE PAYMENT GUARANTEE.

THIS BEING PREMISED, WE, DEUTSCHE BANK AG, HERFORDER STRASSE

23, 33602 BIELEFELD, F.R. GERMANY, HEREBY IRREVOCABLY UNDERTAKE

TO PAY YOU WITHOUT DELAY ON YOUR FIRST WRITTEN DEMAND FOR

PAYMENT AN AMOUNT UP TO EUR15,000.00(SAY EURO FIFTEEN

THOUSAND ONLY), PROVIDED YOUR DEMAND FOR PAYMENT IS

SIMULTANEOUSLY SUPPORTED BY YOUR WRITTEN STATEMENT

(WHETHER IN THE DEMAND ITSELF OR IN A SEPARATE

DOCUMENT(S) ACCOMPANYING THE DEMAND AND REFERRED

TO IN IT) STATING

A) THAT THE PRINCIPAL IS IN BREACH OF HIS OBLIGATION(S) UNDER

THE UNDERLYING CONTRACT, AND

B)THE RESPECT IN WHICH THE PRINCIPAL IS IN BREACH, AND

C)THAT THE OBLIGATION(S) IN RESPECT OF WHICH THE PRINCIPAL IS

IN BREACH IS/ARE COVERED BY THE PRESENT GUARANTEE AND THAT YOU

ARE THEREFORE ENTITLED TO DEMAND REPAYMENT OF THE ADVANCE

PAYMENT UP TO THE AMOUNT OF THE DEMAND FOR PAYMENT.

THIS GUARANTEE SHALL ENTER INTO EFFECT IF AND TO THE EXTENT THE

ADVANCE PAYMENT OF EUR15,000.00 IS CREDITED IN FULL WITHOUT RESERVE TO PRINCIPAL'S ACCOUNT NO. 2825420 HELD WITH US IN MINDEN, IBAN NO. 4907 0028 0282 5420 00 WITH REFERENCE TO THIS GUARANTEE AT HIS FREE DISPOSAL.

THIS GUARANTEE SHALL EXPIRE ON SEPTEMBER 15, 2009, UNLESS YOUR WRITTEN DEMAND UNDER THIS GUARANTEE IN ACCORDANCE WITH THE ABOVE MENTIONED CONDITIONS HAS REACHED US IN BIELEFELD BY THE END OF THAT DAY.

THIS GUARANTEE IS TRANSFERABLE WITH OUR WRITTEN CONSENT ONLY.

THE ISSUANCE OF THIS GUARANTEE IS PERMITTED ACCORDING TO GERMAN LAW. THIS GUARANTEE IS SUBJECT TO GERMAN LAW.

DEUTSCHE BANK AG

THIS IS AN OPERATIVE INSTRUMENT AND NO MAIL CONFIRMATION FOLLOWS.

KIND REGARDS

DEUTSCHE BANK AG

TRADE FINANCE GUARANTEES, REICHSTE

--------------------------- Message Trailer ------------------------

{5:{CHK:B76B8B1832BF}{MAC:00000000}}

　　作为该保函的通知行，交通银行审核该保函后，缮制通知面函，并连同正本保函通知书交给保函的受益人。通知面函如下，假设通知银行编号是 GA200900002，通知费是 EUR18.00。

ADVICE OF LETTER OF GUARANTEE

致(TO): NANJING QINGTIAN CO., LTD. NANJING 南京青田有限公司	我行编号(OUR REF. NO.):	GA200900002
	通知日期(DATE):	20090110
来自(FROM): DEUTSCHE BANK AG BIELEFELD, HERFORDER STRASSE 23, 33609 BIELEFELD	保函号码(GUARANTEE NO.):	123456
	开立日期(ISSUING DATE):	20090107
	保函金额(AMOUNT):	EUR 15,000.00
敬启者: 　　欣告贵司，我行从上述银行收到一张以贵司为受益人的其真实性已经证实的电传/信函/SWIFT 开立的文件，敬请注意下列事项:		

(Dear sirs:

We take a pleasure in notifying you that we have received an authenticated telex/mail /SWIFT GUARANTEE message in your favor from a/m bank. Please note the following item(s):)

(•)一张保函 (A GUARANTEE)

(•)根据保函规定，我行相关通知费用 EUR18.00 由贵司承担。

(As per stipulation of the GUARANTEE, our bank's advising commission EUR 18.00 is for your a/c.)

(•)联系业务时，务请提供我行编号 GA200900002。

(When corresponding, please always mention our reference number:GA200900002.)

要项(Important)

　　如贵司发现该保函中有任何条款难以接受，请径与保函申请人联系以便及时修改，避免单据提示时可能发生的问题。

　　(If you find terms and conditions which you are unable to comply with in this GUARANTEE, please directly contact applicant in order to make timely amendment and avoid any difficulties which may arise when documents are presented.)

　　图 5.1 为案例 5.1 的业务流程图。

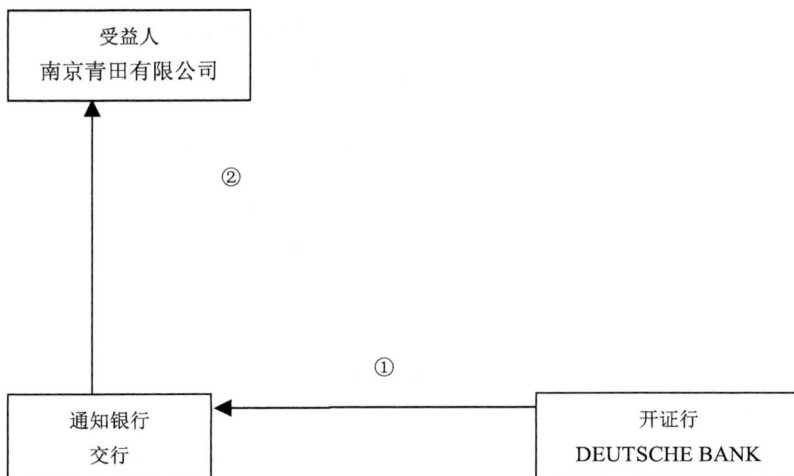

图 5.1　案例 5.1 的业务流程图

① 通知银行交行收到 DEUTSCHE BANK 开来的保函。

② 交行审核保函之后通知受益人南京青田有限公司。

二、风险控制

作为通知行，首先应该审查保函的真实性，以防虚假保函。虽然保函有多种，但其真实性是第一位的。

案例 5.1 中是 DEUTDE3BXXX 银行开来的 ADVANCE PAYMENT GUARANTEE(预付款保函)，函中表明了 DEUTDE3BXXX 银行的保证条款(WE, DEUTSCHE BANK AG, HERFORDER STRASSE 23, 33602 BIELEFELD, F.R. GERMANY, HEREBY IRREVOCABLY UNDERTAKE TO PAY YOU WITHOUT DELAY ON YOUR FIRST WRITTEN DEMAND FOR PAYMENT AN AMOUNT UP TO)，受益人与申请人 (PLUEMAT MASCHINENBAU VERTRIEBSGESELLSCHAFT M.B.H., DR. MAX-ILGNER-STRASSE 19, 32339 ESPELKAMP, F.R. GERMANY)之间有一基础合约(UNDER REF. NO. PLB 10 03 004)，所涉及金额(EUR150,000)，效期(EXPIRE ON SEPTEMBER 15, 2009)，索偿时的相关要求(SUPPORTED BY YOUR WRITTEN STATEMENT (WHETHER IN THE DEMAND ITSELF OR IN A SEPARATE DOCUMENT(S) ACCOMPANYING THE DEMAND AND REFERRED TO IN IT) STATING...)。该保函强调了适用法律(THIS GUARANTEE IS SUBJECT TO GERMAN LAW)。通过上述要点我们可以看出整个业务的基本全貌。为了在保函实际操作中更好地防范风险，对 ICC458 及 ISP98 的学习是必需的，其中应注意的要点如下。

(1) 独立性。实际业务中的保函基本全是独立保函，即保函一旦开出，就是独立于基础合约的。若涉及反担保函，则其应该既独立于基础合同，也独立于保函本身。

(2) 保函单据化特性。凭单付款，不涉及基础交易调查，因此对相关单据一定要能够提供且内容明确。

(3) 担保人只负责文件表面与保函要求相符。

(4) 所涉及的法律。尽量在谈判时选择熟悉的法律以便维护自身利益，案例 5.1 中是 GERMAN LAW。

(5) 如果合同金额有递减条款应特别注意。例如：保函金额随 xxx 合同项下履行金额递减。这些条款如果使用不当可能会使银行卷入与被保证人的纠纷中，或在银行承担保证责任后无法得到相应额度的追偿。因为每个业务时点银行应承担的最高限额是变化的，而银行并不知情，若出现索赔情况时，被保证人可能以超过应承担的限额为由抗辩，从而使银行无法行使追索权。

(6) 保函的生效条款。一般来说，保函自开出之日起即生效。但是，实际业务中，保函常表明可以在未来的某个确认的日期生效，也可依附合同生效之类的事实要件而生效。如目前常见的预付款退款保函、履约保函就常以"保函申请人实际收到预付款"或"待保函申请人与受益人根据 xxx 格式签订 xxx 合同"为生效条件。

此外，对保函内容应特别注意，以防产生风险。在实际业务中应注意银行一般不接受以下情况。

(1) 一般不接受没有明确限额的保函。因缺少保证责任金额最高限制条款，如果是从属性保函，那么，保函出具银行的责任风险可能会失控。如有的保函约定：保证范围包括 xxx(本金)及相关利息。这种情况下，由于利息的计算时间没有约定，实际上担保金额处于一个不确定的状态，是属于银行不可接受的条款。

(2) 不接受保证范围涉及道德风险的条款。因保函业务中，银行对道德风险难以进行评估和预测，因此银行不应接受此类条款。

(3) 银行不接受保函中约定保证期间的起始日早于银行出具保函的日期。如银行出具保函的日期是 2010 年 6 月 1 日，而保函中的保证期间的起始日为 2010 年 4 月 30 日。这种保函条款风险较大，而且可能保证责任实际已经先于保函出具日产生。

(4) 不明确的保证期间条款不接受。例如：本履约保函有效期自保函签发之日至合同条款规定的质量保证期满之日。保证期间难以明确界定，不利于银行控制风险。再者，向受益人赔款后，再向保函申请人追索时，保函申请人可能会以保证期间不明确为由拒绝付款，从而导致纠纷的产生。

三、总结思考

保函分类有多种，按其最重要的属性是第一性付款责任还是第二性付款责任，可以分为见索即付保函和从属性保函。实际业务中的保函基本全是见索即付的独立保函，因此在总结时，对此提示两点。

(1) 见索即付保函包括多方当事人之间互相独立和互相交织的多个法律关系。银行应慎重处理基于基础合同关系的抗辩。

(2) 银行应正确执行保函付款指令。

由于见索即付保函的付款条件是关于银行在何条件下承担付款责任，因此，作为通知银行应关注是否存在以下情形：保函对索偿单据种类、数量、内容的约定不明确；保函对索偿单据的提交时间约定不明；保函对单据的提交方式约定不明；保函规定指示方对单据负有实质审核义务等。如果存在上述情形，则可能会给保函索付带来困难，甚至使银行陷入基础交易纠纷。

最后，我们将保函与备用信用证的异同之处列出来，以便于对比和掌握。

保函与备用信用证的类同之处：

	见索即付独立保函	备用信用证
法律当事人方面	一般包括申请人、担保人或开证行、受益人。三者之间的法律关系是：申请人与担保人或开证行之间是契约关系，二者之间的权利义务关系是以开立保函申请书来确定的；开证行与受益人之间的法律关系则是以保函或备用信用证条款为准。	
应用范围及目的方面	备用信用证是作为保函的替代方式而产生的，它所达到的目的自然与保函有一致之处。	
性质	第一，担保银行或开证行的担保或付款责任都是第一性的；第二，一旦开立，则独立于基础合同；第三，是纯粹的单据交易，只凭单付款。	

保函与备用信用证的不同之处：

	保　函	备用信用证
特点	有从属性保函和见索即付保函之分	独立性，纯粹单据交易
适用的法律规范和国际惯例	ICC458 等	ISP98

四、实训操练

练习 5.1

如果通知银行交行在 2009 年 8 月 8 日收到 DEUTSCHE BANK 开来的保函 MT760。经过审核后，如何填制银行的保函通知书呢？假设银行通知费是 EUR18，银行编号是 GA200900009，保函金额是合同标的的 20%。

MT760 电文

-------------------------- Message Header --------------------------

Swift Output　　　: FIN 760 Guarantee/Stdby Letter Credit

Sender　　　　　: DEUTDE3BXXX

Receiver　　　　: COMMCNSHNJG

-------------------------- Message Text --------------------------

　27 Sequence of Total

　　　Number 1

　　　Total 1

20 Transaction Reference Number

    3300900494

23 Further Identification

    ISSUE

30 Date

    090807

40C Applicable Rules

    Type NONE

77C Details of Guarantee

    PLEASE FORWARD THE FOLLOWING GUARANTEE TO BENEFICIARY,

    ATTN. MR. JI　ENGINEERING DEPT.

    WITHOUT ANY ENGAGEMENT ON YOUR PART AND WITHOUT ANY CHARGES FOR

    US.

    BENEFICIARY:

    NANJING QINGTIAN CO., LTD.

    NO.9 LOUHUI ROAD, NANJING ECONOMIC AND

    TECHNOLOGICAL DEVELOPMENT ZONE,

    NANJING, JIANGSU, 210038

    P.R. CHINA

    ADVANCE PAYMENT GUARANTEE NO. 3300900494

    DEAR SIRS,

    WE HAVE BEEN INFORMED THAT A CONTRACT, HEREINAFTER CALLED
    'UNDERLYING CONTRACT', HAS BEEN CONCLUDED BETWEEN BENE. AND
    MEDISEAL GMBH FLURSTR 65, 33758 SCHLOSS HOLTE-STUKENBROCK,
    FEDERAL REPUBLIC OF GERMANY UNDER CONTRACT NO. 20090801 NANJING
    DD. 01.08.2009 FOR 'ONE COMPLETE SET OF BLISTER PACKING
    LINE MODEL CP400 + P3000' AT A TOTAL PRICE OF EUR750,000.00
    AND
    THAT THE UNDERLYING CONTRACT STIPULATES THAT AN ADVANCE PAYMENT
    IN THE AMOUNT OF 20 PERCENT OF THE TOTAL PRICE BE EFFECTED
    AGAINST AN ADVANCE PAYMENT GUARANTEE.
    THIS BEING PREMISED, WE, DEUTSCHE BANK AG, HERFORDER STRASSE
    23, 33602 BIELEFELD, FEDERAL REPUBLIC OF GERMANY, HEREBY

IRREVOCABLY UNDERTAKE TO PAY YOU WITHOUT DELAY ON YOUR FIRST

WRITTEN DEMAND FOR PAYMENT AN AMOUNT UP TO EUR 150, 000.00

(IN WORDS: EURO ONE HUNDRED AND FIFTY THOUSAND ONLY),

PROVIDED YOU SUBMIT TO US AT THE SAME TIME AND TOGETHER WITH YOUR DEMAND AN ADDITIONAL COPY OF AN AWARD IN ENGLISH LANGUAGE MADE UNDER THE RULES OF CONCILIATION AND ARBITRATION OF THE CHINA INTERNATIONAL ECONOMIC AND TRADE ARBITRATION COMMISSION, CERTIFIED TRUE BY THE SECRETARY-GENERAL OF THE ARBITRATION COURT OF THE CHINA INTERNATIONAL ECONOMIC AND TRADE ARBITRATION

COMMISSION, IN WHICH IT IS HELD WITHOUT ANY RESERVE, THAT THE

VENDOR OWES YOU THE REPAYMENT OF A CERTAIN EUR ADVANCE PAYMENT

AMOUNT UNDER CONTRACT NO. 20090801 NANJING CTTQ-MS DD.

01.08.2009 WHICH AMOUNT MUST NOT BE LESS THAN THE EUR AMOUNT

CLAIMED UNDER THIS GUARANTEE.

THIS GUARANTEE SHALL ENTER INTO EFFECT AS SOON AS THE ADVANCE

PAYMENT AMOUNTING TO EUR 150, 000.00 IS RECEIVED IN FULL BY US,

WITH REFERENCE TO THIS GUARANTEE, IN FAVOUR AND AT THE FREE

DISPOSAL OF THE VENDOR IN HIS ACCOUNT NO. 1245323,

IBAN DE05 4807 0020 0124 5323 00 SWIFT CODE DEUTDE3B

THIS GUARANTEE SHALL EXPIRE ON APRIL 30, 2010, UNLESS YOUR

DEMAND UNDER THIS GUARANTEE IN ACCORDANCE WITH ITS

CONDITIONS HAS REACHED US IN BIELEFELD BY THE END OF THAT DAY.

THIS GUARANTEE IS TRANSFERABLE WITH OUR WRITTEN CONSENT ONLY.

THE ISSUANCE OF THIS GUARANTEE IS PERMITTED ACCORDING TO GERMAN LAW.

THIS GUARANTEE IS SUBJECT TO GERMAN LAW.

DEUTSCHE BANK AG

THIS IS THE OPERATIVE INSTRUMENT, NO MAIL CONFIRMATION FOLLOWS.

THANK YOU VERY MUCH AND KIND REGARDS

DEUTSCHE BANK AG

TRADE FINANCE GUARANTEES

ADVICE OF LETTER OF GUARANTEE

致(TO):	我行编号(OUR REF. NO.):	
	通知日期(DATE):	
来自(FROM):	保函号码(GUARANTEE NO.):	
	开立日期(ISSUING DATE):	
	保函金额(AMOUNT):	

敬启者：

　　欣告贵司，我行从上述银行收到一张以贵司为受益人的其真实性已经证实的电传/信函/SWIFT 开立的文件，敬请注意下列事项：

（Dear sirs:

We take a pleasure in notifying you that we have received an authenticated telex/mail /SWIFT GUARANTEE message in your favor from a/m bank. Please note the following item(s):)

(•)一张保函(A GUARANTEE)

(•)根据保函规定，我行相关通知费用　　　　由贵司承担。

(As per stipulation of the GUARANTEE, our bank's advising commission　　　　is for your a/c.)

(•)联系业务时，务请提供我行编号

(When corresponding, please always mention our reference number:　　　　)

要项(Important)

　　如贵司发现该保函中有任何条款难以接受，请径与保函申请人联系以便及时修改，避免单据提示时可能发生的问题。

　　(If you find terms and conditions which you are unable to comply with in this GUARANTEE, please directly contact applicant in order to make timely amendment and avoid any difficulties which may arise when documents are presented.)

参考答案:

ADVICE OF LETTER OF GUARANTEE

致(TO):	我行编号(OUR REF. NO.):	GA200900009
NANJING QINGTIAN CO., LTD. NANJING 南京青田有限公司	通知日期(DATE):	20090808
来自(FROM):	保函号码(GUARANTEE NO.):	3300900494
DEUTSCHE BANK AG, BIELEFELD,	开立日期(ISSUING DATE):	20090807
HERFORDER STRASSE 23, 33609, BIELEFELD	保函金额(AMOUNT):	EUR150,000.00

敬启者:

欣告贵司,我行从上述银行收到一张以贵司为受益人的其真实性已经证实的电传/信函/SWIFT 开立的文件,敬请注意下列事项:

(Dear sirs:

We take a pleasure in notifying you that we have received an authenticated telex/mail /SWIFT GUARANTEE message in your favor from a/m bank. Please note the following item(s):)

(•)一张保函(A GUARANTEE)

(•)根据保函规定,我行相关通知费 EUR18.00 由贵司承担。

(As per stipulation of the guarantee, our bank's advising commission EUR18.00 is for your a/c.)

(•)联系业务时,务请提供我行编号 GA200900009。

(When corresponding, please always mention our reference number:GA200900009.)

要项(Important)

如贵司发现该保函中有任何条款难以接受,请径与保函申请人联系以便及时修改,避免单据提示时可能发生的问题。

(If you find terms and conditions which you are unable to comply with in this GUARANTEE, please directly contact applicant in order to make timely amendment and avoid any difficulties which may arise when documents are presented.)

练习 5.2

备用信用证的通知与保函的通知相同。假设通知银行交行于 2010 年 2 月 19 日收到 BAYERISCHE HYPO-UND VEREINSBANK AG–HYPOVEREINSBANK NUERNBERG (SWIFT No.：HYVEDEMM460)开来的以下备用证 MT760。经过审核后，如何填制银行的备用证通知书呢？假设银行通知费是 USD30，银行编号是 SA201000001。

MT760 电文

```
-------------------------- Message Header -------------------------
Swift Output        : FIN 760 Guarantee/Stdby Letter Credit
Sender              : HYVEDEMM460
Receiver            : COMMCNSHNJG
-------------------------- Message Text -------------------------
```

27	Sequence of Total	
	Number	1
	Total	1
20	Transaction Reference Number	
	03601000775	
23	Further Identification	
	ISSUE	
30	Date	
	100218	
40C	Applicable Rules	
	Type	NONE
77C	Details of Guarantee	

VERY URGENT

INSTALLATION AND WARRANTY STANDBY L/C NO. 03601000775 FOR USD 11,475.00 DEAR SIR OR MADAM,

BY ORDER OF OUR CLIENTS, SIEMENS AG, HEALTHCARE SECTOR, PLEASE FIND BELOW THE WORDING OF OUR UNDERTAKING NO. 03601000775 , WHICH WE KINDLY ASK YOU TO ADVISE TO THE BENEFICIARY WITHOUT ANY OBLIGATION ON YOUR PART, AND TO CONFIRM THE AUTHENTICATION OF THE SWIFT-MESSAGE.

QUOTE

JIANGSU INTERNATIONAL I/E CORP., LTD.

ROOM 222, BUILDING B

256 GANZHOU AVENUE

210005 NANJING CITY

JIANGSU PROVINCE

PEOPLE'S REPUBLIC OF CHINA

DEAR SIRS,

REFERENCE IS MADE TO THE CONTRACT NO. 10MCD(2)-21000010GE DATED
JANUARY 22, 2010 CONCLUDED BETWEEN YOU AS THE BUYER AND
SIEMENS AKTIENGESELLSCHAFT, HEALTHCARE SECTOR, HENKESTRASSE 127,
91052 ERLANGEN, GERMANY (THE SELLER) FOR THE SUPPLY OF ONE SET
MR MAGNETOM AVANTO IN THE TOTAL AMOUNT OF USD114,750.00.
ACCORDING TO THE SAID CONTRACT, THE SELLER HAS TO FURNISH A
PERFORMANCE GUARANTEE SECURING THE CONTRACTUAL WARRANTY
SERVICE OBLIGATIONS IN THE AMOUNT OF USD 11,475.00
CORRESPONDING TO 10 PER CENT OF THE TOTAL CONTRACT VALUE.
BY ORDER OF SIEMENS AKTIENGESELLSCHAFT, HEALTHCARE SECTOR,
HENKESTRASSE 127, 91052 ERLANGEN, GERMANY, WE, BAYERISCHE HYPO-UND
VEREINSBANK AG – HYPOVEREINSBANK NUERNBERG, HEREBY ESTABLISH THIS
GUARANTEE AND UNDERTAKE
IRREVOCABLY TO PAY TO YOU ANY AMOUNT NOT EXCEEDING
USD11,475.00 (IN WORDS: UNITED STATES DOLLARS
ELEVEN THOUSAND FOUR HUNDRED AND SEVENTY FIVE ONLY)
UPON YOUR FIRST WRITTEN DEMAND STATING THAT THE SELLER HAS NOT
FULFILLED HIS CONTRACTUAL WARRANTY SERVICE OBLIGATIONS. YOUR
DEMAND FOR PAYMENT MUST ALSO BE ACCOMPANIED BY AN ORIGINAL
CERTIFICATE ISSUED BY AQSIQ (ADMINISTRATION OF QUALITY
SUPERVISION, INSPECTION AND QUARANTINE OF THE PEOPLE'S REPUBLIC
OF CHINA) CERTIFYING THAT THE SELLER HAS FAILED TO FULFILL HIS
CONTRACTUAL WARRANTY SERVICE OBLIGATIONS.
OUR LIABILITY UNDER THIS GUARANTEE WILL EXPIRE AS SOON AS THIS
LETTER OF GUARANTEE IS RETURNED TO US, AT THE LATEST, HOWEVER,
ON 10 JUNE 2011. ANY CLAIM HEREUNDER MUST HAVE REACHED US BY
LETTER BEFORE THE CLOSING HOURS OF THAT DAY.
THE ORIGINAL OF THIS LETTER OF GUARANTEE SHOULD BE RETURNED TO
US ON EXPIRATION OR UPON FULFILLMENT OF OUR UNDERTAKING.

THE RIGHTS RESULTING FROM THIS GUARANTEE ARE ONLY ASSIGNABLE
WITH OUR CONSENT.
OUR GUARANTEE IS ISSUED IN CONFORMITY WITH THE LEGAL REGULATIONS
VALID IN THE FEDERAL REPUBLIC OF GERMANY.
YOURS FAITHFULLY,
HYPOVEREINSBANK
UNQUOTE
MANY THANKS AND BEST REGARDS

72　Sender to Receiver Information
THIS MESSAGE IS THE OPERATIVE
INSTRUMENT, NO MAIL CONFIRMATION
WILL FOLLOW. PLEASE ADVISE WITHOUT
ANY OBLIGATION ON YOUR PART.

ADVICE OF LETTER OF STANDBY L/C

致(TO):	我行编号(OUR REF. NO.):	
	通知日期(DATE):	
来自(FROM):	备用信用证号码(STANDBY L/C NO.):	
	开立日期(ISSUING DATE):	
	备用信用证金额(AMOUNT):	

敬启者：
　　欣告贵司，我行从上述银行收到一张以贵司为受益人的其真实性已经证实的电传/信函/SWIFT 开立的文件，敬请注意下列事项：
（Dear sirs:
We take a pleasure in notifying you that we have received an authenticated telex/mail / swift standby L/C message in your favor from a/m bank. Please note the following item(s):)

(•)一张备用信用证(A STANDBY L/C)
(•)根据备用信用证规定，我行相关通知费　　　　由贵司承担。
(As per stipulation of the standby L/C, our bank's advising commission　　is for your a/c.)
(•)联系业务时，务请提供我行编号
(When corresponding, please always mention our reference number:　　　　　)

要项(Important)
如贵司发现该备用信用证中有任何条款难以接受，请径与备用信用证申请人联系以便及时修改，避免单据提示时可能发生的问题。
(If you find terms and conditions which you are unable to comply with in this STANDBY L/C, please directly contact applicant in order to make timely amendment and avoid any difficulties which may arise when documents are presented.)

参考答案：

ADVICE OF LETTER OF STANDBY L/C

致(TO): JIANGSU INTL I/E CORP., LTD. NANJING	我行编号(OUR REF. NO.):	SA201000001
	通知日期(DATE):	20100219
来自(FROM): BAYERISCHE HYPO-UND EREINSBANK AG. – HYPOVEREINSBANK NUERNBERG	备用信用证号码(STANDBY L/C NO.):	03601000775
	开立日期(ISSUING DATE):	20100218
	备用信用证金额(AMOUNT):	USD11,475.00

敬启者：
欣告贵司，我行从上述银行收到一张以贵司为受益人的其真实性已经证实的电传/信函/SWIFT 开立的文件，敬请注意下列事项：
(Dear sirs:
We take a pleasure in notifying you that we have received an authenticated telex/mail /swift standby L/C message in your favor from a/m bank. Please note the following item(s):)

(·)一张备用信用证(A STANDBY L/C)

(·)根据备用信用证规定，我行相关通知费用 USD30.00 由贵司承担。

(As per stipulation of the standby L/C, our bank's advising commission USD30.00 is for your a/c.)

(·)联系业务时，务请提供我行编号 SA201000001。

(When corresponding, please always mention our reference number:SA201000001.)

要项(Important)

如贵司发现该备用信用证中有任何条款难以接受，请径与备用信用证申请人联系以便及时修改，避免单据提示时可能发生的问题。

(If you find terms and conditions which you are unable to comply with in this STANDBY L/C, please directly contact applicant in order to make timely amendment and avoid any difficulties which may arise when documents are presented.)

练习 5.3

如果通知银行交行 2009 年 4 月 1 日收到 DEUTSCHE BANK(SWIFT No.：DEUTDE3BXXX)开来的以下保函 MT760。经过审核后，如何填制银行的保函通知书呢？假设银行通知费是 EUR18，银行编号是 GA200900004。

MT760 电文

```
---------------------- Message Header ----------------------
Swift Output    : FIN 760 Guarantee/Stdby Letter Credit
Sender          : DEUTDE3BXXX
Receiver        : COMMCNSHNJG
-------------------------- Message Text ----------------------
    27    Sequence of Total
          Number          1
          Total           1
    20    Transaction Reference Number
          3371000018
    23    Further Identification
          ISSUE
    30    Date
          090331
    40C   Applicable Rules
```

Type   NONE

77C   Details of Guarantee

ATTN.:

BANK OF COMMUNICATIONS

NANJING BRANCH, NO. 124

NORTH ZHANGSHAN ROAD, NANJING

CHINA

PLEASE FORWARD THE FOLLOWING GUARANTEE TO BENEFICIARY,

ACCOUNT NO. 320006664010123001665 WITH YOURSELVES WITHOUT ANY

ENGAGEMENT ON YOUR PART AND WITHOUT ANY CHARGES FOR US.

QUOTE

TO: NANJING QINGTIAN CO., LTD.

NANJING, CHINA

ADVANCE PAYMENT GUARANTEE NO. 3371000018

WE HAVE BEEN INFORMED THAT A CONTRACT HAS BEEN SIGNED BETWEEN

YOU AND PLUEMAT MASCHINENBAU VERTRIEBSGESELLSCHAFT M.B.H.,

DR. MAX-ILGNER-STRASSE 19, 32339 ESPELKAMP, F.R. GERMANY,

HEREINAFTER CALLED PRINCIPAL, FOR

"ONE SET OF AUTOMATIC FORM-FILL-SEAL PRODUCTION LINE FFS 892HS

MACH.-NO. 2157, DETAILS AS PER APPENDIX I SCOPE OF SUPPLY AND

TECHNICAL SPECIFICATION" AT A TOTAL PRICE OF EUR697,000.00

AND THAT THE UNDERLYING CONTRACT STIPULATES THAT AN ADVANCE

PAYMENT IN THE AMOUNT OF 10 PERCENT OF THE TOTAL PRICE BE

EFFECTED AGAINST AN ADVANCE PAYMENT GUARANTEE.

THIS BEING PREMISED, WE, DEUTSCHE BANK AG, HERFORDER STRASSE

23, 33602 BIELEFELD, F.R. GERMANY, HEREBY IRREVOCABLY UNDERTAKE

TO PAY YOU WITHOUT DELAY ON YOUR FIRST WRITTEN DEMAND FOR

PAYMENT AN AMOUNT UP TO

EUR69,700.00(SAY EURO SIXTY NINE THOUSAND SEVEN HUNDRED ONLY),

PROVIDED YOUR DEMAND FOR PAYMENT IS SIMULTANEOUSLY SUPPORTED BY

YOUR WRITTEN STATEMENT STATING

A) THAT THE PRINCIPAL IS IN BREACH OF HIS OBLIGATION(S) UNDER

THE UNDERLYING CONTRACT, AND

B)THE RESPECT IN WHICH THE PRINCIPAL IS IN BREACH, AND

C)THAT THE OBLIGATION(S) IN RESPECT OF WHICH THE PRINCIPAL IS

IN BREACH IS/ARE COVERED BY THE PRESENT GUARANTEE AND THAT YOU

ARE THEREFORE ENTITLED TO DEMAND REPAYMENT OF THE ADVANCE

PAYMENT UP TO THE AMOUNT OF THE DEMAND FOR PAYMENT.

THIS GUARANTEE SHALL ENTER INTO EFFECT IF AND TO THE EXTENT THE ADVANCE PAYMENT OF EUR69,700.00 IS CREDITED IN FULL WITHOUT RESERVE TO PRINCIPAL'S ACCOUNT NO. 2825420 HELD WITH US IN MINDEN, IBAN DE23 4907 0028 0282 5420 00 WITH REFERENCE TO THIS GUARANTEE, AT HIS FREE DISPOSAL.

THIS GUARANTEE SHALL EXPIRE ON SEPTEMBER 15, 2009, UNLESS YOUR WRITTEN DEMAND UNDER THIS GUARANTEE IN ACCORDANCE WITH THE ABOVE MENTIONED CONDITIONS HAS REACHED US IN BIELEFELD BY THE END OF THAT DAY.

THIS GUARANTEE IS TRANSFERABLE WITH OUR WRITTEN CONSENT ONLY.

THE ISSUANCE OF THIS GUARANTEE IS PERMITTED ACCORDING TO GERMAN LAW.

THIS GUARANTEE IS SUBJECT TO GERMAN LAW.

DEUTSCHE BANK AG

UNQUOTE

THIS IS AN OPERATIVE INSTRUMENT AND NO MAIL CONFIRMATION FOLLOWS.

KIND REGARDS

DEUTSCHE BANK AG

TRADE FINANCE GUARANTEES

ADVICE OF LETTER OF STANDBY L/C

致(TO):	我行编号(OUR REF. NO.):	
	通知日期(DATE):	
来自(FROM):	备用信用证号码(STANDBY L/C NO.):	
	开立日期(ISSUING DATE):	
	备用信用证金额(AMOUNT):	

敬启者：

欣告贵司，我行从上述银行收到一张以贵司为受益人的其真实性已经证实的电传/信函/SWIFT 开立的文件，敬请注意下列事项：

（Dear sirs:

We take a pleasure in notifying you that we have received an authenticated telex/mail / swift GUARANTEE message in your favor from a/m bank. Please note the following item(s):)

(•)一张备用信用证(A GUARANTEE)

(•)根据备用信用证规定，我行相关通知费   由贵司承担。

(As per stipulation of the GUARANTEE, our bank's advising commission   is for your a/c.)

(•)联系业务时，务请提供我行编号

(When corresponding, please always mention our reference number:)

要项(Important)

    如贵司发现该备用信用证中有任何条款难以接受，请径与备用信用证申请人联系以便及时修改，避免单据提示时可能发生的问题。

    (If you find terms and conditions which you are unable to comply with in this GUARANTEE, please directly contact applicant in order to make timely amendment and avoid any difficulties which may arise when documents are presented.)

参考答案：

ADVICE OF LETTER OF GUARANTEE

致(TO): NANJING QINGTIAN CO., LTD. NANJING 南京青田有限公司	我行编号(OUR REF. NO.):	GA200900004
	通知日期(DATE):	20090401
来自(FROM): DEUTSCHE BANK AG, BIELEFELD, HERFORDER STRASSE 23, 33609, BIELEFELD	保函号码(GUARANTEE NO.):	3371000018
	开立日期(ISSUING DATE):	20090331
	保函金额(AMOUNT):	EUR 69,700.00

敬启者：

    欣告贵司，我行从上述银行收到一张以贵司为受益人的其真实性已经证实的电传/信函/SWIFT 开立的文件，敬请注意下列事项：

(Dear sirs:

We take a pleasure in notifying you that we have received an authenticated telex/mail /swift GUARANTEE message in your favor from a/m bank. Please note the following item(s):)

(·)一张保函(A GUARANTEE)

(·)根据保函规定，我行相关通知费 EUR18.00 由贵司承担。

(As per stipulation of the GUARANTEE, our bank's advising commission EUR18.00 is for your a/c.)

(·)联系业务时，务请提供我行编号 GA200900004。

(When corresponding, please always mention our reference number:GA200900004.)

要项(Important)

如贵司发现该保函中有任何条款难以接受，请径与保函申请人联系以便及时修改，避免单据提示时可能发生的问题。

(If you find terms and conditions which you are unable to comply with in this GUARANTEE, please directly contact applicant in order to make timely amendment and avoid any difficulties which may arise when documents are presented.)

第二节　开立进口备用信用证

一、业务场景与操作

备用信用证一经开立便是一项不可撤销的、独立的、要求单据的、具有约束力的承诺。

银行开立备用信用证时的资信审核，如进口国与进口商品等的审查，在前文进口开证部分已经介绍，这里不再重复。下面将从备用信用证自身的特点来设计操作并提示风险。

案例 5.2

2010 年 3 月 5 日，A 公司与 B 公司签订编号为 B22 的合同，从 B 进口价值 USD162000.00 的货物，A 公司预先支付 10%的货款，B 公司在收到预付款后发货。但 A 公司要求 B 公司提供备用信用证作为担保，保证其收到预付款后履行合同，否则 A 公司可通过备用证索偿预付款。B 公司通过 C 银行开立备用证给 A 公司，由 D 银行通知。(因各家银行保函和备用信用证皆有自己经过法律部门审核的标准格式，这里仅是举例说明。)

1. 申请开立备用信用证

B 公司填写备用信用证申请书，并交给开证行 C 银行。

开立备用信用证申请书

STANDBY L/C FOR ADVANCE PAYMENT

In view of the contract No. (基础交易合同编号)B22 (hereinafter referred to as the contract)signed between you and ___(申请人名称)B 公司___ (hereinafter referred to as the applicant)covering (基础交易合同标的) goods .

We, (担保人名称) C bank , hereby unconditionally and irrevocably issue this standby letter of credit No.(备用信用证编号)SLC1001 in your favor for account of the applicant for maximum amount(最大担保金额)USD16200.00 (say (最大担保金额大写)USD sixteen thousand two hundred only) (hereinafter referred to as the guaranteed amount)as guarantee for the advance payment and interest incurred under the contract.

Documents required:

Your draft(s) at sight drawn on us bearing the clause "drawn under irrevocable standby letter of credit No. (备用信用证编号) SLC1001 of (担保人名称)C bank ";

Your signed statement stating the effect and the aspect of the applicant's default in fulfillment of any of his obligation for which the advance payment is made.

We engage with you that draft(s) drawn under and in compliance with terms of this credit shall be duly honored on due presentation to us. We shall pay you, within 5 banking business days after receiving above-mentioned documents, the amount specified in your draft(s) drawn on us.

All banking charges other than opening charges of this standby are for account of the beneficiary.

Except as expressly stated herein, this undertaking is not subjected to any contract, agreement, condition or qualification. The obligation and liabilities of us under this credit shall be independent.

Unless expressly consented by us, this standby L/C is not transferable or assignable.

This credit will come into effect upon our receipt of the statement by the applicant stating that it receives the advance payment, and shall be binding on us as a continuing guarantee until ___(备用信用证到期日) 20101231___. Any claim should reach our counter on or before that day. This standby letter of credit shall automatically become null and void upon expiry, whether it is returned to us or not .

Except so far as otherwise expressly stated, this credit is subject to___(备用信用证选用的国际惯例) ISP98___.

2. 开立备用信用证

如 B 公司已经在 C 银行取得了相关的授信额度，并且授信条件已经全面落实，这时 C 银行将根据 B 公司提供的"开立保函/备用信用证申请书"开立备用信用证。

在实际业务中，每家银行的备用信用证都有经过其法律部门审核的固定格式。如果申请人要做变动，添加或取消某条款时，应该通过其法律部门的审核之后方可进行，这部分不同于前文所介绍的开立一般信用证时对单据等条款的增添和改动。

在实际业务中，备用信用证常采取电开和函开两种形式。在电开时，由于 SWIFT 没有单独为备用信用证设立格式，因而常见用 MT760 开立的备用证，注明受 ISP98 或 UCP600 约束，也有用 MT700 及 MT799 开立的备用证。而电文也不全是受 ISP98 约束，实际业务中，电文中注明受 UCP600 约束的也较多。

下面是开证行根据 B 公司的申请开立的备用信用证。

MT760 电文

```
-------------------------- Message Header ------------------------
Swift Output    : FIN 760 Guarantee/Stdby Letter Credit
Sender          : C bank              发送方 SWIFT
Receiver        : D bank              接收方 SWIFT
-------------------------- Message Text --------------------------
27    Sequence of Total
      Number        1
      Total         1
20    Transaction Reference Number
      SLC1001
23    Further Identification
      ISSUE
30    Date
      20100305
40C   Applicable Rules
      Type      ISP98
77C   Details of Standby Letter of Credit
      IN VIEW OF THE CONTRACT NO. B22 (HEREINAFTER
      REFERRED TO AS THE CONTRACT) SIGNED BETWEEN YOU
      AND B COMPANY (HEREINAFTER REFERRED TO AS THE
      APPLICANT)COVERING GOODS.
      WE, C BANK, HEREBY UNCONDITIONALLY AND
      IRREVOCABLY ISSUE THIS STANDBY LETTER OF CREDIT
      NO. SLC1001 IN YOUR FAVOR FOR ACCOUNT OF THE
      APPLICANT FOR MAXIMUM AMOUNT USD16200.00 (SAY US DOLLARS
      SIXTEEN THOUSAND TWO HUNDRED ONLY) (HEREINAFTER
      REFERRED TO AS THE GUARANTEED AMOUNT)AS GUARANTEE
```

FOR THE ADVANCE PAYMENT AND INTEREST INCURRED
UNDER THE CONTRACT.

DOCUMENTS REQUIRED:

YOUR DRAFT(S) AT SIGHT DRAWN ON US BEARING THE
CLAUSE DRAWN UNDER IRREVOCABLE STANDBY LETTER OF
CREDIT NO. SLC1001 OF C BANK.

YOUR SIGNED STATEMENT STATING THE EFFECT AND THE
ASPECT OF THE APPLICANTS DEFAULT IN FULFILLMENT
OF ANY OF HIS OBLIGATION FOR WHICH THE ADVANCE
PAYMENT IS MADE.

WE ENGAGE WITH YOU THAT DRAFT(S) DRAWN UNDER AND
IN COMPLIANCE WITH TERMS OF THIS CREDIT SHALL BE
DULY HONORED ON DUE PRESENTATION TO US. WE SHALL
PAY YOU, WITHIN 5 BANKING BUSINESS DAYS AFTER
RECEIVING ABOVE-MENTIONED DOCUMENTS, THE AMOUNT
SPECIFIED IN YOUR DRAFT(S) DRAWN ON US.

79	Narrative

ALL BANKING CHARGES OTHER THAN OPENING CHARGES OF
THIS STANDBY ARE FOR ACCOUNT OF THE BENEFICIARY.
EXCEPT AS EXPRESSLY STATED HEREIN, THIS
UNDERTAKING IS NOT SUBJECTED TO ANY CONTRACT,
AGREEMENT, CONDITION OR QUALIFICATION. THE
OBLIGATION AND LIABILITIES OF US UNDER THIS
CREDIT SHALL BE INDEPENDENT.

UNLESS EXPRESSLY CONSENTED BY US, THIS STANDBY
L/C IS NOT TRANSFERABLE OR ASSIGNABLE.

THIS CREDIT WILL COME INTO EFFECT UPON OUR
RECEIPT OF THE STATEMENT BY THE APPLICANT STATING
THAT IT RECEIVES THE ADVANCE PAYMENT, AND SHALL
BE BINDING ON US AS A CONTINUING GUARANTEE UNTIL
20101231. ANY CLAIM SHOULD REACH OUR COUNTER
ON OR BEFORE THAT DAY. THIS STANDBY LETTER OF
CREDIT SHALL AUTOMATICALLY BECOME NULL AND VOID
UPON EXPIRY, WHETHER IT IS RETURNED TO US OR NOT.
EXCEPT SO FAR AS OTHERWISE EXPRESSLY STATED, THIS

CREDIT IS SUBJECT TO ISP98.

图 5.2 为案例 5.2 的业务流程图。

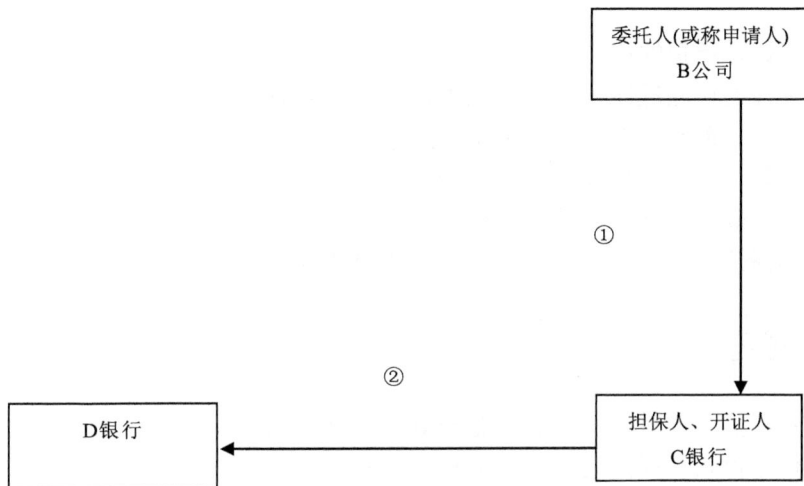

图 5.2　案例 5.2 的业务流程图

① C 银行根据 B 公司开立备用信用证的申请审核其授信额度和条件的落实情况后开立备用信用证。

② C 银行选择 D 银行作为通知行，通过 D 银行通知给受益人 A 公司。

二、风险控制

1. 法律风险

了解备用信用证的法律性质对防范风险是十分重要的。备用信用证的法律性质主要有以下几点。

(1) 不可撤销性：开证人不得修改或撤销其在该备用信用证下的义务。

(2) 独立性：备用信用证一经开立即独立于赖以开立的申请人与受益人之间的基础交易合约，又独立于申请人和开证人之间的开证契约关系。

(3) 单据性：备用信用证项下必须有单据要求，但与跟单信用证所提交的单据(如提单)等要求不同，"单单相符"的原则对备用信用证并不是必要的。

(4) 强制性：一经开立，即对开证人具有强制性的约束力。

2. 当事人的风险

1) 来自受益人的风险

开证行在开立备用信用证之前，需要调查受益人的资信，防止其在备用信用证的有效期内借故提示单据，要求开证行付款。另外还应注意备用信用证中的单据条款的严谨性，严格规定受益人出具证明的格式与内容，防止因条款描述的疏忽而造成损失，使受益人有了可乘之机。尤其是所要求的单据容易得到时，如果遇到恶意受益人索汇，则会使银行陷入麻烦。

2）开证银行承担的风险

备用信用证的风险远比一般信用证大，因为一旦开出，便不可撤销地承担独立付款的责任，而且由于大部分的备用信用证都不用提交运输单据，因此不能通过掌握货权来最大限度地避免风险。另外在付款时，只凭相符但却很简单的单据付款，很容易被资信不良的开证人和受益人骗取资金。因此开证行在开证时，应充分了解开证申请人的资信和交易的背景，按国际惯例办事，以避免损失。最后还要注意对国家风险的防范。

三、总结思考

在使用备用信用证时，一定要注意对其风险加以防范。同其他结算方式一样，备用信用证并不是保证付款和履约的仙丹，同样也存在风险，有操作风险、诈骗风险等，有实际业务中的风险，也有难以预测的国家风险等特殊风险，如果处理不好就会造成难以估计和挽回的损失，因此既要了解备用信用证的作用，又要对其风险加以防范。下面将银行备用信用证与跟单商业信用证做简单比较，以便于在实际业务中加以区分。

1. 功能不同

跟单商业信用证一般以清偿货款为目的，充当的是合同价款的支付手段，它常常作为货款收付方式出现在基础合同的支付条款之中。

备用信用证一般是以融通资金并起到担保作用为目的，它用于在申请人未能履约时银行负责赔款。备用信用证充当的不是支付手段，而是发挥了一种担保作用。

2. 适用范围不同

跟单商业信用证主要适用于国际货物买卖领域，从其产生那天起就与国际贸易领域紧密相连。

备用信用证已发展成为适用于各种用途的融资工具，比跟单商业信用证适用领域更广。

3. 付款责任不同

在跟单商业信用证业务中，开证行的付款责任是第一性的，受益人履行交货义务后由银行付款。

备用信用证则是在申请人未履行其义务时由开证人赔款。尽管备用信用证的开证人形式上承担着见索即付的第一付款责任，但其开立意图实质上是第二性的，具有银行担保的性质。

4. 所要求的单据不同

跟单商业信用证下，一般要求正本货运单据，它代表货物的所有权，能切实保障开证行取得偿付的权益。

在备用信用证下，因其不需提交货运单据而需要提交拒付证明，因而对开证行权益保障较弱。正因为如此，银行开立备用信用证的风险会比开立跟单商业信用证的风险大得多。

四、实训操练

练习 5.4

2010 年 3 月 1 日，Y 公司将参与 E 公司组织的竞标，合同号 SC20100301，标的价值 USD350000.00。E 公司要求 Y 公司提供备用信用证，保证其在中标后履行合同，否则 E 公司有权凭证获得补偿。Y 公司为顺利竞标找到 C 银行开立相关备用证，通知行为 D 行，且相关授信已经落实到位。请根据下列申请书开立履约备用信用证。假设备用信用证的金额是标的价值的 10%。

开立保函/备用信用证申请书如下：

STANDBY L/C FOR PERFORMANCE

In view of the contract No. (基础交易合同编号) SC20100301 (hereinafter referred to as the contract) signed between you and (申请人名称) Y Co. (hereinafter referred to as the applicant)for (基础交易合同标的)USD350000.00 .

We, (担保人名称) C bank , hereby unconditionally and irrevocably issue this standby letter of credit No.(备用信用证编号) SA2010002 in your favor for account of the applicant for maximum amount(最大担保金额)USD35000.00 (say (最大担保金额大写)USD thirty five thousand only) (hereinafter referred to as the guaranteed amount)representing (担保金额占基础交易合同金额的百分比) 10 percent of the contract price.

Documents required:

Your draft(s) at sight drawn on us bearing the clause "drawn under irrevocable standby letter of credit No. (备用信用证编号)SA2010002 of (担保人名称) C bank ;

Your signed statement stating the effect and aspect of the failure of performance by the applicant.

We engage with you that draft(s) drawn under and in compliance with terms of this credit shall be duly honored on due presentation to us. We shall pay you, within 5 banking business days after receiving above-mentioned documents, the amount specified in your draft(s) drawn on us, provided that the aggregate claimed amount does not exceed the guaranteed amount.

All banking charges other than opening charges of this standby are for account of the beneficiary.

Except as expressly stated herein, this undertaking is not subjected to any contract, agreement, condition or qualification. The obligation and liabilities of us under this credit shall be independent.

Unless expressly consented by us, this standby L/C is not transferable or assignable.

This credit will come into effect from issuance and shall be binding on us as a continuing guarantee until (备用信用证到期日) 20101231_____. Any claim should reach our counter on or before that day.

Except so far as otherwise expressly stated, this credit is subject to (备用信用证选用的国际惯例) ISP98_____.

假设通知行为交通银行纽约分行，开证行为 C 银行，请根据上面的开立保函/备用信用证申请书填制用 MT760 格式开立的备用信用证电文。假设银行编号是 SA2010002。

MT760 电文

```
--------------------------- Message Header ------------------------
Swift Output        : FIN 760 Guarantee/Stdby Letter Credit
Sender          :           发送方 SWIFT
Receiver        :           接收方 SWIFT
--------------------------- Message Text ---------------------------
    27      Sequence of Total
            Number
            Total
    20      Transaction Reference Number

    23      Further Identification
            ISSUE
    30      Date

    40C     Applicable Rules
            Type
    77C   Details of Standby Letter of Credit
```

79   Narrative

参考答案：

MT760 电文

```
-------------------------- Message Header ------------------------
Swift Output    : FIN 760 Guarantee/Stdby Letter Credit
Sender        : C bank        发送方 SWIFT
Receiver       : D bank        接收方 SWIFT
-------------------------- Message Text ---------------------------
    27    Sequence of Total
          Number           1
          Total            1
    20    Transaction Reference Number
          SA2010002
    23    Further Identification
          ISSUE
    30    Date
          100301
    40C   Applicable Rules
          Type          ISP98
    77C   Details of Standby Letter of Credit
          STANDBY L/C FOR PERFORMANCE
          IN VIEW OF THE CONTRACT NO. SC20100301
          (HEREINAFTER REFERRED TO AS THE CONTRACT) SIGNED
          BETWEEN YOU AND Y CO. (HEREINAFTER REFERRED TO AS
          THE APPLICANT)FOR USD350000.00.
          WE, C BANK, HEREBY UNCONDITIONALLY
          AND IRREVOCABLY ISSUE THIS STANDBY LETTER OF
          CREDIT NO. SA2010002 IN YOUR FAVOR FOR ACCOUNT
          OF THE APPLICANT FOR MAXIMUM AMOUNT USD35000.00
          (SAY US DOLLARS THIRTY FIVE THOUSAND ONLY) (HEREINAFTER
          REFERRED TO AS THE GUARANTEED AMOUNT) REPRESENTING
          10PCT OF THE CONTRACT PRICE.
```

DOCUMENTS REQUIRED:

YOUR DRAFT(S) AT SIGHT DRAWN ON US BEARING THE CLAUSE DRAWN UNDER IRREVOCABLE STANDBY LETTER OF CREDIT NO. SA2010002 OF C BANK.

YOUR SIGNED STATEMENT STATING THE EFFECT AND ASPECT OF THE FAILURE OF PERFORMANCE BY THE APPLICANT.

WE ENGAGE WITH YOU THAT DRAFT(S) DRAWN UNDER AND IN COMPLIANCE WITH TERMS OF THIS CREDIT SHALL BE DULY HONORED ON DUE PRESENTATION TO US. WE SHALL PAY YOU, WITHIN 5 BANKING BUSINESS DAYS AFTER RECEIVING ABOVE-MENTIONED DOCUMENTS, THE AMOUNT SPECIFIED IN YOUR DRAFT(S) DRAWN ON US, PROVIDED THAT THE AGGREGATE CLAIMED AMOUNT DOES NOT EXCEED THE GUARANTEED AMOUNT.

79	Narrative

ALL BANKING CHARGES OTHER THAN OPENING CHARGES OF THIS STANDBY ARE FOR ACCOUNT OF THE BENEFICIARY.

EXCEPT AS EXPRESSLY STATED HEREIN, THIS UNDERTAKING IS NOT SUBJECTED TO ANY CONTRACT, AGREEMENT, CONDITION OR QUALIFICATION. THE OBLIGATION AND LIABILITIES OF US UNDER THIS CREDIT SHALL BE INDEPENDENT.

UNLESS EXPRESSLY CONSENTED BY US, THIS STANDBY L/C IS NOT TRANSFERABLE OR ASSIGNABLE.

THIS CREDIT WILL COME INTO EFFECT FROM ISSUANCE AND SHALL BE BINDING ON US AS A CONTINUING GUARANTEE UNTIL 20101231. ANY CLAIM SHOULD REACH OUR COUNTER ON OR BEFORE THAT DAY.

EXCEPT SO FAR AS OTHERWISE EXPRESSLY STATED, THIS CREDIT IS SUBJECT TO ISP98.

练习 5.5

2010 年 4 月 5 日,F 公司与 M 公司签订合同购买 MICROFIBRE,标的价值 USD670000.00,分三批交货。M 公司要求 F 公司提供备用证，保证其履行合同，按约定时间和数量购买货物，否则 M 公司有权凭证获得 10%的补偿。F 公司找到 C 银行开立相关备用证，且相关授信已经落实到位。假设通知银行是 D 银行。开立备用信用证申请书如下：

STANDBY L/C FOR PERFORMANCE

In view of the contract No. (基础交易合同编号) SC20100405 (hereinafter referred to as the contract) signed between you and ___(申请人名称)F Co.___ (hereinafter referred to as the applicant) for (基础交易合同标的)USD670000.00___ .

We, (担保人名称) C bank___, hereby unconditionally and irrevocably issue this standby letter of credit No.(备用信用证编号)SD11 in your favor for account of the applicant for maximum amount(最大担保金额)USD67000.00___ (say (最大担保金额大写)USD sixty seven thousand only___) (hereinafter referred to as the guaranteed amount)representing (担保金额占基础交易合同金额的百分比) 10 percent of the contract price.

Documents required:

Your draft(s) at sight drawn on us bearing the clause "drawn under irrevocable standby letter of credit No. (备用信用证编号)SD11 of (担保人名称) C bank___ ";

Your signed statement stating the effect and aspect of the failure of performance by the applicant.

We engage with you that draft(s) drawn under and in compliance with terms of this credit shall be duly honored on due presentation to us. We shall pay you, within 5 banking business days after receiving above-mentioned documents, the amount specified in your draft(s) drawn on us, provided that the aggregate claimed amount does not exceed the guaranteed amount.

All banking charges other than opening charges of this standby are for account of the beneficiary.

Unless expressly consented by us, this standby L/C is not transferable or assignable.

This credit will come into effect from issuance and shall be binding on us as a continuing guarantee until (备用信用证到期日) 20101231___ . Any claim should reach our counter on or before that day. This standby letter of credit shall automatically become null and void upon expiry, whether it is returned to us or not .

Except so far as otherwise expressly stated, this credit is subject to (备用信用证选用的国际惯例) ISP98___ .

请根据上面的开立备用信用证申请书用电开格式开立备用信用证。假设银行编号是 SD11。

MT760 电文

```
------------------------- Message Header -------------------------
Swift Output      : FIN 760 Guarantee/Stdby Letter Credit
Sender            :              发送方 SWIFT
Receiver          :              接收方 SWIFT
------------------------- Message Text -------------------------
```

27   Sequence of Total

        Number

        Total

20   Transaction Reference Number

23   Further Identification

        ISSUE

30   Date

40C   Applicable Rules

        Type

77C   Details of Standby Letter of Credit

79   Narrative

参考答案：

MT760 电文

-------------------------- Message Header ----------------------------

Swift Output	: FIN 760 Guarantee/Stdby Letter Credit	
Sender	: C bank	发送方 SWIFT
Receiver	: D bank	接收方 SWIFT

-------------------------- Message Text ---------------------------

    27   Sequence of Total

           Number   1

Total   1

20   Transaction Reference Number
      SD11

23   Further Identification
      ISSUE

30   Date
      100405

40C   Applicable Rules
      Type   ISP98

77C   Details of Standby Letter of Credit
      STANDBY L/C FOR PERFORMANCE
      IN VIEW OF THE CONTRACT NO. SC20100405
      (HEREINAFTER REFERRED TO AS THE CONTRACT)SIGNED
      BETWEEN YOU AND F CO. (HEREINAFTER REFERRED TO AS
      THE APPLICANT)FOR USD670000.00.
      WE, C BANK, HEREBY
      UNCONDITIONALLY AND IRREVOCABLY ISSUE THIS
      STANDBY LETTER OF CREDIT NO. SD11 IN YOUR FAVOR
      FOR ACCOUNT OF THE APPLICANT FOR MAXIMUM AMOUNT
      USD67000.00 (SAY US DOLLARS SIXTY SEVEN THOUSAND ONLY)
      (HEREINAFTER REFERRED TO AS THE GUARANTEED
      AMOUNT) REPRESENTING 10PCT OF THE
      CONTRACT PRICE.
      DOCUMENTS REQUIRED:
      YOUR DRAFT(S) AT SIGHT DRAWN ON US BEARING THE
      CLAUSE DRAWN UNDER IRREVOCABLE STANDBY LETTER OF
      CREDIT NO. SD11 OF C BANK.
      YOUR SIGNED STATEMENT STATING THE EFFECT AND
      ASPECT OF THE FAILURE OF PERFORMANCE BY THE
      APPLICANT.
      WE ENGAGE WITH YOU THAT DRAFT(S) DRAWN UNDER AND
      IN COMPLIANCE WITH TERMS OF THIS CREDIT SHALL BE
      DULY HONORED ON DUE PRESENTATION TO US. WE SHALL
      PAY YOU, WITHIN 5 BANKING BUSINESS DAYS AFTER
      RECEIVING ABOVE-MENTIONED DOCUMENTS, THE AMOUNT

SPECIFIED IN YOUR DRAFT(S) DRAWN ON US, PROVIDED
THAT THE AGGREGATE CLAIMED AMOUNT DOES NOT EXCEED
THE GUARANTEED AMOUNT.

79 Narrative

ALL BANKING CHARGES OTHER THAN OPENING CHARGES OF
THIS STANDBY ARE FOR ACCOUNT OF THE BENEFICIARY.
UNLESS EXPRESSLY CONSENTED BY US, THIS STANDBY
L/C IS NOT TRANSFERABLE OR ASSIGNABLE.
THIS CREDIT WILL COME INTO EFFECT FROM ISSUANCE
AND SHALL BE BINDING ON US AS A CONTINUING
GUARANTEE UNTIL 20101231. ANY CLAIM SHOULD REACH
OUR COUNTER ON OR BEFORE THAT DAY. THIS STANDBY
LETTER OF CREDIT SHALL AUTOMATICALLY BECOME NULL
AND VOID UPON EXPIRY, WHETHER IT IS RETURNED TO
US OR NOT.
EXCEPT SO FAR AS OTHERWISE EXPRESSLY STATED, THIS
CREDIT IS SUBJECT TO ISP98.

练习 5.6

2010 年 5 月 9 日，Z 公司将参与 K 公司组织的竞标，标的价值 USD880000.00。K 公司要求 Z 公司预先支付 20%的金额作为竞标成功后履约的保证。Z 公司为顺利竞标找到 C 银行开立相关备用证。通知行为 D 银行，且相关授信已经落实到位。请用电开格式开立。

开立保函/备用信用证申请书如下：

STANDBY L/C FOR PAYMENT

In view of the contract No. (基础交易合同编号) SC20100509 (hereinafter referred to as the contract) signed between you and (申请人名称) Z Co. (hereinafter referred to as the applicant).

We, C bank, hereby unconditionally and irrevocably issue this standby letter of credit No.(备用信用证编号) EF1 in your favor for account of the applicant for maximum amount(最大担保金额) USD176000.00 (say (最大担保金额大写)USD one hundred seventy six thousand only) (hereinafter referred to as the guaranteed amount)covering (担保金额占基础交易合同金额的百分比)20 percent of the contract price.

Documents required:

Your draft(s) at sight drawn on us bearing the clause "drawn under irrevocable standby letter of credit No. (备用信用证编号) EF1 of C bank";

Your signed statement stating that the applicant fails to make payment wholly or partially in accordance with the contract, and the amount drawn represents the unpaid balance of indebtedness due to you by the applicant.

We engage with you that draft(s) drawn under and in compliance with terms of this credit shall be duly honored on due presentation to us. We shall pay you, within 5 banking business days after receiving above-mentioned documents, the amount specified in your draft(s) drawn on us, provided that the aggregate claimed amount does not exceed the guaranteed amount.

The guaranteed amount will reduce automatically and proportionally to the sum already paid by the applicant, if we've received the document evidencing that the applicant has made the said payment, or by us.

All banking charges other than opening charges of this standby are for account of the beneficiary.

This credit will come into effect upon our receipt of the documents evidencing that the applicant has received the equipment in accordance with the contract and shall be binding on us as a continuing guarantee until (备用信用证到期日) 20101220   . Any claim should reach our counter on or before that day. This standby letter of credit shall automatically become null and void upon expiry, whether it is returned to us or not .

Except so far as otherwise expressly stated, this credit is subject to   (备用信用证选用的国际惯例) ISP98   .

请根据上面的开立保函/备用信用证申请书用电开格式开立备用信用证。
MT760 电文

```
------------------------- Message Header ------------------------
Swift Output      : FIN 760 Guarantee/Stdby Letter Credit
Sender            :              发送方 SWIFT
Receiver          :              接收方 SWIFT
------------------------- Message Text -----------------------
```

27	Sequence of Total
	Number
	Total
20	Transaction Reference Number
23	Further Identification
	ISSUE
30	Date
40C	Applicable Rules
	Type

77C　Details of Standby Letter of Credit

79　Narrative

参考答案：

MT760 电文

-------------------------- Message Header ----------------------------

Swift Output　　　　: FIN 760 Guarantee/Stdby Letter Credit

Sender　　　　　: C bank　　　发送方 SWIFT

Receiver　　　　: D bank　　　接收方 SWIFT

-------------------------- Message Text ----------------------------

27　Sequence of Total

　　Number　　　　1

　　Total　　　　1

20　Transaction Reference Number

　　EF1

23　Further Identification

　　ISSUE

30　Date

　　100509

40C　Applicable Rules

　　Type　　　　ISP98

77C　DETAILS OF STANDBY L/C FOR PAYMENT

IN VIEW OF THE CONTRACT NO. SC20100509

(HEREINAFTER REFERRED TO AS THE CONTRACT) SIGNED

BETWEEN YOU AND Z CO. (HEREINAFTER REFERRED TO AS

THE APPLICANT).

WE, C BANK, HEREBY UNCONDITIONALLY

AND IRREVOCABLY ISSUE THIS STANDBY LETTER OF

CREDIT NO. EF1 IN YOUR FAVOR FOR ACCOUNT OF THE

APPLICANT FOR MAXIMUM AMOUNT USD176000.00

(SAY US DOLLARS ONE HUNDRED SEVENTY SIX THOUSAND ONLY)

(HEREINAFTER REFERRED TO AS THE GUARANTEED

AMOUNT) COVERING 20 PERCENT OF THE CONTRACT PRICE.

DOCUMENTS REQUIRED:

YOUR DRAFT(S) AT SIGHT DRAWN ON US BEARING THE

CLAUSE DRAWN UNDER IRREVOCABLE STANDBY LETTER OF

CREDIT NO. EF1 OF C BANK.

YOUR SIGNED STATEMENT STATING THAT THE APPLICANT

FAILS TO MAKE PAYMENT WHOLLY OR PARTIALLY IN

ACCORDANCE WITH THE CONTRACT, AND THE AMOUNT

DRAWN REPRESENTS THE UNPAID BALANCE OF

INDEBTEDNESS DUE TO YOU BY THE APPLICANT.

WE ENGAGE WITH YOU THAT DRAFT(S) DRAWN UNDER AND

IN COMPLIANCE WITH TERMS OF THIS CREDIT SHALL BE

DULY HONORED ON DUE PRESENTATION TO US. WE SHALL

PAY YOU, WITHIN 5 BANKING BUSINESS DAYS AFTER

RECEIVING ABOVE-MENTIONED DOCUMENTS, THE AMOUNT

SPECIFIED IN YOUR DRAFT(S) DRAWN ON US, PROVIDED

THAT THE AGGREGATE CLAIMED AMOUNT DOES NOT EXCEED

THE GUARANTEED AMOUNT.

THE GUARANTEED AMOUNT WILL REDUCE AUTOMATICALLY

AND PROPORTIONALLY TO THE SUM ALREADY PAID BY THE

APPLICANT, IF WE HAVE RECEIVED THE DOCUMENT

EVIDENCING THAT THE APPLICANT HAS MADE THE SAID

PAYMENT, OR BY US.

79   Narrative

ALL BANKING CHARGES OTHER THAN OPENING CHARGES OF

THIS STANDBY ARE FOR ACCOUNT OF THE BENEFICIARY.
THIS CREDIT WILL COME INTO EFFECT UPON OUR
RECEIPT OF THE DOCUMENTS EVIDENCING THAT THE
APPLICANT HAS RECEIVED THE EQUIPMENT IN
ACCORDANCE WITH THE CONTRACT AND SHALL BE BINDING
ON US AS A CONTINUING GUARANTEE UNTIL 20101220.
ANY CLAIM SHOULD REACH OUR COUNTER ON OR BEFORE
THAT DAY. THIS STANDBY LETTER OF CREDIT SHALL
AUTOMATICALLY BECOME NULL AND VOID UPON EXPIRY,
WHETHER IT IS RETURNED TO US OR NOT .
EXCEPT SO FAR AS OTHERWISE EXPRESSLY STATED, THIS
CREDIT IS SUBJECT TO ISP98.

第六章

贸 易 融 资

学习目标：

了解和掌握贸易融资中福费廷和出口押汇业务的操作流程；知晓在完全让渡福费廷业务中如何编写与包买银行之间的相关文件电文，合理确定利率和宽限期；知道如何控制福费廷和出口押汇业务中的相关风险；掌握福费廷和出口押汇业务中的每一个环节和步骤。

第一节 福 费 廷

福费廷业务是基于进出口贸易的一种融资方式，指银行从出口商那里无追索权地买断通常由开证行承诺付款的远期款项。以信用证方式叙做福费廷业务为例，其叙做的方式有三种(假设出单行为交行)：包买商自己买断，即交行自行买断；风险参加，即由交行出资，包买商承担风险；完全让渡，即交行完全让渡该笔出口业务给包买商，包买商出资并承担风险。实际业务中如果开证行在出口方银行有叙做福费廷的同业额度，则出口方银行自己买断；如果开证行在出口方银行没有叙做福费廷的同业额度，则出口方银行采用完全让渡的方式比较多，这样做一方面是利用包买商对相关地区风险能够掌控的优势，另一方面可以缓解人民币升值所带来的筹资紧张。本节中我们仅介绍信用证项下的完全让渡形式的福费廷业务。

一、业务场景与操作

案例 6.1

出口商南京 ABC 公司与进口商印度 SUDAR 公司就进口文化纸签订了合同，双方约定采用远期信用证方式结算，期限为 B/L 后 120 天，金额为 60000 美元，B/L 日期为 2010 年 7 月 4 日。印度 ICICI BANK 作为开证行开立了信用证，信用证号为 MLC25910，交通银行为出口交单行，发票号为 100707。

1. 完全让渡福费廷业务操作

交行于 2010 年 7 月 10 日邮寄出口商单据，编号为 BP201000062，并于 7 月 17 日收到开证行 ICICI BANK 的承兑电，称其将于 10 月 4 日付款。

交行向 CITIBANK, HONG KONG 询价，得到答复为利率为 LIBOR 加 155 点，最低 120 美元，另有 200 美元的处理费。融资时间超过两个月，少于三个月，需按三个月 LIBOR 计算，当时三个月 LIBOR 为 0.35%。交行向受益人报价为 LIBOR 加 230 点，所以包买行与交行的利率分别为 1.9%和 2.65%。由于 10 月 4 日是国庆假期，故融资期限延长至 10 月 8 日，办理融资日为 7 月 22 日。

所以包买行收取利息为 USD 60000×1.9%×78/360 = USD247.00，另有处理费 USD200。交行收取客户的总费用为利息加处理费，即 USD60000×2.65%×78/360+USD200= USD344.5 +USD200。交行利润为 USD344.5-USD247 = USD 97.5。

交行将利率和费用报送至客户确认，出口商南京 ABC 公司认可并和交行签订业务申请书和融资合同。由于超过最低收费，所以按实际利息收取。

福费廷报价确认书

基本信息	报价信息
L/C 号：　MLC25910	利率：Libor(0.35)+2.30%
发票号：　100707	宽限期：4 WORKING DAYS
我行业务编号：BP201000062	外资银行费用：USD200
融资金额：　USD60000.00	

我司同意以上报价

南京 ABC 公司(签字盖章)

说明：

(1) 外资银行预扣的费用 USD200 中涵盖了预算开证银行付款时所扣的费用。若开证银行所扣费用小于 USD200，则外资银行将多余款项作为其收益，一般不退回；若所扣费用大于预扣的 USD200，此时，有些外资银行会再向受益人收取。选择哪种方式，在报价时会做说明，为了便于练习，关于此费用我们将不展开说明。

(2) 关于最低费用 USD120，此业务中，由于包买银行利息是 USD247，大于 USD120，故按实际收取。在一些实际业务中，由于期限短、金额小，有时利息小于最低报价的利息(如 USD120)，此时，则按 USD120 收取，而不是按实际算出的低于 USD120 的利息收取。为了便于练习，关于此费用我们将不展开说明。

(3) 由于现行银行在叙做此业务时，一般不收取承诺费，因此，关于此费用我们同样不展开说明。

操作步骤如下。

步骤一：出口商南京 ABC 公司向出口交单银行交行提出办理福费廷业务申请，交行接受申请后，根据业务的特点选择完全让渡福费廷的方式，然后开始选择包买商，进行询价。交行在询问了多家包买商后，选择 CITIBANK, HONG KONG 作为包买商(一般选择下款快、利率低、收费少的包买商)。

步骤二：交行依照包买银行 CITIBANK, HONG KONG 预先提供的报价(一般是 LIBOR 加上一定的点数。开证行情况、期限、地区因素等都可能影响报价和融资期限)再加上一定利润，向出口商出具福费廷业务报价确认书。 确认书主要写明 L/C 号、发票号、交行业务编号、融资金额和利率、宽限期、银行费用等，并要求申请方盖章确认。融资期限一般是承兑到期日加上合理的宽限期，一般为 2～4 天。

步骤三：出口商接受以上融资条件后填制福费廷申请书，与交行签订福费廷业务合同，明确办理要素以及双方相关权利义务。

步骤四：交行向包买银行 CITIBANK, HONG KONG 确认办理福费廷后，交行向包买行传真承兑电文以及信用证，同时发送让渡电文。在实际业务中，每个包买商所要的文件不大相同，也有一些包买行还要求传真发票、运输单据等相关单据，所有单据须经有权签字人签字后方为有效等，具体需按包买商要求办理。

2. 让渡权利

让渡权利主要是指让渡该信用证项下的各有关权利。各包买商的要求不同，但基本上是要让渡者做出以下的承诺：WE HEREBY IRREVOCABLY AND UNCONDITIONALLY ASSIGN ALL OUR RIGHTS, TITLE, INTEREST AND CLAIMS TO YOU.WE HEREBY REPRESENT AND WARRANT TO YOU THAT WE ARE THE SOLE LEGAL AND BENEFICIAL OWNER OF THE RIGHTS HEREBY ASSIGNED, WHICH ARE FREE AND CLEAR OF ANY PLEDGE, SECURITY INTEREST, CLAIM, SET-OFF OR COUNTERCLAIM OR ANY OTHER CHARGE.

各家包买商具体用词有所差异，但基本意思如前所述。

让渡权利的业务操作是通过分别给包买商和开证行发送相关的电文来实现的。操作步骤如下所述。

步骤一：交行依照包买商提供的格式向包买商 CITIBANK, HONG KONG 发出加押 SWIFT 报文，证实该笔款项的权益已经完全让渡给其，同时向承兑银行 ICICI BANK 发加押电，告知交行已经将款项转让，请其将款项付至包买商 CITIBANK, HONG KONG。发送电文后，交行须将发至开证行的报文签字后传真给包买商。

步骤二：包买商 CITIBANK, HONG KONG 收到相关报文后，扣收相关利息和费用后，将款项支付交行。交行在扣除其相关利息和费用后，将余款支付给出口商。

步骤三：承兑到期日，开证行 ICICI BANK 将款项直接付给包买商 CITIBANK, HONG KONG，完成整个业务流程。

所涉及的具体电文如下。

1) 让渡电文

假设选择向 CITIBANK, HONG KONG 让渡权利，交通银行给 CITIBANK(包买行)发转让权益电文，向其让渡权利。电文内容如下：

MT799 电文

-------------------------- Message Header --------------------------

Swift Output   : FIN 799 Free Format Message

Sender   : COMMCNSHNJG

Receiver   : CITIHKHHXXX

-------------------------- Message Text --------------------------

RE OUR REF. NO. BP201000062

YOUR REF FSH100323 此处为 CITIBANK 报价时提供的业务相关编号

LETTER OF CREDIT NO. MLC25910

FOR A TOTAL AMOUNT OF USD60000

ISSUED BY ICICI BANK

WITH REFERENCE TO THE ABOVE L/C, WE HEREBY

CONFIRM THAT YOUR OFFER LETTER IS

ACCEPTED AND AGREED BY US. WE HEREBY IRREVOCABLY

AND UNCONDITIONALLY ASSIGN ALL OUR RIGHTS, TITLE,

INTEREST AND CLAIMS TO YOU. WE HEREBY REPRESENT

AND WARRANT TO YOU THAT WE ARE THE SOLE LEGAL AND

BENEFICIAL OWNER OF THE RIGHTS HEREBY ASSIGNED,

WHICH ARE FREE AND CLEAR OF ANY PLEDGE, SECURITY

INTEREST, CLAIM, SET-OFF OR COUNTERCLAIM OR ANY

OTHER CHARGE. THIS ASSIGNMENT SHALL BY NO MEANS

TRANSFER OUR OBLIGATION AND DUTY UNDER THE ABOVE

L/C TO YOU.

2) 通知电文

在选定让渡权利的包买行 CITIBANK 后，交行在向包买行发送让渡权利电文的同时要向开证行发通知电文，告知其权利的让渡。

MT799 电文

-------------------------- Message Header --------------------------

Swift Output   : FIN 799 Free Format Message

Sender   : COMMCNSHNJG

Receiver   : ICICIHKHXXXX

-------------------------- Message Text --------------------------

RE YOUR L/C NO. MLC25910

BILL FOR USD60,000.00 DULY ACCEPTED BY YOUR BANK

TO BE MATURE ON 20101004

OUR REF.: BP201000062

WE REFER TO THE ABOVE BILL DULY ACCEPTED BY YOUR

BANK UNDER SUBJECT L/C AND YOUR AUTHENTICATED

ACCEPTANCE OF REF. NO. MLC25910.

PLEASE NOTE THAT THE SUBJECT BILL HAVE BEEN

ASSIGNED TO:CITIBANK HONG KONG

SWIFT ADDRESS: CITIHKHH

WE HEREBY INSTRUCT YOU TO PAY ON MATURITY

DIRECTLY TO THEIR ACCOUNT AS FOLLOWS: CITIBANK,

NEW YORK (SWIFT:

CITIUS33XXX) ACCOUNT NO.:03118

IN FAVOR OF CITIBANK, HONG KONG

QUOTING REF. NO.: BP201000062

图 6.1 为案例 6.1 的业务流程图。

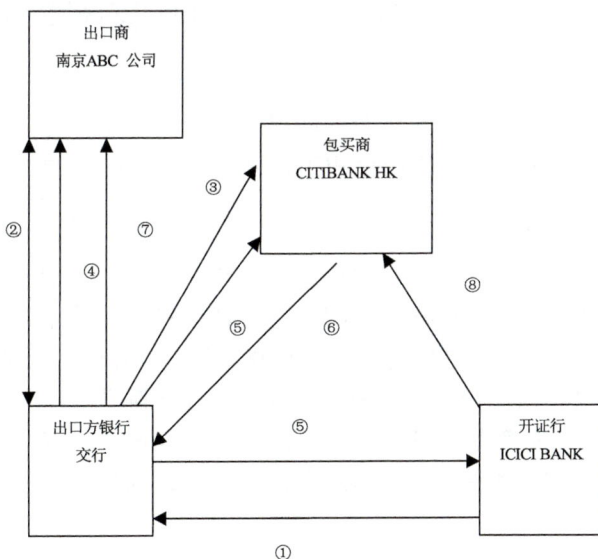

图 6.1　案例 6.1 的业务流程图

① 开证行 ICICI BANK 对此笔业务向交行发了承兑电。

② 交行及时将承兑电通知给出口商南京 ABC 公司后，出口商向交行提出叙做福费廷的申请(也可在出单时就提出申请)。

③ 交行向多家包买商询价后，选定其中一家包买商 CITIBANK, HONG KONG 的报价。

④ 交行在此报价上加点后与出口商南京 ABC 公司联系，得到确认后，与包买商确定价格。

⑤ 交行分别向包买商 CITIBANK, HONG KONG 和开证行 ICICI BANK 发出电文，确认款项让渡事宜，并通知开证行，该款项已让渡给包买商，请其直接联系包买商支付货款。

⑥ 包买商扣除报价中的相关利息和费用后，将款项支付给交行。

⑦ 交行将其相关利息和费用扣除后，及时将款项结汇／原币划给出口商。一般来讲，包买商与出口商之间的福费廷合同关系到贴现付款阶段就结束了，出口商取得款项后银行无权追索。

⑧ 付款到期日，开证行 ICICI BANK 直接付款给包买商 CITIBANK, HONG KONG。

二、风险控制

1. 贸易背景的真实性

对出口商来说，叙做福费廷业务的前提是有真实的贸易背景，严格遵照国家外管政策法规。如果经常与进口商发生商业纠纷，无法正常收汇，以及以往有虚假贸易行为等，是不能通过银行对融资的审核的。出口商在与进口商签订贸易合同之前就应该做好融资的准备，与出口方银行联系，询问银行是否可以做此业务，如果做，报价大致是多少，这样出口商可以核算成本，在与进口商谈判签约时可将延期付款利率打入成本中。

2. 叙做的条件

目前银行叙做的福费廷业务仅限于远期出口信用证项下，且已收到开证银行发来的加押电文表明承兑后才可叙做，出口托收和出口光票项下不能叙做。

3. 操作风险

首先，信用证 DRAWEE 应该是银行，如果 DRAWEE 是开证申请人，开证行在电文中就会以开证申请人的名义承兑并就此推卸自己责任，包买商是不接受这种信用证做福费廷的。银行只接受开证行以自己的名义所做的承兑。其次，开证行承兑电文一定是加押电文，如 MT799、MT752 等，MT999 一般是不接受的。在实际业务中，又常遇见这种情况，远期信用证项下提交的单据存在不符点，后经出口商担保出单，开证行拒付后又以申请人的名义承兑了单据。这种同样是开证行推卸自己的责任，这种承兑电文包买商也是不接受做福费廷的。

4. 福费廷当事人之间的法律关系

福费廷合同一旦成立，包买商和出口商均应对这笔融资交易承担契约责任。因此，如果其中一方因某种特殊情况单方中止交易，那么其须承担违约责任。如果是出口商提出中止，则包买商为提供融资而发生的筹资费用以及为消除业务风险而在金融市场上采取防范措施发生的业务费用应全部由出口商承担；如果是包买商的原因，则出口商由于要重新安排融资，并且通常是成本更高的融资而发生的费用和利息损失也要由包买商承担。

三、总结思考

福费廷这种出口融资工具，其实质是出口商将因远期收汇而可能发生的风险全部转嫁给买断行，同时获得买断行的即期付款。通过福费廷，出口商确实得到了益处，从而能够最大限度地规避国际贸易中的风险。

银行从自身利益出发也会意识到，在处理涉及某些发展中国家的业务时，常对相关政策、规则等认识不够，存在一定的地区风险，因此对一些高风险地区一般选择完全让渡福费廷方式，与一些有优势的包买商合作，从而有效地转嫁国家和地区风险。(以交通银行为例)实际业务中常见的福费廷分为交通银行委托包买银行买断和交通银行自行买断两种。只有在收到开证行承兑付款通知后，方可办理福费廷业务。前文已经讲述了交通银行作为中间商，完全让渡给包买商买断的福费廷业务。在实际业务中，交通银行自己也会作为包买商买入福费廷业务，其操作流程如下：交通银行在收到开证行/保兑行的承兑电后，自行确定对开证行/保兑行是否有授信额度可以办理，由于没有另一家包买银行的参加，所以不需传真单据报文以及发送确认转让报文。其余步骤同完全让渡他行买断的流程，因此不再重复。

四、实训操练

练习 6.1

南京 EFG 公司欲在远期信用证 LC123 项下办理福费廷，开证行为 BOTKJPJT，金额 USD90000，交通银行编号为 BP201000060，期限为 6 月 21 日至 8 月 29 日，融资当天的 LIBOR 为 0.45%，包买行报价为 LIBOR+200 点，交通银行报价为 LIBOR+250 点，包买行预扣 USD500(多退，少不补)，宽限期为 2 天。如果让渡银行为交通银行，请计算融资期限、出口商入账金额和交行受益。假设包买商是 CITIHKHH，融资编号是 F1。

请填写：

日期　　　天

包买行收取利息：

交通银行收取客户的总费用：

交通银行利润为：

出口商入账金额：

交通银行将利率和费用报送至客户确认，出口商认可并和交行签订业务申请书和融资合同。假设电报费为 USD20.00。

福费廷报价确认书

基本信息   报价信息

L/C 号：   利息：

发票号：   宽限期：

我行业务编号：   外资银行费用：

融资金额：   预扣费：

我司同意以上报价   公司

参考答案：

日期 71 天 (6 月 21 日至 8 月 29 日的天数再加上 2 天宽限期)

包买行收取利息为 USD 90000×2.45%×71/360 = USD434.875

交通银行收取客户的总费用为 USD90000×2.95%×71/360+USD500 = USD523.62+USD500 = USD1023.62

交通银行利润为 USD 523.62-USD434.87 = USD88.75

出口商入账金额：USD90000-USD523.62-USD500-USD20 = USD88956.38

福费廷报价确认书

基本信息   报价信息

L/C 号： LC123   利息： Libor(0.45)+2.50%

发票号： 12345   宽限期： 2 WORKING DAYS

我行业务编号：BP201000060 外资银行预扣费：USD500

融资金额： USD90000.00

我司同意以上报价 南京 EFG 公司

出口商确认价格后，交行分别向包买商 CITIHKHH 和开证行 BOTKJPJT 发出款项让渡的电文。请填写以下电文：

给开证行的 MT799 电文

---------------------------- Message Header ------------------------

Swift Output   : FIN 799 Free Format Message

Sender   :

Receiver   :

---------------------------- Message Text ------------------------

RE YOUR L/C NO.

BILL FOR　　　DULY ACCEPTED BY YOUR BANK

TO BE MATURE ON　　　OUR REF:

WE REFER TO THE ABOVE BILL DULY ACCEPTED BY YOUR

BANK UNDER SUBJECT L/C AND YOUR AUTHENTICATED

ACCEPTANCE OF REF NO.

PLEASE NOTE THAT THE SUBJECT BILL HAVE BEEN

ASSIGNED TO:

SWIFT ADDRESS:

WE HEREBY INSTRUCT YOU TO PAY ON MATURITY

DIRECTLY TO THEIR ACCOUNT AS FOLLOWS:

(SWIFT:　　　) ACCOUNT NO.:

IN FAVOR OF

QUOTING REF NO.:

给包买行的 MT799 电文

-------------------------- Message Header --------------------------

Swift Output　　　　: FIN 799 Free Format Message

Sender　　　　　　:

Receiver　　　　　:

-------------------------- Message Text --------------------------

RE OUR REF NO.

YOUR REF

LETTER OF CREDIT NO.

FOR A TOTAL AMOUNT OF

ISSUED BY

WITH REFERENCE TO THE ABOVE L/C, WE HEREBY

CONFIRM THAT YOUR OFFER LETTER IS

ACCEPTED AND AGREED BY US. WE HEREBY IRREVOCABLY

AND UNCONDITIONALLY ASSIGN ALL OUR RIGHTS, TITLE,

INTEREST AND CLAIMS TO YOU. WE HEREBY REPRESENT

AND WARRANT TO YOU THAT WE ARE THE SOLE LEGAL AND

BENEFICIAL OWNER OF THE RIGHTS HEREBY ASSIGNED,

WHICH ARE FREE AND CLEAR OF ANY PLEDGE, SECURITY

INTEREST, CLAIM, SET-OFF OR COUNTERCLAIM OR ANY

OTHER CHARGE. THIS ASSIGNMENT SHALL BY NO MEANS

TRANSFER OUR OBLIGATION AND DUTY UNDER THE ABOVE
L/C TO YOU.

参考答案：

给开证行的 MT799 电文

------------------------- Message Header -------------------------
Swift Output　　　　: FIN 799 Free Format Message
Sender　　　　　　 : COMMCNSHNJG
Receiver　　　　　 : BOTKJPJT
------------------------- Message Text -------------------------
RE YOUR L/C NO. LC123
BILL FOR USD90,000.00 DULY ACCEPTED BY YOUR BANK
TO BE MATURE ON 20100829 OUR REF: BP201000060
WE REFER TO THE ABOVE BILL DULY ACCEPTED BY YOUR
BANK UNDER SUBJECT L/C AND YOUR AUTHENTICATED
ACCEPTANCE OF REF NO. LC123
PLEASE NOTE THAT THE SUBJECT BILL HAVE BEEN
ASSIGNED TO: CITIBANK, HONG KONG
SWIFT ADDRESS: CITIHKHH
WE HEREBY INSTRUCT YOU TO PAY ON MATURITY
DIRECTLY TO THEIR ACCOUNT AS FOLLOWS: CITIBANK,
NEW YORK (SWIFT:
CITIUS33XXX) ACCOUNT NO.: 03118
IN FAVOR OF CITIBANK, HONG KONG
QUOTING REF NO.: BP201000060

给包买行的 MT799 电文：

------------------------- Message Header -------------------------
Swift Output　　　　: FIN 799 Free Format Message
Sender　　　　　　 : COMMCNSHNJG
Receiver　　　　　 : CITIHKHH
------------------------- Message Text -------------------------
RE OUR REF NO. BP201000060
YOUR REF F1

LETTER OF CREDIT NO. LC123

FOR A TOTAL AMOUNT OF USD90,000.00

ISSUED BY BOTKJPJT

WITH REFERENCE TO THE ABOVE L/C, WE HEREBY

CONFIRM THAT YOUR OFFER LETTER IS

ACCEPTED AND AGREED BY US. WE HEREBY IRREVOCABLY

AND UNCONDITIONALLY ASSIGN ALL OUR RIGHTS, TITLE,

INTEREST AND CLAIMS TO YOU. WE HEREBY REPRESENT

AND WARRANT TO YOU THAT WE ARE THE SOLE LEGAL AND

BENEFICIAL OWNER OF THE RIGHTS HEREBY ASSIGNED,

WHICH ARE FREE AND CLEAR OF ANY PLEDGE, SECURITY

INTEREST, CLAIM, SET-OFF OR COUNTERCLAIM OR ANY

OTHER CHARGE. THIS ASSIGNMENT SHALL BY NO MEANS

TRANSFER OUR OBLIGATION AND DUTY UNDER THE ABOVE

L/C TO YOU.

若到期开证行扣费 USD300.00，则包买商将退多少金额？假设电报费是 USD20.00。

金额 ＝

参考答案：

USD500−USD300−USD20 ＝ USD180

交通银行将二次结汇或原币划转此金额给出口商(EFG 公司)。

练习 6.2

南京 YUFAN 公司欲在远期信用证号码 LC456 项下办理福费廷，开证行为 MIDLGB22，金额 USD120000，出单行编号 BP201000067，期限 3 月 31 日至 7 月 26 日，融资当天的三个月 LIBOR 为 0.35%，四个月 LIBOR 为 0.45%，让渡银行为交通银行，包买行报价为 LIBOR+300 点，交通银行报价为 LIBOR+400 点，宽限期 3 天。请计算融资期限、出口商入账金额和交行受益。假设包买商是 CITIHKHH，电报费为 USD20.00。

请填写：

日期　　　　　　　　天

包买行收取利息为：

交通银行收取客户的总费用为：

交通银行利润为：

出口商入账金额为：

交通银行将利率和费用报送至客户确认，出口商认可并和交通银行签订业务申请书和融资合同。

福费廷报价确认书

基本信息   报价信息

L/C 号：   利息：

发票号：   宽限期：

交通银行业务编号：   外资银行费用：

融资金额：

我司同意以上报价   公司

参考答案：

日期 120 天，LIBOR 四月

包买行收取利息为：USD120000×3.45%×120/360 = USD1380.00

交通银行收取客户的总费用为：USD120000×4.45%×120/360 = USD1780.00

交通银行利润为：USD1780−USD1380 = USD400

出口商入账金额为：USD120000−USD1780−USD20 = USD118200

福费廷报价确认书

基本信息   报价信息

L/C 号：   LC456   利息：Libor(0.45)+4.00%

发票号：   567   宽限期：3 WORKING DAYS

我行业务编号：BP201000067   外资银行费用：无

融资金额：   USD120000.00

我司同意以上报价   南京 YUFAN 公司

出口商确认价格后，交行分别向包买商 CITIHKHH 和开证行 MIDLGB22 发出款项让渡的电文。请填写以下电文：

给开证行的 MT799 电文

-------------------------- Message Header -------------------------

Swift Output   : FIN 799 Free Format Message

Sender   :

Receiver   :

-------------------------- Message Text --------------------------

RE YOUR L/C NO.

BILL FOR   DULY ACCEPTED BY YOUR BANK

TO BE MATURE ON   OUR REF:

WE REFER TO THE ABOVE BILL DULY ACCEPTED BY YOUR

BANK UNDER SUBJECT L/C AND YOUR AUTHENTICATED

ACCEPTANCE OF REF NO.

PLEASE NOTE THAT THE SUBJECT BILL HAVE BEEN

ASSIGNED TO: CITIBANK, HONG KONG

SWIFT ADDRESS:

WE HEREBY INSTRUCT YOU TO PAY ON MATURITY

DIRECTLY TO THEIR ACCOUNT AS FOLLOWS:

(SWIFT:) ACCOUNT NO.:

IN FAVOR OF

QUOTING REF NO.:

给包买行的 MT799 电文

------------------------- Message Header ------------------------

Swift Output   : FIN 799 Free Format Message

Sender   :

Receiver   :

------------------------- Message Text ------------------------

RE OUR REF NO.

YOUR REF

LETTER OF CREDIT NO.

FOR A TOTAL AMOUNT OF

ISSUED BY

WITH REFERENCE TO THE ABOVE L/C, WE HEREBY

CONFIRM THAT YOUR OFFER LETTER IS

ACCEPTED AND AGREED BY US. WE HEREBY IRREVOCABLY

AND UNCONDITIONALLY ASSIGN ALL OUR RIGHTS, TITLE,

INTEREST AND CLAIMS TO YOU. WE HEREBY REPRESENT

AND WARRANT TO YOU THAT WE ARE THE SOLE LEGAL AND

BENEFICIAL OWNER OF THE RIGHTS HEREBY ASSIGNED,

WHICH ARE FREE AND CLEAR OF ANY PLEDGE, SECURITY

INTEREST, CLAIM, SET-OFF OR COUNTERCLAIM OR ANY

OTHER CHARGE. THIS ASSIGNMENT SHALL BY NO MEANS
TRANSFER OUR OBLIGATION AND DUTY UNDER THE ABOVE
L/C TO YOU.

参考答案：

给开证行的 MT799 电文

------------------------ Message Header ------------------------

Swift Output	: FIN 799 Free Format Message
Sender	: COMMCNSHNJG
Receiver	: MIDLGB22

------------------------ Message Text ------------------------

RE YOUR L/C NO. LC456

BILL FOR USD120000.00 DULY ACCEPTED BY YOUR BANK
TO BE MATURE ON 20100726 OUR REF: BP201000067

WE REFER TO THE ABOVE BILL DULY ACCEPTED BY YOUR
BANK UNDER SUBJECT L/C AND YOUR AUTHENTICATED
ACCEPTANCE OF REF NO. LC456

PLEASE NOTE THAT THE SUBJECT BILL HAVE BEEN
ASSIGNED TO: CITIBANK, HONG KONG

SWIFT ADDRESS: CITIHKHH

WE HEREBY INSTRUCT YOU TO PAY ON MATURITY
DIRECTLY TO THEIR ACCOUNT AS FOLLOWS: CITIBANK,
NEW YORK (SWIFT:

CITIUS33XXX) ACCOUNT NO.: 03118

IN FAVOR OF CITIBANK, HONG KONG

QUOTING REF NO.: BP201000067

给包买行的 MT799 电文

------------------------ Message Header ------------------------

Swift Output	: FIN 799 Free Format Message
Sender	: COMMCNSHNJG
Receiver	: CITIHKHH

------------------------ Message Text ------------------------

RE OUR REF NO. BP201000067

YOUR REF

LETTER OF CREDIT NO. LC456

FOR A TOTAL AMOUNT OF USD120000.00

ISSUED BY MIDLGB22

WITH REFERENCE TO THE ABOVE L/C, WE HEREBY

CONFIRM THAT YOUR OFFER LETTER IS

ACCEPTED AND AGREED BY US. WE HEREBY IRREVOCABLY

AND UNCONDITIONALLY ASSIGN ALL OUR RIGHTS, TITLE,

INTEREST AND CLAIMS TO YOU. WE HEREBY REPRESENT

AND WARRANT TO YOU THAT WE ARE THE SOLE LEGAL AND

BENEFICIAL OWNER OF THE RIGHTS HEREBY ASSIGNED,

WHICH ARE FREE AND CLEAR OF ANY PLEDGE, SECURITY

INTEREST, CLAIM, SET-OFF OR COUNTERCLAIM OR ANY

OTHER CHARGE. THIS ASSIGNMENT SHALL BY NO MEANS

TRANSFER OUR OBLIGATION AND DUTY UNDER THE ABOVE

L/C TO YOU.

第二节　出口押汇

　　一般来说，银行办理出口押汇有两种方式：一种是纳入对申请人的综合授信管理，申请人应获得银行授予的出口押汇授信额度，并在额度内提出申请，办理出口押汇；另一种是对部分单证相符，且开证行和申请人符合有关其他条件的出口押汇业务，可以纳入对开证行的同业授信管理，不占用申请人的出口押汇授信额度。本节中介绍的是纳入申请人综合授信管理的出口押汇业务。

一、业务场景与操作

案例 6.2

　　出口商南京 TGB 公司向德国客户出口玩具，双方签订合同，约定以远期议付信用证方式交易，期限为 B/L 后 90 天，开证行为 DEUTSCHE BANK, FRANKFURT，信用证号为 LC2145，装期为 2010 年 5 月 31 日，效期为 2010 年 6 月 21 日，金额为 USD50000.00，发票号为 WS1135，发票金额为 USD50000。现该司于 2010 年 6 月 1 日来 ABC 银行办理出口交单业务后，要求办理押汇融资，相关流程如下所述。

1. 填写出口押汇申请书

ABC 银行出口押汇申请书

编号：

<table>
<tr><td rowspan="12">申请单位填写</td><td colspan="2">申请单位</td><td colspan="5">中文：南京 TGB 公司</td></tr>
<tr><td colspan="2">名　称</td><td colspan="5">英文：NANJING TGB CORPORATION</td></tr>
<tr><td colspan="2">申请单位外汇账号</td><td colspan="5" rowspan="2">123456</td></tr>
<tr><td colspan="2">(押汇账号)</td></tr>
<tr><td colspan="2">申请单位人民币账号</td><td colspan="5">147258</td></tr>
<tr><td colspan="2" rowspan="2">法定代表人</td><td>信用证</td><td>2010 年 5 月</td><td>信用证</td><td colspan="2">2010 年 6 月</td></tr>
<tr><td>装　期</td><td>31 日</td><td>效　期</td><td colspan="2">21 日</td></tr>
<tr><td colspan="2">信用证号</td><td colspan="2">LC2145</td><td>信用证金额</td><td colspan="2">USD50000.00</td></tr>
<tr><td colspan="2">发票号</td><td colspan="2">WS1135</td><td>发票金额</td><td colspan="2">USD50000.00</td></tr>
<tr><td colspan="2">申请押汇
金额和币种</td><td colspan="5">(大写) USD FIFTY THOUSAND　(小写)USD50000.00</td></tr>
<tr><td colspan="2">申请押汇期限</td><td colspan="2">90 天</td><td>押汇日期</td><td colspan="2">2010 年 6 月 1 日</td></tr>
<tr><td>汇票</td><td>发票</td><td>装箱单</td><td>提单</td><td>保险单</td><td>产地证</td><td></td></tr>
<tr><td></td><td>2/2</td><td>4/4</td><td>3/3</td><td>3/3</td><td></td><td></td><td></td></tr>
</table>

ABC 银行：

　　本公司谨以本出口信用证项下全套已装船单据提交贵行，申请叙做出口押汇，并保证履行与贵行签署的《XX 银行出口押汇合同》(编号：A001)，承诺本出口项下款项一经收妥，立即用于归还贵行的押汇本息及费用；如开证行拒付，本公司保证在接到拒付通知后三个工作日内，偿还押汇本息和贵行各项费用。否则，贵行有权自开证行拒付之日起，按实际融资天数和中国人民银行有关规定收取罚息或处置单据和货物。若仍不足以偿还押汇本息、罚息及贵行的各项费用，贵行对本公司仍有追索权。本公司确认贵行办理此项业务的依据为国际商会最新修订的《跟单信用证统一惯例》(UCP600)。

申请单位(公章)：

2010 年 6 月 1 日

2. 审查押汇资格

　　(1) 出口商品必须在申请人的主营范围之内，产品应适销对路，价格波动小；来证中无软条款。

　　(2) 应严格审查申请人的授信额度情况和授信条件，在相应的额度内和规定的授信条件下为申请人办理出口押汇业务。

(3) 信用证开证行必须资信良好，经营作风稳健，符合银行代理行政策。

3. 审查信用证

(1) 对自由议付或指定银行为议付行的即期/远期信用证或开证行即期付款信用证，可以办理出口押汇。

(2) 对承兑信用证、延期付款，一般应在收到开证行的承兑通知书/延期付款到期确认书后办理出口押汇；因特殊情况在收到承兑通知书/延期付款到期确认书之前办理的，申请人在银行的出口押汇额度条件中应该容许。

(3) 对限制他行议付信用证、转让信用证或其他被银行认为不宜办理出口押汇业务的信用证，一般不得叙做出口押汇。

(4) 信用证条款应清晰明了。信用证不能包含对银行收汇不利的软条款。

(5) 出口押汇原则上叙做银行应该掌握货权。对提交非货权运输单据，应在客户取得出口押汇授信额度时在授信条件中列明允许。

(6) 出口押汇的币种应为信用证币种，出口押汇的期限根据收汇情况，参照下述期限确定。一般即期：近洋 8～12 天；远洋 15～20 天。远期：相应即期天数加远期期限，但整个融资期限不得超过 180 天。出口押汇利息实行多退少补原则。

4. 计息入账

审查完毕后，计算押汇的相关费用并将押汇款项经过核查之后入客户账。

假设案例 6.2 的议付费为 USD50，邮费为 USD30，融资利率为 3%，融资利息和入账金额计算如下(假设银行在做押汇时，设定寄单行在东南亚等地区为近洋，根据其邮程时间的估算，一般在融资天数上加 15 天，其他地区设定为远洋，加 30 天)：

远洋 90+30 天

押汇利息 USD50000×120/360×3% = USD500

入账金额 USD50000-USD500-USD50-USD30 = USD49420

5. 还款

(1) 利息的计算问题：实际业务中，由于银行所给的融资时间通常是信用证的付款期限加邮程，再加开证银行处理单据的时间估算出来的，因此，实际的收汇时间与融资的到期日一般会有一个出入。为了准确计算利息，银行押汇实际利息是在放款时按银行预计的收汇天数计算，先行扣除，等到从开证行收汇时，再按实际收汇天数重新计算利息，多退少补。

(2) 国外扣费方面(开证行等银行扣费问题)，最后实际融资行收到的金额一般会比出单的金额略少，这里面有开证银行的处理费用、不符点费用、账户行费用等，而押汇发放时融资行是按全额发放的。对于这块费用，也是按照实际情况多退少补。

就案例 6.2 而言，假如实际融资 115 天后收到开证行款项，收到头寸金额为 USD49900，那么最后归还融资时应重新计算押汇利息如下：

押汇利息应为 USD50000×115/360×3% = USD479.17

而融资银行在放款时已经收取 USD500，那么，银行应退还申请人多收的利息 USD500−USD479.17 = USD20.83。

再看国外扣费方面，融资行只收到 USD49900，而放款时是按全额 USD50000 发放的，因此还应向申请人要回 USD100，凑足 USD50000。

综合这两项后，最后银行在做押汇还款时，还应该向申请人账户收取 USD100−USD20.83 = USD79.17。

图 6.2 为案例 6.2 的业务流程图。

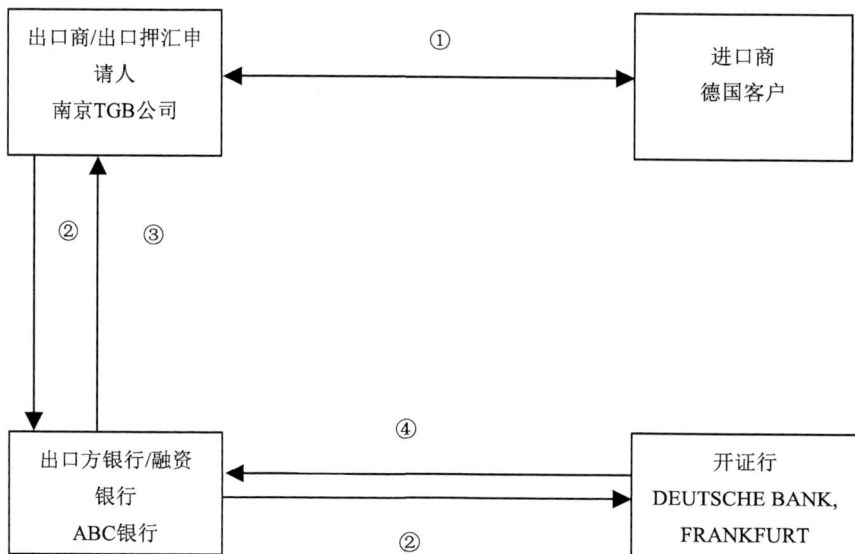

图 6.2　案例 6.2 的业务流程图

① 进出口双方签订贸易合同，同意按信用证方式结算。

② 出口押汇申请人南京 TGB 公司收到国外信用证 LC2145 后，按信用证要求缮制单据，提交给出口方银行 ABC 银行。该行审单后，按信用证的规定寄单给开证银行/寄单行/保兑行 DEUTSCHE BANK, FRANKFURT。

③ 出口方银行接受出口押汇申请人的押汇要求，双方签订合同，签署申请书等文件，然后办理押汇，将款项扣除利息和银行相关手续费后，付给出口押汇申请人。

④ 开证行付款给出口方银行。出口方银行收到款项后，对利息重新计算，多退少补。如果有国外扣费，则还需重新计算后再决定是否扣收申请人账户。

二、风险控制

1. 贸易融资风险

叙做押汇的银行应严格审查申请人的授信额度的使用情况和授信条件的落实情况，对是否有不符点以及是否拥有完全货权等应该在授信条件中加以明确。

2. 信用证风险

叙做押汇的银行要严格审核开证行的资信状况和经营作风，开证行所在国家的政治及经济情况，确认信用证的真实性且没有软条款。

3. 单据审核风险

叙做押汇的银行要求单证必须满足出口押汇客户授信额度中的授信条件，原则上应掌握货权。同时要向出口商强调，要其充分了解信用证的各项条款，并按要求制作单据，做到"单证一致、单单一致"，不能有实质性的不符点。

4. 拒付风险

出口押汇发放后应注意安全收汇，如遇开证行无理拒付，应及时根据国际惯例与开证行据理力争。

三、总结思考

与普通外汇贷款相比，出口押汇以出口单据作为抵押，因此操作手续简便，尤其在当前人民币升值的趋势下。前文已经将整个业务做了简单介绍，这里再强调两点。

(1) 严格押汇审批手续，加强金融风险防范。所有的押汇业务都应该在授信额度项下办理。

(2) 对于贸易融资项下的贷款，应定期跟踪，尤其是对大额的押汇单据应事先与运输公司、海关等部门联系，对运输单据进行核实，以防欺诈等风险。

四、实训操练

练习 6.3

出口商南京 KATA 公司向美国客户出口货物，双方签订合同，以即期付款信用证方式交易，开证行为 JPMORGAN CHASE BANK, NEW YORK，信用证号为 S15092，装期为 2010 年 1 月 31 日，效期为 2010 年 2 月 21 日，金额为 USD35000，发票号为 JP3358，发票金额为 USD20000。现该司来交通银行办理出口议付交单业务后要求办理押汇融资。出口押汇申请书如下：

交通银行出口押汇申请书

编号：

	申请单位 名 称	中文：南京 KATA 公司					
申 请 单 位 填 写		英文：NANJING KATA CORPORATION					
	申请单位外汇账号 (押汇账号)						
	申请单位人民币账号						
	法定代表人		信用证 装 期	2010 年 1 月 31 日	信 用 证 效 期	2010 年 2 月 21 日	
	信用证号	S15092		信用证金额		USD35000.00	
	发票号	JP3358		发票金额		USD20000.00	
	申请押汇 金额和币种	(大写) USD TWENTY THOUSAND　(小写)USD20000.00					
	申请押汇期限	30 天		押汇日期	2010 年 2 月 1 日		
	汇票	发票	装箱单	提单	保险单	产地证	
	2/2	3/3	3/3	3/3			

交通银行南京分行：

　　本公司谨以本出口信用证项下全套已装船单据提交贵行，申请叙做出口押汇，并保证履行与贵行签署的《交通银行出口押汇合同》(编号：A002)，承诺本出口项下款项一经收妥，立即用于归还贵行的押汇本息及费用；如开证行拒付，本公司保证在接到拒付通知后三个工作日内，偿还押汇本息和贵行各项费用。否则，贵行有权自开证行拒付之日起，按实际融资天数和中国人民银行有关规定收取罚息或处置单据和货物。若仍不足以偿还押汇本息、罚息及贵行的各项费用，贵行对本公司仍有追索权。本公司确认贵行办理此项业务的依据为国际商会最新修订的《跟单信用证统一惯例》(UCP600)。

申请单位(公章)：

2010 年 2 月 1 日

如果你是办理押汇的人员，在审查了相关授信条件和单证方面的要求后，请计算押汇利息和入账金额。假设此笔业务的议付费为 USD20，邮费为 USD30，融资利率为 2%，融资期限按 30 天计算。(假设押汇天数是信用证付款期限加远洋天数 30 天。)

押汇利息：

入账金额：

押汇还款如何计算，假设实际融资期限为 25 天，实际收到头寸 USD19950，最后应如何跟客户结算？

实际押汇利息：

应退还客户：

应向客户收取：

参考答案：

押汇利息：USD20000×30/360×2% = USD33.33

入账金额：USD20000−USD33.33− USD20− USD30 = USD19916.67

实际押汇利息：USD20000×25/360×2% = USD27.78

应退还客户：USD33.33−USD27.78 = USD5.55

应向客户收取：USD20000−USD19950−USD5.55 = USD44.45

练习 6.4

出口商南京 YUFAN 公司向日本客户出口货物，双方签订合同，以远期承兑信用证方式交易，开证行为 BANK OF TOKYO-MITSUBISHI UFJ, TOKYO，信用证号为 D658，装期为 2010 年 5 月 21 日，效期为 2010 年 6 月 11 日，金额为 USD60000，发票号为 CS82，发票金额为 USD45000，该笔出单于 2010 年 5 月 20 日承兑，承兑金额为 USD44850，到期付款日是 6 月 8 日。现该司来交通银行办理出口议付交单业务后要求办理押汇融资。出口押汇申请书如下：

交通银行出口押汇申请书

编号：

申请单位填写	申请单位名称	中文：南京 YUFAN 公司					
		英文：NANJING YUFAN CORPORATION					
	申请单位外汇账号(押汇账号)						
	申请单位人民币账号						
	法定代表人		信用证装期	2010 年 5 月 21 日	信用证效期	2010 年 6 月 11 日	
	信用证号	D658		信用证金额	USD60000.00		
	发票号	CS82		发票金额	USD45000.00		
	申请押汇金额和币种	(大写) USD FORTY FOUR THOUSAND EIGHT HUNDRED AND FIFTY ONLY (小写)USD44850.00					
	申请押汇期限	20 天		押汇日期		2010 年 5 月 30 日	
	汇票	发票	装箱单	提单	保险单	产地证	
	2/2	3/3	3/3	3/3	2/2		

交通银行南京分行：

　　本公司谨以本出口信用证项下全套已装船单据提交贵行，申请叙做出口押汇，并保证履行与贵行签署的《交通银行出口押汇合同》(编号：A004)，承诺本出口项下款项一经收妥，立即用于归还贵行的押汇本息及费用；如开证行拒付，本公司保证在接到拒付通知后三个工作日内，偿还押汇本息和贵行各项费用。否则，贵行有权自开证行拒付之日起，按实际融资天数和中国人民银行有关规定收取罚息或处置单据和货物。若仍不足以偿还押汇本息、罚息及贵行的各项费用，贵行对本公司仍有追索权。本公司确认贵行办理此项业务的依据为国际商会最新修订的《跟单信用证统一惯例》(UCP600)。

申请单位(公章)：

2010 年 5 月 30 日

　　如果你是办理押汇的人员，在审查了相关授信条件和单证方面的要求后，请计算押汇利息和入账金额。假设此笔业务的议付费为 USD45，邮费为 USD15，融资利率为 2.5%，承兑后一般按承兑金额办理，近洋客户。

押汇利息：

入账金额：

押汇还款如何计算？假设实际融资期限为 18 天，实际收到头寸 USD44850，最后应如何跟客户结算？

实际押汇利息：

应退还客户：

应向客户收取：

参考答案：

押汇利息：USD44850×20/360×2.5% = USD 62.29

入账金额：USD44850−USD62.29−USD15−USD45 = USD44727.71

实际押汇利息：USD44850×18/360×2.5% = USD56.06

应退还客户：USD62.29−USD56.06 = USD6.23，不向客户收取费用

第七章

个人外汇买卖

学习目标：

掌握个人外汇买卖的基本知识和流程及买卖外汇操作；知道如何控制相关业务中的风险。

一、业务场景与操作

我国是外汇管制的国家，近几年来随着经济的发展，国家的外汇政策有了较大的改变。目前按国家有关政策规定，银行只能进行实盘外汇买卖，暂不能进行虚盘外汇买卖，所以个人外汇买卖业务均为实盘交易(不能进行透支、保证金等交易)。个人在银行规定的交易时间内，通过柜面或其他电子金融服务方式，进行实盘外汇买卖。银行接受客户的委托，按照银行个人外汇买卖业务的报价，为客户把一种外币买卖成另一种外币。目前人民币还未实现完全可自由兑换，人民币与外汇之间还不能进行自由买卖。居民个人可持现钞去银行开户，也可将已有的现汇存款转至开办个人外汇买卖业务的银行。在交易手段上，既可以到银行柜台办理，也可以通过电话、因特网进行外汇买卖。

1. 外汇交易基本内容

(1) 外汇交易中的实盘交易是一种现货交易。它要求客户持有多少外汇才能做相应金额的交易，客户在完成交易后即持有另一种货币，因此它除了提供利用汇率波动赚取差价的机会外，还可满足客户的兑换需求。

(2) 交易时间：理论上居民个人可 24 小时办理外汇买卖。

(3) 交易货币：均为自由兑换货币。

(4) 资金结算时间：外汇交易的结算时间短，因此当日可进行多次反向交易，起息日采取 T+0 方式，即居民个人可把当天买入(卖出)的货币当天卖出(买入)，交易次数没有限制。

(5) 交易渠道：通过柜面交易、电话交易、网上交易、手机银行交易和自助终端交易五种渠道进行。

2. 外汇标价方式

外汇标价方式分为两种：直接标价法与间接标价法。

(1) 直接标价法。以美元为基本货币的报价方式称为"直接标价法"，例如 USD/JPY。包括中国在内的世界上绝大多数国家目前都采用直接标价法。如日元 119.05，即一美元兑119.05 日元。在直接标价法下，若一定单位的外币折合的本币数额多于前期，则说明外币币值上升或本币币值下跌，这称为外汇汇率上升；反之，如果用比原来较少的本币即能兑换到同一数额的外币，这说明外币币值下跌或本币币值上升，这称为外汇汇率下跌，即外币的价值与汇率的涨跌成正比。

(2) 间接标价法又称应收标价法。以美元为目标货币的报价方式称为"间接标价法"，例如 EUR/USD，如欧元 0.9705，即一欧元兑 0.9705 美元。在间接标价法中，本国货币的数额保持不变，外国货币的数额随着本国货币币值的对比变化而变动。如果一定数额的本币能兑换的外币数额比前期少，这表明外币币值上升。本币币值下降，即外汇汇率下降；反之，如果一定数额的本币能兑换的外币数额比前期多，则说明外币币值下降、本币币值上升，即外汇汇率上升。即外币的价值和汇率的升跌成反比。外汇市场上的报价一般为双向报价，即由报价方同时报出自己的买入价和卖出价，由客户自行决定买卖方向。买入价和卖出价的价差越小，对于投资者来说意味着成本越小。

需注意的是，外汇汇率的标价通常由 5 位有效数字组成，从右边向左边数过去，第一位称为"X 个点"，它是构成汇率变动的最小单位，第二位称为"X 十个点"，如此类推。例如：1 欧元 = 1.1010 美元；1 美元 = 120.50 日元。欧元对美元从 1.1010 变为 1.1015，称欧元对美元上升了 5 点；美元对日元从 120.50 变为 120.00，称美元对日元下跌了 50 点。

3. 外汇实盘交易成本

外汇实盘交易的交易成本体现在买卖点差。银行根据国际外汇市场行情，按照国际惯例报出买价和卖价。银行针对不同币种的汇率设置了不同的买卖点差。以 EUR/USD 为例，买卖点差一般为 30 点。即银行给出的买价为 1.2830，给出的卖价为 1.2860。客户如果想用持有的美元买入欧元，需要接受 1.2860 的价格；如果想用持有的欧元买入美元，需要接受1.2830 的价格。刚刚接触外汇实盘交易的人不容易分辨清楚到底哪个是银行的买价，哪个是银行的卖价。窍门是，银行总是低买高卖，它不会赔本吆喝。

4. 业务操作

交易方式分为即时交易和挂盘交易两种，即时交易是指按银行公布的买卖报价，实时完成客户买卖申请的交易方式。挂盘交易是指客户指定买卖币种、交易金额及成交价格，银行按价格优先、时间优先的原则受理客户指令，一旦银行报价优于或等于/劣于或等于客户指定的价格，即执行客户指令，实际的成交价格为客户指定价格。目前有盈利挂盘、止损挂盘、双向挂盘和组合挂盘四种挂盘方式。

1) 盈利挂盘

盈利挂盘是指客户指定买卖币种、卖出金额及盈利挂盘价格，根据国际市场汇率变动情况，一旦银行即时报价达到或优于盈利挂盘价格，即受理客户的盈利挂盘申请，实际成交价格为客户指定的盈利挂盘价格。

例如，一客户持有美元，希望兑换成日元，在挂盘时银行即时报价为 116.40，盈利挂盘价格可设为 116.80。当银行即时报价达到或优于 116.80 时，该笔盈利挂盘申请即以 116.80 成交。

2)　止损挂盘

止损挂盘是指由客户指定买卖币种、卖出金额及止损挂盘价格，根据国际市场汇率变动情况，一旦银行即时报价达到或劣于止损挂盘价格，即受理客户的止损挂盘申请，实际成交价格为客户指定的止损挂盘价格。

例如，一客户持有美元，希望兑换成日元，若挂盘时银行即时报价为 116.40，止损挂盘价格可设为 116.00(小于 116.40)。当银行即时报价达到或劣于 116.00 时，该笔止损挂盘申请即以 116.00 成交。

3)　双向挂盘

双向挂盘是指客户可以对一笔交易金额同时设定盈利挂盘价格和止损挂盘价格，根据国际市场汇率变动情况，一旦银行即时报价先达到盈利挂盘价格，即受理客户的盈利挂盘申请，实际成交价格为客户指定的盈利挂盘价格，其止损挂盘申请同时撤销；一旦银行即时报价先达到止损挂盘价格，即受理客户的止损挂盘申请，实际成交价格为客户指定的止损挂盘价格，其盈利挂盘申请同时撤销。

例如，客户持有美元，希望兑换成日元，若挂盘时银行即时报价为 116.40，盈利挂盘价格可设为 116.80(大于 116.40)，止损挂盘价格可设为 116.00(小于 116.40)。一旦银行即时报价达到或优于 116.80 时，即受理该盈利挂盘申请，并以 116.80 成交，止损挂盘同时撤销；一旦银行即时报价达到或劣于 116.00，即受理该止损挂盘申请，并以 116.00 成交，盈利挂盘同时撤销。

4)　组合挂盘

组合挂盘是指客户在单向盈利或止损挂盘的基础上，再增加一笔同币种反方向的双向挂盘的挂盘方式。即若该笔组合挂盘中，前一笔单向盈利或止损挂盘成交，则后一笔反方向的双向挂盘申请才能生效。在设定交易价格时，组合挂盘后一笔双向止损挂盘价格与首次单向挂盘价格的差价必须为该组交易货币的买卖双边点差。

例如，一客户持有美元，希望先兑换成日元，再兑换回美元，挂盘时银行即时报价为 116.40。在设立美元兑日元盈利挂盘价格 116.80 的同时，设立日元兑美元的双向挂盘价格，其中盈利挂盘价格可设为 116.60，止损挂盘价格可设为 117.30。一旦银行报价达到或优于 116.80 时，美元兑日元盈利挂盘申请即以 116.80 成交，则日元兑美元的双向挂盘申请立即生效，客户可继续等待后笔双向挂盘成交，也可以人工撤销或修改。

在对外汇买卖有了基本理解后，下面以业务流程图(如图 7.1 所示)来说明个人外汇买卖的开户流程及实际办理过程(以甲银行为例)。

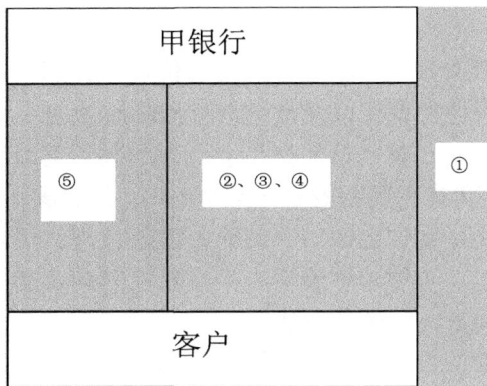

图 7.1　个人外汇买卖的业务流程图

①　选择开户银行：在进入个人外汇买卖之前，根据个人偏好选择开户银行。
②　开户并存入外汇：本人携带有效身份证明到银行开立外汇买卖账户，签署《个人实盘外汇买卖交易协议书》，存入外汇；办理网上交易和电话委托交易开户手续。如果采用柜台交易，各银行可能会有不同的开户起点金额的限制。如甲银行交易金额起点为 50 美元或其他等值外币，交易的最高限额为 200 万美元或其他等值外币。
③　确定交易策略和制定交易计划。
④　建立日常的汇市信息来源渠道。
⑤　实际买卖交易。

二、风险控制

市场利润与风险的辩证关系决定了在利润增加时风险亦在同步增加，且没有任何策略可以颠覆这一关系。无论是投资国内还是国外市场，投资的基本策略是一致的。虽然，每个人的投资策略不同，但其中的一些方法是相通的。下面的一些总结对各种投资者来说，都可以参考和借鉴。

(1) 以闲余资金投资。如果投资者以家庭生活的必需费用来投资，万一亏损，则会直接影响家庭生计，心理上已处于下风，故在决策时亦难以保持客观、冷静的态度。

(2) 知己知彼。需要了解自己的性格，容易冲动或情绪化倾向严重的并不适合这个市场。

(3) 切勿过量交易。要成为成功的投资者，其中一项原则是随时保持 3 倍以上的资金以应付价位的波动。假如资金不充足，应减少手上所持的买卖合约，否则，就可能因资金不足而被迫"斩仓"以腾出资金，纵然后来证明眼光准确亦无济于事。

(4) 正视市场，摒弃幻想。一位美国期货交易员曾经说过，一个充满希望的人是一个美好和快乐的人，但他并不适合做投资者，一位成功的投资者是可以分开他的感情和交易的。

(5) 勿轻率改变主意。预先订下当日入市的价位和计划，勿因眼前价格涨落影响而轻易改变决定，基于当日价位的变化以及市场消息而临时做出决定是十分危险的。

(6) 适当地暂停买卖。日复一日的交易会令你的判断逐渐迟钝。一位成功的投资者曾经说过：每当他感到精神状态和判断效率低至 90%时，开始赚不到钱，而当其状态低过 90%时，便开始亏本，这时候，他便会放下一切而去度假数周。可以说暂短的休息能令你重新认识市场，重新认识自己，更能帮你看清未来投资的方向。当太接近森林时，甚至不能看清眼前的树，即所谓当局者迷，旁观者清吧。

(7) 切勿盲目。成功的投资者不会盲目跟从别人的意思。当每个人都认为应买入时，他们会伺机沽出。当大家都处于同一投资位置，尤其是那些小投资者亦都纷纷跟进时，成功的投资者会感到危险而改变路线。这和逆反的理论一样，当大多数人说要买入时，阁下就该伺机沽出。

(8) 当不肯定时，暂抱观望态度。并非每天均需入市，初入行者往往热衷于入市买卖，但成功的投资者则会等机会，当他们入市后感到疑惑时亦会先行离市。

(9) 当机立断。投资外汇市场时，导致失败的心理因素很多，一种颇为常见的情形是投资者面对损失，亦知道已不能心存侥幸时，却往往因为犹豫不决，未能当机立断，因而愈陷愈深，损失增加。

(10) 订下止蚀位置。这是一项重要的投资技巧。由于投资市场风险颇高，为了避免万一投资失误而带来损失，在每一次入市买卖时，都应该订下止蚀盘，即当汇率跌至某个预定的价位，还可能下跌时，立即交易结清，因而这种订单是限制损失的订单，这样我们便可以限制损失的进一步扩大了。

三、总结思考

叙做个人外汇买卖的动因是想通过外汇买卖，卖出手中持有的外币，买入存款利率较高或处于升值中的另一种外币，从而获取更高的利息收益或者获得外汇升值的好处，避免汇率风险。如买入利率较高且处于升值中的货币，可获得汇差、利息两方面的收入。通过外汇买卖，个人还可以调整手中所持外汇的币种结构，既方便使用，也有利于保值。

由于目前全球汇率体制主要是浮动汇率，加之国际外汇市场受国际上各种政治、经济因素以及各种突发事件的影响，汇率波动已经成为一种正常现象，有时甚至会出现大幅波动。国际外汇市场汇率涨跌幅没有限制。汇价波动给个人外汇买卖业务既带来机遇，也带来风险。那么，决定外汇汇率走向的根本原因是什么？外汇汇率的波动，虽然千变万化，归根到底是由供求关系决定的。在国际外汇市场中，当某种货币的买家多于卖家时，买方争相购买，买方力量大于卖方力量，卖方奇货可居，价格必然上升；反之，当卖家见销路不佳，竞相抛售某种货币，市场买方力量占了上风，则汇价必然下跌。因此，在做个人外汇买卖时，应注意以下几点。

(1) 通过外汇买卖可以规避汇率变动所造成的损失，增加利息收入，但同时又具有风险。因而在参与外汇买卖前，应做充分的准备。

(2) 了解影响汇价变动的基本因素：各国基本经济、金融因素，政治和传媒因素，各国央行的政策因素，心理及市场预测因素。这四个基本因素促使了汇率的变动。实盘的外汇买卖尤其应注重中长期判断。

(3) 对全球外汇市场基本情况要有所了解。例如，外汇市场的形成，外汇市场有哪些参与者，参与者的动机各是什么等。

四、实训操练

练习 7.1

李先生在银行存有 10000 美元，并办理了外汇交易手续。假设美元/日元价格为1/109.25，李先生预期日元将会升值，采用止损挂盘交易，止损价格定位为110.05。若汇率走势不如李先生预料，美元/日元价格变为 1/111.75，请帮李先生计算其盈亏状况。

参考答案：

李先生卖出美元，买入日元 USD10000×109.25 (JPY/USD)= JPY1092500

汇率变动后因超过止损点，所以按止损点价格成交，以避免更大损失。卖出日元，买入美元 JPY1092500/110.05(JPY/USD) = USD9927.31

李先生亏损 USD10000− USD9927.31= USD72.69

练习 7.2

王女士在银行办理了外汇交易手续，现有港币 HKD500000，王女士预料港币将会下跌，日元将会升值，于是要卖出港币，买入日元。但为了预防风险，王女士采取盈利挂盘方式交易。假设当时的汇价是 HKD/JPY = 1/12.54，王女士设定的止盈点为 12.20，之后汇价果如王女士预料，变为 1/12.15，试计算王女士盈利情况。

参考答案：

卖出港币，买入日元 HKD500000×12.54(JPY/HKD) = JPY6270000

卖出日元，买入港币 JPY6270000/12.20(JPY/HKD) = HKD513934.43(盈利挂盘，采用止盈点价格 12.20)

盈利 HKD513934.43−HKD500000 = HKD13934.43

练习 7.3

刘小姐在银行存有欧元 50000 元并办理了外汇交易手续，其预料美元将会上升，于是要卖出欧元，买入美元。但为了控制风险，刘小姐采取双向挂盘方式交易。假设当时的欧元汇价是 1.0344，即 1 欧元兑换 1.0344 美元，王女士设定的止盈点为 1.0285，止损点为 1.0394。之后汇价并未如刘小姐预料，变为 1.0412。试计算刘小姐盈亏情况。

参考答案：

卖出欧元，买入美元 EUR50000×1.0344 (USD/EUR) = USD51720

美元汇价下跌，超出止损点 1.0394，按止损点挂盘交易平盘，盈利挂盘取消。

卖出美元，买入欧元 USD51720/1.0394 (USD/EUR) = EUR49759.48

亏损 EUR50000-EUR49759.48 = EUR240.52

练习 7.4

张先生在 A 银行开户存入美元并办理外汇买卖手续，选择实时交易方式。假设此时银行美元对日元汇价为 105.87，张先生预计日元有上升空间，于是用 10000 美元买入日元，他获得多少日元？

之后，汇价如张先生预期，日元升值，汇价为 103.12。如果这时张先生卖出日元，又可获多少美元？盈利多少美元？

参考答案：

卖出美元，买入日元 USD10000 × 105.87(JPY/USD) = JPY1058700

卖出日元，买入美元 JPY1058700/103.12(JPY/USD) = USD10266.68

盈利 USD10266.68- USD10000 = USD266.68

附录

账户行一览表

此处所列信息非真实数据，仅供练习时参考。

银　行	币　种	账　号
WELLS FARGO BANK USA	USD	27128383
BANK OF COMMUNICATIONS CO., LTD. FRANKFURT	EUR	94753260500268
CITIBANK USA	USD	36044455
BKCHUS33XXX	USD	7201-1000101-006-001
MRMDUS33	USD	173142
MIDLGB22	EUR	123456
BANK OF COMMUNICATIONS HK	HKD	9475326

参 考 文 献

1. 关于审核跟单信用证项下单据的国际标准银行实务(ISBP681).

2. 苏宗祥. 国际结算. 北京：中国金融出版社，2008.

3. 蒋琴儿，秦定. 国际结算：理论·实务·案例(双语教材). 北京：清华大学出版社，2006.

4. 金融专业英语证书考试教材(现代银行业务). 北京：中国金融出版社，2002.

5. 周树玲. 外贸单证实务. 北京：对外经济贸易大学出版社，2002.

6. 吴百福. 进出口贸易实务教程. 第 4 版. 上海：上海人民出版社，2003.

7. Caves R E，et al. World Trade and Payments. 北京：中国人民大学出版社，2004.

8. 沈瑞年，尹继红，庞红. 国际结算. 北京：中国人民大学出版社，1999.

9. 林孝成. 国际结算实务. 北京：高等教育出版社，2004.

10. 汇天结算网. http://www.10588.com/.

11. 新华网. http://news.xinhuanet.com.

12. 中国人民银行网站. http://www.pbc.gov.cn/zhifutixi/.

13. 百度网站. http://www.baidu.com/.

14. 香溢担保. 浅析非格式银行保函常见的法律风险及对策(转载).

15. 审单手册.